D0072519

Assured Victory

Assured Victory

How "Stalin the Great" Won the War, but Lost the Peace

Albert L. Weeks

 PRAEGER

AN IMPRINT OF ABC-CLIO, LLC
Santa Barbara, California • Denver, Colorado • Oxford, England

10/17/11
WW
$44.95

Copyright 2011 by Albert L. Weeks

All rights reserved. No part of this publication may be reproduced, stored in a retrieval system, or transmitted, in any form or by any means, electronic, mechanical, photocopying, recording, or otherwise, except for the inclusion of brief quotations in a review, without prior permission in writing from the publisher.

Library of Congress Cataloging-in-Publication Data

Weeks, Albert Loren, 1923-
  Assured victory : how "Stalin the Great" won the war but lost the peace / Albert L. Weeks.
     p. cm.
  Includes bibliographical references and index.
  ISBN 978-0-313-39165-1 (alk. paper) — ISBN 978-0-313-39166-8 (ebook)
  1. World War, 1939–1945—Soviet Union. 2. Stalin, Joseph, 1879–1953—Military leadership. 3. World War, 1939–1945—Diplomatic history. 4. Soviet Union—Foreign relations—1917–1945. 5. World War, 1939–1945—Campaigns—Eastern Front. I. Title.
  D764.W44   2011

  940.53'47—dc22   2010039732

ISBN: 978-0-313-39165-1
EISBN: 978-0-313-39166-8

15 14 13 12 11   1 2 3 4 5

This book is also available on the World Wide Web as an eBook.
Visit www.abc-clio.com for details.

Praeger
An Imprint of ABC-CLIO, LLC

ABC-CLIO, LLC
130 Cremona Drive, P.O. Box 1911
Santa Barbara, California 93116-1911

This book is printed on acid-free paper ∞

Manufactured in the United States of America

Contents

Preface   ix

Note on Transliteration   xv

Introduction   xvii
   Fallout from the Medvedev Decree   xxii
   Poll on Stalin's Greatness   xxiii
   Revising School Textbooks   xxiv
   Historiographers' View Toward Writing History   xxviii

PART ONE: Age of Dictators   1

1   Stalin: The Twentieth Century's Second Dictator   3
   Unique Dictator   3
   Advantages Enjoyed by Stalin   4
   Contrasts with Western Leadership   6
   Stalin Uses Diplomacy as a Weapon   7
   Stalin's Personal Qualities   9
   Dealing with the West and America   11
   Stalin's Use of Bluff   13
   A "Master Politician"   13

2   Stalin's Methods and Accomplishments   17
   The Stalin Cult   17
   Machiavellian Methods   21
   Legacy of the Cautious Leader   23

3 The *Vozhd'* Prepares for War   25
   Consolidating the Home Front   25
   Were the Purges Justified?   27
   The Kirov Case   28
   Mainstream Historiography on the Purges   30
   The Watershed Year   31

4 The World as Seen from Stalin's Kremlin   37
   Foundation of German-Soviet Relations   38
   Red Army-German Military Collaboration   41
   Soviet-Fascist Totalitarian Kinship   44
   Treacherous Currents of Europe   48

5 Soviet Two-Track Policy   51
   Counterpoint of Early Soviet Diplomacy, 1918–1930s   52
   Peredyshki   55
   Fomenting Inter-Imperialist Tensions   56
   Diplomacy in Stalin's Industrialization   57
   Stalin's Emphasis on Defense   60
   Trail of Broken "Friendship" Treaties   62
   Comintern Factor   64
   United Front (Lenin)/Popular Front (Stalin)   66

6 Soviet Pro-German Posture   71
   Early Roots   71
   The Brest-Litovsk Precedent (1918)   72
   Straws in the Wind   76
   The "Communazi" Factor   78
   Stalin Navigates European Waters   81
   Far East Dangers   82

PART TWO: Stalin Prepares for War   85

7 The Myth of Collective Security   87
   League Weaknesses   90
   Soviet View toward the League   91
   Stalin's Cautiousness   99

8 America in Stalin's Future   105
   Stalin Watches America's Slide toward War   106
   Stalin's American Affinities   109
   Stalin at the Eighteenth Party Congress   111

Stalin's Defensism 112
Stalin on the West's Plans 113
The Significance of Stalin's Hints 114
Stalin and the CPUSA 115
American "Colossus" 116
Stalin's Hoped-for Lend-Lease 119
A "Strange" U.S.-Soviet Alliance 123
Stalin Defends State Interests 126
Stalin and FDR 131
Spies and Agents of Influence 132
Stalin among the Big Three 134

9 Nazi-Soviet Pacts and Aftermath 143
Controversy over Stalin's Defense Policies 144
Specifics of Nazi-Soviet Pacts and Protocols 146
Carving up the World 149
New Tensions 151
Gaining Territory by the Pacts 159

10 Pre-Barbarossa War Plans 161
Stalin's First Reactions 162
Early German Successes 163
Stalin's Behavior on the Dramatic Day 164
Development of Historiography on Stalin's Reactions 168
New Versions of Stalin's Behavior on June 22 172
Additional Observations and Issues 182

PART THREE: The War and Its Aftermath 191

11 Stalin Bluffs and Defeats Wehrmacht 193
Reassessing Stalin 193
Stalin Bluffs in the "Great Game" 198
Barbarossa Materializes 200
Stalin's Not-So-Blind Eye 201
The "Bluff" 202
Stalin's Costly Errors 205
Soviet Weaknesses 206
Stalin Approves a Modified Kutuzov Strategy 208
Did the Bluff Pay Off? 209
Preventing a Russian "Gleiwitz" 210
Stalin's Military Defense Plan 211
How "Unprepared" Was the RKKA? 211

12   Epilogue: Winning the War, Losing the Peace   215
     Hints of a Coming Cold War, 1946   216
     Cold War Chronology   219
     A "New" Stalin?   222
     Today's Russian Historians on the Cold War   223
     Assessing Stalin's Alleged Greatness   225

Appendix I: Stalin, Soviet Premier, Broadcast to the People
         of the Soviet Union   229

Appendix II: Stalin's Biography in Current Russian
         Military Encyclopedia   235

Appendix III: Stalin's Speech at the Reception in the Kremlin
         in Honor of the Commanders of the Red Army   237

Bibliography   239

Notes   253

Index   273

Preface

In canvassing Stalin's supporters' claim of the *Vozhd''*s (leader's) greatness and the controversial treatments of the dictator by today's Russian historians from their differing perspectives, we single out seven authors and their books for examination. Other authors, leading Western, Russian, and other writers, will also be examined. Some of the works by the highlighted Russian historians or memoirists have appeared in English and other languages. Others have been published only in Russian.

All of the seven authors to some degree are critical, often harshly so, of Stalin for his bloodstained record of leadership of the Soviet Union before, during, and after World War II. None of the authors, including even Vyacheslav Molotov, can be described as biased to the point of being entirely useless as a source of a number of valuable insights into the leadership of the Soviet dictator. A case in point here is memoirist Sergo Beria. He is of importance not only for being the son of a top Soviet official in Stalin's inner circle, Lavrenti Beria, secret police tsar and overseer of the Gulag. Beria's son was also an adult in Stalin's most productive years. On many occasions he was in Stalin's company and was privy to inside information about the *Vozhd'* and Stalin's policies as related confidentially by his father, to whom the son was close and with whom he had numerous revealing conversations. Sergo's experience was firsthand. As it concerns Stalin, his account does not seem unduly biased one way or the other, especially since his father was targeted for purge by the dictator.

The above-cited Russian memoirists and historians represent various approaches to the Stalin era and the leader's legacy. Although they are in many ways critical of the dictator, the information and insights they provide are occasionally extremely useful. In some cases, the historians' research is commendable because of its depth and originality. Moreover, the writers are valuable sources in that for the most part they represent, quite naturally, a variety of perspectives and "interests" relating to their own time and place in the Soviet as well as in the post-Soviet period.

Below is a list of these authors together with brief descriptions of their writings as well as biographic information about them:

- **Dmitri Volkogonov**: Late, retired Soviet Army General, former chief of the main political administration of the armed forces in charge of military indoctrination during the time of Leonid Brezhnev. Volkogonov was one of the first top Soviet officials who, after the demise of the USSR in 1991, enjoyed access to various archives. His books include biographies of Stalin, Lenin, and Trotsky. He also authored a study entitled *Autopsy of an Empire: The Seven Leaders Who Built the Soviet Empire*, as well as writing articles for the post-Soviet civilian and military post-Soviet press before his death in 1995 by natural causes. To say he was a bitter critic of Stalin is an understatement.
- **Georgi K. Zhukov,** the so-called "Soviet Eisenhower," was appointed by Stalin to head the Soviet General Staff in the critical early months of 1941. During the war, Zhukov served as commander of various war fronts, especially in the crucial defense of Moscow against the Germans' Operation Typhoon that reached a peak in December 1941. Zhukov played a major operational role in the final Soviet victory in taking Berlin in the spring of 1945. Marshal Zhukov earned a reputation as field commander on the Eastern Front as an outstanding tactician as well as a most demanding and some would say brutally tough disciplinarian. Zhukov published more than 10 editions (in three lengthy volumes) of his extended memoirs before he died in retirement in 1974. His recollections contain both negative and positive references to Party General Secretary/Commander-in-Chief/Premier Stalin. For the most part, Zhukov, a loyal Communist to the end, endorsed in retrospect most of Gensek Stalin's domestic and foreign policies as well as his diplomatic maneuvers of the 1930s and 1940s. On the whole, the marshal commended the fearsome *Vozhd'*

for his prescient prewar and able, hands-on wartime leadership. Zhukov's generally favorable treatment of Stalin—the marshal, after all, had nothing to fear from Stalin over a generation after his death!—tends to be overlooked by his biographers and historians.

- **Vyacheslav Molotov**'s unique 439-page memoirs, *Molotov Remembers: Inside Kremlin Politics,* were published in the form of extended interviews with writer Felix Chuev in 1969. Molotov died in 1986, an octogenarian in peaceful retirement on a government pension, tending his rose gardens and occasionally being seen in the streets of Moscow. His comments on Stalin are candid and at times even critical. Molotov especially emphasized the "great game," as he called it, played by Stalin just before the German invasion in June of 1941. Like some other historians, who are often overlooked in Western accounts, Molotov viewed Stalin's "bluffing" of Hitler as a clever, deceptive ploy on Stalin's part that was intended to make unmistakable that it was Hitler and the Wehrmacht, not the Red Army, that started the war on the Eastern Front in mid-1941. No "pretext," he told Chuev, should be given Hitler in June 1941 that would offer Hitler a phony excuse to invade the USSR on the model that the fuehrer had contrived in the German-rigged "provocation" in Gleiwitz, Germany, on the German-Polish frontier. This ploy had been used to try to justify the Wehrmacht's invasion of Poland on September 1, 1939. Stalin was determined that this trick would not be played on him.

- **Sergo Beria,** author of the 400-page *Beria My Father: Inside Stalin's Kremlin,* is a widely read account of the Stalin years through the eyes of the son of one of the infamous but also best-informed members of the Stalin regime. His is by no means a flattering, monochromatic account of Stalin and those around the dictator. Sergo's personal acquaintance with the Soviet leader and with members of the leader's inner circle gave Beria's adult son unique access to information of great interest to historians. Beria reproduces significant conversations he had had with his powerful father, Lavrenti, as well as disclosing what he had learned from other Stalin cohorts.

- **V. A. Zolotarev**: Russian historian, author, and editor of several histories, one of the most prestigious and relatively objective of which is the 600-page volume he edited, *Miroviye voiny XX veka* (*World Wars of the 20th Century*), published in Moscow in 2002. Its contributors consisted of a team of writers including himself and the well-known mainstream historians **A. O. Chubaryan, L. V. Pozdeyev,** and **O. A.**

Rzheshevsky, all prominent, respected Russian authorities in their fields and/or in some cases ranking members of the Russian Academy of Sciences.

- **Yakov Verkhovsky** and **Valentina Tyrmos**, co-authors of the controversial study *Stalin: Tainiy "tsenariy" nachala voiny* (*Stalin: Secret "Scenario" of the Start of the War*), the widely read, 608-page history published in Moscow in 2006. The authors' research was conducted for more than 10 years under the auspices of the Moscow Institute for Scientific Research. The authors had access to government archives. They implicitly praise Stalin, e.g., for his successful buildup of Soviet defenses before the war and most particularly for assuring a Soviet victory by closing ranks with the capitalist West. Yet the co-authors do not spare criticism of the dictator's mistakes and his cruelty, including his anti-Semitism. One of the authors' main contentions, which they derive from Soviet sources, is that Stalin was bluffing Hitler by making peaceful overtures to Berlin in the immediate run-up to the German invasion of June 22, 1941. Stalin engaged in such appeasement, the historians claim, in order to depict the Soviet Union as the hapless victim of "Fascist aggression." Thereby the Soviets were assured of winning Allied support in the war against Nazi Germany. With his ruse, Stalin went to great pains—using NKVD special operations for this purpose—to forestall Hitler from concocting frontier incidents in order to falsely depict the Soviets as the aggressors. As it turned out, Hitler nevertheless verbally resorted to this pretext in his Barbarossa invasion address to the world on June 23, 1941. In his speech, Hitler claimed that the USSR had been planning a "preventive war" against Germany. The latter's armies, Hitler claimed, responded by preempting Stalin. Yet thanks to Stalin's appeasement bluff, the fuehrer could provide no concrete proof of such Soviet preemption. In fact, there was none.

- **A. B. Martirosyan**, prolific contemporary Russian military historian, is evidently favored, as Verkhovsky-Tyrmos presumably are, by the Putin-Medvedev government in Moscow. Martirosyan's perspectives on Stalin are wholly positive with few reservations. He does not entirely endorse the most extreme measures employed by the dictator's security police, headed by such oppressors as Yagoda, Yezhov, and Beria. Yet he deems warranted Stalin's draconic program to secure and enforce absolute party and national unity under a one-man dictatorship by rooting out and punishing, by means of purges and purge trials, those who were suspected—according to the historian on questionable evidentiary grounds—of opposing the Stalin regime. The author generally gives Stalin credit, his faults and mistakes aside, for being a successful and necessarily Machiavellian leader under the circumstances and who had foreseen the danger of Hitlerism, had prepared his country, often mercilessly, for the coming "inevitable" war, and who, above all, successfully guided the Russian state to victory on the Eastern Front from 1941 to 1945. Stalin had saved the Russian state for posterity.

The above historians and the other writers referenced in this book are themselves critiqued by this author. While the interpretations of some of the writers, whether Russian or Western, of Stalin's most inscrutable, controversial plans and deeds may sound at least partly convincing, others do not. A sorting-out process in the chapters that follow may help readers make their own choices among several possible interpretations as to the degree, deserved or not, of Stalin's putative greatness. At the same time, a definition of and criteria for establishing historic greatness are in order. (See the introduction that follows.)

In the concluding chapter, the author, using a number of sources, shows how Stalin, although he had won the war, lost the peace.

Albert L. Weeks

Note on Transliteration

This book follows conventional rules of transliteration from the Cyrillic to the Latin alphabet.

When a Russian name is familiar to Western readers, the usual English spelling is used. Generally in transliteration to English, the Cyrillic letter **ы** is written with an "i"; the Russian letter **й** with a "y." However, a Russian family name ending in "-skiy" is commonly rendered in English as "-sky" in the case of famous persons, like "Belinsky" or "Stravinsky." However, when the Russian name may not be commonly known to Westerners, transliteration rules will be followed for the person's family name and given name. As, for example, with first names like "Anatoliy" or "Yevgeniy."

For convenience throughout this text, author-historian Yakov Verkhovsky's name is spelled in the usual English way.

Introduction

In the current reassessment of the Russian Federation of Stalin's 25-year reign in Soviet Russia, the Russian government is calling on the nation's historians to once again "rewrite history."

Josef Stalin is today being restored in some history texts and Russian mass media as a "great leader" who saved Russia in the four-year war against Nazi Germany, from 1941 to 1945. Even his most brutal methods in the purges of 1930s in preparing the USSR for war as well as his role of warlord defending the state when the Wehrmacht swept into the country in late June 1941 are now being rationalized by some historians as tributes to the Soviet leader's greatness. The British military historian Chris Bellamy rationalizes somewhat Stalin's harsh measures as follows:[1]

> "The survival of the Soviet Union in 1941–42 and its resilience in the face of shattering defeats can be ascribed to the character and patriotism of its people, especially the Russians, or to the draconian measures imposed by Stalin, Beria, and their lieutenants. In fact, it must be ascribed to both. . . . The system was able, using a mixture of terror and propaganda, to mobilize the latent patriotism of the nation. One recent analysis acknowledged that 'without Stalin, we would not have won. But if it had not been for Stalin, in all probability the war would not have happened.'"

Other, more mainstream historians currently praise the former "Soviet government" (under Stalin) for a number of decisions that were taken in foreign policy, such as the deals struck with Hitler in

August 1939 or Stalin's huge military buildup that was begun in the 1920s.

Contemporary recasting of the Soviet past by Russian historians is evidently encouraged by President Dmitri Medvedev and Prime Minister Vladimir Putin. These two top leaders have voiced support for a thorough rewriting of Soviet history in order, they say, to enhance patriotic feeling in the Russian Federation (RF). In this ongoing rewrite, even the Nazi-Soviet (Molotov-Ribbentrop) pacts and secret protocols of August–September 1939, one of Stalin's most controversial if not egregious maneuvers on the foreign front in the prewar years, are being touted by the Medvedev-Putin government and by a new crop of Russian historians. The Russian officials tend to regard as understandable and necessary the drastic measures undertaken by Stalin in the perilous times of the 1930s. They claim such draconic policies were in order to defend Russian national security and, as they phrase it, the "Russian state" (omitting the word "Soviet").

Such Orwellian-like recasting of the past in ways that serve present interests and political demands may not always be historically truthful. Such falsification of the past was customary in the Soviet period. The treatment of Soviet leader Stalin in published histories in the USSR, until 1956, was, of course, totally positive and flattering. With Stalin's death in 1953 and the de-Stalinization campaign opened by First Secretary Nikita Khrushchev at the 20th Party Congress in February 1956, historians began to cast Stalin as a virtual pariah. He did nothing whatsoever good for the Soviet state and its peoples. He was blamed for the "leadership cult," the bloody purges of the 1930s, and later, the arbitrary confinement of innocent people in the Gulag and prisons; for excesses under collectivization; and, above all, for the German victories in the opening phase of the Great Patriotic War on the Eastern Front.

As to his policies in the prewar period just before 1941, historians in the post-Stalin period after 1991 universally condemned the Molotov-Ribbentrop pacts as well as Stalin's utopian ideology, including its promotion of "world revolution." For many post-1991 authors, Stalin's administrative-command system was a prescription for a dystopia and totalitarianism.

By the time of the reign of General Secretary and President Leonid Brezhnev in the 1960s and 1970s, a partially positive reexamination of the Stalin legacy cropped up in the mass media and history books. Emphasis on the Soviet victory in World War II was inspired in part by the personal glorification of Brezhnev as a putative war hero. This literature ran parallel to a renewed interest in military history and Marxist-Leninist (and, in part, Stalinist) ideology. The world's largest military buildup by any country up to that time was under way in the USSR in the 1970s. With it came a militaristic mantra that found room for at least modest praise of Stalin.

Yet that era soon yielded to a return by Russian historians and school textbooks to a mostly negative treatment of the former *Vozhd'* (leader). In the late 1980s under General Secretary and President Mikhail Gorbachev, a period followed by the demise of the USSR and Communist Party rule in 1991, a new twist was given to Russian historiography. Formerly secret archives began to be opened. A process of democratization began under the administrations of Boris Yeltsin and Vladimir Putin (1991–2008). This period saw a generally more objective treatment of Soviet history in Russian mass media, nonfiction histories, and school textbooks.

On Russian bookshelves, a few titles appeared that even touted U.S. Lend-Lease aid to the Soviets during the war with Germany. Lend-Lease, wrote several Russian authors, crucially abetted the Soviet victory over Hitler's Wehrmacht. American aid to Stalin's Red Army in the war had been a delicate topic that had been altogether ignored or treated dismissively in the previous telling of history by Russian authors.[2]

Yet, as suggested by a few Russian historians today, Stalin's preparations for and stunning welcoming of an alliance with the Western capitalist Allies was a shrewd maneuver. It placed the USSR on the side of the "good guys," assured the Soviet victory in the East over the "Fascist hordes," all while erasing the Soviets' "bad reputation" as a Communist pariah. Above all, Stalin's historic maneuver resulted in giving the Soviet Union the status of a superpower along with Josef Stalin's claim of greatness.

One new version of Stalin's ploy on the eve of the German attack depicts the dictator as letting the Wehrmacht attack in June 1941 since, first, Stalin knew that the Red Army was not prepared to halt the invasion. Second, the Soviet leader preferred, as he had indicated on several occasions, that the USSR be perceived—by the world and in particular by its potential Western allies, who would assure its victory in the war with the Germans and the Japanese—as the victim of aggression (see chapter 11).

With the relaxed, post-Soviet atmosphere after 1991 that allowed historical research and the writing of history more in tune with *wie es eigenlicht gewesen* (roughly, "telling-it-as-it-was"), some boiler-plated interpretations of the Stalin period nevertheless continued to hold their ground. The West was still blamed for various shortcomings, such as its appeasement policy toward Hitler's Germany or for showing too much distrust in the USSR. Partially credible alternative interpretations of Stalin's foreign and domestic policies—such as his preparations for war, the positive aspects of his prewar leadership, and as commander-in-chief in the Great Patriotic War—were generally ignored. Today, however, the reluctance to find anything good about Stalin or about much of Soviet history is beginning to erode. Some historians are being encouraged by the Russian government to view the Soviet past in less negative ways and in order to whet patriotism in twenty-first-century Russia. By 2009, the two top Russian leaders themselves raised the issue of the way in which the country's history was being told—that is, in "unpatriotic" and "mythological" ways.[3]

A significant step on the way to still another Russian history rewrite came on May 15, 2009, when Russian President Dmitri Medvedev issued Ukase No. 549. It was a landmark decree since it commissioned Russian historians to—again—rethink the country's Soviet past and "oppose all attempts at falsifying history and harming the interests of Russia." Without being specific, the president ordered that history be presented to the population in terms that enhanced patriotism and removed from national historiography various, as he called them, long-established "myths."

For their part, some scholars and commentators described the Medvedev decree as providing a "juridical basis for waging the struggle for truth and objectivity" in the nation's casting of its history in the twentieth century. As an example of this nationwide mission, the Medvedev administration called on historians and classroom teachers to counter "attempts to minimize the role of the Soviet Union in the fight against Nazism." This "struggle" includes the prewar "anti-Fascist" stance of the Stalin government as well as the mission of the Great Patriotic War as the "world-historical anti-Fascist struggle" against Germany and its Axis allies, from 1941 to 1945.

As will be discussed later, it appears to this author in retrospect that Stalin regarded this military struggle from 1941 to 1945 as a Wartime Popular Front, the analog of the famous 1930s Popular Front. This program embodied tactics that were used by the Communists in Western Europe in order to penetrate the coalition cabinets in those capitals and eventually capture power. In postwar Eastern Europe this was, in fact, the ploy used by Stalin to gain footholds in those half-dozen nations occupied by the Red Army at the end of the war.

From the very beginning, as in Stalin's wartime speeches about the aims of the Great Patriotic War, the Soviet dictator invariably referred to "liberation." No one needed a Soviet political dictionary to realize that this term carried the double meaning of "throwing off the yoke of Fascism," as well as "liberating the masses from capitalism," from which the Western system, according to Marxism-Leninism, the system of Fascism inexorably develops.

In an ominous way, the Soviet leader's language foreshadowed the postwar party line that was unfurled by Stalin in February 1946 (see chapter 12). World War II, he said less than a year after the end of the global conflict, was "no accident." It was the inevitable by-product of capitalism. Moreover, as a threat of another war continued unabated, the Soviet Union, he said in his electoral speech just after World War II, must continue as before the war to emphasize building of its military forces. Stalin's policy emphases made that soon after the war signaled the start of the 40-year Cold War and the "two-camps' struggle" between East and West. This in turn indicated that the peace gained from the six-year global war would be challenged by a newly great power with a global, messianic doctrine, the Soviet Union.

Under Stalin's leadership, the *Vozhd'* was clearly indicating that the Soviet state would again take up the cudgels of Marxist-Leninist militancy and expansionism. This was made undeniably clear just five years after VE Day and VJ Day. With Stalin's military and political support, North Korea, under the Moscow-trained puppet, Kim Il Sung, suddenly on a Sunday morning in June 1950 crossed the 38th Parallel and in full force invaded the Republic of Korea. Stalin, Mao, and Kim Il Sung aimed to paint the Far East red.

The Cold War thus became a very bloody hot war. It signaled the end of whatever hopes were abroad after 1945 for East-West accommodation and partnership that had largely characterized East-West collaboration against the Axis enemy.

Stalin, indeed, had won the war. He had "saved the Russian state," as revisionist historians point out today. Yet he had lost the peace, assuming that it was his intention to keep it. Many standard Russian textbooks now acknowledge Stalin's fault in helping bring about the $10 trillion (the U.S. price was $4 trillion) Cold War. Revisionist historians deny this and fault the United States for the Cold War. Some

Western historians agree. Mainstream Russian historians claim that the fault rests equally on both sides.

FALLOUT FROM THE MEDVEDEV DECREE

After the 2009 commemorations, a number of historians held panels across the RF on "patriotic" themes as called upon by the Medvedev ukase. Among them was a much publicized lecture delivered in Tula to a group of law students that featured revisionist military historian, retired intelligence officer, and prolific author Arsen B. Martirosyan.[4]

Commentaries on the decree throughout 2009 referred in some cases in implicitly positive terms to the Nazi-Soviet Pact, whose seventieth anniversary was commemorated in August 2009. After this world-shaking nonaggression pact and its follow-up Friendship Pact, secret protocols, and trade agreements, there came next month the start of World War II. Germany's invasion of Poland on September 1 was soon followed by the Soviet invasion and occupation of eastern Poland as agreed to with Germany in the secret protocols. Both of these seventieth anniversaries were commemorated with a raft of speeches and articles in the Russian Federation. A memorable speech was given by Prime Minister Vladimir Putin in Poland in late August 2009. For his part, President Medvedev issued official anniversary statements via his online blog.

Both contemporary Russian leaders did their own history rewrite in the manner in which they depicted the threatening situation in 1939–1941. Putin and Medvedev, whose innuendoes are echoed by some of the new revisionist Russian historians, typified by Martirosyan, suggested that Stalin "correctly" surmised the dire danger facing the USSR in the late 1930s. The life-or-death situation demanded, suggested the two Russian officials in agreement with such "revisionist" historians, recourse to bold diplomatic maneuvers that befit the times, the age of dictators. It was widely claimed in such commemorative lectures and articles that Stalin's deals with Hitler successfully deflected Nazi German armies away from the USSR, at least temporarily. By these arrangements, which were facilitated by Stalin, the German dictator could not carry out his stated intentions (e.g., in *Mein Kampf*) to attack and enslave the Soviet Union.

Still, in September 2009 to the audience in Poland, which included German, Polish, and Russian leaders and other top officials, Prime

Minister Vladimir Putin in essence described the Nazi-Soviet deals of 1939 as "immoral" (his term). This was presumably in reference to the secret protocols that accompanied the pacts and that led to the destruction of Poland "as a state," as Soviet Premier/Foreign Minister Vyacheslav Molotov bluntly put it in an address to the USSR Supreme Soviet in August 1939. Yet Putin also suggested that the Molotov-Ribbentrop pacts were understandable given the dire circumstances facing the Soviet (as some historians word it, "Russian") state in that dangerous era.

POLL ON STALIN'S GREATNESS

Today the Russian public is not lagging behind the leadership in its revised attitude toward Stalin. A public opinion poll, taken in early 2009, echoed the thinking of the presidential history commission and, apparently, the top leadership as well as a number of deputies in the Duma (parliament). Sixty-three percent of the sample indicated that it believed the signing of the Nazi-Soviet Pacts and secret protocols of August–September 1939 was a "timely" move by Stalin. Thereby, said the two-thirds majority, the Soviet leader had "avoided [a Soviet] war with Germany [at that juncture] or at very least postponed it." Fifty-seven percent saw "nothing wrong" with the pacts and protocols made by Stalin with Hitler "since the Western powers refused to join forces with the Soviet Union in opposing Germany." Meanwhile, only 25 percent of the poll disagreed with these positive views of the Moscow-Berlin deals (31 percent found such questions "difficult to answer").

Other polls held in Russia in recent years show that at least half of the population now considers Stalin to have been a "great" leader. Only about one-quarter of such polls take a negative view toward the dictator, who reigned for a quarter of a century. The poll and blog feedback suggest that a large majority of Russians now feel that the Soviet dictator earned an honored place in history. This stems in large part from the fact of the dictator's preparing Soviet Russia over several prewar years for the ordeal of war and for having led Russia to victory in the war on the Eastern Front. This popular support of Stalin's legacy should not be conflated with the 10 to 15 percent of the Russian population who say in polls that they support today's Russian Communist Party, among whom may be only a small minority who would favor a return to Stalin's coercive administrative-command, or totalitarian, system.

Today's increasing interest in and positive attitude toward Stalin seems to reflect the release of pent-up Russian nationalism within the society, particularly among some of the youth. It also seems to reflect a desire to erase the "shame" of the Soviet period. It is a trend that is attractive to large numbers of Russian youth and is reflected in the history textbooks used in Russian schools.

REVISING SCHOOL TEXTBOOKS

Under the Medvedev decree, historians, schools at all levels, and pedagogical institutes are being tasked to observe the presidential ukase by correcting any "distortions of the truth or attempts by the West to rewrite history in favor only of itself." Just what this may imply may be detected from the fallout from the presidential decree as found in the Russian press and academic journals and from Russian media coverage of the double anniversaries of August and September 2009. This fallout can be summed up as the government's and public acknowledgement that a new program for rewriting Russian (and Soviet) history is necessary and is actively under way at the present time in the Russian Federation. The purported aim of this history rewrite is to insert in the telling of Russian history elements of patriotism and an appreciation of the accomplishments of the Soviet past.

Some Russian press commentary has noted that such history revisions were common in Stalin's Soviet Union. Moreover, they have been common throughout the post-Stalin period, particularly since the demise of the USSR in 1991. In recent years, droves of history texts have been published, some of which correct the Soviet record in more or less credulous ways. The schools seem to be free in many cases to choose from this bevy of textbooks those volumes—with whatever corresponding interpretations—they wish to assign their students. Other textbooks tack in novel ways through the treacherous seas of the past as they reexamine, and in some cases blatantly endorse, Stalin's most problematic and controversial domestic and foreign policies. (The contents of the new history texts are tailored into the discussion in the upcoming chapters.)

A timely and revealing prestigious lecture on Russian historiography was given in mid-2009 by Russian military historian Arsen B.

Martirosyan, a retired intelligence officer and author of many contemporary books on Soviet foreign policy, military strategy, and Stalin's political biography. The prolific historian framed his talk to students within the context of the Medvedev decree. The lecture presumably reflected official views on Russian history held by the Medvedev-Putin administration, since the lecture was sponsored by the RF Ministry of Justice.

Some of Martirosyan's interpretations and positive evaluations of Stalin's leadership would shock mainline Western historians. As of this writing, the Russian historian's book has not as yet been translated into English. All but totally unknown and unread in the West, a half dozen of Martirosyan's books are bestsellers in Russia. The author is one of about a dozen widely read "new-thinking" historians. One of Martirosyan's latest volumes (in Russian) is *Deal of the Dictators or Breathing Space for Peace?* published in 2009. The main points of the lecture he gave in September 2009 at the Tula branch of the Russian Academy of Law of the RF Ministry of Justice can be summed up as follows:

- Russian historians, in conforming to President Dmitri Medvedev's History Commission's call for rectifying the "myths" of Soviet historiography, must *otdelit' zerna ot plevel*, i.e., sort out the wheat from the chaff, in terms of providing a "truthful" historical treatment of Stalin's prewar and wartime leadership. "Falsifying our history," Martirosyan complained, "harms Russian interests [given] the current information struggle to uncover historical truths as demanded by the Presidential Commission."
- Among these "myths" is the one that sweepingly decries and dismisses Stalin's pacts with Hitler in 1939 as immoral and without historians' objectively considering the era in which the pacts were made, as well as their positive sides, such as providing a "breathing space" for needed defense preparations by the USSR, i.e., time afforded the USSR as a result of the deals of 1939.
- It was hoped in the ruling circles of the West, alleged the historian, that Hitler would turn his Wehrmacht *east*, not west. Stalin was cognizant of this "self-interested" thinking in the Western capitals. He reacted to it rationally while being aware of the fact that the USSR was left to face Hitler alone. In the professor's opinion, the Ribbentrop-Molotov pacts did not "cause World War II," as some historians allege (including a few Russian writers) by allegedly "instigating"

Hitler's *Drang nach Westen*.[5] In any case, Soviet intelligence knew of
Hitler's Polish invasion plans since before the spring of 1939.

- They were a fait accompli. The professor omitted any mention of
  Comintern leader Georgi Dimitrov's diary entry of September 1939
  quoting Stalin to the effect that he relished the idea of a mutually
  destructive war in the West between the "imperialists."[6]
- Stalin's gains under the pacts moved the Soviet frontier hundreds
  of miles westward by which the Soviets picked up well over
  100,000 square miles of geostrategic borderland territory, once
  part of the old Russian Empire. This deal, Martirosyan argued,
  was to the advantage of the USSR, given, as expected by Stalin per *Mein Kampf* and Soviet intelligence, the "inevitable" (the
  term used in Soviet ideology) coming "imperialist" war against
  the Soviet Union. Most Western historians have claimed that this
  westward shift of the Soviet frontier actually worsened the situation for the Soviets since it moved the borders, or "Molotov
  Line," closer to the enemy. Yet, as is now counter-argued by some
  of the new historians, this extra territory actually paid off for the
  defending Red Army (RKKA). This was seen in what occurred
  on June 22, 1941, when the new territories were violated by the
  invading Wehrmacht. It turned out that the defending RKKA
  needed territory in which to carry out tactical and strategic
  retreats.
- Stalin's Five-Year Plans and the great purges of the late 1930s were
  brutal. Yet, claims Martirosyan, the brutality stemmed mainly from
  the fact that "there was actual anti-Stalin plotting going on within
  the USSR"—i.e., he claims, within the party and the military. This
  debilitating subversion harmed Soviet security interests. Martirosyan alleges—as do other Russian historians of his persuasion and
  who in this respect are in conflict with the Western consensus about
  the Stalin purges—that this sedition included an anti-Stalin plot supported by Marshal Tukhachevsky, a "cohort" of Trotsky. The marshal
  was executed along with other RKKA senior officers in the period
  of the Great Purges of 1936–1938 and in following years. Thus, the
  professor disputes the widely held opinion in the West as well as
  among most post-Stalin Russian historians that all charges against
  Tukhachevsky and other RKKA senior officers were fabricated with
  Stalin's approval by the NKVD. Disputing the opinion that evidence
  was fabricated, the historian sketches out what he calls concrete
  evidence of an anti-Stalin military plot that is proved among other

sabotage, he maintains, by culpable RKKA commanders' suspicious dismantling of the old Stalin line of defenses.

Martirosyan also singles out Trotsky's many supporters, or "remnants," within the Communist Party, including the military, as a dangerous, subversive element. This, too, runs counter to the long-held Western view that all such charges against the party and military epigones from 1936 to 1941 had been trumped up under Stalin's orders by the NKVD, headed by Nikolai Yezhov, then by Lavrenti Beria. Yet Martirosyan indicates in his books that he does not entirely subscribe to Stalin's bloody methods: "We do not forgive Stalin for his criminal acts," he told the Tula students. Nevertheless, the historian comes close to rationalizing Stalin's methods, as he said, "given the circumstances of the times" and the fact, as he claims, that Trotskyites and other subversive elements who with foreign support from the capitalist West constituted a deadly threat to Soviet security at a time when the very continued existence of the Soviet Union as a state was on the line because of hostile states that sought its demise.

In short, what is found here in Martirosyan and implicitly in the Medvedev-Putin recasting of Russian history is a total departure from the traditional assumptions about Stalin that date from the de-Stalinization campaign of *"protivo-staliniana"* (anti-Staliniana, a neology) initiated by Nikita Khrushchev and more or less continued intact up until recently, in histories published in both the East and the West. In some sense, the revised historiography is a throwback to the Stalin days of the 1940s and 1950s, when the dictator enjoyed a full-blown cult in his name. It is relevant that most of the Russian population, the post-1953 "new generation" as well as present Russian officialdom, have no personal recollection of "life under Stalin." Fortunately for them, they did not personally witness any of the events of the 1930s, 1940s, and early 1950s. An old Soviet joke describes how Lenin himself was luckily free of Stalinism. "He slept peacefully in the Mausoleum through the First Five-Year Plan, the Second Five-Year Plan, the Purges, the Great Patriotic War . . . etc."

The fact is today many Russian citizens of all ages appear to believe that Stalin strengthened the USSR in the face of the mortal danger the country faced—and did so largely alone. Soviet war hero Marshal Zhukov himself in his extended memoirs gives much credit to Stalin's leadership throughout his whole tenure of a quarter of a century. Zhukov lavishes such praise (note: doing so a generation after Stalin's death) despite the fact that the dreaded *Khozain* (boss) when he was alive was a terror to the marshal personally as well as to the other RKKA staff and field senior officers. For example, Zhukov once said of the Soviet dictator:[7]

> "Stalin's very appearance, moderately-toned voice, the concreteness and depth of his decisions, his familiarity with military issues, his attention span . . . all made a profound impression on me."

Also, after the war Stalin had relegated Zhukov in 1945 to a lowly status by sending him to routine duty "out in the provinces" as a military district administrator. Zhukov's many-sided praise of Stalin in particular in his memoirs, as far as I know, has not been cited in Western literature. This may be because authors were not using the fuller text of his memoirs available only in Russian in the later 1990s edition, when significant, formerly omitted material was added.

HISTORIOGRAPHERS' VIEW TOWARD WRITING HISTORY

How truthful in the full, historiographic sense are these latest recast treatments of Stalin and Soviet history? A number of classical, historiographic issues are involved.

By way of introducing such discussion, even rationalizing the rewriting of history, the current Russian history rewrite campaign reflects the perennial urge among all historians worldwide to reach a consensus on major events when summing up a war, revolution, a historic leader's reign, and so on. The question of the worthiness or not of an outstanding historical figure will quite predictably spark spontaneous controversy among independent-minded historians. It would take a whole book to catalog even half of these raging controversies, past and present. Taken together, such disputes and rival interpretations perhaps illustrate the futility of any forced attempt to cast a single, moralistic, monochromatic picture of the past, of world historical events, and in portraits of the historical persons who compose the picture. On this point, Harvard history professor David Fischer catalogs what he calls the "fallacies of the herd," i.e., those disputable conclusions drawn by some historians that unfortunately become boilerplated as allegedly infallible history. Fischer especially singles out what he calls the "moralistic fallacy." By this he means those many historians who condemn this or that event or historical person as "indisputably" evil. This has certainly been the case with the treatment of Stalin by historians.

For his part, the highly reputed historian E. H. Carr recalls that the eminent historian Benedetto Croce once insisted that "the historian is not a judge, still less a hanging judge." Carr added that, indeed, the standpoints of the historian and of the moralist are in no way identical. "History is a process of struggle," he writes, "in which results, whether we judge them good or bad, are achieved, . . . at the expense of others. The losers pay." Moreover, he continues, "suffering is indigenous in history."

Books on historiography, "the historian's craft," written by philosophically minded historians like Carr, Croce, Louis Gottschalk, Marc Bloch, R. G. Collingwood, Ernst Breisac, and others are seldom assimilated by less thoughtful, yet widely read historians. Nevertheless, it is the former historians and historiographers who seriously urge their colleagues and those who have a serious interest in reading history to conjure up as much objectivity as possible.

Historians and their readers must not to succumb to stereotypes, least of all to government orders to write history in a monochromatic way in the name of patriotism or any other imposed political standard. Only by way of free, uninhibited inquiry can historians develop a balanced, well-rounded view of the complex ebb and flow of the "dead," yet resuscitated and synthetically constructed past.

Still, is moral relativism really an acceptable posture for the historian and his or her readers to adopt? Do readers really wish to consume whitewashed accounts of Julius Caesar, Napoleon, or Stalin? Is the historian expected to show utter indifference toward the intense, often bloody struggles and their tragic outcomes on the battlefields and in the graveyards of the past in many cases resulting from the policies of leaders? The human urge, of course, is to distinguish good from evil, to condemn, and to judge and punish highly placed perpetrators of crimes past and present. It is established in contemporary civilization to mount judicial trials of war criminals, as at Nuremberg in 1946 and by the War Crimes Tribunal at Brussels today. These are justifiable responses to empowered authorities, civilian or military, who have perpetrated wars, massacres, and atrocities like genocide. Yet Carr, Fischer, and other historians wonder if this adequately sums up the calling of historians *per se*—that is, *that* they pronounce tendentiously *post facto* judgments on historical persons. Yet a Nero, Napoleon, Lenin, Mussolini, Hitler, Stalin, Pol Pot, etc., are historic figures toward whom a posture of cold moral indifference by anyone, including the historian, seems to be totally out of order.

Perhaps what the above seasoned historians ask us to do is not to forswear any judgmentalism whatsoever. They do not expect historians to indulge in mindless, amoralistic fence-sitting. The historians and historiographers are merely pleading for *as broad and open-minded interpretation as possible of a given past war, revolution, or leader's reign.* Could it even be true, they ask, that out of an "evil King John" something positive or good nevertheless emerged? Might even Napoleon, odd and contradictory as it may seem, combine in his reign a progressive spirit of liberation, yet crossed with raw aggression? Could the good and great President Abraham Lincoln have combined elements of rank opportunism with pure idealism? Likewise, might even dictator Stalin's prewar domestic and foreign policies, brutal and immoral as many of them were, nevertheless have ultimately played a positive role in some respects by unifying the country and in a sense guaranteeing the survival of the USSR and, hence, of its successor, the Russian Federation? Many popular treatments of Stalin in Russia and in the West depict his prewar policies and his leadership in the Great Patriotic War, as he chose to name the bloody conflict on the Eastern Front, as flawed and evil. Some of these denunciations appear to stand in need of reexamination.

One might ask if the macro-scale complexities of history are something like the inscrutable processes of nature. Anatole France, Nobel Peace Prize laureate and definitely no lover of wars, despotism, or inhumanity, once wrote that "nature has no principles. She furnishes us no reason to believe that human life is to be respected. Nature, in her indifference, makes no distinction between good and evil." Is history perhaps the analog of nature by its being similarly "indifferent"? Someone might object, "That may be true of nature. But is it true of *human* nature or of our moralistically toned perspectives on human history?" We might at least agree that such questions, especially painful ones about the role of the historian and the issues related to controversial historical personages like Stalin, deserve more than sweeping judgmentalism or a dismissive attitude based mainly on the given historic person's repugnance. Historian Michael Oakeshott warned against historians who act like "whippets in a meadow on Sunday afternoon . . . exercising their moral and political opinions" about the past. The great Roman chronicler Tacitus once wrote: "Let no worthy action go uncommemorated." But how does one define "worthy"? Yet, by violating this axiom, Tacitus himself at times distorted his renderings of past events to suit his own predispositions—namely, about his fellow Romans as well as about the invading German tribes toward whom he showed something less than a historian's objectivity. Fisher notes that the moral judgments offered by Tacitus in *Germaniae* were "dysfunctional" to his allegedly dispassionate interpretations of the Romans, whom he singled out pejoratively by treating the Romans with "sarcastic side comments." Fischer concludes: "From the age of Tacitus to our own time, the moralistic fallacy [in writing history] has flourished in a thousand forms."

Historians are not respected when they engage in postmortem prosecutions of a historic person by denouncing him as "evil, *period.*" It is alleged that "nothing good whatever came out of his reign." As the anti-Fascist poet of World War II, John Betjeman, wrote: "History must not be written with bias. . . . Both sides must be given, even if 'there is only one side.'" Another World War II historian, Marc Bloch, himself a former Nazi prisoner, agreed with Betjeman's sentiment. Most everyone remembers Thomas Carlyle's emphatic statement: "History is the biography of great men." But did Carlyle mean to omit bloodthirsty scoundrels from his great historic persons? Cynical comments about the historians' work are also in abundance. For instance, Napoleon, the inventor of morale-building wartime propaganda, claimed that "history is merely a set of lies that are *agreed upon.*"

Among social scientists, the historian's craft is unique. The "past" that historians examine is intangible. It is not "found" intact. Rather, it is *constructed* (not "reconstructed") by a judicious combination of the historian's imagination and objectivity. In contrast to sleuths or *natural* scientists, historians' "evidence" is largely invisible. Historiography, after all, is about the *dead* past. Moreover, the most relevant, yet inscrutable historical data consist mainly of mental phenomena. These take the form of the hidden desires, motives, and plans of statesmen that in turn may act as causative factors in the course of events. It is, after all, the leaders' and commanders'-in-chief inner impulses and motivations that underlie their policies and decisions. The soldiers themselves harbor their own inscrutable motivations and feelings. Who can discern their inner thoughts with complete accuracy? There is, after all, no "rock" that can be lifted up to reveal a set of obscured "concrete truths" about the past.

In *constructing* the past, the historian is said to "find," or better, *select* factors of his own choosing out of an infinitude of relevant data as he goes about tailoring his research into *his* story, *his* version of the past. The historiographer Collingwood put it that the "historian makes history." By this, he did not mean that the analysis of the dead past, followed by a synthetic construction of that intangible, absent past, necessarily becomes simply "anyone's subjective opinion." By "makes history," Collingwood explained that he meant that the professional historian confronts a vast amount of chronicled data that laymen (and some unthinking historians) like to describe inaccurately as "*the past.*" He must make crucial choices out of the plethora of recorded and unrecorded or purported data. Not all of this data may even be entirely accurate as to time, place, and nature of occurrence. The historian chooses which threads and colors of threads he will weave into his tapestry. His choices in telling his story are myriad.

This is precisely why treatments of Stalin's plans for making war with Germany in the East in mid-1941 are subject to varying points of view. It is also the reason why some historians, especially those among the new crop of Stalin apologists, can find any number of arguments in support of their positive view toward Josef Stalin. Analyses of the run-up to the Great Patriotic War are replete with controversy. The disputes over this among professional historians in Russia as well as those in other countries has been going on since the end of World War II. However, for the historian as for the natural scientist, there are bound to be missing links, anomalies, vagaries, and even imponderables. Just as the science, say, of medicine has its obvious limitations, so also does the scientific discipline of history. This is because in "doing history" the basic subject matter of the "past" is mostly intangible. In an anguished mood, Augustine, the fifth-century AD theologian who was deeply read in Greek and Roman philosophy, wrote in his *Confessions* that he did not know even what is meant by "Present, Past and Future."[8] Each of these three states of consciousness, he pleaded, seems fantastic, and its flux, as known or constructed in the mind, is impossible to fix. Siegfried Kracauer, a Swiss historian with an interest in cinematography, addressed in his seminal work *History: The Last Things Before the First*, the many problematical aspects of doing history, of piecing together the static "frames" of historical time in order to project the illusion of movement and change, and in some cases even of progress. As he wrote:[9]

> "Our preoccupation with historical 'reality' may certainly attain to a level of above mere opinion; but [it] does not convey, or reach out for ultimate truths, as do philosophy and art proper. [Written histories] share their inherently provisional character with

the material they record, explore, and penetrate. . . . Historiography differs from philosophy [and morality]. Instead of proceeding from, or climaxing in, statements about the meaning, or, for that matter, meaninglessness, of history as such, it is a distinctly empirical science which explores and interprets historical 'reality' in exactly the same manner as the photographic media render and penetrate the physical world about us. History is much closer to the practically endless, fortuitous, and indeterminate *Lebenswelt*—Husserl's term for the basic dimension of daily life—philosophy. Consequently, the historian would not dream of assigning to his findings and conclusions the kind of generality and validity peculiar to philosophical [or moral] statements. [The historian] is unconcerned for high abstractions and absolutes; at least he does not primarily care about them."

In the above, perhaps over-lengthy exegesis on historiography, the author of this book is conveying the idea that in treating Soviet history and Stalin's alleged greatness as a prewar and wartime leader, his own telling of the story, including the "denouement" of the story of the Cold War, will be as independently objective as his research leads him. In his construction of the past, he will not act, as Croce put it, as a "hanging judge." Yet he will not have his literary transmission set at neutral.

PART ONE

Age of Dictators

1

Stalin: The Twentieth Century's Second Dictator

Josef Stalin inherited the mantle of Vladimir Lenin, modern times' first dictator, to become the twentieth century's second dictator of the world's largest country.

As the years passed, Stalin kept steadily increasing his authority. By the crucial pre-World War II years of 1938–1939, Stalin's dictatorial rule had reached a peak. By then, his power more than matched that of the supreme leaders of Italy, Germany, Japan, or Spain, as well as of the dictator-led countries of eastern Europe. This was, after all, the age of dictators. Stalin, leader of a wide, contiguous empire with 11 time zones, most of whose population was ethnically non-Russian, operated in those times more effectively than any of the rest of the autocrats of the era.

In many ways, his style of leadership was quite different from any of the other modern dictators. This was especially seen in the way Stalin dealt with the rest of the world. He executed his grand strategy carefully and thoughtfully while displaying a high degree of foresight of the type used in playing chess, or, better, the Oriental game of Go.

UNIQUE DICTATOR

Above all, no reckless adventurer, the *Vozhd'* always kept two goals in mind: namely, using all means to preserve his personal power while protecting at whatever cost the security of the Soviet state against any perceived internal and external enemies. In defending his country against the menace of the aggressive, well-armed Axis, his foreign policy outclassed the slow-moving democracies of the time as well as the other armed dictatorships that became enemies of the USSR. In the end, Stalin defeated all of the Axis powers that had threatened his country while far outliving their leaders.

The key to Stalin's and the Soviet army's victory over Germany by 1945 was the foresight the Soviet dictator had shown in the prewar period. He had adroitly steered Soviet policy in such a way as to lead to an "assured victory." This would be guaranteed, above all, by the Soviets' joining forces with the powerful Western bloc of states, including especially the powerful United States, in fighting the Axis on a global scale.

Yet for the Soviets, perceived widely as a "Communist threat," to be so welcomed by the West as an ally, the USSR had to be, above all, perceived as the victim of Axis aggression, not as the initiator of a pre-emptive, or preventive, war of the type, say, that it had waged against Finland beginning in December 1939.

Stalin's unique brand of hands-on authoritarianism and the "monolithic unity" of his subjects gave him enviable leverage and dispatch (*operativnost'*) to see through his inventive and at times zigzagging policies. Through persuasion and terror, he had molded his population into a largely obedient mass. Stalin rudely compared the "workers, peasants, and intellectuals" to what he called "screws" in the huge machine of the Soviet Leviathan-state. The process of indoctrination that he established was aided by his exploitation of "engineers of human souls," i.e., the "stratum" of obedient intellectuals and artists tasked with instilling in the populace the values of national unity, patriotism, and obedience to Stalin and the Communist Party.

Any challengers to his one-man leadership—as, say, by the fractious, anti-Stalin "Trotskyites" or anti-Stalin Old Bolsheviks of the 1930s—were liquidated. Such "enemies of the people" were consigned to the gulag or to the cellar of the Lubyanka, Moscow, headquarters of the NKVD. Anyone caught as much as verbally criticizing the leader would suffer punishment, including death.[1]

ADVANTAGES ENJOYED BY STALIN

Under such "ideal" social-political conditions for consolidating tyranny, Stalin's crafting of foreign and defense policy enjoyed exceptional *operativnost'* and flexibility. He suffered no parliamentary interference or questioning by the press, which he controlled, or from any quarter of organized public opinion.[2] Thus unimpeded by institutions outside his control (in fact, none really was), he effected his stratagems and freely made his secret deals and treaties with other dictators or with statesmen in the democracies. He had his commissar of foreign affairs craft impressive-sounding speeches delivered in the forum of the world organization, the League of Nations. These were much-publicized addresses delivered in an era when European populations yearned for peace. These addresses touted "collective security" and peace and attracted much world attention and praise.

On the home front, in the great purges of the late 1930s, Stalin had so cleansed the country of any potential "interferers" or "wreckers"—civilian, military, and within the party and economic administration and foreign ministry—that he was positioned in the Kremlin to exploit maximum latitude in the life-or-death actions he undertook in the perilous times just before the outbreak of World War II. Russian historians such as Martirosyan praise Stalin by name for the use of such power that the historian claims was absolutely necessary at that time in order to protect the threatened Soviet state's internal and external security. Other contemporary Russian historians tend implicitly to praise the dictator for these defensive efforts, but without mentioning his name.[3]

The acquisition of absolute power by Stalin was nicely timed, apparently deliberately so. As we will see in the next chapter, events by the late 1930s had reached an ominous crescendo, in particular with respect to the imminent threats to the security of the Soviet state posed by the Axis powers or by alleged plotting by Western European powers. Martirosyan and others claim that some Western policymakers wished to surround the USSR with hostile states that in the case of Nazi Germany would constitute a deadly threat to the Communist state's very existence.

Democratic countries suffered certain disadvantages given the challenges presented by dictators. Under these circumstances, any foreign leader whose authority might be "checked and balanced," as in whatever democratic European country, say, France or England, was put at a distinct disadvantage. Moscow took advantage of uncontrolled fluctuations in Western parliamentary politics as well as of the turn of the capitalist business cycle, those countries' local social and economic conditions, and of other factors that by the nature of their political systems could not be manipulated as by an authoritarian government.[4]

CONTRASTS WITH WESTERN LEADERSHIP

Stalin was fully cognizant as to the vulnerabilities of the Western democracies in respect to their "hamstrung" situation. For instance, a mixed, if short-term, left-wing "Popular Front" government in France (that included Communists as well as pacifist Socialists) was hampered in developing strong foreign and defense policies that were capable of opposing Nazi Germany and Fascist Italy. This weakness obviously stemmed from the inherently democratic nature of that country's political system, a flaw when viewed in the context of an era in which dictators enjoyed maximum *operativnost'* in their own nation-states.

In England, a Conservative leader, Sir Neville Chamberlain, headed a shaky coalition. In this democracy, Chamberlain's main preoccupation was satisfying and catering to the British public's overwhelming demand for peace. Opinion polls, conducted in the late 1930s, reflected very large percentages against war. Both countries' weaknesses led by a red thread to appeasement of Hitler, who also exploited the democratic system in these countries and whose ruling circles he called "worms." The Munich Conference in 1938 capped this disabling appeasement process and amounted to a nonaggression pact signed with a leader whose record and intentions for doing the opposite were quite obvious.

From his vantage point far to the east in Moscow, Stalin closely observed this state of affairs in the West. He saw the condition of near paralysis in the democracies as Hitler grabbed territory, as Mussolini bombed the capital of Abyssinia, and as the League of Nations remained powerless, which like its successor, the United Nations, lacked *compulsory jurisdiction* and *compulsory adjudication* in enforcing international law or its charter. The Soviet dictator drew the necessary conclusions.

All the while Nazi Germany gave every sign of regarding the Communist Soviet Union as its main, potential enemy. Under such conditions, reasoned Stalin, the USSR would proceed—alone—strictly according to its own interests and by using its own drastic methods. In crafting domestic and foreign policy, Stalin's authoritative free hand thus gave him many advantages, even over Hitler's authority in Germany. The latter was sometimes questioned or partly blocked on occasion by his top military and other power blocs and interests within German society whenever the fuehrer sought to press ahead with his most ambitious plans. Any such plans, especially those involving war, demanded expediency and total loyalty by Nazi Party comrades, by the military brass (many of whom were old Prussian foot-draggers), and by the population.

Yet despite his charisma and authority, Hitler did not always achieve the desired 100 percent loyalty. In fact, plans to assassinate him continually arose, and two came close to success. For his part, Stalin never had that problem. His intimidation was total, his personal security unbreachable.[5] But the price paid to him to attain such authority was extreme.

STALIN USES DIPLOMACY AS A WEAPON

As one studies the conduct of Stalin's favorite business in the Kremlin, namely, diplomacy, it is important to keep the leader's various personal characteristics in mind.

Diplomacy to Stalin was to be used with utmost seriousness, like a well-tooled weapon. To Stalin's mind, all-out war was not always necessary or preferable to achieve Soviet state aims. Diplomacy, toward which by contrast Hitler had little patience, could prove its effectiveness, Stalin thought, short of a clash of arms. In fact, in brandishing diplomacy like a weapon, often in tandem with scarcely cloaked extortion, Stalin calculated that the Soviets could reap the impressive rewards via diplomacy—together with the enhancement of the international prestige of the Union of Soviet Socialist Republics and the extension of Soviet influence and territory—that might not otherwise have been achieved through risky armed conflict.

In going along so readily with U.S.-donated Lend-Lease, as he did so promptly in July 1941, just days after the German attack, Stalin had obviously calculated that as a powerful dictator, he could control the risky "fallout" of friendliness toward the popular capitalist donor-country. As he knew, such gratitude would inevitably be felt among his own subjects toward this well-known aid from "*Amerika*," that rather romantic place to many ordinary Soviet citizens. Russian historians today admit that Lend-Lease had a tremendously positive effect on the morale of Soviet civilians and soldiers. Stalin himself, aware of this, not unpainfully, was not above expressing gratitude for the American aid—for public consumption, at home and in America. Later in the war and especially after 1945, all that was forgotten in Soviet propaganda.

Some historians have observed that Stalin considered diplomacy to be "the continuation of war by other means." This Clausewitzian-Leninist formula certainly did underlie Stalin's diplomacy. At the same time, when diplomacy did not or could not get the desired results under urgent conditions as sought by the *Vozhd'* in the short term, he would resort to arms. A case in point was his three-month war against Finland, begun by the Soviets in December 1939. This was a case that resembled the earlier, enforced sovietization of the former Russian imperial borderlands through the 1920s—in which Stalin, the Georgian, personally played an important part as Commissar of Nationalities. In such cases that affected the borderlands and former tsarist territories, Stalin would not hesitate to use arms when a victorious outcome was assured.

Well after World War II and into the years of 1952–1953, Stalin showed signs of increased militancy, both in his domestic as well as foreign policies. Some observers have even detected signs of Stalin's planning a World War III. Yet other historians find evidence for the opposite, even in the early 1950s: that is, a tendency in Stalin's policy in late 1952, for example, to seek accommodation with the West. It was then that the aging dictator showed signs of wishing to hold a new summit, namely with Winston Churchill, who had returned as prime minister in 1951. At that time when he was in his early 70s, Stalin's suspiciousness, perhaps outright paranoia, especially when directed at his comrades in the Politburo and Secretariat, may not have been entirely misplaced. His hatred of Jews was also on the rise at that time.

As to the Winter War against Finland from 1939 to 1940, actual fighting was in that case one such last resort. He had tried the diplomatic route (to win leases of bases for defense of the Soviet Union) but had been adamantly turned down by the Finnish government.

To Stalin, war inevitably entailed dangers that as a rule he was not willing to face. The Winter War against Finland had been a virtual debacle for the USSR. It perhaps made the Soviet dictator extra cautious in his next moves to defend the USSR as the Hitler menace mounted. In contrast to Hitler, Stalin seldom acted impetuously like a risk-taking gambler. This was seen in the days of the civil war when it was Stalin who, opposing his gung-ho generals like Tukhachevsky, opposed mounting a Red Army campaign to go all out to take Warsaw in 1920. Moreover, Stalin, then a minor figure, seems also to have been skittish about the Bolshevik armed coup of November 1917, leaving it to others, especially to Trotsky, to engineer the seizure of power, or as called in Bolshevik propaganda, the "revolution."

As to the Winter War: It had come about this way. In his application of forceful diplomacy to acquire the Finnish territory he wanted from Helsinki in the autumn of 1939, the usually cautious Stalin, in launching a war against "little Finland," had counted on the Red Army's risk-free, large superiority in numbers of men and arms. With such assets, he reasoned, his armies could easily overpower the enemy. Yet his aggression failed, an embarrassing travesty in the field of battle that left an indelible mark on the Soviet dictator along with a low opinion of the fighting capabilities of his military. Of course, in the end the sheer weight and firepower of the Soviet army brought a Finnish surrender.

Casualties in the war had mounted astronomically on the Soviet side. So Stalin again resorted to diplomacy to see through his territorial demands on Finland, with the result that the treaty with that scrappy country to the north, signed in March 1940, gave the dictator only half a loaf—less than the large swatches of Finnish territory, if not the whole of Finland as an additional Soviet Republic, that apparently he had originally sought, although this is disputed. The compromise peace with the Finns assured that this bloody war—especially for the Soviets—would not continue. With the war had come a mounting antipathy abroad toward the USSR along with the perception that the RKKA was not as mighty and invincible (a weakness that was closely observed in Berlin) as Soviet propaganda had claimed. At the same time, Marshal Kirill A. Meretskov, the strategist who had drawn up the Soviet Finnish invasion plan, wrote in his postwar memoirs that he had been ordered by Stalin after the March peace treaty to develop a further plan for capturing and annexing all of Finland. Whether that aim is true or not—Meretskov is not necessarily a credible source, especially given his loathing of the dictator and his clashes with the leader, who had intimidated him—Stalin never in the future entertained such expansionism against Finland. This restraint on Stalin's part was seen even during the Great Patriotic War when Finland was a fighting ally of Nazi Germany and might have been expected to be conquered and occupied by Stalin's armies just as other Baltic countries and east European Axis allies were.

The Winter War and the treaty with Finland significantly marked the final abandonment, in fact, of overt Soviet attempts ever again to try to convert Finland into a vassal state or Soviet Republic. In its way, the settlement of March 1940 and its aftermath became a symbol of the way in which Stalin operated.

STALIN'S PERSONAL QUALITIES

Stalin totally lacked the emotional instability—that is, on the job—that interfered so disastrously with Hitler's distorted sense of reality. Stalin's alleged "paranoia" is often cited by biographers and historians, whether Russian or Western. Yet the less clinical expression with which to describe the dictator's or any tyrant's eagle eye might better be "suspiciousness." In any case, this trait seldom interfered with the Soviet leader's conduct of foreign affairs. If and when it did, it arose only near the end of his life in 1952–1953. This was when Stalin definitely showed signs of pathological paranoia. This was seen in his irrationally blaming Jews for plotting various nonexistent conspiracies and crimes, and planning, as some speculate, a World War III against the capitalist world.

Yet even in 1952–1953, when he was in his early 70s, Stalin's suspiciousness, when directed at his "comrades" in the Politburo and Secretariat, was hardly misplaced. It may even have been warranted. For, as it turned out, evidence of active plotting against Stalin among his cohorts, especially by 1952, has surfaced through recent historical research. Some evidence points to Stalin's murder in early 1953 by means of a plot centered around Lavrenti Beria and Georgi Malenkov, along with others at the top.

The Soviet dictator's workday started mid-to late morning. He would then work far into the night and early morning hours. His day could last anywhere from 10 to 12 or even 15 hours. At "dinners" toward midnight at his nearby dacha 15 minutes from the Kremlin or at his "distant" dacha twice the time away, Stalin would often hold informal, semiofficial meetings with a half-dozen key members of the Politburo. At these informal conclaves, most of the other comrades would down large amounts of vodka. Stalin, however, generally kept to Georgian wine, a regimen that some believe permitted him to keep his cool while observing his colleagues as they got progressively drunker. They would perhaps thereby reveal some unpleasant things that Stalin should know about. (It is said that Stalin's physicians recommended wine as a remedy for the dictator's notorious insomnia.) Only on rare occasions would Stalin allow himself to cross the line.

Unlike many of his cohorts, Stalin was frugal in his private life. His two dachas were modestly furnished. At Kremlin banquets in honor of foreign dignitaries during World War II, Stalin would pretend to be drinking toasts of 100-proof vodka like the rest of the Politburo and the guests. Actually, however, his glass most often contained wine of low alcoholic content. In talks with American negotiators as Lend-Lease and collaboration in the war got under way in 1941–1942, Stalin would let the guests drink while keeping himself sober. Stalin was always in control of himself and, as he hoped, others, not infrequently in order to take them in or as happened several times during the war, as when he insisted on the Western Allies' opening of a second front in Europe. The next day he would be all smiles, prompting observers to describe Stalin as a consummate actor.

To make this system work efficiently in the Soviet Union and for the Soviets ultimately to triumph over their external enemies as events played out before and during war on the Eastern Front in World War II, Stalin in his person possessed the necessary leadership qualities of determination, intelligence, and skill. Above all, he had to show caution (one of his well-known traits in politics) when dealing with the volatile complexities and vagaries of world affairs, which also meant coping with adventurous types like Adolf Hitler or with the militarist clique in Tokyo or, often unsuccessfully, as it sometimes happened, with the bumptious *Il Duce* of Italy.

According to intimates, Stalin's work habits reflected his extraordinary determination and daily application to his job. He toiled diligently on a virtual "18/7" basis and into late night hours. To quote the Russian proverb, which might apply to Stalin's punctiliousness, *Rabota ne volk, v les ne rubezhit*, "Work is not a wolf that runs away into the forest." Stalin habitually would arrive at his Kremlin office in late morning. Sometimes he had previously slept in his private Kremlin quarters, as he apparently did on the eve of the German attack, June 21–22, 1941. Or he was driven to the Kremlin from one of his two dachas, the one (*blizhnaya*) near Moscow's outskirts, the other farther away.

DEALING WITH THE WEST AND AMERICA

When it came to the appeasement-obsessed ruling circles of the Western European countries in the 1930s as well in the World War "Big Three" summits, Stalin was particularly adept in following an unnerving "dialectic." At times he would woo partners, at other times taunting the Allied countries' leaders and attempting to manipulate Western public opinion. These were the techniques of psychological warfare that seemed to come natural to Stalin. Such methods kept his adversaries and their electorates guessing. America presented a special case in Stalin's maneuvers, including the way he "handled" President Franklin D. Roosevelt.

Even as he struck deals with Hitler, however, Stalin never entirely broke off relations or lost interest in maintaining links with the Western allies-to-be. This was true even as he hurled epithets of "bourgeois" or "imperialist" at them. It was as if for Stalin the Western Bloc was his ace in the hole. In Stalin's superficial use of ideological and propagandistic sloganeering, the Western democracies were the "bourgeois-democratic states" who, in war with the Axis after September 1, 1939, tried on their own to defeat Hitler's aggression. At the time—at least until mid-1940—Stalin thought this intra-"imperialist" armed struggle in the West, begun in September 1939, would last for many more years, during which the USSR itself would have time to prepare to confront German aggression and "tip the scales" in its favor.

However, the war in the West ended abruptly (by his or anyone's reckoning) with the fall of Paris in June 1940 to the Nazis. Hitler soon indicated (as detected by Soviet foreign intelligence) that he would postpone the invasion of the British Isles and instead turn the Wehrmacht against Soviet Russia. Stalin, also clearly taken by surprise by the suddenness of Hitler's victories in the West, set about revising his own plans after mid-1940 for meeting the German thrust toward the East, which Stalin had earlier calculated would be Hitler's ultimate strategy. Meanwhile, both Germany and the Soviets knew that America sooner or later would enter the war. America under President Franklin D. Roosevelt had steadily edged toward war with the Axis by the spring of 1941 and had become a de facto semi-participant. Indeed, by the spring of 1941, Lend-Lease aid was flowing to Britain. By December, the United States was fully at war with both Japan and the European Axis powers. As everyone knew, when America did enter the conflict, a colossal tipping of the scales in the Allied favor was bound to follow. Consequently, each side, Germany and Russia, was getting ready for this watershed turning point in the war. For his part, Hitler knew that America's entry into the struggle would save England and also bring Russia into the war on the side of the Allies. His only recourse, he calculated, was to seize the initiative by invading and occupying Russia and thereby fulfill the classic geopolitical goal of dominating Eurasia as the all-determining "world island." Once in control of this huge, well-resourced land mass, even America could be outflanked and neutralized.[6]

Did not Stalin reason in the same geopolitical/geostrategic way? However, in Stalin's reckoning, America had best be on the Soviet side, not cast as an enemy.[7]

STALIN'S USE OF BLUFF

In his political-diplomatic maneuvering and posturing, Stalin showed that he was adept, above all, at bluffing. Maneuver and bluff, of course, are both often used in the military context. This was a frame of reference all too familiar to Stalin, who was well schooled in military tactics from his experience as hands-on commissar on the dozen-member Council of Workers' and Peasants' Defense (simply *Sovet Oborony*, or Defense Council). This was the key organ that under Lenin's leadership conducted the Civil War, 1918–1921, and that saved Soviet power. In politics, as in war, Stalin would tack and execute maneuvers and gambits—e.g., as in his "friendly" gestures toward Berlin during the 21-month "honeymoon" after the Nazi-Soviet pacts of August–September 1939 or toward the Western Allies during the height of World War II. Winston Churchill once described Stalin as a consummate tactician. The British Prime Minister remarked ironically, "What a pleasure it was to work with that great man ... the 'father of his nation.'" Yet all those "acts" and Stalinite moves were simply part of what Molotov, the dictator's closest aide, called in his retirement the "great game" that Stalin chose to play in the serpentine way he did. As we will see, this "game" also included another game, one of bluff, played by the Soviet leader on the eve of the German invasion in June 1941.[8]

A "MASTER POLITICIAN"

In all, Josef Vissarionovich Djugashvili (Stalin) possessed to an impressive degree the entire gamut of biographical prerequisites for unqualified dictatorial leadership under Soviet conditions. His fit into his times, the age of dictators, was all but perfect. As a few Western biographers along with the statesmen who dealt with the Soviet leader have acknowledged, for his times and circumstances, Stalin was *the* "master politician" who knew how to navigate the stormy seas and treacherous currents better than any of his contemporary heads of state. For his part, Marshal Georgi Zhukov commended the party and Stalin for the latter's "wisdom" and his "farsighted" foreign and domestic policies that, alleged Zhukov, "laid the basis for our victories in the Great Patriotic War." It was Stalin, by the way, who aptly gave the Eastern Front war that historic name, derived from the term, "Patriotic War," used for Tsar Alexander I's war against Napoleon. Stalin added the word "great."

To be sure no "close friend" of Stalin's, Zhukov nevertheless fulsomely endorsed Stalin's grand strategy and tactics that the Soviet leader used before and during the war. The marshal noted that in the war, these tactics were sometimes defensive (*oboronitel'niye*) in nature, at other times offensist (*nastupatel'niye*). According to the retired marshal, Stalin's prewar and wartime leadership combined qualities of cool calculation and wary cautiousness.[9]

The "boss" (*Khozain*) and "leader" (*Vozhd'*) were names applied to him by his cohorts and propagandists. These cognomens indeed caught the essence of Stalin's nature and style. A true tyrant, like Ivan the Terrible in Russian fact and legend, Stalin was not satisfied unless he had penetrated and controlled tyrannically every facet of Soviet society, including especially the minds of his immediate aides. Ivan was known to scrutinize a comrade's face and manner during a banquet to see if a given aide or boyar was paying attention to the tsar or appeared in to be plotting against him. Stalin was said to employ the same kind of eye scrutiny of his Politburo cohorts during late-night parties held at one of his dachas. In so many respects in his success as supreme leader, Stalin far outshone his colleague-dictator, Adolf Hitler. Stalin's aides' show of loyalty to him, as toward Tsar Ivan III from his obedient entourage, was a matter of life and death to them. Stalin made sure that they all understood that.

Stalin's curiosity about key foreign countries and their systems, leaders, and exploitable vulnerabilities knew no bounds. An important part of Soviet espionage was to feed back information to the Stalin Kremlin on the workings of foreign political systems and their leading officials. This was especially true in connection with Stalin's deep interest in America—as the second-most (after Germany) major helper in Soviet industrialization and also possibly a future Soviet ally and donor of vital military aid in the "inevitable" war to come. That Stalin perceived this possibility, if not likelihood, by 1940–1941 now seems undeniable.

As concerned the United States, the Soviet leader inserted himself into every possible aspect of that country's relations, present or future, with the USSR. This fact struck American Lend-Lease negotiators in Moscow. They discovered to their surprise from the very opening of the talks in July 1941 how well informed Stalin was on all things American. As to war supplies, this included Stalin's command of every single item to be shipped as listed on his first, long Lend-Lease wish list. The inclusion of those items, obviously, he had been contemplating for some time, perhaps even months.

Once briefed on whatever matter, Stalin considered himself to be an expert (although this was not always true, the dictator nevertheless gave the impression of being a polymath). This putative expertise included everything from *belles-lettres* and linguistics to military science, biology, agronomy, and constitutional law to particular types and specs of military equipment, as in the case of technology to be sent to the Soviet Union via Lend-Lease. His memory—for detail and persons (e.g., "party cadres")—has been described as prodigious by those who knew him well. Although his manner was certainly authoritarian, he would arrive at his conclusions as a rule only after consulting professional specialists. He would even hear out other members of the Politburo before drawing his own final conclusions and making decisions. Later in the war, he did the same with his military commanders. Once he had immersed himself in the nitty-gritty of whatever endeavor or subject, Stalin would make the final decision absolutely on his own. He chose whichever plan, conclusion, tactics, and strategy or work of art—along with any given assassination or execution—that he thought best fit the bill or served the best interests of the state. This procedure, of course, buttressed his own personal power, which he viewed as being in tandem with the country's interests as well; "the state is me," he seemed to think. At the same time, whatever policy he and his aides crafted toward other countries had to in some manner ultimately advance the Soviet global cause of world revolution and Soviet domination.

It is generally testified by Soviet army memoirists that this likewise was his procedure as commander-in-chief when conducting sessions within the councils of the military high command, or Stavka, during the war. Unlike Hitler during the Russian campaign, Stalin—at least, by 1942, during the Great Patriotic War—would carefully weigh what his commanders had to say before making the final decision. Poets and novelists, architects, economists, cinematographers, composers, scientists, marshals, admirals and generals, and diplomatic service officials—anyone performing a public function in the society and for the state—knew that whatever party line or decision would be reached, it would be Stalin alone who would ultimately color it and approve it. And woe to those who did not take this into account. Perhaps this is what Hitler meant when he described his Soviet counterpart as an outstanding organizer and administrator.

Stalin would likewise keenly observe how policy was being carried into effect. This, too, directly affected Lend-Lease. Sometimes this occurred in counterproductive ways, since lower officials, especially senior officers of the RKKA, feared to act unless they thought the boss would approve. Similarly, junior RKKA officers would show little initiative and awaited detailed commands from senior officers (this became less so as the war progressed). Initiative and decision making at lower levels was thus often hamstrung. Typically heavy-handed, totalitarian bureaucracy, developed to the nth degree in Stalin's administrative-command system in Soviet Russia, also complicated execution of Lend-Lease assistance at the middle and grassroots levels. Everyone was expected to think and work as Stalin thought they should. The penalty for failing to "understand" Stalin's methods and the system could mean, and often did, torture, prison, the gulag, or the firing squad.

Unlike some of the other dictators in history, Stalin set very high standards of *rabotosposobnost'* (capacity for work, diligence). Lenin (Vladimir Ilyich Ulyanov) by comparison was considered to have been quite lazy. Yet his party name was not derived from the Russian word for "lazy," *leniviy*. It was derived from the Lena River, where he had spent a relatively leisurely exile in Siberia from 1897 to 1900. Vacations for the boss were working ones. He was an indomitable toiler at his job. Any number of foreign diplomats, such as those discussing Lend-Lease and other sensitive matters with the Soviet leader in 1941 or participating in summits with him throughout the war, noticed how shrewdly and intelligently the well-informed Stalin conducted himself and the affairs of state. Naturally, his information was buttressed by electronic bugs secretly installed in the temporary residences of his official guests, as in Yalta, Crimea, in 1945.

Whatever the hidden electronic bugs may have failed to pick up, Stalin likely heard with his own ears and kept tucked away in his extremely keen memory.

2

Stalin's Methods and Accomplishments

Following Lenin's death in January 1924, Stalin immediately created the self-serving "Lenin Cult."[1] To this campaign he associated his own person as the supreme protector of the Leninist tradition. Moreover, he had been the lead speaker at Lenin's funeral. Through his party propaganda machine (much admired by Josef Goebbels as well as by Hitler), Stalin began being touted as the only true Leninist and interpreter of the Lenin credo.

It is sometimes alleged that while he was alive, Lenin was modest about his own importance and potential historicity as "creator of Bolshevism," and "founder of the world's first socialist state." In contrast to Ilyich's alleged modesty, it is claimed, Stalin was boastful, a self-glorifier. The truth, however, is that while he was still alive, Lenin never actually discouraged or put a stop to the glorification of his own person. Adoration of the leader was in place in Lenin's own lifetime. It had noticeably blossomed in the years just before Lenin's death in January 1924. The famous party-condoned red and black Futurist and Constructivist posters alone of the 1920s with their eulogies to Lenin and Bolshevism tell the story of this self-glorification (such totalitarian art was later copied in Fascist Italy and Nazi Germany). Portraits and busts of Lenin were displayed ubiquitously in homes and offices throughout the Soviet Union—posthumously as well as in his lifetime.

THE STALIN CULT

The flattering, Stalin-inspired Lenin biographies of the 1920s and 1930s whitewashed all this evident conceit in the deceased national hero. Instead, Ilyich was depicted as "modest" and "unassuming." He was often pictured wearing a plain white shirt and tie and a black worker's *kepka*. In motion picture sequences shot in the Kremlin, Lenin was shown smiling and petting a tabby cat (*polasataya koshka*) sitting contentedly on his lap. Or he was shown speaking animatedly in the street with a comrade-in-arms. Here was the "caring," "affectionate," "personable," comradely Vladimir Ilyich.

Meanwhile, however, beyond the Kremlin walls, innocent people were being shot simply for being non-Communist Socialist-Revolutionaries, alleged spies, or what Lenin called "counterrevolutionary scum" and "insects." Lenin gave instructions to the police to kill ever more public enemies in order to drive home the tangible intimidation by means of what he proudly called the "Red Terror" in imitation of the Robespierre model in the French Revolution. Orthodox priests were strung up on trees and lampposts as Lenin called for more of the same. Citizens were taken hostage by the Cheka secret police or they were sentenced to death by the drumhead "revolutionary tribunals" (presaging the summary justice meted out by latter-day Communist regimes in Maoist China, North Korea, Cuba, Cambodia, etc.). Suspect writers were imprisoned or exiled, among them the "George Orwell" of Soviet Russia, Yevgeny Zamyatin, author of the science fiction novel *We*. During the Lenin years, thousands were put in prison or sent to Siberian concentration camps. Millions of citizens died of starvation, victims of Lenin's harsh "War Communism" policies of seizing peasants' land and food supplies. Suspect "petty-bourgeois businessmen"—shopkeepers and small businessmen, many of whom were Jews—were forced in many cases to wear yellow cards in their hats so that they were publicly stigmatized as potential or actual "enemies of the people." Similarly, Hitler used star-shaped yellow labels pinned on stigmatized people, as displayed on the coats worn by Jews or pasted on their shop windows.[2]

Although much vaunted by Western leftists, the Soviet republic had become a modern police state. Besides enforcing "revolutionary justice," it was replete with such accoutrements as regime scapegoats and hostages that were used to enforce absolute rule. Indeed, Lenin's efficient, totalitarian methods for exerting power were to be widely imitated abroad in the 1930s. So was the cult of the leader.

A little-known fact until recently about Lenin was his mental impairment from 1923 until his death in January 1924. Official photos of him at the time were doctored to show a recuperating Lenin with a normal if grim and sad expression on his face as he sat covered with a blanket in a wheelchair. Yet at the time these pictures were taken in the city of Gorky and published in the Soviet press and abroad, the leader's mind was deranged. Hardened, sclerotic cerebral veins and arteries had reduced his speech to that of babbling like a baby; his cognitive faculties had become involved.

Meanwhile, with Lenin away in Gorky, Stalin and his aides availed themselves of the partial vacuum in the Kremlin. The general secretary had taken personal control of Lenin's terminal "recuperation." Falsely promised by Stalin and his cohorts for public consumption was Lenin's "ultimate recovery." Stalin and others would visit the ailing Lenin at his suburban retreat on a daily basis. Stalin's men carefully "skinned" and censored Lenin's mail whole taking note of his declining mental acuity. At one point, as the records show, Stalin preempted Lenin's plans, openly expressed by Ilyich himself, to commit suicide. Lenin had obtained poisoned potassium cyanide capsules. But, alas, Stalin allegedly prevented the leader's suicide, boastfully informing the party central committee of his timely intercession.

Lenin's last testament, withheld by Stalin, strongly criticized the Gensek. (Some of today's Stalin apologists claim that there was no such testament, that its existence was invented by Trotskyites and Western "Trotsky toadies," like, they say, Max Eastman.)[3] Lenin's wife, Nadezhda Krupskaya, treated rudely by Stalin personally and his cronies, was not on speaking terms with the "crude" Georgian. Stalin and his efficient party machine had all such mumbled criticism and dissatisfaction with the Gensek's methods suppressed.

Stalin's political machine to the contrary, deep dissatisfaction with him nevertheless was known to be widespread among top Old Bolsheviks and party insiders. Intra-party dissent became one of the reasons why Stalin by the 1930s chose to liquidate such persons. Trotsky's active, ubiquitous anti-Stalin organization abroad also poured out a steady stream of bitter recriminations against Stalin, which the latter combated for some 15 years until he successfully had Trotsky assassinated in Mexico.[4]

Stalin's hagiography about Lenin's last months was finally rectified with the demise of the USSR in 1991. With the partial opening of the archives, authentic photos of Lenin, formerly kept out of sight, were released. They showed the deranged leader as he looked in 1923–1924 with his dazed, blankly staring eyes and his distorted facial appearance. It was during this period of terminal cerebral infirmity in 1923 when some of Lenin's, the party's, and the Cheka's most draconic measures were inflicted on the Russian population. They had been devised or at least formally approved by the mentally deranged Lenin, who often lost his temper and was virtually out of his senses.

Lenin's much touted humility and modesty aside, we now know—as did Stalin in the 1920s—that Vladimir Ilyich did not object to the wide, immodest adoption of "Lenin," "Leninsky," "Ilyich," "Bol'shevistskiy," etc., being attached to the names of factories, streets, schools, works of art, and towns that had lost their traditional geographic designations. Parents gave their sons and daughters first names that bore some form of Lenin's name or words related to his career, family, etc.: viz., "Ulyanov," "Ulyanova," "Kommunist," "Bolshevik," "Partiiyets," "Komsomoly-ets," "Rabochiy," etc. As Gensek in charge of the party *apparat*, Stalin, of course, encouraged this bathos about the deceased Lenin. It was a device of which, in fact, he himself would later make use for his own self-glorification. Lenin's title of *Vozhd'* was later bestowed on Stalin, ostensibly by comrades, not by himself.

Abroad in Berlin in the 1920s, meanwhile, an ambitious and ardent nationalist named Josef Goebbels was recording in his earliest diary that he found Lenin to be just the right national leader for the stressful times after World War I.[5] Goebbels was just about to join Hitler's budding movement, later to become Hitler's propaganda minister, and wrote that he admired Lenin's authoritarian style, his nationalistic pride, even the Leninist ideology of Soviet socialism. Goebbels himself had even once flirted with adopting the principles of Soviet Communist ideology. Above all, young Goebbels was attracted to Lenin's authoritative manner and the Russian dictator's upright arm as a salute and rallying gesture pointing to a glorious future for his huge country. He admired Bolshevik militancy, Lenin's fiery radio speeches and film clips, and, of course, the dramatic, full-length Soviet propaganda films of the 1920s, with their propagandistic varnishing or distortions of historical truth (an early form of feature-length "docudramas"). Goebbels was also struck by the way Russian youth idolized the Russian *Vozhd'*, Lenin, in the Communist Youth (*Komsomol*) organizations named after him.

Such Soviet public organizations were later duly copied by the Nazis, as with their *Jugend* adoration of Hitler. Lenin, as Goebbels suggested in his diary, truly embodied the "leadership principle"

(*Füherprinzip*). In a later speech, entitled *Lenin oder Hitler?*, Goebbels obliquely showed his admiration of the Soviet dictator by promoting in propaganda Hitler's own expression of the leadership principle, the German embodiment of the original Lenin-Stalin *yedinonachaliye* (or "one-man leadership" principle), invented and touted in Soviet Russia after 1918. The Soviet authorities, at Lenin's urging, had openly adopted this basic principle of exalting one-man, heroic leadership as they backed away from sugarcoated promises of "workers' control" as touted in Lenin's pre-Bolshevik coup pamphlet, *State and Revolution* (August 1917). All such deviousness undoubtedly impressed Stalin.

The above raises the issue of the great contrasts between Stalin and Hitler's propaganda methods. Whereas Stalin emphasized the "positive" features of utopian Sovietism and the happy workers and peasants, Hitler focused on discipline, awe, and fear. Put another way, Stalin was clever to conceal the brutalities of his regime, whereas Hitler appeared for all but advertised the "Teutonic" might and fearsomeness of his new order. All of this is another way of saying that Stalin was trying to *sell* his system to Western "bourgeois" countries. Hitler, by contrast, aimed at instilling fear and trembling in subject populations. This difference in turn reflected Stalin's usual expansionist tactics of bringing out his new order via a "creeping toward Sovietism" represented by the Popular Front tactics employed in Western countries in the 1930s. Stalin likewise emphasized the importance of converting countries to socialism gradually by well-timed stages. He especially singled out Poland and Romania in this context. He viewed colonial countries in the Third World as being at the "pre-bourgeois stage" in their development. For Hitler, on the other hand, it was a case of simply marching in with panzers and infantry. Not that Stalin never used similar methods!

MACHIAVELLIAN METHODS

As sometimes stressed in Western and Russian literature, Stalin was suspicious of and impulsively vengeful toward some of the Red Army commanders—as, for instance, at the very beginning of hostilities in 1941. He used intimidation and fear-mongering as a tool to guarantee obedience to him. His summary actions in brutally punishing by shooting some of the top RKKA officers (such as Gen. D. G. Pavlov and Pavlov's chief of staff of the Western Special Military District,

Gen. V. Ye. Klimovskikh, and others) are hard to rationalize even as "understandable" severity demanded by wartime urgency and for the purpose of setting an example for other Red Army field and staff officers, not to mention the effect of such intimidation on the rank and file.

Stalin demanded that his military show nothing less than superb skill and maximum courage in trying to halt the Wehrmacht's advance. Especially in the earliest months of the war, Stalin was totally intolerant of what he perceived as the slightest show of "cowardice" or proclivity of RKKA commanders to retreat in the face of fire. Actually, there was considerable defection in the ranks and desertions in the early weeks of the war, although RKKA men and women mostly fought bravely under extremely adverse conditions. Stalin would make some of the officers sacrificial lambs to drive home his point about his demand for courage and bravery. RKKA GIs, or *Vanki,* were shot in the back of the head if they tried to retreat from fighting the enemy. During later months of the war, Stalin showed less intolerance and brutality toward his professional military, who themselves, however, were no less intolerant of the slightest breach in discipline or the bravery of their men. Unlike Hitler in the latter years of the war, Stalin after 1942 appeared increasingly willing to listen to the advice of his field and staff officers. He would generally agree to their tactics in a given battle situation and would even sometimes yield to their arguments, changing his own views to conform to theirs. In their memoirs, some military officers commended Stalin for this.

It might be admitted that, above all, Stalin's Machiavellian methods, brutal as they were, generally succeeded. Whether under some other less firm and authoritarian Soviet leader the USSR would have been saved from disaster in 1941–1945 is a matter of conjecture. In any case, it appears to be true that the country—the party, the military, and the society—were more united in Soviet Russia on the eve of the German attack in June 1941 than at any other period up to that point in the 24-year history of that vast, multi-ethnic state. However, the price paid to attain this desired unity was, to say the least, high.

The consolidation of a highly heterogeneous population and instilling in it via a single, ruling party unimpeachable solidarity were the results of Stalin's draconic measures. This was no small, if also morally reprehensible, accomplishment. In place of the rampant political heresies and diverse movements within the ruling party and the society that characterized the immediate post-Lenin period after 1924, Stalin had managed to weld together a largely obedient society. Molotov, number two to Stalin, was perhaps not entirely exaggerating in observing in his retirement in the 1980s:[6]

"We slashed right and left. We scored victories, yet latter enemies of various stripes survived, and as we were faced by the growing danger of Fascist aggression, [these internal enemies] might have united. Thanks to 1937, there was no Fifth Column in our country during the war. Even among the Bolsheviks, you know, there were some—there still are some—who are loyal and dedicated as long as the nation and the Party face no danger. But as soon as something dangerous appears, they first waver and then switch sides."

LEGACY OF THE CAUTIOUS LEADER

In terms of his global strategy, Stalin can be accused of many things, but not of reckless adventurism or of a lack of inspired shrewdness and foresight. In some respects, even his signs of paranoia, so tangible if not needless in the years following the war, paid dividends. His pre-war suspicion toward putative enemies, foreign or domestic, was not infrequently on target. No few enemies were locked up or shot. Even whole peoples, such as Soviet Germans and Turkic Chechen-Ingush ethnic groups, were uprooted from their native locales, put into railroad boxcars, and shipped off to be "resettled" far from any combat zone so that they could not collaborate with the enemy. These were precautions. Were such dire measures entirely necessary?

Stalin made mistakes, some of which were very costly. Yet on the whole he proved that nothing wins like victory and that nothing serves better as leadership, at least under the Soviet system of the 1930s and 1940s, than absolute control buttressed by large doses of terror and fear. The point is that objective historians might be obliged to agree that his brutal, immoral methods did pay off.

In March 1953, after ruling the USSR for some 25 years, the "genius," "Coryphaeus," and "Generalissimus" died at age 72. He had been world history's most brutal tyrant. Yet under his rule, his state played the key role in the military defeat of the Axis Powers in World War II (e.g., as much as 80 percent of the Wehrmacht was tied up in fighting the war on the Eastern Front). Certainly one of his greatest accomplishments was to have put the former "outcast" USSR on the global map by the 1940s and 1950s. It had become a nation-state that was fast assuming the rank of a superpower, rivaling even the United States.

To quote the often-repeated boast heard in Moscow up to the mid-1980s, "No decision in world politics can be made without the participation of the Soviet Union." This was a far cry from the Soviet Union's lowly prewar status as an outcast at a time when a major Munich conference and other summits in Europe of the period excluded the USSR as a participant. At that time, the Soviet Union was an outright pariah-state ignominiously expelled from the league in 1939. For their part, Nazi Germany and Fascist Italy voluntarily withdrew from the league just as the Soviet Union was entering it.

Yet expulsion aside as a pro tem setback for Soviet prestige and the marketability of Sovietism, it seems that under the circumstances of the late 1930s, Stalin appeared rather to prefer a policy for his country of going-it-alone—at least for the interim, up until Soviet involvement in the "big war." In some ways, the Soviet dictator had no other choice. The West both feared and despised, and for good reasons, the "Marxist-Leninist" empire with its goal of establishing a Soviet federation of the whole world. In 1919, Lenin had founded the Communist International, or "General Staff" of world revolution, as a subversive base for the express purpose of undermining of "bourgeois-democratic" regimes worldwide as well as sovietizing "imperialist-ruled colonies" of the Third World. Stalin once candidly described his construction plans for the USSR as "establishing the base for world revolution."

As to autarchy, the Soviet leader even touted, somewhat disingenuously given extensive Soviet trade with capitalist countries, an economic policy of self-dependence. This would dovetail with Stalin's diplomatic line of neutrality. The latter especially meant no "binding" ties with other states in an international arena that was inexorably moving toward a major war.

After his appointment by Lenin in 1922 as general secretary (Gensek) of the Russian Communist Party, a key position, Stalin set about using and improving upon the dictatorial power that he had seen Vladimir Ilyich employ successfully. Ilyich's 13 years as authoritative and oracular Bolshevik party leader plus his seven short years as Soviet head of state and nominal party chief were instructive models to Stalin.

Lying ahead for Stalin were years of momentous decisions that he would have to make in an international environment replete with fighting and threats of worse to come, especially for the USSR.

3

The *Vozhd'* Prepares for War

Stalin had readied himself for the tricky political maneuvers called for on the stormy international front. These were the universal dictators' tactics that were so characteristic of the mid-1930s. By then fully in command of the Communist Party and the Red Army military—following the party and military purges, respectively, of the early and later 1930s and into the 1940s—Stalin was fully equipped to meet by means of absolute authority the many challenges of that tumultuous prewar era. Stalin's accretion of power seemed to follow Montesquieu's principle that the larger the given nation, the greater the ruling power must be.

CONSOLIDATING THE HOME FRONT

What were these foreign and domestic threats? How did the Soviet dictator cope with them? Given the supreme power he had acquired, did he adequately prepare his country for what Lenin-Stalin ideology called the coming "inevitable war"? Some post-Stalin criticism of the late dictator claimed that Stalin had not sufficiently prepared the country for the German onslaught. What about the blatant immorality of the bloody methods Stalin had employed to meet the challenges of war in the 1930s? Stalin had met this enormous task of unifying the ruling party and the country by liquidating most of the party's Old Guard. As to the need to unite the Communist Party, which lacked airtight solidarity in the early 1930s, Stalin's drastic measures took the form of the infamous purge trials (most were held in 1936–1937). Famous Bolsheviks like Bukharin, Radek, Rykov, Zinoviev, Kamenev, et al., who had been close, "lips-to-teeth" comrades of Lenin and who had held high positions, were accused of anti-party—read: anti-Stalin—treason as well as of embracing the ideology of Trotskyism. The latter was a catchall epithet describing a heinous "political crime." It was exploited in a vague, elastic way. Yet it was one that did contain some "concrete" meaning, to use a Marxist term.[1]

Although exploited exaggeratedly by Stalin, who obsessed over Trotsky the renegade, there nevertheless was evidence backing up the allegation of Trotskyism as a disorienting heresy. Widespread Trotskyism in various forms did detract from the kind of monolithic unity that Stalin sought and that he regarded as necessary to enhance his autocratic power as well as to gird up the expansive country for the coming big war. Moreover, some Old Bolsheviks actually did adhere to some of Trotsky's ideology about domestic policy and world revolution. Some even favored Trotsky's formal readmission into the Russian Communist Party (from which he had been expelled since the late 1920s).

Combined with persistent, pro-Trotsky sentiments top to bottom within the party was, of course, widely spread dislike and fear of Stalin and his ham-handed methods. By the summer of 1932, Gensek "Koba" Stalin was fully aware that well-organized opposition to his policies was growing throughout the country. He was by then strong enough to adopt draconic measures against his disuniting foes. Through the *apparat*, which he tightly controlled, Stalin was able to engineer various measures to defeat his opponents at such forums as party congresses and plenums of the Central Committee—especially by packing both bodies with a sufficient number of loyal Stalinites. (In the 1970s, Saddam Hussein in Iraq, an emulator of Stalin, used the same methods to eliminate foes within the Baathist Party and unite its ranks under his autocracy.)

In reviewing the above events, some of today's Communist-tinged as well as non-Communist apologists for the "struggle against Trotskyism" in the USSR view Stalin's campaign against the number two leader of the Bolshevik coup d'etat of November 7, 1917, as "understandable." They claim that under prevailing conditions, Stalin's campaign was "justifiable" in eliminating tenacious, fractious opposition to the Soviet leader's policies of the dangerous late 1930s.

In his biography of Stalin, Martirosyan claims that Stalin was a "de-Leninizer" as well as an advocate of the "realistic, farsighted" program of "building socialism in one country." The historian claims that one of Stalin's monumental achievements was to rid Soviet realpolitik of the "utopian," "Cominternist" idea of world revolution.[2] For its part, the Comintern, brainchild of Lenin and Trotsky, he alleges, was an organ mainly used by Stalin as a tool in his foreign policy of diplomatic maneuvering among adversaries and for the purposes of recruiting spies. Stalin, Martirosyan says, rarely lent verbal support to the notion of world revolution. Instead, he worked assiduously to industrialize the country and build the economic foundations toward developing the state's military defenses while following a policy of uniting the party and the country. In pursuing his program of "socialism in one country," Stalin in effect rejected the Lenin-Trotsky idea of Russia's being merely the "tool" of foreign revolutionaries and domestic utopians. These latter "dreamers" thought that Russia itself was inherently incapable of being a power in its own right. Stalin thus "de-Leninized" the country's policies.

WERE THE PURGES JUSTIFIED?

In this context and that of building socialism, Martirosyan and others of his persuasion view Stalin's mission against the Lenin-Trotsky legacy and the Old Bolsheviks as one of "de-Westernizing" Soviet policy. That is, he claims, Stalin put the emphasis on Russia's own capabilities. The Old Bolsheviks along within the purged military, he writes, denied the possibility of "building socialism in one country," Stalin's adopted slogan by the late 1920s. Instead, these officials counted on revolutionary conquest of the rich, industrialized countries as a shortcut to achieving industrialization in Soviet Russia.

In making these accusations against those whom Stalin purged in the three major public trials in 1937–1938, the historian goes so far as to suggest that the Comintern and its leading officials were financed by foreign enemies, as represented by the Jewish bankers, Warburg and Rothschild. Fearing sovietism and Communism, these powerful foreign elements influenced their respective governments, especially in Germany, into adopting hostile policies toward the young Soviet republic. Stalin, on the other hand, a Russophile to his core, was onto this foreign intrigue, he alleges. He attempted to counter it by asserting Russia's own native strengths and capabilities. Martirosyan particularly singles out for criticism such party epigones as Trotsky, Bukharin, Radek, Rykov, and Zinoviev in language that more than smacks of anti-Semitism. (For instance, throughout his book he inserts the term "Zionist" in the context of the policies of these officials, whom Stalin later purged—"rightfully so," Martirosyan maintains.)

Moreover, the historian describes Khrushchev, who initiated the de-Stalinization campaign in 1956, as a "neo-Trotskyite," a line also proffered by Molotov in his interview with Chuev and other pro-Stalinites. All contemporary "Stalin restorers" are bitterly hostile toward Khrushchev. They criticize Western biographers of Khrushchev, like William Taubman, for singing the praises of the "anti-Russian de-Stalinizer," Khrushchev. The Russian author, moreover, claims that these Stalin-initiated, Russian nationalist-oriented policies worked. They resulted in such successful achievements, he notes, as large-scale industrialization and collectivization of the peasant farmers, the latter making possible assured supplies of food to the workers, who were newly settling in the industrializing urban centers. Anti-Stalin, "anti-Party elements" had endangered the ruling party's solidarity as well as unity within the population, the historian alleges, at a crucial time when the need for national consensus and loyalty to the leader was at a peak. These were years when well-armed external enemies were closing in on the Soviet Union. In some cases, the "encirclement" and anti-Soviet hostility were egged on by appeasement-minded Western governments that were content to see Hitler's Wehrmacht turn eastward rather than toward the West.

THE KIROV CASE

Another element in Stalin's campaign to achieve absolute authority and regime solidarity involved a popular "comer," Sergei Kirov, a young party leader from Leningrad. Kirov had once openly challenged Stalin on the latter's call to censure, expel, or put on trial the Old Bolsheviks, many of whom loathed Stalin and had fought against his rise in the party during the succession struggle after 1924.

Stalin, of course, never forgot Kirov's initial questioning of the Gensek's methods vis-à-vis the old guard. On December 1, 1934 (ironically, the same year of the notorious "Night of the Long Knives," in Nazi Germany, in which Hitler liquidated his own party enemies), Kirov was assassinated. Stalin's apparatus claimed Kirov had been murdered in a personal love triangle involving a rival to his wife's affections. Yet Kirov's death had occurred under suspicious circumstances that hinted at Stalin's personal involvement in the popular party official's liquidation. It had not been helpful to Stalin's nascent autocracy that the dynamic Kirov, who, incidentally, was as much of a hardliner as Josef Vissarionovich, was earning a personal following within the party. (Throughout his reign, Stalin was known to employ various carefully disguised methods for eliminating rivals under his or the NKVD's suspicion: e.g., by means of phony traffic, aircraft, surgical-medical, and other types of so-called "mishaps.")

With Kirov out of the way in the mid-1930s and with the appointment of the unscrupulous Nikolai Yezhov as head of the punitive NKVD, replacing his equally notorious predecessor, Genrikh Yagoda, who was liquidated, the way was cleared for Stalin to stage the major purge trials of the late 1930s.

These three "show trials" led, first, to the liquidation of the above party epigones. Later in 1937–1938 came the purging of most of the top staff officers and commanders of the RKKA. As a result of these severe measures against the Old Bolsheviks and the military, Stalin had achieved for the first time a degree of party unity and control at the top that was crystallized around his person to an extent that not even Lenin had been able to attain.

In retrospectively analyzing these developments, some "new" Russian historians today, while for the most part anti-Communist writers who condemn the extreme methods employed by Stalin, by the *Yezhovshchina*, and by Lavrenti Beria's methods in the NKVD, and who reject Marxism-Leninism ideology, nevertheless stress what they insist is the other side of the coin of these purges. This is the need, as they put it, to *otdelit' zerna ot plevel* ("separate the wheat from the chaff"). Namely, that the trials of fractious, foreign-plotting Old Bolshevik Party bigwigs, humbled and publicly excoriated by Stalin in previous years before the trials, were one of the first "necessary," if dire, steps toward empowering Stalin in order to unify and prepare the country for the approaching life-or-death war.

This the Soviet leader had accurately foreseen, it is alleged, looming at the western and eastern horizons of the state since the early 1930s. While in some cases by no means admirers of Stalin's person, some writers currently claim in their studies, interviews, and school textbooks that the strengthening of Stalin's absolute leadership was "essential." It was, they say, the *sine qua non* for meeting the demanding, dangerous circumstances facing the USSR just before and during World War II. A disunited party and divided country would not have been able to confront such an extreme challenge to the country as total war, they insist. They point out that by the late 1930s, the Soviet Union stood alone in confronting an aggressive Axis poised with their armies on two widely separated fronts—in eastern Europe as well as in the Far East abutting Axis partner Japan's satrapy of Manchuria.

Yet such historians do not necessarily condone all aspects of the Lenin-Stalin authoritarian/totalitarian system, or "model," as it had evolved by the prewar years. Instead, they place it within the context of the times before World War II. Historians like Martirosyan tend to view the system as a "cruel fact," a product of the real circumstances of those times and not simply the subjective result of Stalin's personality cult or his egregious political machine. It was in any case, some of the historians maintain, a viable system, like it or not, that was then prevailing and within which the leadership, the military, and the population were obliged to operate, almost as if the whole nation were on autopilot. To weaken this authoritarian system in any way given the mortal threat to the very survival of the Soviet Union was impermissible.

Nor was it lost on the Stalin regime that Hitler explicitly sought to entirely liquidate the "Russian state" as a geographic entity. Had he and his Axis partners succeeded in their campaign, there would be today quite a different world, as Martirosyan and others maintain. The "world-island" of Eurasia under Axis totalitarian control would have acquired quite a different complexion from what it became after 1945 and by the 1980s. Too, there certainly would be no contemporary, quasi-democratic, post-1991 Russian Federation.

MAINSTREAM HISTORIOGRAPHY ON THE PURGES

The new, pro-Stalin historiographic treatment of the purges clashes with the burden of research and books on the topic, whether published abroad or in Russia. Perhaps the most widely read of all accounts of the open and secret trials of Old Bolsheviks and Red Army officers is by Russian Academy of Sciences member Robert Conquest. His book, *The Great Terror: A Reassessment*, is considered to be the standard text on the topic.[3]

For Conquest and the many Soviet and post-Soviet authors who make the same assessment of the purges, the three show trials and the secret executions of these top officials were based on fabricated evidence. In some cases, it is alleged, the defendants were forced to confess by means of torture or through the verbal tricks used by the chief prosecutor, Procurator Andrei Vyshinsky. Defendants were induced into making what appeared to be confessions, yet in some cases were not full-fledged admissions of guilt (which was particularly the case with Bukharin). In Tukhachevsky's case, the whole process, if it can be called that since there were no open trial and no published transcripts, was carried out in secret, with the marshal being shot, apparently in the basement of NKVD headquarters.

At the same time, Conquest writes that there is still much that remains unknown about the trials as well as presumably about the purported guilt or innocence of the accused. He cites those individuals, among them *New York Times* Moscow correspondent Walter Duranty and U.S. ambassador to the USSR Joseph E. Davies, as persons who believed that the defendants were guilty, at least to some degree, of plotting against Stalin and/or collaborating with the Germans. Conquest notes that some "people opposed to the principles of Communism accepted the official version."[4] He concludes that the purges stemmed from the fact that "Stalin's genius consisted precisely in this: He recognized no limitations, either moral or intellectual, in his methods of securing power. His calculation about the effect [of the trials] abroad was on the whole sound. It is true that the frame-ups were clumsy fabrications. . . . Stalin had a clearer idea of the state of the public mind both in Russia and in the West. It is only too plain that he was right. Those who were prepared to believe his story believed it regardless of its peripheral faults, and rejected accounts put out by people who had had access to the correct information."

THE WATERSHED YEAR

In the crucial year of 1939, the year of the first round of purges, Germany and Soviet Russia made concerted approaches to each other, many of them in secret. Simultaneously, Stalin began to respond, it now appears disingenuously, to intense British and French feelers aimed at possibly closing ranks with Stalin in opposing Hitler. The latter by now was all but universally perceived as a menace to peace. As Russian historian Edvard Radzinsky writes, from Stalin's vantage point, "Hitler was really drawing Europe into war and Germany would bring down in ruins the whole capitalist system. It was no longer a [Marxist-Leninist] mirage, no longer a dream—world revolution

was advancing on empire. All that was needed was to egg Hitler on."
NKVD foreign-intelligence officer Pavel Sudoplatov, as we saw, con-
firms this Stalin ploy in his memoirs.

Thus, Stalin began playing a new game well beyond the frontiers of
his own country and its "geopolitical borderlands." Besides opening
the way to an accord with Germany, the Soviet dictator began simul-
taneous negotiations with France and England—in effect, creating a
kind of ersatz "Popular Front at the top." This was a "typical Stalin
ploy," Radzinsky writes. He continues:

> "He knew in advance that the Western democracies [against whom
> he had directed so many venomous attacks] would never trust the
> new Genghis Khan. He inspired in them only fear and revulsion. The
> talks [between the French and British and the Soviets in Moscow]
> were meant to gain leverage on Hitler. This gambit worked. Fearing
> an alliance between the Stalin and the Western democracies, Hitler
> was soon responding to Soviet advances. The customary fulminations
> against the USSR disappeared from official German statements, and
> the campaign of mutual insult petered out. A new phase had begun:
> the irreconcilable foes seemed to have stopped noticing each other."

In mid-summer 1939, Hitler told Nazi Propaganda Minister Josef
Goebbels that he no longer expected London and Moscow ever to
reach an agreement, "that leaves the way open for us," Goebbels wrote
in his unpublished diary. "Stalin doesn't want either a won or lost war.
In either case, he'd be history."

Goebbels cleverly ordered German editors not to express glee
at Stalin's stalling of the Anglo-French negotiations in Moscow, nor
to comment on differences emerging between Moscow and Tokyo.
Newspapers were also told to ignore German-Soviet trade talks. After
the first, August 23rd Nazi-Soviet agreement, Goebbels' comment was
laconic: "How times change," he wrote.

However, a few weeks later Hitler fully described to Goebbels the
deal he had made with Stalin. To the fuehrer, "the question of Bolshevism," Goebbels wrote in his diary, "is for the time being of lesser
importance." Then to the press he controlled Goebbels ordered: "You
can indicate that the purpose of this [non-aggression] pact is to enable
Germany and Russia alone to settle all outstanding problems in the
Lebensraum [living-space] between them, i.e., in eastern Europe. . . .
Newspapers are permitted to display a degree of *Schadenfreude* [mali-
cious pleasure], though not in their editorial columns."

Nineteen thirty-nine, as already indicated, was the cardinal year in the process of forming an active Soviet-German alliance. Early that year it was Stalin who sounded the first, undeniable hint of impending Soviet-German rapprochement at the highest level. It was a hint so strong that during the Nazi-Soviet negotiations in Moscow in August 1939, Ribbentrop in Stalin's presence specifically referred back to it as the spur to Hitler that got rapprochement going between Germany and the USSR. To Ribbentrop's observation, Stalin replied, "That was precisely my intention." Speaking from the rostrum of the Eighteenth Party Congress in the Bolshoi Theater on March 10, 1939, Stalin made his several startling statements. He had entirely rewritten the draft of the speech he was to give and that had been prepared for him, as usual, by the administrative department of the Communist Party Central Committee. The gist of his speech was that the French and British were trying to poison relations between the USSR and Germany by means of "malicious rumors." In fact, he went on, nothing stands in the way of sharply improving those relations.

He reassured his audience that Germany had no base designs against Soviet Russia, least of all any plans to seize the Ukraine. Referring to Western hopes of Soviet cooperation in stopping Hitler and dashing such hopes to pieces, Stalin bluntly asserted: "We will not allow our country to be drawn into conflicts by warmongers [*podzhigatel'yami voiny*] who are accustomed to getting others to pull chestnuts out of the fire for them."

To make sure Berlin understood what Stalin was saying in Aesopian language between the lines, he ordered the Soviet press to soften its "anti-Fascist" line. Then he made an undeniably friendly gesture: On May 3, he fired Maxim Litvinov, formerly promoted as a collective-security advocate, as long-time Soviet Commissar of Foreign Affairs. Stalin even removed him from the Central Committee. In Litvinov's place he appointed his closest aide, Vyacheslav Molotov (real name Scriabin, a Great Russian, who was untainted in Nazi eyes since he was not, as Litvinov was, Jewish; that Molotov was married to a Jewish woman was of little concern).

As soon he was in charge of that ministry, Molotov (who had in any case supervised the ministry for many years) weeded out some of the deputy commissars and other officials closely associated with Litvinov. As we will see, Litvinov, always willing to oblige the boss, was later—after the German attack on the USSR in June 1941—brought out of limbo and appointed ambassador to the United States. By that time, it was useful to have such a personality in Washington helping to arrange Lend-Lease aid for Soviet Russia.

Berlin got this politically telegraphed message, too. During the Nazi-Soviet honeymoon, German officials acknowledged that the departure of Litvinov (as well as that of the Jewish Soviet Ambassador to Berlin, Georgi Astakhov) was welcome news. It signified, they concluded, that Stalin was adopting a form of "national Bolshevism" and was virtually "de-ideologizing" his foreign policy and returning it to a "non-Jewish-Bolshevik, great Russian orientation" without global pretensions. This, obviously, was a foolish assumption on the Germans' part.

The details and events immediately leading up to the signing of the final Nazi-Soviet nonaggression pact are related in many books. A brief summary follows here.

Marshal Voroshilov had been assigned to sound out the Germans on the precise designs of the ensuing agreements; Molotov, too, was active in the preparatory period of July and early August. All told, two major pacts and several other agreements together with several secret protocols came out of the August–September negotiations in Moscow in which Stalin personally always played a key role. (Documents made available to researchers since 1991 show a pattern of the Soviet dictator's deep, personal involvement in all aspects of Soviet foreign policy as well as defense policy.)

Before the memorable day of August 23 arrived, Stalin ordered all talks with the French and the British—this "silly game," as he called the negotiations—to be terminated. Diplomats like the pro-Soviet British Ambassador Sir Stafford Cripps were enraged and disillusioned. They had tried for months to win Stalin over, little suspecting that the Soviet dictator, as it turned out, had bigger game in his crosshairs. Such talks with the British and French by now, of course, had become pointless, if they were not from the start.

First came the Soviet-German Nonaggression Pact, signed on August. 23. The secret protocol attached to it, whose existence was denied by the Soviets up to and including the Gorbachev period of putative *glasnost*, was designated top secret (*sovershenno sekretno*) for good reason. The Polish state was to be utterly destroyed. Its corpse was to be divided in two—Germany acquiring the western half, the Soviets the eastern, but with the eastern demarcation line drawn to Soviet advantage considerably farther west of the old post-World War I "Curzon Line."

Furthermore, with Germany's blessing, Moscow won its long-prized "spheres of influence" in the Baltic region as well as to the south bordering Romania. (Previous attempts under Lenin in 1918 to sovietize the Baltics had failed; the three countries had been independent ever since. Lenin, earlier in 1917, had disingenuously acknowledged their independence.) This meant that soon Estonia, Latvia, and Lithuania would be absorbed into the Soviet Union, thus increasing the number of Soviet Republics to 16. Bessarabia, to which Stalin laid claim without any historical basis for it, likewise was assigned to the Soviet sphere and was duly absorbed in 1940 to become the thirteenth Soviet Republic, the Moldavian SSR.

Thus, what publicly was touted as a "nonaggression pact" actually turned out to be a deal for joint Soviet-German carving up and occupation of foreign lands. The pact was duly ratified by the rubber-stamping Soviet "parliament," the USSR Supreme Soviet, at its next meeting, August 31. In his speech to the assembly, Molotov described the pact as being "in the interests of universal peace [that every sincere supporter of peace will realize]. . . . It is a turning-point in the history of Europe, and not only of Europe." Within a month that same speaker was to announce that Poland "has ceased to exist as a state."

Too, it was ironic that the text of the first Nazi-Soviet agreement, unlike the texts of other nonaggression treaties signed by Moscow with several other countries in the 1920s and 1930s, stated that the provisions should apply only in the case of *defensive* war. This suggested that if either Germany or the Soviet Union launched an offensive war against whatever other state, it would not affect their agreement.

The "booty" thus acquired by the USSR by 1940 via its deal with Germany was considerable: at least 130,000 square miles of land, counting Carpathian Ruthenia, where the Soviets were granted sovereignty. Populations in the new territories totaled about 16 million.

Stalin himself had predicted the Soviet rationale for such seizures. Back in 1920, he had written:

"Central Russia, that hearth of World Revolution, cannot hold out long without assistance from the border regions [former territories of the tsarist empire], which abound in raw materials, fuel, and foodstuffs. The border regions of Russia in their turn are inevitably doomed to imperialist bondage unless they undergo the political, military, and organizational support of the more developed Central Russia."

4

The World as Seen from Stalin's Kremlin

The Paris Peace Conference of "victors" in 1919, followed by the Versailles Treaty, did not include Russia (by then Soviet Russia) as a participant or, of course, the defeated Germany. The Versailles world-makers decided to enforce the following basic principles:

1. The countries defeated in World War I should be financially punished, deprived of some of their long-held territory, and overall be emasculated as the geopolitical entities they once were before 1914.

2. The former ally, tsarist Russia, now the Soviet republic under Bolshevik Lenin's leadership, had in early 1918 summarily pulled its armies out of the fight in the East. This had allowed the Germans to shift their forces to the Western Front to fight against the beleaguered Allies just as the American Expeditionary Force had landed in France. Bolshevik Russia, by way of Versailles punishment, as it were, for deserting the Allied cause, was stripped of much of its former, tsarist-controlled borderlands. This loss included Poland, Finland, the Baltic states of Estonia, Latvia, and Lithuania, as well as territory in Czechoslovakia and Romania. Despite Moscow's aspirations (particularly as voiced by Stalin, by 1918 holding the key portfolio of Commissar of Nationalities, also member of the Defense Council in charge of conducting the Soviet Civil War that included annexing former tsarist territories) to attach these borderlands to the new Soviet state. However, these territories and peoples, promised autonomy in an autumn 1917 decree issued by the Lenin regime, became proud, independent nation-states. They viewed themselves as beneficiaries of the Versailles principle of "self-determination" that was so strongly backed by President Woodrow Wilson.

Germany and Soviet Russia thus became mutual losers in the postwar territorial settlements made by the victors in Paris. The two "deprived" powers also became de facto allies of a new, revisionist type and soon began to actively cooperate.

FOUNDATION OF GERMAN-SOVIET RELATIONS

The Soviet-German Brest-Litovsk Treaty of 1918, followed by the Treaty of Berlin (1926), were harbingers of future, significant bilateral cooperation between the two "loser" states.

Brest-Litovsk became the symbol of Soviet diplomatic flexibility forced under dire circumstances upon the emergent revolutionary state. It became a precedent in which the Soviets had struck a temporary deal "in league with the devil" in order to enhance Soviet Russia's own national interests and external security—at others' expense—regardless of appearances. Ironically, Germany in 1939 again became such a devil when Stalin made a second Brest-Litovsk-like deal with the leader of the Nazi German state, including discussion of even a broader Soviet pact with the German-led Axis to divide up the world between the other totalitarian states— Germany, Italy, and Japan—including the USSR as a recipient. (In 1940, Stalin rejected this arrangement.)

Significantly, the Brest-Litovsk deal was struck with Germany, the birthplace of Hegel, Lenin's favorite philosopher, and of Marx and Engels, the holy ghosts of Leninism-Stalinism. It was the country Lenin most admired for, among other things, its socialist-like wartime economy designed by Gen. Erich von Ludendorff. The latter, incidentally, was the author of the influential military writing, *Notes on Offensive Battles*, an important work in military science that impressed Lenin, a zealous reader of military theory (as per his deep reading of Karl von Clausewitz, author of *On War*).

Moreover, Lenin was a dedicated Germanophile (on his mother's side, the family name was Blank, so he was aware of having "German blood"). Above all, Germany was the Central European linchpin country that Lenin considered to be the indispensable linchpin country and launching pad for pan-European revolution. "When you see a Soviet of Workers' and Soldiers' Deputies in Berlin," Lenin remarked in 1918, "you will know that the proletarian world revolution has been born."

Indeed, this was the Germany, then under Kaiser rule during World War I, that had first recognized Lenin's notoriety and influence in world politics. It was Berlin in 1917 that had provided the funds to the anti-war agitator, Lenin and his Bolshevik cohorts in Switzerland, to board the famous "sealed train" (a misnomer; it was not "sealed") traveling safely through the battle fronts in Germany, then by ship and rail to Sweden, finally to Finland, and on to Petrograd, Russia. This was in April 1917, the momentous time, when Lenin gave a monumental speech, known as the "April Theses," on the train station platform. In the speech, he called for the overthrow of the provisional government under Prince Lvov.

Long before the train trip, Lenin from his base in Switzerland had been penning inflammatory articles opposing Russian participation in the "imperialist war"—a story told in historical fiction form in Alexander Solzhenitsyn's *Lenin in Zurich*. The "subversive" train trip had been perpetrated by Berlin just a month after the overthrow of Tsar Nicholas II. By means of this journey back to Russia, the kaiser wanted that Allied country to be embroiled in internal strife. The German officials said that they regarded Lenin as a "bacillus," who would "infect" Russia. Berlin hoped that Lenin's subversive work in his home country would keep it paralyzed and take it out of the war. It was a shrewd and effective game played by the German leaders.

Well after April 1917, the Germans continued to subsidize the subversive Lenin as well as his subsequent Bolshevik regime into 1918. Lenin's opponents called him a "German spy." He was not. He merely took advantage of the Kaiser's "generosity" and exploited the subsidies for his own purposes in seizing and holding power in Russia. The details of the large funding and the way the money was laundered and reached Lenin and his comrades in Petrograd (to fund Bolshevik newspapers, propaganda, demonstrations, and so on throughout 1917) were all disclosed as Communist archives began to be opened in Moscow under *glasnost* in the mid-1980s and then to a much greater degree after 1991. The post-Soviet weekly, *Argument I Fakty*, under the headline "Reich marks for the Dictatorship of the Proletariat" (No. 3, 1992, p. 4) was among the first large-circulation publications in Russia to provide complete evidence on the German funding of Lenin and Bolshevism. The paper noted the dates, locations, and amounts of the bank deposits made in Russia and included photostats of Soviet memoranda concerning the actual depositing of the checks. Along with this article, *AiF* published a photomontage depicting Lenin in a German World War I helmet replete with *pickelhaube* (ice-pick point).

The Treaty of Brest-Litovsk (1918) became another milestone in Soviet-German relations. By the treaty, 70 German divisions that had been fighting against Russia on the Eastern Front in the Great War were transferred by rail to the West European front. Thanks to this addition of German forces, the German army at one point had driven within 35 miles of Paris. Moreover, with Lenin's encouragement and initiative, post-World War I Weimar Germany in 1922 eagerly became the first major country to have entirely normal relations with the young Soviet republic. In his diaries of the mid-1920s, cited earlier, Josef Goebbels, some eight years later to become Hitler's propaganda minister, had written that he relished the advent of German-Soviet cooperation.

It should be recalled that Russian-German cooperation had begun back in tsarist times. This was a process that went back to the eighteenth century, when Peter the Great encouraged close relations with Prussia. The Russian army, in fact, copied Prussian tables of organization and Prussian uniforms and drills as well as adopting a high-stepping goosestep, which the Red Army also adopted. (In the Yeltsin-Putin period after the demise of the USSR in 1991, the Russian Federation continued the tradition of German-Russian friendship. In his years as a KGB official, Vladimir Putin's base of operations, notably, was in East Germany. Putin speaks German.)

With German unification after 1871, Russia historically had again closed ranks with Germany. Under the German chancellor Bismarck, the "Reinsurance Treaty" was concluded with Russia and protected Germany's eastern rear in the case of trouble in the west with France and Britain. The latter were being alienated by Bismarck's expansionist ambitions, especially into the Near East. After the chancellor was dismissed in 1890, Kaiser Wilhelm let the Reinsurance deal with Russia decline. This decision paved the way toward World War I, in which Austria became allied with Germany in a common front against Russia and the Western Allies.

Finally, after World War I, as a sequel to the postwar Genoa Conference (1922), came fruitful diplomatic Soviet-German negotiations. Then followed a historical treaty with Lenin's Russia and secret clauses, signed between the Soviets and Germans at Rapallo in 1922. This opened the way to broad German-Soviet collaboration that lasted up to and even beyond Hitler's assumption of power in 1933. In fact, this process of Soviet-German collaboration never really ceased except for a few ups and downs right up until the momentous events of June 22, 1941.

The history of that period after World War II shows that Lenin, and particularly Stalin and his closest collaborators, like Molotov and Marshal Voroshilov, were always attracted to Soviet-German friendship. These

Soviet officials regarded the two countries to be what they termed "natural allies." Germany and Russia, they said, confronted a "common enemy" in the form of the victorious, vengeful victors who wrote the Versailles Treaty of 1919. Well before Hitler came to power, it became obvious that the two Soviet dictators, Lenin and Stalin, relished the fact that Germany was a have-not capitalist state that was bent upon revenge against the capitalist-imperialists of World War I. For the Kremlin, Germany thus became useful as a spearhead directed at its old enemies in the West. Moscow, moreover, fully concurred with Berlin that German lands had been "extorted" by the Versailles Treaty makers from a "defenseless" Germany. The treaty drafters, said Lenin, "were robbers with knives in their hands."

RED ARMY-GERMAN MILITARY COLLABORATION

Always in awe of German efficiency, industriousness, and the Prussian military, Lenin in the 1920s closed ranks with Weimar Germany on several levels and with several purposes in mind. Among other actions, he invited German military (Reichswehr) officers to come to Soviet Russia, despite strict Versailles Treaty prohibitions against German rearmament to practice their two countries' arts of war on the broad plains of Russia.[1]

This they proceeded to do efficiently and to their mutual profit beginning in 1924. This decade-long active collaboration continued up to 1933. The top secret, illegal (under the Versailles Treaty) German-Soviet military collaboration was based on the clandestine follow-up agreements of the Rapallo Treaty of April 1922. The names of the German and Soviet senior military officer-participants on both sides later became famous in World War II. They were among those purged in Stalin's purges of Red Army general staff and line commanders in 1937–1938.

On the German side in this early Soviet-German military cooperation were noted generals, marshals, chiefs-of-staff, and various Nazi army commanders to-be. These included World War II German staff officers and commanders like Brauchitsch, Guderian, Blomberg, Marcks, Model, Horn, Mannstein, Kestring, and others. Figuring in the collaboration on Soviet soil with the Germans were noted RKKA strategists and commanders such as Tukhachevsky, Triandafillov, Blyukher, Yakir, Svechin, Frunze, Voroshilov, Kork, Alksnis, Budyenny, and Shaposhnikov. Directly supporting this "strictly secret" (*sovershenno sekretno* or *strogo sekretno*, i.e., the highest degree of Russian secrecy)

Soviet-German military collaboration from the Communist Party and civilian-administrative side were Lenin, Stalin, Trotsky, Radek, Rozengoltz, Krestinsky, and others Their names appear on documents disclosed in archives that have been opened since the demise of the Soviet Union in 1991.

This had been a prolonged period of bilateral cooperation between the RKKA and the German Reichswehr. They had pioneered development of tactics of what was later to become mobile, "blitzkrieg" warfare, or as the Red Army called their own form of it, "deep-battle operations" (*glubokiye operatsii*) conducted "with engines." These operations tested in Soviet Russia in the 1920s practiced air-ground support by tactical aircraft and the use of mechanized armor and tanks (in German parlance, "panzers") as well as airborne paratrooper formations. To carry out these German-Soviet war games, the Russians had laid out a large airfield at Lipetsk, south of Moscow. Under the secret agreement between Berlin and Moscow and carried out under the supervision of Stalin-appointed overseers, this spacious area was transformed into a modern airbase replete with hangars, repair shops, and stands and rigs for testing aircraft engines.

Other facilities consisting of several hundred acres of grounds included dispensaries, barracks, and administrative buildings. The whole area was designated off-limits and was surrounded with thick barbed wire. It was guarded by sentries around the clock. Soviet citizens in the neighboring town could only guess what was going on. One revealing episode in 1923 saw German Gen. Paul Haze's 100 advanced Fokker D-XIII aircraft purchased from Holland that were flown to Russia. In addition, the budding German aircraft industry, already famous from World War I, began building new experimental craft. These planes, too, were secretly flown to Russia from a secluded airbase at Echlin, Germany.

By the mid-1920s, some 60 German pilots and flight instructors had been assigned to Limpets, Russia. During some summers, the contingent of German airmen reached 100 men. The trainees were replaced every six months by others who had graduated from basic training at Reichswehr or Luftwaffe schools in Germany. The entire German unit was masqueraded with the misleading cognomen of "Fourth Squadron of the Red Air Force." Out of this secret nest in Soviet Russia came 120 outstanding German fighter pilots and 450 flight personnel. All had been thoroughly trained along with their Soviet counterparts.

In the Hitler years, these personnel were to serve as the core of Hitler's Luftwaffe. One can only guess as to how many of the Limpets cadre themselves sat behind the controls of German military

Messerschmitt and Fokwulfe aircraft—the fighters, dive-bombers, and medium bombers that were engaged in combat with the Red Air Force in the skies over the USSR during the Great Patriotic War and before that with Allied planes in combat in western Europe in 1940.

Thanks to Lipetsk and Soviet-German military collaboration in general, Nazi Germany's aircraft industry was able to draw up and test aircraft designs that otherwise could not have been developed until the time when Hitler, after 1935, began openly rearming Nazi Germany. The famous screaming Junkers Stuka dive-bomber (Ju-87) was actually first produced in a Soviet factory. Moreover, poison-gas warfare was tested in the German-Soviet war games. According to Luftwaffe Gen. Helm Speidel, who worked in the administrative sector of the so-called "Zentrale Moskau," the most lasting contribution made via Soviet collaboration to Hitler's Luftwaffe was the conceptual foundation laid for the future Luftwaffe in its actual flying practice.

On the ground, blitzkrieg-like tactics were played out on the Russian steppe. From such games and trial maneuvers in ground operations, the Germans and the Soviets together learned valuable lessons in mobile, panzer-led warfare. As airfields and aircraft factories were built, tank and flying schools and defense-production facilities were constructed. Soviet-German collaboration also involved both their navies. Out of this cooperation came the German "pocket battleships" as well as advanced submarine designs. The clandestine Soviet-German military relationship of these years up to 1933, in blatant violation of international law embodied in treaties (although the Germans and Soviets could claim they were not signatories of the Paris accords), was obviously mutually beneficial to both states.

Of course, such war planning made a mockery of Soviet Russia's much-touted "peaceful intentions." Ironically, this was also the time when Lenin first unfurled the Soviet term, "peaceful coexistence" (he used the term "cohabitation") as the earliest form of often-employed Soviet "peace offensives." He also predicted that war with the capitalist states of the West was "inevitable," that peaceful coexistence was merely a temporary breathing spell during which Soviet Russia could prepare for war. In this early period, the wily People's Commissar of Foreign Affairs Georgi V. Chicherin became Lenin's conduit in this respect by helping design "two-track" Soviet foreign policy of talking peace while planning for "revolutionary war" through the Third Communist International (Comintern) (see chapter 5). Chicherin, the "diplomat," was at the same time an ardent advocate of Marxist-Leninist global expansionism.

Finally, when British Prime Minister David Lloyd George later got wind of the Soviet-German collaboration, he wrote in his memoirs in the 1930s: "The greatest threat at present consists, to my mind, in that Germany can bind its destiny with Bolsheviks and may place all its material and intellectual resources, all its huge organizational talents at the service of revolutionary fanatics, whose dream is conquest of the world by force of weapon for Bolsheviks. Such a threat is not chimera."

The outstanding feature of the weapons development and the war games in Russia, including tactics first developed in theory by such Red Army senior officers as Mikhail Tukhachevsky and Vladimir Triandafillov, was seen in the employment of the element of surprise. Attacks against the enemy would be carried out by the massive use of tank-based motorized units together with air-ground offensives and paratroop drops.

The Soviets actually applied these offensist methods for the first time on a large scale in combat against the Japanese in 1939. These were the two major armed skirmishes fought along the frontier of the Soviet client state of the People's Republic of Mongolia bordering Japanese-occupied Manchuria. The smaller Japanese forces in Kwantung, Manchuria, were overwhelmed and decimated, especially once Red Army Gen. Georgi K. Zhukov had taken command of the Soviet forces there mid-year. Back in the Kremlin, Stalin became aware of Gen. Zhukov's successes in the Far East. The dictator was immensely impressed with commander Zhukov, who was soon transferred to Moscow, then promoted to higher positions. By early 1941, he was chosen by Stalin to be chief of the general staff.

SOVIET-FASCIST TOTALITARIAN KINSHIP

It is not Germany that will turn Bolshevist, but Bolshevism will become a sort of National Socialism. Besides, there is more that binds us to Bolshevism than separates us. There is, above all, genuine revolutionary feeling. —*Adolf Hitler*

After he had outmaneuvered his political rivals among the Old Bolsheviks and had all but taken over the helm in the Kremlin by the late 1920s as the largely unchallenged yet not entirely absolute leader, Stalin embarked the country on a concerted program of building the USSR into a world-class industrial power, especially in the military sense. This was to become the program for achieving "socialism in one country"—but with other countries in mind. That is, in the sense that

Stalin intended for the USSR to outclass and overpower other European countries, especially in the military sense as well as becoming what he called expansively as the "base of world revolution." One of Stalin's pet slogans was "catching up to the USA."

The ensuing Five-Year Plans after 1929 were geared, above all, to building a heavy industrial base of producer goods. From this base, defense production would be given top priority, as Category A, while consumer goods would be relegated to what was designated as the lower Category B. The whole thrust of Stalin's program of economic construction was aimed in the long term at making the Soviet Union a major player on the world scene in both the political and military sense, or as the Soviets called it, in "politico-military" terms. Some Western writers suggested that in this ambitious program, Stalin was acting with a typical dictator's megalomania that was motivating these policies. Others allege that Josef Vissarionovich Djugashvili, who adopted the name "Stalin" (from the Russian word *stal*, which means "steel"), was a devout Russophile, at least ostensibly so. For him, his Georgian roots were scarcely a source of pride. The trait of Russophilia, even "Great Russian chauvinism" in Stalin was noticed by a number of his comrades as early as 1912, the Russist-racist equivalent of Hitler's Germanism. Several writers and film producers in the 1930s flattered the ethnic-Georgian dictator by comparing him—apparently with his own prompting—to the Russian tsars Ivan the Terrible and Peter the Great. Hitler himself acknowledged that he and Stalin were the most impressive leaders in the modern world. Mussolini, Churchill, and Roosevelt all paled, the fuehrer said, in comparison to the authoritarian Stalin. This was true even if, as Hitler also remarked to comrades, the Soviet Russian state was a "house of cards." At the opening of the Nazi-Soviet honeymoon in 1939, the *Vozhd'* Stalin returned the compliment to Hitler by praising the fuehrer—disingenuously, of course—for his leadership of the German people, who Stalin said, "love their leader." The Soviet Commissariat of Foreign Affairs congratulated the Germans in 1940—with apparent disingenuousness—for their "splendid" military victories against the "plutocratic," "warmongering" countries of France and England.

For his part, in *Mien Kampf*, Hitler praised the "Marxists" for their one-party dictatorship; their ubiquitous political police; punitive labor camps; "world-girdling" ideology; one-man dictatorship; and glorification of the leader as well as Bolshevik etatization of the trade unions, press, schools, and all other social, political, and economic institutions. Soviets were implicitly praised as the Nazis imitated so many of their methods: the rubber-stamp "parliament"; glorified militarism and military march-pasts as the leaders watched in the reviewing stands; singling out of a scapegoat, pariah-class (as Hitler did with the Jews and Lenin did analogously with the "bourgeoisie"); creation of youth movements; ideologizing education with indoctrination; etatization of labor unions and the media; and censorship. Too, the Soviets' huge sports extravaganzas, military rallies, and parades staged in Moscow's Red Square, demonstrations much favored by the Stalin regime, likewise were copied by the Italian Fascists and German Nazis (not to mention by the People's Republic of China in 2009 on the occasion of the sixtieth anniversary of the foundation of the Communist regime on the mainland). Even the Soviet use of the color red on the banners and their utterly new (as a state symbol) hammer and sickle were specifically praised by Hitler in *Mein Kampf*.

These colors and symbols were emulated by the Nazis with the latter's red, black, and white banners emblazoned with their own invented symbol, the novel swastika, rivaling the novel Communist hammer and sickle. Mussolini had adopted his own particular symbol, the ancient Roman ax with fasces. To Mussolini, Stalin was a "crypto-Fascist" while Hitler said in his "bible," "We must learn from the Marxists." The men who were the best Nazi recruits in Germany, Hitler added, were ex-Communists. In Benito Mussolini, Lenin found much to admire in Italian fascism—an early example of the affinities between totalitarian states. The "Blackshirts" were notorious in Lenin's lifetime. Yet the Soviet republic eagerly opened relations with Fascist Italy toward which it made friendly overtures. This Moscow initiative was a harbinger of Stalin's continuing efforts to develop ties with Nazi Germany.

As to Mussolini, he had made his triumphant march on Rome in 1923, six years after Lenin had seized power in Petrograd. Having passed through a phase of internationalist, Bolshevik-like socialism in his pre-World War I political evolution, Mussolini later adopted a strictly nationalistic platform, realizing that this appealed more to Italians. When he became Italy's *Il Duce*, he developed a form of corporate state socialism that was derived from his earlier prewar Marxist socialist and Bolshevist views. Ironically, like Lenin, Mussolini spent years away from his native country in Switzerland, where, like Lenin, who was nearby in the same country, he refined his political program. In the Italian Fascist system, dictatorship of the proletariat, which a younger Mussolini had once supported in his "Marxist-socialist" period before

World War I, would be transformed into a centralized dictatorship state running most affairs in the country from the center. This Fascist system prompted Lenin's admiration for the Italian regime just as he had admired Gen. Ludendorff's centralized war economy in Germany. On his part, Mussolini, like Goebbels in the 1920s, was impressed with Lenin's one-man leadership. "The masses," *Il Duce* once wrote in the fascist newspaper *Il Popolo d'Italia*, "need a hero." (In the early 1930s, Molotov, Stalin's right hand, was to pen an identical observation concerning the need for a powerful leader like Stalin.)

Moreover, like Lenin and Stalin, Mussolini had no use for "bourgeois liberalism" and "bourgeois democracy." These political ideas likewise are condemned by modern Marxists (e.g., in Cuba, Venezuela, Bolivia, Nicaragua, etc.) as "neo-liberalism": "[We] throw the noxious theories of so-called liberalism on the rubbish heap," Mussolini once said, "[along with] the more or less putrid body of the Goddess of Liberty." Hitler agreed. Whereas Lenin and Stalin created "Soviet Man," Mussolini sought to create the "Fascist Man" just as Hitler was later to create the new "Aryan Man." In 1921, in the Chamber of Deputies in Rome, Mussolini declared: "I recognize that between us and the Communists [there are] intellectual affinities."

Italian-Fascist affinities with Leninism aside, the main point is that totalitarian similarities existing between the Nazi Germans and the Soviets, i.e., the "Communazi"/"Red-Brown" kinship, seem definitely to have played a seminal role in the Soviet-German coming together in late 1939 in some ideological sense. This appears to be true even if the ideological comradeship in those instances was largely *pokazukha*, i.e., "for show." At one point in the Ribbentrop negotiations with Stalin, the German foreign minister blurted out over a toast in the Kremlin on the night of August 22–23, 1939, after the signing of the first of the Nazi-Soviet agreements that he felt "comfortable" in the camaraderie of his Soviet hosts. It was, he said, as if he were "among old party comrades." At other times, Soviet and German spokesmen let it be known that the two states and their regimes had more in common than not, despite verbal on-again/off-again propaganda wars between them. Stalin returned the German foreign minister's words by observing that "we had dumped garbage on each other" but, he said, that lay in the past.

Again, was this not an indication of how lightly Stalin regarded ideology when it came to conducting serious diplomatic summits and the best interests of the Soviet state? To Stalin, the latter's priorities were uppermost even over any ideological pretenses.

TREACHEROUS CURRENTS OF EUROPE

In the interwar period, many conflicting tidal currents were flowing between the states of Europe. Some of them were new "Versailles"-born nation-states, such as Czechoslovakia, Hungary, Romania, and the three Baltic states, which were newly established since World War I. One such ebbing current put Germany and the Soviet Union on the same side of the barricades. This stemmed from the fact that the Versailles Treaty had drawn the boundaries of several countries—among them France, Czechoslovakia, and Poland—in ways that disadvantaged, in the latter's perceptions at least, both Germany and Soviet Russia as the so-called twin "losers" from the Great War.

In the coal-rich Ruhr in the west, Germany had lost vital land and industrial assets to France. On its eastern borders, Germans had been "arbitrarily" included within the new, Czechoslovak-ruled territory of the Sudetenland. Former German territory and people were also packaged into an enlarged, postwar Poland. This was when Versailles decreed that part of Silesia with its German population would become Polish territory. Also, Poland gained while Germany lost a valuable port on the North Sea and with it the "Polish Corridor" that, by the Versailles Treaty, had separated Prussia from cretinized Germany to Poland's advantage.

On the Russian side, an enlarged Poland also "encroached" on Russian territory in the east, land that was formerly part of White (Byelo-) Russia or Ukraine and of the Russian Empire. Moreover, the Baltic States of Estonia, Latvia, and Lithuania, former duchies of tsarist Russia, were granted independence but not without Lenin's Red Army contemplating forceful reannexation of these lands to the Soviet Republic. In 1918, Russia also lost Bessarabia to Romania, another fledgling state created out of the old Ottoman Empire on the basis of the fuzzy Wilsonian concept of "self-determination."

Yet the Paris peace treaty had not only offended Germany and Russia. It had likewise aggravated tensions between minority peoples throughout Europe. This was especially true in cases where new boundaries drawn under the Versailles regime put people unwillingly under "foreign" rule.

Stalin, like Hitler later in German terms, observed this process with interest. He saw in it tinder for unrest that in turn could be exploited for Soviet expansionism. As we will see, Stalin later used such ethnic tensions arising in volatile East European politics to excuse Soviet non-participation in efforts to allow passage of Red Army troops over such lands in the name of enforcing "collective security," which Moscow used as a propaganda tool (see chapter 7). This Soviet game was played, for example, during the German-Czech crisis of 1938–1939. Collective security was an idea to which Stalin's foreign policy devoted considerable verbiage. Yet it was crossed with Soviet inaction.[2]

In sum, it was inconceivable that the two large states of Germany and Soviet Russia would ever accept their position of inferiority as the result of the "bandits'" treaty of 1919. Not surprisingly, when both powers had regained their strength, nationalist-minded elements within the two "deprived" countries proclaimed their intention to rectify the "injustices" of the so-called Versailles victors. As a consequence, Europe became divided into states and political movements that on the one hand included territorial "revisionists," and on the other "anti-revisionists." As revisionist capitals, both Berlin and Moscow, therefore, sought to create a New Order for Europe that would replace the Versailles Treaty's allegedly "artificial" one. It was against the backdrop of these tensions and common interests that helped drive Germany and Russia together.

Far from the European arena, the Soviet Union faced several dangers in the Far East. As a contiguous empire stretching a width of 11 time zones, any Russian leader had a full political-military strategic agenda in planning the defense of both ends of this gigantic entity. (See chapter 6 for an analysis of this threat to Soviet security.)

Still, the Soviets' main strategic focus was on Europe, in particular on Germany. The German-Russian connection was a permanent fixture during periods of Lenin's, Stalin's, and their successors' reigns. Going back to Peter the Great, Russians had always respected German efficiency and public administration. In the Soviet period, this extended to appreciation of and exploitation of traditional German militarism via the German-Soviet military collaboration of the 1920s and beyond, including the trade deals that followed the Nazi-Soviet pacts of 1939. The German half of these agreements included export to the Soviets of the latest military models (e.g., aircraft). Berlin mostly reneged on its end of the bargain. Toward Hitler's Germany, Stalin seemed both cooperative and wary. As will be seen, there is little doubt that Stalin sought to get the better of Hitler by the terms of the Nazi-Soviet agreements of 1939–1940 as well as by exploiting Germany's own involvement in war with the Western Allies. He had told intimates that while Hitler thought he had tricked him with the Molotov-Ribbentrop pacts and protocols, it was Stalin who had tricked Hitler.

However, the "stab in the back" that Hitler himself executed before, as some historians claim, Stalin could realize his own apparently offensist plans against Germany in 1941 was Hitler's big miscalculation. Stalin's long-range intentions, some historians contend today, called for the eventual trumping of the Nazi dictator's control of Europe—the continent that both Lenin assigned as the prime target of revolution. This was to be accomplished in a big war in which the USSR would have some powerful allies.

Even today with the fading of the German militarist tradition at the end of World War II and the birth of a democratic Germany, Russian admiration of Germany by no means ceased. It was already visible in the time of Brezhnev in the 1970s. In the present, post-Communist period in Russia, Moscow's ties with Germany can be described as stronger than as with any other Western state. Moreover, since Vladimir V. Putin came to power in 2000, the Russian leader, who once served as a KGB officer in East Germany and as Lenin did has voiced his admiration for this key central European state, Russo-German amity has grown tighter.

In conclusion, what Stalin observed at either end of his sprawling empire were threats to Soviet external security and the brewing of another great war. Apparently guided by basic Marxist-Leninist doctrine on "imperialism" and the "inevitability of war as long as capitalism exists," Stalin knew what the Soviet Union must do in order to save itself and his own grip on power. This was to prepare for the inevitable, both in domestic as well as foreign policy.

One might well ask, did Stalin need Marxist-Leninist doctrine to foresee the coming of a second global war that would be preceded by a major war on the continent of Europe? It can be speculated that even without Marxist ideology—given the political climate of extremism in those days and the age of dictatorship and the power to carry out such programs as the Tanaka Plan and the ambitious plans stated in *Mein Kampf*—that vulnerable, neighboring states, particularly the resource-rich USSR, would be advised to keep their powder dry.

War, and not only in the form of small, local conflicts, seemed very likely to lie in the immediate future. Stalin's preparations for it were timely.

In an ironic way, it was the dogmas of Marxism-Leninism itself that actually played a hand in alerting their believers in Soviet Russia to get ready for war—even if the philosophical dogmas upon which this expectation rested were, to say the least, questionable.

5

Soviet Two-Track Policy

Several Russian history textbooks published since 2000 during the terms in office of Presidents Boris Yeltsin and Vladimir Putin reflect revision in the way post-Soviet historians view Soviet foreign policy in retrospect. At the same time, these books, which are intended mainly for secondary school and technical institute students, echo in some respects the interpretations of world events found in late Soviet-era histories. This is particularly evident in their treatment of Soviet foreign policy in the 1930s, in which Soviet foreign policy tends to be touted as having been reasonable under the circumstances. Yet in these histories, Stalin is not singled out for praise. Instead, the Soviet government is commended for its policies.

In history textbooks now being assigned to classrooms in the Russian Federation, such as the 2010 textbook by A. I. Yur'ev, *Noveishaya istoriya Rossii: Fevral' 1917 goda—nachalo XXI veka* (*Newest History of Russia: February 1917 to the Beginning of the 21st Century*), there are new traces of revisionism that cast Stalin as Soviet leader, at least implicitly, in a less derogatory way than was seen throughout the final years of Soviet rule, and certainly less negatively than during the Khrushchev-initiated de-Stalinization campaign and its fallout that was reflected in most Soviet history texts from 1956 to the Brezhnev period (1956–1965).[1]

Yur'ev's and the somewhat earlier Yeltsin and Putin period histories do not go as far as, say, does historian Arsen Martirosyan, along with lesser-known authors of his persuasion in their books, interviews, or articles today. These are writers who all but re-glorify Stalin as an indispensably great leader who saved Russia from the "Fascist horde" and whose policies above all advanced the cause of Russian statehood—a line on the "Russian state" that parallels that of the Putin-Medvedev regime. Views expressed by some historians on the seventieth anniversaries hint of departures in the telling of the Soviet past and of Stalin as a leader. Not all of the claims of such Russian writers, some of whom are educators, may seem farfetched, although some are unsupported by what other historians have long regarded as proven facts (as, for example, concerning the Stalin purges, his spring 1941 "denial" of the German preparations for invasion, the slow response to the German attack in June of 1941, and so on).

COUNTERPOINT OF EARLY SOVIET DIPLOMACY, 1918–1930s

Some historical background is needed as a framework for past and current trends in Soviet and Russian historiography and for critiquing the claim for Stalin's greatness.

After their coup d'etat and the formation of the first Soviet Republic in 1918, the Bolshevik leaders announced that all traditional ways of conducting diplomacy were to be changed. In fact, Moscow was going to be the center of an entire remaking of the world.

As far as foreign relations were concerned, the Soviet Republic would make no secret treaties or deals with foreign powers. It would publicly reveal all past tsarist diplomatic secrets. The Lenin regime also promised independence to former tsarist borderland territories, meaning especially Poland, the Baltic countries, and Caucasus republics like Georgia and Armenia. How long such promises were going to be respected in the long term by the Bolsheviks is well known. The flimsiness of such proclamations under Lenin is told quite frankly in some cases in post-Soviet histories used in Russian schools and institutes.[2]

When Lenin strode triumphantly down the center aisle of the Tavrida Palace in Petrograd (later Leningrad, now St. Petersburg) to open the first, post-November 7 Second Congress of Soviets, he announced that, in his words, a "New Order" had been established by the Bolshevik revolution. This was not mere ideological posturing. Lenin had explicitly set out profoundly to change his country root and branch, and with it, as he said, the whole world. The Russian and, in fact, pan-European *ancien regime,* as French revolutionaries called the departing system in France, was to be buried and with it would go many customary "bourgeois" institutions composing what Marx called the capitalist "superstructure." Among these institutions were diplomacy and the "old way" of doing things in world politics.

With several ensuing decrees and pronouncements during the weeks following the Communist seizure of power, Lenin and his associates let it be known that, like it or not, Soviet relations with foreign states would be cast in totally new, "militant" ways. Old treaties would be torn up, debts written off, and the tsarist diplomatic tradition repudiated. The Old Order worldwide would be replaced by socialist construction. "Much remains in the world that must be destroyed by fire and steel," said Lenin during World War I, "in order that emancipation of the working class may be achieved. . . . Do not listen to sentimental whiners who are afraid of war." Or be afraid of world revolution.

By "war," Lenin not only meant clashes between nation-states, or as he put it between proletarian and bourgeois states, which he considered the wave of the future. Diplomacy, too, was regarded as a "weapon" for advancing "the Cause" worldwide. Lenin's tactics called for advance-and-retreat, or what he called taking "one step backwards in order to make two steps forward." Yet by 1918, Lenin was prepared under certain circumstances to look at interstate relations in quite conventional ways as viewed from the parapets of the Kremlin, the Soviet government's new home (as of March 11, 1918, when the regime was officially moved there from Petrograd). Despite their revolutionary rhetoric and the adoption of radically sounding governmental titles like "commissar" (an invention of Trotsky's), the leaders of the Soviet Republic began to confront traditional problems of Realpolitik along with their preoccupation with their much-touted revolutionary messianism. As this mix was being prepared, the Third Communist International, significantly, was founded the very next year, 1919.

Of utmost immediate importance to the Bolshevik leaders, however, was the defense of their "revolution." The regime was acquiring increasing numbers of domestic armed and unarmed enemies—especially within the restive working class itself. Lenin had prorogued the democratically elected constituent assembly that the new Soviet police state had allowed to meet for only one day, on January 18, 1918. In the voting throughout the country, the Bolsheviks had won only about one-quarter of the seats. The oppressive Cheka police (from the Russian acronym for Extraordinary Commission to Combat Counterrevolution) and its drum-head, firing-squad tribunals had already been set up in the preceding December, a few weeks following the coup civil war. The latter began to rage as domestic and foreign enemies harangued and fought against the "revolution" and the Lenin dictatorship. By 1921, on Kronstadt Island in Petrograd, Lenin's Red Army was mowing down workers and sailors, i.e., his staunchest, former Bolshevik supporters. Throughout the rest of the country, the Red Army and the Cheka tribunals went about liquidating "counterrevolutionaries" and brutally suppressing peasant revolts.

The later, half-hearted, short-term Allied intervention in the Civil War (1918) further complicated the young Soviet Republic's external security. The aim of the Allied intervention, which was to be carried out only while World War I was still raging, had been intended mainly to defend against Bolshevik seizures of the large Allied stores of weapons and ammunition bunkered at such Russian wharves and depots as Murmansk, Archangel, and Odessa, as well as in the Far East. Bolshevik propaganda, often later Little Sir Echoed in the West, depicted this limited enterprise solely as a concerted effort by the Western powers to snuff out Communist rule. George V. Kennan, a witness to these events, described such propaganda about the "counterrevolutionary intervention" as just that, propaganda. Still, for a time, the intervention did have an anti-Bolshevik edge.

In early January 1918, Russia was still formally engaged in hostilities against the Central Powers in World War I. Soldiers on both sides died in this interval following the Bolshevik seizure of power in November 1917. In this continued fighting on the Eastern Front, Germany was about to fully occupy Ukraine and with it to gain control over 40 percent of Russia's total industry and 70 percent of her iron and steel-producing capacity. The bulk of Russian-exported grain was produced in this "breadbasket."

How to extract the Soviet state with its emerging Red Army from World War I with minimal damage to the integrity of the New Order became central to Lenin's diplomacy. Ukraine was not yet totally in German hands. It was Berlin's price demanded of the Lenin regime for German withdrawal from Russia in exchange for Russian closure of the Eastern Front against the Germans. By a narrow margin of voting in the party's Central Committee in which Trotsky at first opposed Lenin, the latter's plan to sacrifice the entire Ukraine to Germany was adopted. Yet it was Trotsky and other officials of the Commissariat of Foreign Affairs, touting the line "neither peace nor war," who thereupon traveled in Western-style civilian clothes (but without top hats or striped pants) to Brest-Litovsk in

German-occupied Poland for the purpose of working out the deal with the German emissaries in closing down the Eastern Front.

This agreement became the famous Brest-Litovsk Treaty of March 1918, abbreviated simply as Brest-Litovsk. It became a cardinal symbol, an early example of Soviet willingness to compromise on the diplomatic front (although Lenin seemingly had no other choice). In particular, it struck a deal with the Germans that gave the Bolsheviks a breathing spell in which top leaders consolidated their power. Historians like Martirosyan claim that Stalin above the rest of the leadership supported such a line since preservation of "Russian statehood" was of prime importance to him. This contrasted with the "Comintern internationalists" who did not make this their priority.[3]

PEREDYSHKI

As noted above, Brest-Litovsk also signified winning of what became boiler plated in Soviet tactics as a "breathing space" (*peredyshka*), or time to recoup in order to later resume the revolutionary offensive following a Brest-Litovsk-like "retreat." Zigzagging was a well-known Bolshevik device, part of the "code of the Politburo."[4] Lenin said at the time: "If you are not able to adapt yourself, if you are not prepared to crawl in the mud on your belly, you are not a revolutionary but a chatterbox." Such retreating, as with Brest-Litovsk or the new economic policy launched in 1921, did not mark the end of the Bolsheviks' revolutionary socialist mission. It only represented a pause. It was a useful one in several respects, especially having lasting influence on Stalin's political tactics when dealing with foreign affairs or the necessity of using *peredyshki* to prepare for and cope with future contingencies.

Lenin had just barely sold his comrades on the usefulness of the treaty. Yet he had convinced a majority by arguing that German troops fighting on the Eastern Front would be transported westward to fight the "capitalist imperialist" states of France, Britain, and the United States. (The latter had been dispatching units of the American Expeditionary Force into France since early 1917.) The Germans soon carried out the deployment to the disadvantage of the Allied war effort against the Central Powers. It is interesting to speculate whether Stalin's deals with Hitler in August–September 1939 likewise redirected a German threat to Soviet Russia westward to similarly plague the Western capitalist states.

FOMENTING INTER-IMPERIALIST TENSIONS

In any case, Brest-Litovsk provided an example of dovetailing what looks superficially like reason-of-state (*ragione dello stato*) diplomacy—namely, ending the war on Russia's western frontier and saving the nascent Soviet Republic—along with the dictates of Leninist ideology: namely, encouraging inter-imperialist "contradictions" and inter-imperialist fratricidal war. Here was established in 1918 a lasting precedent, a harbinger of what was to become a perennial Soviet tactic in foreign relations—namely, helping the Western capitalist states self-destruct. As Lenin advised: In diplomacy, "We must exploit the contradictions and divergencies in view between any two imperialisms, between two groups of capitalist states, pushing one against the other." The "pushing" included instigation of war between them.

Pondering Lenin's words and Stalin's later deeds with realist versus traditionalist-ideological points of view in mind, the question arises whether this "instigation" policy was motivated by non-ideological "geopolitical interests" alone. Divide-and-conquer is not necessarily a Communist invention or whether it was based on Bolshevist-Communist revolutionism. It would seem that both factors were operating in tandem. Yet without ideological underpinning about the "laws" of capitalist imperialism, the policy of fomenting intra-imperialist tensions would have lacked a perspective and an ideological motivation.

Because of the transfer of German troops to the Western Front, Germany in the spring of 1918 seemed to have come near to winning the war against the Allies, with its 200 divisions poised to drive on to Paris—at one point, the invaders were only some 35 miles from the French capital. However, French and American reinforcements succeeded by the summer of 1918 in stopping the last of Ludendorff's several offensives. By November, the war was over.

Out of such internecine struggle within the imperialist camp of "bourgeois" capitalist states, as noted, Lenin hoped that strife and socialist revolution would grow. War, as Marx and Engels taught, is a catalyst of unrest and destruction out of which comes socialist construction. Later, the Soviet leader gave Japan as an example of such a state with which the Soviets could help instigate future hostilities against capitalist America. He added that war between these two states in any case was "inevitable." Referring to Japan, Lenin said: "To put it bluntly, we have incited Japan and America against each other and so gained an advantage." In a speech to the Moscow party *aktiv* on December 6, 1920, Lenin further declared:

> "Until the final victory of socialism throughout the whole world, we must apply the principle of exploiting contradictions and opposition between two imperialist power groups, between two capitalist groups of states inciting them to attack each other. . . . If it should prove impossible to defeat them both, then one must know how to rally one's forces so that the two begin to fight each other. For when two thieves quarrel, honest men have the last laugh. . . . As soon as we are strong enough to defeat capitalism [worldwide], we will seize it at once by the scruff of the neck."

As will be seen, in the 1920s and 1930s, Stalin enlarged on this Leninist concept of Soviet encouragement of divide-and-conquer via intra-capitalist-sphere war. At the same time, Stalin endeavored to unite ideology with the national interests of the "Russian" (i.e., Soviet) state. The policy as applied to the Far East was to include Japan. This would become a war that ultimately began at Pearl Harbor and in the South Pacific in December 1941 and involved the capitalist powers, America, Britain, and its allies. It may be assumed that months in advance of December 7, 1941, Stalin had intelligence about the impending attack on Pearl Harbor, but did not share that information with Washington. This, after all, would have violated the tactic of helping capitalist states commit fratricide. Shrewd as this overtly "non-ideological" Soviet diplomacy was, it was in tune with the regime's ideology as a tool by which in an important way Soviet fundamental national goals could be realized.

DIPLOMACY IN STALIN'S INDUSTRIALIZATION

"Trade diplomacy," the art of winning trade partners and achieving profitable trade deals that would strengthen the Soviet Republic, especially in the military sense, had been an integral part of Soviet foreign policy at least since the inauguration of the New Economic Policy (NEP, 1921). This was when Lenin ordered his temporary, tactical retreat in Soviet domestic and foreign policy under NEP. By this means he sought to repair some of the economic damage wrought by the previous three-year stint of radicalized utopian "War Communism" and by the disruptive civil war of the same period. The Soviet leader thereupon began to a degree to open up the young Soviet state to intercourse with capitalist nations. This presaged the period of intense Soviet-German military collaboration (see chapter 6) that established a lasting precedent right up to 1939 and the Molotov-Ribbentrop pacts.

After Lenin's death and Stalin's subsequent consolidation of power, elaboration of Lenin's commercial opening to the West was effected by Stalin. This partial rapprochement with the capitalist states, although confined mainly to commerce, was linked to Stalin's industrialization program that was initiated with the first Five-Year Plan in the late 1920s.

Josef Stalin well understood that for the USSR to become a major player in the world arena, which he repeatedly indicated was his principal goal, it would have to be powerful in the military-industrial sense. He was not satisfied to relish the Soviet Union as the model socialist state merely in the idealistic sense, or as an isolated "Soviet garden" lacking influence on the global chessboard. As Stalin once asked matter-of-factly about the Vatican, the capital of Western Catholicism and a fountain of myths, "So, how many divisions does the Pope have?" Spiritual monumentality alone did not impress Stalin—except as propaganda icing on the cake. Heavy industry and motorized infantry divisions were what really mattered.

Before Stalin could supply the Red Army with guns, tanks, motorized infantry vehicles, aircraft, naval ships, and ammunition, it was necessary, of course, to develop the basic producer goods or heavy industries of mining, power (energy), iron and steel, and machine-building of several types. Here again diplomacy would come to the rescue. This case took the form of fostering foreign trade and on-site aid together with sales of foreign patents to the Soviets.

It is sometimes forgotten that the process of industrializing Russia had already proceeded at an impressive pace under the tsars before World War I in the 1890s to 1914. But the devastation of that war had set back this impressive, nascent Russian industrial growth. Stalin picked up where the tsars had left off. Now, however, the Soviet leader's emphasis was on defense production, which after Stalin's death in 1953 had left per capita food and consumer goods output in Soviet Russia where the tsarist Russian economy had been 40 years earlier, in 1913. (First, Secretary

Nikita Khrushchev was obliged to disclose this embarrassing fact in September 1953, perhaps at Premier Georgi Malenkov's urging.)

During the Five-Year Plans, Stalin repeatedly emphasized what the basic intentions of the Soviet buildup were and what its sacrifices were for. As he proclaimed, Soviet Russia would become a major power, in his words the "prototype of the future world socialist Soviet Republic," calling it the "base for world revolution." The Russian proletariat, he said, "is the vanguard of the international proletariat." In order for it (meaning Russia) to fulfill that role, it must become a world power. Moreover, in so doing, the USSR would be more than able to defend itself against the "capitalist encirclement." Stalin appeared to ignore the fact that with the end of the war-related Allied intervention, this "encirclement" had been distinctly passive since 1918. All of Soviet Russia's "defense needs," Stalin promised, would be met by the completion of the several Five-Year Plans. By then, as the giant that came last, the country would be ready to meet any expediency—war being the most likely such event, as the ideology and as Stalin himself had predicted.

As Mr. X (George Kennan) documented in his famous essay in 1949, with numerous citations directly from Lenin and Stalin's speeches and writings, both Lenin and Stalin on many occasions predicted that a new world war was "inevitable." They anticipated that it would be one, they claimed, in which imperialism would perish—with Soviet help. For the Soviets, developing weapons of war was not, in their view, simply a case of militarism, Soviet-style. The policy flowed from geopolitical as well as ideological premises formulated in Moscow.

Foreign economic assistance to the Soviet Union, i.e., aid that was developed through trade diplomacy, became crucial for the process of industrializing the USSR. Significantly, although not surprisingly, the Soviets' main supplier in the 1920s and 1930s was Germany. The United States was a close second. It is no exaggeration to say that the Soviet power industry (represented, above all, by the great Dnepropetrovsk Dam in Ukraine, built with U.S. help and equipment), its manufacturing industries (including not only heavy industry, but also textiles), its mining and oil-drilling equipment, its railroad construction, its tractor-, tank-, and aviation-production facilities, and much else, could not have developed apace without this foreign assistance. The Soviets likewise purchased foreign patents when needed. (When this author visited the USSR as late as

1966, he still saw old foreign trade marks stamped on metal labels affixed to factory machinery—in this case, at Zhelyabov Textile Factory, a major plant in Moscow.) All of this American aid was never forgotten by Stalin.

STALIN'S EMPHASIS ON DEFENSE

As the Red Army was training and equipping itself largely for a mobile war, during 1934–1939 alone the Red Army's fleet of tanks tripled. Before the Soviet-German war began in June 1941, Soviet tank production already was up to 12,000 per year with the total number of the fleet reaching 24,000 by the summer of 1941.[5] This was a defense-production feat far exceeding even Germany's let alone the combined levels of tank production in France, Britain, and, not surprisingly, in the United States in its defense-poor, pre-Pearl Harbor years. By means of the heavy industries that made all of this possible, the USSR boosted itself to first, second, or third place in the world in the production of various kinds of electrical power (thermal and hydroelectric) as well as crucial raw and manufactured materials—iron, coal, and steel being among them.

Soviet tank, plane, and many types of field weapons production at that time exceeded the production of all the major Western countries combined! That is, of course, before U.S. arms production made the United States the "arsenal of democracy" by 1942–1943. But even during World War II, the USSR far outproduced the United States in machine guns and mortars as well as cannons and tanks. Also, the unique, multiple-rocket-firing Katyusha (or mobile "organ" artillery, so named because of its resemblance to a nest of organ pipes) was coming on line as the Great Fatherland War began. Like other new, world-class weaponry just starting to come off Soviet assembly lines in 1941, the Katyusha ultimately played a major role in Soviet victories.

Among the new Soviet tanks was the low-profile, diesel-driven, amphibious T-34, developed in the late 1930s. This was the only such tank of its kind in battle in 1941 and was the envy of the Wehrmacht. Early Soviet artillery likewise was impressive as were several other types of ground-force weaponry, including mortars, infantry guns, and vehicles (the hardiness of the latter under Russia's severe winter conditions became a crucial factor). Moreover, the Soviet aircraft industry was developing apace. Many innovations and some world-flight records were chalked up by the Red Air Force in the 1930s. (Pre-1917 Russian progress in aviation is, of course, well known to anyone who has ever heard the names Mozhaisky, Tsiolkovsky, or Sikorsky.)

Not the least of the impressive new Soviet aircraft were the twin- and four-engine medium and long-range bombers and transport aircraft, the latter especially for transporting airborne troops. The long-range, heavy bomber TB-3, to cite one example, could carry four light aircraft mounted atop its wings or slung below them and the fuselage. Such Red Air Force planes, powered by impressive engines, could carry more weight than any foreign equivalent. In some ways, the power plants of these planes were the forerunners of the powerful rocket engines developed in the USSR in the 1950s.

From 1940 to mid-1941, the Soviet aviation industry was mass-producing the MiG-3, Yak-1, LaGG-3, Il-2, Pe-2, and other aircraft. In that mere one-and-a-half-year period, the total fighters and bombers produced in the USSR came to 1,200 MiG-3s, 400 Yak-1s, 250 Il-2s, and 460 Pe-2s. According to British and other military analysts, the Soviet planes in some cases were, indeed, world-class. Also, the rate of their production in the USSR in the late 1930s, even before Operation Barbarossa was launched against the USSR in the summer of 1941, exceeded German aircraft production by a ratio of four to one. These machines included the Ilyushin-2, or "Shturmovik" air-ground support fighter; the heavily armed fighter Polikarpov (Po-2) that saw service in the Spanish Civil War; the Ilyushin-16, Version 17, a Polikarpov design appearing in 1938, an outstanding aircraft with ShKAS machine-guns mounted atop the engine cowling plus two 20-mm cannons mounted in the wings, firing 1,600 rounds/minute with a muzzle velocity of 2,700 feet/second. These were exceptional specs for its time. The Il-16's armament and ordnance weight exceeded that of the Messerschmitt 109-E1 by double, and that of the British Spitfire by triple.

The specs of several other types of Soviet planes also led their equivalents worldwide. Some broke records in long-distance flight and in the power of their engines. Red Air Force fighters could attain speeds of up to 260 mph and outclassed in several respects the German single- and twin-engine Me-109, FW-190, Ju-87, and Ju-88.

By mid-1941, the total Red Air Force fleet consisted of 10,000 planes, with a monthly production rate of 1,630 aircraft. By 1942, this latter figure had risen to 2,120 on the production base already established during the two preceding years. The designers of such world-class aircraft included A. S. Yakovlev, S. A. Lavochkin, A. I. Mikoyan, N. E. Zhukovsky,

V. M. Petlyakov, N. N. Polikarpov, S. V. Ilyushin, G. M. Beriyev, A. N. Zhuravchenko, D. A. Ventsel', V. S. Pugachev, and G. I. Pokrovsky.

Soviet defense-production organization and experience became vital when the German penetration of the industrial Ukraine in the opening weeks of the Great Fatherland War in June–July 1941 forced the Soviets to step up the moving of their production facilities to the rear to the Ural Mountains industrial region, the easternmost boundary of European Russia. At this time, the Soviets' own production of war materiel rather dwarfed subsequent Lend-Lease aid—as vitally important, however, as the latter was, as per Stalin's public postwar admission to U.S. Lend-Lease administrator, Eric Johnston.

TRAIL OF BROKEN "FRIENDSHIP" TREATIES

As the Soviets built up their industrial and military strength, their diplomatic relations with the outside world appeared confusing.

In the pre-World War II years, the "dialectical" twists and turns and zigzags of Soviet tactics became standbys in Soviet diplomacy. Some Western analysts even thought that the Soviets were using such mind-boggling on-again/off-again tactics as a form of psychological warfare to baffle and "wear down" the adversary. The Soviet policy toward the League of Nations is one of many examples of this zigzagging. The "Nazi-Soviet honeymoon," suddenly inaugurated in August 1939 to the world's surprise and certainly to that of the world's Communist Party apparatuses, was only the latest of a string of such policy gyrations.

At times, such zigzag behavior profoundly disoriented foreign observers, especially pro-Soviet ones and fellow travelers. Why, some might ask, would Stalin and the Soviet Union conclude a friendship treaty with each of the Baltic states—Estonia, Latvia, and Lithuania— while at the same time using Communist Party legals and illegals in those same countries to overturn their capitalist system, private ownership of property, and political order? Indeed, as early as 1918 and in the 1920s Lenin followed a policy of attempting to sovietize countries as far to the west as Hungary and Germany. Was this merely old-fashioned realpolitik based on the basic Russian geopolitical situation? Or did the regime's expansionist ideology serve as more than a contributing factor to such behavior?

The same could be asked about Moscow's overtures to and agreements with Poland, Czechoslovakia, Romania, and other nation-states among the Little Entente in Eastern Europe with whom Moscow made non-aggression, friendship, or mutual-assistance treaties in the 1930s while at the same time fomenting unrest in these same countries. Eventually, the post-World War II period saw Stalin ordering the region into Soviet satrapies. A U.S. Senate staff study compiled in 1959 found that in 38 short years after 1917, the USSR "had broken its word to virtually every country to which it ever gave a signed promise. It signed treaties of nonaggression and friendship with neighboring countries then in some cases absorbed these states. It signed promises to refrain from revolutionary activity inside the countries with which it sought friendship. [One may] seriously doubt whether during the whole history of civilization any great nation has ever made as perfidious a record as this in so short a time."

Trade was a strong motivating factor in such diplomatic intercourse, to be sure, although not the only one. Not even trade—say, as embodied in the Anglo-Soviet trade pact of 1921—was allowed to interfere with Moscow's pursuit of world revolution and subversion in all of the countries without exception with which it had diplomatic, et al., dealings.

The several precedents in this respect established in Soviet behavior in the 1920s and 1930s shed light on Soviet serpentine maneuvering throughout 1939. This was at the time, namely, when negotiations, including trade deals, were held simultaneously with the Germans on one hand and the French and British on the other. In these negotiations, the Soviets would secretly share with Berlin the texts of their confidential political talks with the British and French to win the favor of Germany as well as give preference to the latter. They did not bestow this favor on the other two capitalist states by disclosing to them Soviet talks with the Germans. By contrast, that summer on occasion the British kept Moscow informed of its talks with the Germans—and, of course, informed Stalin in 1941 of some of the contents of Enigma-machine intercepts of German general staff-coded messages. These decrypts pointed to the opening of German hostilities against the USSR in June 1941. (The British and Americans never revealed, of course, the top-secret source of their information. Yet it is alleged by some authors that Soviets had penetrated Bletchley Park.)

The United States was also the object of two-track duplicity. In 1933, in Moscow, via the Soviet Commissar of Foreign Affairs, Maxim Litvinov, the same accomplished, wily Old Bolshevik who had taken part in the Rapallo negotiations with Germany. It was he, despite his Jewish ancestry, who favored Soviet-Nazi rapprochement and who spoke for his government in disingenuously agreeing to terminate Communist Party-supported activities in the United States. This was in exchange for recognition of the Soviet Union by the Roosevelt administration. Yet this promise, too, was to be broken despite repeated U.S. protests.

COMINTERN FACTOR

Lenin was a uniquely innovative political actor in several respects. Not the least of his extraordinary accomplishments was the founding of the modern world's first totalitarian state. Another such innovation was his establishment in 1919 of the Third Communist International— the "General Staff of World Revolution."

Under Lenin's influence, world politics witnessed an entirely new phenomenon. Now organized, global subversion by a major power would cast a shadow over the ways in which the diplomatic game had been played traditionally in Europe since the 1600s. Lenin had broken entirely new ground by creating this world-girdling subversive organization with its headquarters in Moscow.

A good deal more than a Kremlin toy but less than a world-revolutionary Red Army ready to march against the world, the Comintern and its mission assumed several effective forms. It cannot be underestimated as an influential tool used by the Kremlin in order to promote Soviet interests and ideology on a global scale. Specifically, the Comintern was tasked to:

1. Propagate Soviet-style communism that Lenin described as the sole model for all bourgeois and colonial societies in order to make the transition to socialism via the dictatorship of the proletariat on the Soviet model.
2. Establish Communist-led vanguard political forces in the target countries, capitalist and pre-capitalist, that would unite with subsidiary "front" organizations in order more broadly—e.g., via parliamentary struggle, through the trade unions, etc.—to wage class war to bring down bourgeois democracy.
3. To use the "citadel" of the Soviet Union, or "base of world revolution" (Stalin), as a guide and leader of the world movement, even using its

military force, the Red Army "of liberation," wherever appropriate or feasible to bring about the Communist revolution in a given country or region. This was known as exporting revolution on the "tips of Red Army bayonets."

4. To exploit pacifism by the use of peace campaigns to sap and stop armed, defensive containment of Soviet-sponsored world revolution in capitalist countries, above all in Britain, France, and the United States. (An old piece of barracks humor in the Soviet Union had it that "one day the Soviet peace effort will be so successful that not a brick will be left standing anywhere.")

5. To recruit spies and subversives within capitalist or colonial countries.

The Comintern's life span was 25 years—from 1919 to 1943. During that time, it was far from successful in its ongoing labors to trigger world revolution. Yet, at the very least, it was the source for recruiting numbers of effective spies and agents of influence. It also helped promote pro-Sovietism and *poputchikestvo* ("fellow-travelership") within the politics of the given targeted foreign nation. This it did not only in the industrialized capitalist countries, but also throughout the Third World.

Actually, the Comintern acted as an arm of the Soviet secret police (OGPU, GPU, later NKVD), which had thoroughly penetrated the organization. Moreover, with clever operatives like Soviet Comintern agent Willi Münzenberg—who organized outwardly non-Communist, though Communist-backed, movements and demonstrations in the Western democracies—an impressive number of left-wing people and organizations were bamboozled into accepting various Communist-supported radical stands. A number of very well-known Western intellectuals were taken in. Comintern policy stands revolved about such issues as opposing Western rearmament and military defense preparations; supporting unqualified Soviet friendship even if it meant disloyalty to one's home country; and smoothing the way via innocuous-looking "fronts" toward spreading Communist propaganda and influence within the target societies.

The Comintern's work combined with that of the national Communist Party's activities worldwide succeeded in some places in thoroughly penetrating labor unions, youth groups, and even the media. However, it had much less success in those days making inroads in the United States than it had in such European countries as Britain, and particularly France, Italy, and the Lowlands.

UNITED FRONT (LENIN)/POPULAR FRONT (STALIN)

Much has been written about the Popular Front tactic developed within the Comintern in the mid-1930s—a line that Stalin attentively crafted. Historians have described how this party line transitioned into the Comintern-backed anti-Fascist movement.

Actually, Lenin invented the front tactic back in 1922, calling it at that time the United Front tactic. Later under Stalin's tutelage after 1924, the Comintern began sharply to distinguish Communist parties from Social-Democratic parties (SDs). Under Stalin's direction, it sought, for the most part, to put them on diametrically opposite sides of the barricades. The SDs were stigmatized as "social fascists" by Stalinite parties throughout Europe and the Americas.

By thus following Stalin's orders in the Comintern, the German Communist Party adamantly refused to cooperate with the popular Social Democratic Party, which opposed Hitler's and the Nazis' rise to power. With this in mind as well as displaying his usual penchant for believing that "worse is better"—for Communism and world revolution—Stalin instructed in the late 1920s that:[6]

> It is necessary that Social Democracy be unmasked and defeated and be reduced to being supported by an insignificant minority of the working class. Without this happening, it is impossible to speak of establishing a dictatorship of the proletariat. . . . The most favorable circumstances for a revolution in Germany would be an internal crisis and a significant increase in the forces of the Communist Party accompanied by serious complications within the camp of Germany's external enemies.

It is now a consensus view held among Russian historians—a view that began to surface under "glasnost'" near the end of Communist rule in the USSR—that Stalin's aversion to democratic socialism as represented by the SDs helped pave the way to Hitler's ascent to power in 1933 and with it German military aggression. Stalin believed that Hitler's Nazis would only aggravate the German class struggle in ways he thought useful to the Soviets. Because of Stalin-decreed splittism within the German Left, the anti-Hitler camp in Germany became divided. The German Communists refused to join forces on the left to block the Brownshirts.

When Lenin's United Front tactic was refurbished and unfurled again as the Popular Front at the Seventh Congress of the Comintern in August 1935, the organization's leader, Georgi Dimitrov, described it as a boring-from-within tactic to be used among Communist-supported, left-wing forces worldwide in order to attract supporters of the USSR and of world revolution. These front groups were designed ultimately to fall under the leadership of the Communists. (This writer actually witnessed such a stratagem in the postwar period. It was used by Communists within the Chicago chapter of a World War II veteran's organization, known as the American Veterans Committee [AVC]. The AVC's elected leaders got wind of this tactic and expelled the Communists. Similar episodes occurred within U.S. labor union executive bodies.)

Dimitrov explained the tactic quite candidly in his widely distributed pamphlet with its yellow, red, and black cover titled *The Working Classes Against Fascism*:

> Comrades, you will recall the ancient tale of the capture of Troy.... The attacking army was unable to achieve victory until, with the aid of the famous Trojan Horse, it managed to penetrate to the very heart of the enemy camp.

Dimitrov was quite frank about the fact that the forming of popular fronts with leftist-minded collaborators was not an end in itself. It was a step, he said, toward eventually capturing power for the Communists.

As to the anti-Fascist side of the Popular Front, this side, or thrust, of the movement did not in the least deter Stalin's efforts to close ranks with the German Nazis (see chapter 3). This was true despite mutually hostile propaganda attacks shared between both parties' propagandists, those of the Reds and of the Browns, throughout the 1930s. And despite Hitler's plans, as stated in his bible, *Mein Kampf*, to seize territory from Russia for the purpose of securing German "Lebensraum." As author Stephen Koch explains:[7]

> Münzenberg's apparatus, in turn, was ordered to transform the 'peace' movement and use it to mount a new, worldwide anti-Fascist campaign.... The Soviet state under Stalin was assuming the moral high ground. Or so it seemed.... As such, communism seemed to represent the only real resistance to the new horror so obviously taking shape [in Nazi Germany]. The democracies, through their real or supposed inaction, were depicted as bound by capitalism either to the ineffectiveness of liberalism—or worse, to a secret sympathy for the Nazis, 'Fascist brothers under the skin.' This myth therefore assigned moralized roles, casting the struggle between the two states

as the definitive struggle between good and evil in the century. In it, the Stalinist line became good or at least necessary to the good, by virtue of its supposed opposition to Hitler's evil. . . . The tremendous moral credit inuring to this myth, which was added to (and was much greater than) the already existing moral credit of the Revolution itself, came flowing toward the Soviets at exactly the moment that Stalin's government was moving toward its most sinister and brutal phase. Paradox? It was not a paradox born in coincidence. It was a deception, and it was planned. For this great confrontation between the [two] totalitarian powers was itself a deception, and in every way a very different thing from what it appeared to be.

Soviet aide Karl Radek, who had supervised the anti-Fascist line (and who had been approached by representatives of the German General Staff when he was briefly in prison in Germany in the 1920s and who urged him to promote Germano-Soviet collaboration), had made the same points to Walter Krivitsky. He disclosed to Krivitsky the grand deception of the anti-Fascist movement sponsored worldwide from Moscow: "Only fools," Radek said, "could imagine we would ever break with Germany. What I am writing here [of an anti-Fascist nature] is one thing. The realities are something else. No one can give us what Germany has given us. For us to break with Germany is simply impossible." Stalin shared these sentiments.

Koch adds that just as Münzenberg was placing himself in Paris in charge of executing the Popular Front line in France, Radek was sent by Stalin into top-secret contacts with the German ambassador in Moscow, Radek acting as the Soviet dictator's direct, confidential emissary. These confidential discussions, in which the Soviets were the initiators, took place without the knowledge of the Soviet diplomatic service or of the army. The contents of the talks amounted to negotiations based on mutual benefit. In other words, they were the prelude to the Nazi-Soviet negotiations of 1939, in which the Soviets once again were the initiators.

In July 2000, the Russian journal *Voprosy Istorii* published for the first time long excerpts from the diary of the head of the Comintern, Georgi Dimitrov. The document was unearthed by Russian Academy of Sciences historian F. I. Faros from the Archive of the Soviet Communist Party Central Committee. Classified "strictly secret", the Dimitrov diary contains many revealing facts about Stalin's attitude toward world revolution, the capitalist states, Germany, and the coming war.

We learn, for instance, that far from downgrading the importance of the Communist International's activities at any juncture in its history, Stalin took a special interest in its work. In remarks to Dimitrov on September 7, 1939, he explained the rationale behind the Nazi-Soviet agreements that, superficially at least, seemed only to help Germany. As Stalin explained:[8]

> War between the two groups of capitalist states (poor ones vs. rich ones in terms of their colonial possessions, raw materials, etc.) is taking place for the redivision of the world and for world domination! We won't prevent them at all from fighting among themselves all they wish as they go about damaging and bringing down the capitalist system. Communists who are in power take a different position from those who are in opposition [seeking power]. We are masters in our own household. The Communists in capitalist countries, on the other hand, are in opposition to the bourgeois boss. So, we are able to maneuver, pitting one [bourgeois state] side against the other so that they will fight all the harder with each other. The [Nazi-Soviet] Nonaggression Pact helps Germany to a degree but at the next juncture spurs on the other side.

Here Stalin was suggesting that in helping Germany with the formidable shipments of Soviet materiel to buttress the German war machine (see chapter 4), the Soviets thereby aggravated the military balance between Germany and its potential enemies (World War II began September 1, 1939; it did not become a truly fighting war in Western Europe until the next year).

On the sixteenth anniversary of Lenin's death held in the Bolshoi Theater, January 21, 1940, Stalin defined world revolution under the new conditions of actual, ongoing war as follows:

> World revolution seen as a single act is pure nonsense. It proceeds through several stages at various times in the several countries. Actions by the Red Army also are part of the world revolution.

On November 25, 1940, Dimitrov heard Stalin say the following in discussions between him and Foreign Commissar Molotov upon the latter's return from Berlin:

> In the lands destroyed by the occupation of German troops we will pursue a course there of carrying on our work but not screaming from the rooftops what we're up to. We would not be

Communists if we did not follow this course. The thing is to do this quietly.

Stalin closed down the Comintern in 1943 after almost a quarter century of its playing the role as something more than a mere disposable tool of the Kremlin.

For some authors, the Comintern's demise, on Stalin's orders, testified to the dictator's demeaning of its importance. Yet the Comintern's *functions* did not cease as the USSR allied itself with the Western powers in World War II. On the contrary, Comintern-like activities were continued. They were even strengthened in the name of spreading Soviet-style socialism worldwide by the Comintern's successors, the Cominform and the CPSU Central Committee's International Department, which was run by former Comintern executives. These "internationalist" organs by no means were vestigial. Their program for global subversion and Soviet expansionism was solidly within the traditions of the Com intern, the "General Staff of World Revolution."

6

Soviet Pro-German Posture

Stalin's program to industrialize the Soviet Union and build its military defenses for the coming "inevitable" war required safe external conditions during this protracted period of vast construction. Soviet foreign policy's primary goal was to prevent any hostile coalition of foreign powers forming at its expense. The Soviet Union would keep out of any and all international conflicts until such time as it would be strong enough herself to enter them without risk and with maximum profit to itself. Toward that end, the Soviet-German Brest-Litovsk Treaty of 1918, followed by the Treaty of Berlin (1926), became harbingers of future significant bilateral cooperation between the two "loser" states.

EARLY ROOTS

Historically, Russian-German cooperation began in tsarist times. It is a long story that goes back to the eighteenth century, when Peter the Great encouraged close relations with Prussia. The Russian army began copying Prussian uniforms and drills and adopted the goosestep (which the Red Army also adopted). With German unification after 1871, Russia again closed ranks with Germany. Under the German chancellor, Bismarck, a reinsurance treaty was concluded with Russia that protected Germany's rear in the case of trouble with France and Britain, who were being alienated by Bismarkian expansionist ambitions. After Bismarck was dismissed in 1890, Kaiser Wilhelm let the reinsurance deal with Russia flounder. This decision paved the way toward World War I, in which Austria united with Germany against Russia and the Western Allies.

In the post-World War I environment in Europe, the two-state bloc between Germany and the Soviet Republic would, for the Bolshevik leaders, serve to deter any West European powers from penetrating toward the USSR. It would also keep in line the Little Entente states of Eastern Europe, created by Versailles as "bastard children," as perceived by Berlin and Moscow. (For active German-Soviet military collaboration after World War I, see chapter 4.) This bilateral accord affecting the heart of Europe was in its way a kind of eastern Axis. Also, Brest-Litovsk became the symbol of Soviet diplomatic flexibility that was forced on Moscow under dire circumstances of an emergent "revolutionary state" whose subversive, expansionist ideology was viewed abroad as threatening the security of other states.

THE BREST-LITOVSK PRECEDENT (1918)

Brest-Litovsk became a classic precedent in which the Soviets had struck a temporary deal "in league with the devil" in order to enhance Soviet Russia's own national interests and external security regardless of "appearances." In 1939, Germany again became such a devil when Stalin made a second deal, this time with the leader of the Nazi German state. At the mid-point in 1940 during the 21-month "Nazi-Soviet honeymoon" begun in August 1939, discussion between Berlin and Moscow looked toward an even broader pact. This four-way coalition was to be based on the farfetched Age of Dictators plan to divide up the world between the USSR and the other totalitarian states—Germany, Italy, and Japan—thus leaving the United States alone and isolated. Not surprisingly, however, given his own, more far-seeing, plans, Stalin would have no part of such an arrangement with the aggressive Axis. The taint of such a global alliance with "Fascists and militarists"—not to mention the risks of trusting in such an alliance with the likes of a Hitler, Mussolini, or the Japanese militarists—could hardly figure seriously in the Soviet leader's own more realistic long-range global strategy. Stalin played along with such invitations in order to sound out his potential enemies as well as to keep them at bay until the USSR was strong enough to deal with them as enemies.

Of at least symbolic significance of Soviet ties with Germany was the fact that such a deal would be struck with the nation that was the birthplace of Hegel, Lenin's favorite philosopher and the homeland of Marx and Engels, the holy ghosts of Leninism-Stalinism.

Moreover, it was the country Lenin most admired for, among other things, its socialist-like wartime economy designed by Gen. Erich von Ludendorff. The latter, incidentally, was the author of the influential military writing, *Notes on Offensive Battles*, a work doubtlessly familiar to Lenin, a zealous reader of military theory (e.g., as per his deep reading of Carl von Clausewitz).

Lenin, moreover, was a dedicated Germanophile.[1] In geostrategic terms and Soviet expansion, Germany was the pivotal Central European country that he considered to be the linchpin of the pan-European revolution. "When you see a Soviet of Workers' and Soldiers' Deputies in Berlin," Lenin remarked in 1918, "you will know that the proletarian world revolution has been born."

This was the same Germany, then under Kaiser rule, that had recognized Lenin's notoriety and influence on world politics from his base of exile in Switzerland. In April 1917, Berlin had provided the funds to Lenin and his Bolshevik cohorts to take the famous "sealed train" from Switzerland safely through the battlefields of Germany, thence by ship and rail to Sweden and Finland, and finally on to Petrograd, Russia. The trip was perpetrated just a month following the overthrow of Tsar Nicholas II and the establishment of the shaky provisional (temporary) government in Petrograd. The Kaiser, naturally, wanted Russia out of the war as well as embroiled in internal strife to keep it paralyzed and off the German rear as German armies were lurching toward Paris.

The insertion of the firebrand Lenin into the turmoil in Russia was a shrewd and effective game played by the German leaders. Regarded as a useful "bacillus," as German officials described him, Lenin was utilized by Berlin as an agitator-catalyst who would help "neutralize" Russia. Lenin, of course, had been bitterly opposed to Russian participation in the "imperialist war"—a story told dramatically and authentically in Alexander Solzhenitsyn's fictional *Lenin in Zurich*.

Dispatching millions of Reich marks to Russia, the Germans continued well after April 1917 to subsidize the subversive Lenin and to support his Bolshevik regime from late 1917 into 1918. The details of the large funding and the way the money was "laundered" and reached Lenin and his comrades in Petrograd (to fund Bolshevik newspapers, propaganda, demonstrations, etc., throughout 1917) were disclosed as Communist archives began to be opened in Moscow under glasnost. Still more was disclosed about this arrangement between Lenin's Bolsheviks and Berlin after 1991 when secret Soviet archives began to be opened. The post-Soviet weekly, *Argument i Fakty*, under the headline "Reich marks for the Dictatorship of the Proletariat" (No. 3, 1992, p. 4), was among the first large-circulation publications in Russia to provide complete evidence of the German funding of Bolshevism. The paper noted the dates, locations, and amounts of the bank deposits made in Russia and included photostats of Soviet memoranda concerning the banking of the subsidies in Moscow. Along with this article, *Aif* published a photomontage depicting Lenin in a German World War I helmet. Accusations that Lenin was a German spy, however, are doubtful and have never been confirmed.

The details of Treaty of Brest-Litovsk (1918) illustrated the way in which this agreement became a milestone in Soviet-German relations. It also fit Lenin's overall subversive strategy of dividing the enemy camp of capitalist powers. Under the treaty, 70 German divisions that had been fighting against Russia on the Eastern Front in the Great War were transferred to the West European front. It may be safely assumed that if the United States had not entered the war and sent the American Expeditionary Force to Europe to fight alongside the Allies, it is quite possible that Germany would have won the war, or at least the war might have dragged on interminably. At one point, the German army was within 35 miles of the French capital.

Finally, with the establishment of the Weimar government and with Lenin's encouragement and initiative, post-World War I Germany in 1922 eagerly became the first major country to have entirely normal relations with the young Soviet Republic (although a modest Anglo-Soviet rapprochement in the form of a trade deal, later abrogated by London, had been concluded the year before). In his earliest diaries of the mid-1920s, Josef Goebbels, who was to become Hitler's propaganda minister some eight years later, relished the advent of German-Soviet cooperation. Goebbels was about to pen his encomium to both Hitler and Lenin under the title *Lenin oder Hitler?*

As a follow-up from the Genoa Conference (1922) came fruitful diplomatic negotiations and the resultant treaty, including its secret clauses, signed between the Soviets and Germans at Rapallo in 1922. An era of close, active collaboration thereupon opened between the two states. This process, in fact, of Soviet-German collaboration never really ceased—with the exception of a few ups and downs for a while after Hitler consolidated his power in 1933—until June 22, 1941, with the German attack on the USSR.

For their part, Lenin and Stalin were always attracted to Soviet-German friendship, those "natural allies," Germany and Russia, who confronted a "common enemy." As in the Hitler period, the two Soviet leaders relished the fact that Germany was a have-not capitalist state that was bent upon revenge against the capitalist-imperialist victors of World War I. Moscow fully concurred with Berlin that German lands had been "extorted" from a "defenseless" Germany by what Lenin called the Versailles Treaty "robbers with knives in their hands."

Mainline Russian historiographic treatment of Soviet-German relations is found in the widely read text *Miroviye voiny XX veka; Kniga 3; Vtoraya mirovaya voina: Istoricheskiy ocherk (World Wars of the 20th Century: Historical Outline, Book 3; World War II),* published in 2002 in Moscow, edited by V. A. Zolotarev with author contributions by leading Russian historians such as A. Yu. Chubaryan, L. V. Pozdeyev, and Makhmut Gareyev. In general, the authors take an ambivalent but overall favorable line on the foreign policies of what they repeatedly refer to as the "Soviet government"—that is, without mentioning the name of Stalin, who, however, with Vyacheslav Molotov, set that line.

In terms of the new states created by the Versailles Treaty, the text argues that, "The newly created 'Cordon Sanitaire,' consisting of states that were separated from Russia became a barrier blocking the spread of Bolshevism into Western Europe."[2]

On the "loser" powers, Germany and Soviet Russia (note the Russian authors' use of "Russia" in place of "Soviet Republic" or "RSFSR". Significant passages are underlined by the author):

> "Those powers [Germany and the Soviet Republic] could not rely on the League of Nations [to defend their interests] and therefore made friendship treaties between them. . . . [As noted by German General G. Seeckt]: 'Only by establishing lasting relations with Great Russia can Germany count on restoring its status as a world power.' . . . The Russian Republic and Germany established secret collaboration in the military-technology field that resulted in defense production in Soviet Russia valued at 250 million marks, including 140 marks for construction of an aircraft factory. The decision of the Soviet leadership to effect such cooperation with Germany is explained by the fact that the Soviet Republic wished to take the country out of its isolation as well as strengthen Russia in case of renewed military intervention against it."

In a concluding note about close German-Soviet relations in the 1920s, Zolotarev alludes to French occupation of the Ruhr:

> "The government of the USSR was not interested in breaking ties with Germany. Thus, the Comintern instructed German

Communists to put the emphasis on demanding French evacuation of the Ruhr [which it had occupied in 1922–1923] instead of opposing the German Government. . . . In September–December 1924 the Soviet government tried to induce Germany not to join the League of Nations and, instead, to form closer relations with Moscow."

Of the Nazis, Zolotarev contends:

"The program of the Nazi party contained many demands that were in the interests of workers, tradesmen, and small businessmen. The regulatory functions of the German state were increased. . . . The foreign policy of the Nazi leadership was laid out, principally in Hitler's *Mein Kampf*, the first edition of which appeared in 1925. . . . This [and other Nazi books of its type] were replete with racism and aggression. . . . With the coming to power of the Nazis in Germany arose a common threat to neighboring countries in the East as well as in the West. This situation objectively laid the foundation for establishing cooperation between the USSR."

STRAWS IN THE WIND

A number of other straws in the wind in the early 1930s likewise pointed in a friendly direction concerning Moscow and Berlin. This process began when initiatives started emanating from the Soviet side. As per the following events:[3]

- In 1933–1934, Lev Lebedev, a Communist Party Central Committee apparatchik in Moscow, visited Berlin on a secret mission to study Gestapo techniques. This was followed by the transfer to the Germans of the table of organization used by the Soviet Commissariat of Internal Affairs (NKVD) for establishing Soviet labor camps as well as the design for mobile, poison-gas "liquidation wagons," invented in the USSR and used against recalcitrant peasants in Stalin's collectivization drive.
- According to Leon Gelfand, former counselor at the Soviet embassy in Rome, who defected to the United States in 1941, "Stalin had been obsessed with the idea of an agreement with Germany since 1933."
- On a visit to the Ministry of Foreign Affairs in Berlin, December 21, 1935, Sergei Bessonov suggested openly that it would be highly desirable if the neutrality agreement signed between Germany and Soviet Russia in 1926 were supplemented by a "mutual nonaggression

pact," as official German documents from the period show. Bessonov again brought up this idea to German officials in July 1936. In this it is clear, of course, that no Soviet official, especially one on assignment in a foreign country, would ever make such bold statements unless they were approved by the Kremlin.

- Ex-Soviet security officer Walter Krivitsky relates that in 1936, one A. Slutsky, chief of a foreign intelligence section of the Russian secret police, confided in him that, "We have set our course towards an early understanding with Hitler and have started negotiations."
- In December 1936 and February 1937, David Kandelaki, Soviet trade emissary with the cover designation of "commercial attaché" and one of Stalin's personal aides, had an audience with Hitler's finance overseer, Hjalmar Schacht. Kandelaki read a statement, presumably coming directly from Stalin, that said in effect that Soviet-German trade should be stepped up sharply, and with it a bold improvement should be made in overall Soviet-German relations.

There were several other wrinkles in the pre-1939 "feelers" period that signaled significant rapprochement between Moscow and Berlin. Some of the initiatives originated on the Soviet side, others on the German. But the milestone year in the process of forming a Soviet-German alliance, of course, was 1939.

Early in that year, Stalin sounded the first undeniable hint, a hint so strong that during the later Nazi-Soviet negotiations in Moscow in August 1939, Ribbentrop specifically referred to it favorably. So did Stalin.

Speaking from the rostrum of the Eighteenth Party Congress in the Bolshoi Theater, March 10, Stalin made some startling statements. They were delivered in his typically subtle, low-toned, droning way in which the Soviet dictator customarily exploded his verbal bombshells.

First, Stalin blasted the Western democracies for trying to incite, he claimed, the Soviet Union against Germany and "to poison the atmosphere and to provoke a conflict with Germany without any visible grounds." Then after making overtures to Germany, with which the Soviets, he indicated, surely should have better relations than they do presently, he dropped his classic "chestnuts-out-of-the-fire" remark, how, he implied, the Soviets were not about to come to the aid of other threatened capitalist states. The remark clearly indicated that Stalin was not about to engage in any serious collective-security negotiations with the Western capitalist states. This would be the case despite appearances or the fond hopes nurtured among pro-Soviet observers or officials in the West (such as British envoy and ambassador to Moscow, Sir Stafford Cripps).

Both Austria and Czechoslovakia, after all, would have been such "chestnuts" in 1938. In both cases, Moscow reacted more or less disinterestedly in Hitler's bold annexations of both of those states in that preceding year.

The fact that a country had been occupied by Germany did not cause any radical change in Communist tactics. In Czechoslovakia, the Communists accused the government there of being lackeys of French and British capitalism. In France, the Communists spread defeatism.

Later, the memoirs of Czechoslovak and Polish diplomats showed, as the memoirists claimed, a pattern of false Stalin pursuit of "collective security." One of these diplomats reported that he viewed Moscow as actually playing the role of instigator of war. He said he detected a Soviet plan to provoke war with Germany by urging the Czechs to stand fast against the Germans while at the same time ostentatiously offering, while not delivering any military support to the former— support that was never, in fact, forthcoming and which was never intended to be.

No such capitalist-state chestnuts would be pulled out of the fire. The fire of future war, it seemed, was too valuable to Stalin. Or at very least, he intended to keep the Soviet Union out of it until an appropriate time.

THE "COMMUNAZI" FACTOR

Some Western writers have suggested that not only was the leader's typical dictator's megalomania motivating these ambitious policies. They allege that Josef Vissarionovich Djugashvili, who adopted the name "Stalin" (from the Russian word *stal'* meaning "steel"), was a devout Russophile. For him, his Georgian roots were scarcely a source of pride. The trait of Russophilia in Stalin was noticed by a number of his comrades as early as 1912. Several writers and film producers in the 1930s flattered the dictator by comparing him—with his own prompting—to the Great Russian tsars Ivan the Terrible and Peter the Great.

For his part, historian Arsen B. Martirosyan—who, recall, had been chosen by the Putin government to give a major address to the Ministry of Justice Tula Institute in the autumn of 2009, stresses what he calls Stalin's (and Marshal Voroshilov's) "staunch, unwavering" conscientiousness about defending Russian state interests and honoring the Russian past under the tsars (the historian often drops "Soviet" when discussing this aspect of Stalin's "pro-Russian" policies).[4]

Stalin became the first Hitler-like dictator on the world stage of the twentieth century. Later, Hitler himself acknowledged magnanimously that he and Stalin were the most impressive leaders in the modern world. In comparison to them, he said, Mussolini, Churchill, and Roosevelt all paled. During the Nazi-Soviet honeymoon of 1939–1941, Stalin returned the compliment to Hitler by praising the fuehrer for his leadership of the German people. He congratulated him in 1940 on his "splendid" military victories against the "plutocratic," "war-mongering" countries of France and England—common enemies, the Soviets said, of both Germany and the USSR.

By the time Hitler came to power in Germany in 1933, Stalin had set a number of enviable precedents for effective police-state totalitarianism, some of which drew praise from Hitler, Goebbels, and Mussolini. These were one-party dictatorship; the ubiquitous political police; punitive labor camps; an official ideology, or "world outlook," upheld as exclusive and binding with its "world-historical," world-girdling pretensions; one-man dictatorship and glorification of the leader; etatization of the trade unions, press, schools, and all other social, political, and economic institutions; a rubber-stamp "parliament"; ascendant militarism; and singling out of a scapegoat, pariah-class, as Hitler did with the Jews and Lenin with the "bourgeoisie," the bourgeoisie being forced by the Bolsheviks to wear yellow cards (Hitler used yellow stars) in their hats so that the public could recognize and condemn them.

The Soviets' huge sports and military rallies and parades, reviewed by the top party leaders, likewise were copied by the Italian Fascists and German Nazis. Even the Soviet use of the color red on the banners and their utterly new (as a newly invented, unconventional state symbol) hammer and sickle were praised by Hitler in *Mein Kampf*. These were emulated by the Nazis with the latter's red, black, and white banners and their own invented symbol, the swastika. Mussolini had adopted his own particular symbol, the ancient Roman ax-with-fasces.

For good reason, Mussolini called Stalin a "crypto-Fascist" while Hitler said, "we must learn from the Marxists," recognizing the similarities between the two regime's philosophies. The best Nazi recruits in Germany, Hitler added, were ex-Communists.

Speaking of Mussolini, Lenin found much to admire in Italian fascism—an early example of the affinities felt between totalitarian states.[5] The "Blackshirts" were notorious in Lenin's lifetime, and the Soviet Republic eagerly opened relations with Fascist Italy. Mussolini had made his triumphant march on Rome in 1923, just six years after Lenin seized power in Russia. Having passed through a phase of Bolshevik-like socialism in his pre-World War I political evolution, Mussolini later adopted a nationalistic platform. When he became Italy's Il Duce, he developed a form of corporate-state socialism that was derived from his earlier prewar socialist, Marxist-Bolshevist views. In his system, dictatorship of the proletariat would be trans-mogrified into a centralized state running most affairs in the country from the center. Hence, Lenin's admiration for the Italian regime.

Mussolini, like Goebbels in the 1920s, was impressed with Lenin's one-man leadership. "The masses," he wrote in the fascist newspaper *Il Popolo d'Italia*, "need a hero." (In the early 1930s, Molotov was to pen an identical observation concerning the need for a powerful leader like Stalin.) Moreover, like Lenin and Stalin, Mussolini had no use for "bourgeois liberalism" and "bourgeois democracy": "[We] throw the noxious theories of so-called liberalism on the rubbish heap," he said, "[along with] the more or less putrid body of the Goddess of Liberty." Hitler agreed. Whereas Lenin and Stalin created "Soviet Man," Musso-lini sought to create the "Fascist Man" just as Hitler was later to create the new "Aryan Man." In 1921, Mussolini declared in the Chamber of Deputies in Rome: "I recognize that between us and the Communists [there are] intellectual affinities."

Italian-Fascist affinities with Leninism aside, the main point is as fol-lows: The totalitarian affinities between the Germans and the Soviets, that is, the "Communazi"/"Red-Brown" kinship, definitely played a seminal role in the Soviet-German uniting of late 1939. At one point in the Ribbentrop negotiations with Stalin, on the night of August 22–23, 1939, during the signing of the first of several Nazi-Soviet agreements at the Kremlin, the German foreign minister blurted out after a toast or two that he felt comfortable in the camaraderie of his Soviet hosts. It was, he said, as if he were "among old party comrades." At other times, Soviet and German spokesmen let it be known that the two states and their regimes had more in common than not, despite verbal on-again/off-again propaganda wars between them.

There was much between them, in other words, by way of common interest and a type of mutual respect that the powerful feel toward others of similar strength that paved the way to that fateful day of August 23, when the Nazi-Soviet Nonaggression Pact was signed before a broadly smiling Stalin and a grateful Ribbentrop. It was also marked the culmination of a long-brewing close relationship embracing many spheres.

STALIN NAVIGATES EUROPEAN WATERS

In the interwar period, many conflicting tidal currents were flowing between the states of Europe, some of them new Versailles-born nation-states, such as Czechoslovakia, Hungary, and Romania and the three Baltic states, all newly established since World War I. Stalin approached them in the interwar period strictly in terms of "Russian" national interests, as former tsarist-ruled borderlands that were of special geostrategic concern to Moscow.

One such ebbing current put Germany and the Soviet Union on the same side of the barricades. This stemmed from the fact that the Versailles Treaty had drawn the boundaries of several countries—among them France, Czechoslovakia, and Poland—in ways that disadvantaged, in the latter's perceptions at least, both Germany and Soviet Russia, the so-called "losers" from the war.

In the west in the coal-rich Ruhr, Germany lost vital land and industrial assets to France. On its eastern borders, Germans had been "arbitrarily" included in the new, Czechoslovak-ruled territory of the Sudetenland. Former German territory and people were also packaged into an enlarged, postwar Poland when part of Silesia with its German population became Polish territory. Much to Germany's dismay, the "Polish Corridor," also created by the Paris settlement, "artificially" separated Prussia from the "cretinized" postwar Germany.

On the Russian side, the enlarged, post-Versailles Poland also "encroached" on Russian territory in the east, land that was formerly part of White (Byelo-) Russia. Also, the Baltic States of Estonia, Latvia, and Lithuania, former duchies of tsarist Imperial Russia, were granted independence. Russia also lost Bessarabia to Romania, another fledgling state created out of the old Ottoman Empire on the basis of the fuzzy Wilsonian concept of "self-determination."

As noted, the Paris peace treaty had not only offended Germany and Russia, who, of course, were left out of the postwar territorial resettlements concluded at Versailles. It had likewise aggravated tensions between minority people everywhere, especially where new boundaries drawn under the Versailles regime put them unwillingly under "foreign" rule.

It was inconceivable that the two large states of Germany and Soviet Russia would ever accept their position of inferiority as the result of the "bandits'" treaty of 1919. Not surprisingly, when both powers had regained their strength, nationalist-minded elements proclaimed in their countries that they would seek to rectify the "injustices" of the Versailles "victors."

As a consequence, Europe became divided into states and political movements that on the one hand included territorial "revisionists," and on the other, "anti-revisionists." As revisionist capitals, Berlin and Moscow therefore sought to create a New Order for Europe that would replace the Versailles Treaty's "artificial" one. It was against the backdrop of these tensions and common interests that helped drive Germany and Russia together.

We will see in the discussion of the Nazi-Soviet agreements in autumn 1939 that the mutual interests of the two "deprived" states were reasserted in the Nazi-Soviet Friendship Pact concluded in September 1939. In the manner in which the pact's secret protocols carved up Poland between Germany and the USSR (presaging Foreign Commissar Molotov's announcement in the fall of 1939 that "the Polish state has ceased to exist"), long-standing German and Soviet interests dating from 1919 were well served.

FAR EAST DANGERS

Not without relevance in the 1930s kaleidoscope was the Far Eastern picture. To Soviet Russia, affairs in this region looked particularly unfavorable to its national interests. Soviet foreign policy toward the East Asian nations of Japan and China thus displayed those same contradictions as it did toward the West. Perhaps these contradictions were unavoidable considering Moscow's notorious "double track" of illegal export of revolution versus normal diplomatic intercourse.

Thus, in Asia (as later in Africa and South America in the postwar years), Leninist-Trotskyite strategy included the tactic of stirring up the colonial "rear" of the Western "imperialist" nations. This was another way of weakening and bringing down the industrialized capitalist countries, which relied on the natural resources they obtained from what later was called the "Third World." The way to Paris and London, said Trotsky and Sultan Galiyev (who sought to create what he called a "Colonial Comintern"), lay via the West's colonies—the metropolitan countries' sources of raw materials and cheap labor as well as potential cauldrons of revolution.

Playing upon anti-colonialist discontent in, for instance, China in the 1920s—which had been undergoing a nationalist transformation before and after World War I—the Comintern under Stalin's direction allied itself with the Chinese nationalist party, the Kuomintang. While they were allied with the Kuomintang and its leader, Chiang Kai-shek, the Soviets, via their emissary in China, Mikhail Borodin, built up and trained the Chinese nationalist army (the contemporary Taiwanese Army, of the Republic of China, as observed by this author in Taiwan in 1983, still bears traces of this training) and developed the security police. Stalin's plan was to embrace "anti-colonial" nationalist forces in the largest East Asian country. Eventually they would facilitate the Communist seizure of the reins of leadership over the mainland.

However, by the late 1920s, this united front tactic, an updating of Lenin's similar tactic as pursued by Stalin, failed on the mainland. Chiang, sensing what the Soviets and their Chinese Communist Party comrades were up to, turned against his Soviet advisers. He began a bloody liquidation of the Communists in his midst. The failure signified that "the road to Paris and London" that lay through the Far East would not at this time, at least, be able to run westward from Kuomintang Nanking or Beijing.[6]

Meanwhile, farther to the east, Japanese expansionist militarism came to power in Tokyo. This led in 1931–1932 to the Japanese seizure of Manchuria and parts of Mongolia—territory bordering directly on the Soviet Union. (Some three-quarters of Russian territory stretches eastward into Asia from the Ural Mountains.) Relations between Japan and the Soviet Union steadily worsened as the two states soon got on a collision course. Their interests directly clashed, for instance, in Outer Mongolia, which had become by 1921 a Soviet client-state, or "People's Republic." There, local, independently acting Japanese generals, ruling like mandarins in areas, often made their own arbitrary decisions in spreading Japanese control throughout China and Mongolia. However, when the local Japanese commander took on the Soviet "bear" aggressively in Kwantung Province by assaulting Soviet troops across the Mongolian border in the spring of 1939, he and his two division-sized, primitively equipped forces of 40,000 men met from the Russians what the Soviets proudly called a "firm rebuff."

In fact, the Soviet-Japanese conflict on the Mongolian Khalkin-Gol River plain became the occasion for the Red Army to test, successfully, those advanced tactics of the art of utilizing surprise in waging modern, mechanized warfare while employing "overwhelming force," tactics that were so prized by the more offensist-oriented Red Army commanders—meaning by the latter, the then-Gen. Georgi Zhukov, who earned his first laurels as an impressively effective, hard-driving commander at Khalkin-Gol in the summer of 1939.

But, as we saw, the Soviets' main focus remained on Europe, and in particular on Germany.

The German-Russian connection was a permanent fixture during the reigns of Lenin, Stalin, and their successors. Going back to Peter the Great, Russians have always respected German efficiency and public administration. In the Soviet period, this extended to the appreciation of and exploitation of traditional German militarism via the German-Soviet military collaboration of the 1920s and beyond.

Toward Hitler's Germany, Stalin was both cooperative and wary. As will be seen, there is little doubt that the Soviet leader would have liked to get the better of Hitler by the terms of the Nazi-Soviet agreements of 1939–1940 as well as by exploiting Germany's own involvement in war with the Western Allies.

This was the "stab in the back," in other words, that Hitler himself executed before Stalin could perhaps realize his own offensist plans. Stalin's long-range planning, in fact, apparently called for the eventual trumping of the Nazi dictator's control of Europe, the continent that both Lenin and Stalin had long sought for themselves and the cause of world revolution. Yet the looming war was the short-term top priority in Stalin's planning. The dictator was adept at coping with one problem at a time but not at leaping ahead in untimely fashion.

With the fading of the German militarist tradition at the end of World War II and with the birth of a democratic Germany, Russian admiration of Germany by no means ceased. It was already visible in the time of Brezhnev in the 1970s. In the present, post-Communist period in Russia, Moscow's ties with Germany can be described as at least as strong as with any other Western state.

Since the coming of power of Vladimir V. Putin in 2000, the new Russian leader who once served as a KGB officer in East Germany and, as Lenin did, has voiced his admiration for this key central European state. This tradition shows no signs of withering away.

PART TWO

Stalin Prepares for War

Chapter 7

The Myth of Collective Security

The Soviet government, with an eye on its internal situation in Russia and fearing a war on two fronts, must hold aloof from military enterprises [related to enforcing collective security with the Western powers]. [It] is hardly likely to march in defense of a bourgeois state [such as Czechoslovakia].

—German Ambassador to the USSR Count Friedrich Werner von Schulenburg.

The idealistic concept of "collective security" was embodied in the Charter of the League of Nations (1919–1939). It has had a second life in the Charter of the United Nations (1946 to present). Essentially, collective security was founded on the notion that if nation-states will agree to limit their national sovereign power for the sake of the larger promise of ensuring collective safety from aggressive war-making by overtly threatening or pariah powers, the world will be freed of war and become an all-round safer place. Besides the league's charter, a number of agreements were signed in the 1920s that affirmed principles of keeping the peace and disarmament. All of them were flawed or incompletely honored by their customary three-dozen signatories. Some were biased in favor of the great powers, like Great Britain, as in the highly questionable naval ship reductions negotiated in the protracted Geneva Conference, 1932–1934. As for Stalin, in the early 1930s, the Soviets for their part signed a number of friendship and/or nonaggression treaties as well as trade agreements with neighboring states, including Poland and Czechoslovakia. With France, Moscow signed a five-year mutual-assistance pact in 1935. This was supposed to open a period of a virtual Paris-Moscow alliance, as some Western historians contend. Yet the "French connection" was just as fragile in Paris as it was in Moscow, and was overstretched in the geographic distance existing between the two states.

Most of these treaties were actually posturings that were ignored or violated as the years passed. They looked as calico thin as the futile attempts at "reduction and limitation of arms" and the much-touted effort to define aggression via the Kellog-Briand Pact of 1928, which lacked substantive meaning in the sense of its being enforceable. All such gestures contributed nothing tangible to either peace or disarmament. In any case, the notion that war could be prevented by reducing nation-states' arms was—and is—a debatable thesis. Needless to say, the Soviet leaders, and Stalin in particular, placed no stock in such conferences. Still less seriously did he take paper treaties pledging friendship and nonaggression. In fact, Soviet spokespeople occasionally blatantly ridiculed them. For instance, the League of Nations' Preparatory Commission, which was paving the way toward the disarmament powwows of the late 1920s and early 1930s, was greeted cynically in Moscow with the obviously fatuous, typically Soviet demand that all countries sign a "worldwide agreement" for immediate "dissolution of all land, sea and air forces; the scrapping of all armaments; the abolition of military training and the discontinuance of military budgets, defense ministries and general staffs."[1]

A new Russian textbook by Yelena Lapteva, *The History of Russia*, published in 2009 and designed for college-level students, describes the foreign scene in the 1930s as viewed from the perspective of what might be called the "moderate wing" of post-Soviet historiography:[2]

"The 1930s saw the recognition of the USSR. . . . In 1933, the Soviet Union participated along with 10 other states in drawing up a convention on the definition of aggression signed at the London conference.

"Talks were begun with France and the United States on creating a system of collective security. In 1934, the USSR was accepted as a member of the League of Nations. The USSR viewed the basic tasks of international policy in the 1930s to be the establishment of a lasting system of collective security. In 1939, the USSR conducted a diplomatic struggle (*diplomaticheskuyu bor'bu*) and participated in negotiations with England and France. The aim of Soviet diplomacy was to reach agreement on mutual aid against an aggressor. But the USSR viewed these two countries as bourgeois imperialist states. . . . As a result the partners in the talks did not trust each other so that the chance was lost to stop the drift into war. The USSR feared a war on two fronts—in the West and in the East, Czechoslovakia was occupied in 1939. . . . its divided parts becoming protectorates of Germany. . . . In the 1930s the USSR was building its defenses. . . ."

The above excerpt from Lapteva's book displays the rather common writing strategy found in late-period Russian Federation (RF) school textbooks on history. The presentation sounds objective in tone and noncommittal in passing judgment on the wisdom or not of Stalin's foreign policy (that is, when Stalin is mentioned by name). It thus strikes a contrast with texts of two other types being used in Russian classrooms during the periods of the Yeltsin, Putin, and Medvedev administrations, 1991 to the present, which are of (1) the critically anti-Soviet type, which is be coming increasingly rare in school texts used at the secondary and college levels, and those that (2) present a virtually pro-Stalin position, with certain exceptions, in which some of the excesses of the Soviet period are criticized while the accent nevertheless is put on the extreme demands on Soviet security at the time and because of this why and how it was necessary to use extreme means in draconic domestic policies and in maneuvering in diplomacy in order to meet the danger of war posed by the "Fascists." (The latter is a catchall term for the European Axis powers of Fascist Italy and Nazi Germany.)

In this latter, virtually pro-Stalin species of history text, which apparently is becoming more common among published textbooks in the RF, it is sometimes unclear whether the author-historian is defending the Soviet Communist "administrative-command" system and Stalin's leadership. Or whether the historian construes the system under Stalin in the USSR merely as a "necessary evil," given the dire circumstances of the times and in the face of the ineffectual appeasement policies and flaccid inaction shown by the Western powers in their failure to stop Hitler in the 1930s.

Russian textbooks aside, how realistic was the formula of collective security? How did Josef Stalin view its prospects from his vantage point in the Kremlin in the mid-1930s, and what does this reveal about his overall political strategy? It might be better to ask, How willing was Moscow, or for that matter Paris or London, to sacrifice any meaningful degree of sovereign power and national interest in the name of gaining some vague promise of safety for the whole, disparate "world community"?

It does not take a conformed cynic or skeptic to realize, first of all, that there is no "world community." There is no global *Gemeinschaft* of universally shared, communitarian values among a more or less homogeneous people. The real world, divided as it is into "nation-state packages," is by no means the analog of a real, single nation-state with its common values, common language, and "web" of government and law that reflects the shared values of a united people.

The more than 195 nation-states throughout the world with their various types of civilizations, customs, and social and political systems and cultures can, and do, generally agree between themselves on obvious matters as, say, a common system of time zones (with a few exceptions); on using the same slide rule or electronic calculator to solve equations; working with the same geometric tables and mathematical constants in engineering and designing electronic gadgets; and even to agreeing that a standard way to make music is with a combination of 12 full and half tones. Yet beyond that, upon what in the *political sphere* might they agree? Very little, it seems. Even today's European Union (EU), whose parliament functions somewhat vegetatively in Brussels, lacks a dynamic, hands-on reality that reflects a unified "society" agreeing on financial policy, on each country's defense needs, and even on how to cope in a collaborative way with the huge economic recession that began in 2008.

LEAGUE WEAKNESSES

The first premise of an effective world organization committed to guarding the peace was sorely absent in the League of Nations—namely, the world organization's lack of two fundamental legal principles in the context of any *Rechtsstaat*, of law-state: *compulsory jurisdiction* and *compulsory adjudication* coupled to *executive enforcement of the law through effective sanctions*. Stalin, above all, as a national leader, was perfectly aware of the "every-man-for-himself" aspect of international politics of his time.

In other words, the league's judicial organ, the World Court, like its League Council, the league forerunner of the UN Security Council, was doomed to irrelevancy from the very start. It had no ability to extend its power effectively over the world in the form of an all-embracing legal web combined with enforcement of the laws and sanctions. An additional brake on league action was the council's unanimity principle as applied by its big, powerful members.

Were the weaknesses widely perceived—say, in Moscow? To quote a Russian proverb, "Even the sparrows chirped about it." The dictatorial state in Soviet Russia was among the first to quite naturally detect the league's built-in weaknesses in terms of its having any real power. In any case, the Soviets were building a "new world" of their own, even a "world state." Its design had nothing to do with the nether "world" as represented by the League of Nations and its members.

Only by way of the principle of compulsion, or "teeth," could—and can—infringement of international law be stopped throughout the world and any nation-state lawbreakers be prosecuted. Yet what nation-state at that time was—or is today—willing to go that far in ensuring for itself an allegedly peaceful "community"? In fact, no state, East or West, actually recognized the existence of any such world community or law-state in any effective legal sense. There was no world court with compulsory jurisdiction and compulsory adjudication. Without these two premises, how can something approaching enforcement of international law be reached?

Another way of faulting the powers' refusal to get serious about enforcing collective security is to regard the failure as a poor understanding of their own best national interests. As Willard N. Hogan expressed it:[3]

> The debacle of collective security during the 1930s was not due to a refusal to subordinate national interests to collective security, but to mistaken conceptions of what was required to protect national interests.

Perhaps. Yet national interest can be defined in many different and rational ways. Its definition may, for instance, exclude sacrifice of national decision making in committing a country's armed forces and prestige to armed foreign missions of doubtful substance or credibility. This may be true no matter how noble the proposed commitment may be.

SOVIET VIEW TOWARD THE LEAGUE

Least of all did the Soviet Union recognize any such foreign authority or "bourgeois" institution as the league or recognize the legal legitimacy of "bourgeois" arms reductions conventions. Soviet ideology stipulated that its own polity was the sole legal and political model for any government, including a world government, or "world state." Any adulteration of this fundamental Soviet principle undercut the very legitimizing of the Soviet order in Russia as well as in its messianic aspect abroad: that is, the Soviet Republic's, later the USSR's, "revolutionary" mission as the world's model of an entirely new social, political, and economic order designed as the seedling of a new world state of the Soviet socialist type. As Lenin proclaimed on the day after the Bolshevik seizure of power in Petrograd, November 8, 1917: His regime, he said to the handpicked Second Congress of Soviets, was building a "New Order." (The Nazis were to use the same expression for their own "revolution" in Germany 16 years later.)

In the Soviet view, as it evolved through the 1920s and particularly under the influence of Stalin and Molotov, the League of Nations came to be viewed by Moscow as a useful tool. It could serve as an international sounding board or forum for *legally* spreading Soviet influence on a global scale. Such "PR" was irresistible to the Soviet leadership. As a cynic might put it, the league, like its successor on Turtle Bay, could be exploited as a global "talk fest" for all member nations to posture and vent their alleged peaceful intentions for world public consumption in which, however, the Soviet message would ring in revolutionary ways as it resounded throughout the world from the lecterns in Geneva. At the same time, the Soviets, more or less like the rest of the league members, would refuse to take any substantive, collective action against potential or even actual war-making disturbers of the peace. Such substantive collection action might well be seen, as it often was in fact in the 1930s, as going against a state's own best national interests. Or at best it was thought to be too dangerous to put into effect or was seen as unduly restricting the freedom of a state to set its own policies in its own way. And certainly the 1930s demanded that kind of flexibility. An early example of this rejection of collective response was the league's and the Western powers' inaction in 1931 when Japan, a former entente ally in World War I, began its series of conquests of the Chinese mainland province of Manchuria. Japan's aggression continued apace and spread in the years that followed. Yet the league continued to look the other way while Moscow tried to cope with the threat in its own individual ways.

Significantly, Japan became the first but not the last state to voluntarily withdraw (in 1933) from the world organization: a symbolic precedent. In the same year, Nazi Germany also withdrew, while Fascist Italy left the league in 1937. With apparent, intentional irony, just as Hitler's Germany withdrew from the league, Stalin's Soviet Russia *entered* the world organization, and quite ostentatiously so, in the very next year, 1934. This opened an era of peaceful Soviet oratory in the league and other forums, as voiced by Maxim Litvinov, an old Comintern hand, yet

Moscow's newly become number one conventional peace advocate and its voice for rhetorically touting collective security. At this time, Stalin got the USSR involved in European diplomacy full time—while continuing its huge military buildup under Stalin's defense-accented Five-Year Plans as the Soviet leader actively prepared for what he and the ruling ideology described as a future of "inevitable" war—as though this eventuality were a historical law, or as the Marxist-Leninist creed framed it, as "historically determined."[4]

The league's notorious paralysis and inaction were witnessed year after year in the 1930s. Plaints in the United States among pro-league opinion lamented the fact that America had refused to join the world organization in 1919. But what difference would it have made with the United States as one of the paralyzed league members, perhaps becoming even more ineffective by that country's rampant isolationism?

As to Japan, during the decade, that state freely committed aggressive war against China, mercilessly bombing its main, heavily populated cities. Moreover, in the heart of Europe, the world stood by as Italy attempted by war to subdue the sub-Saharan African nation of Ethiopia in order along with Libya to convert a large chunk of Northern Africa into satrapies of Mussolini's new "Roman Empire," and bombed the Ethiopian capital to make the point. The league was powerless as it heard Ethiopia's President Haile Selassie personally voice in Geneva an urgent appeal to the international assemblage to stop Fascist Italy's aggression against his country.

Meantime, the Lenin-Stalin stance toward the post-World War I world organization added a Soviet note of non-starter stultification to the already stalled application of the much-vaunted concept of collective security. Moscow viewed the league as a product of the loathed Versailles Treaty, to which, of course, the Soviets never subscribed nor had even signed. Lenin predictably called the alien world organization a "band of robbers."

Moscow, after all, after the Great War had taken the side of the loser from World War I, Germany. This policy was based in part on the old Lenin formula of divide and conquer.[5] Until the early 1930s, just as Stalin was consolidating his power, Moscow still echoed Lenin's "internationalist," or doctrinal, sentiment toward international law, collective security, and the league. Yet, at the same time, under Stalin and Molotov's guidance, Soviet leadership showed fresh signs of seeking to participate in the Western charade of talking disarmament, indulging in other gestures of what Lenin called "bourgeois pacifism," and concluding various peace and nonaggression treaties, even with countries that could hardly be counted among the Soviet Union's friends.[6] In the strictly legal sense, moreover, the Soviet leaders, including Stalin, could hardly be expected to accept "bourgeois" law in any form as being legally applicable throughout the world or binding on them. That "world" and its system of laws, after all, was the merely perishable "superstructure" of the Old Order. For their part, the Soviets had already begun creating and tirelessly advertising their own New World Order consisting of their "progressive" brand of socialism-leading-to-communism via the dictatorship of the proletariat and one-party rule. This was the pre-programmed autopilot upon which the Soviet state operated.

Meanwhile, Marxism-Leninism's above-the-law revolutionary activity on a global scale via the Communist International was itself carried on illegally in defiance of the system of conventional law embodied in the league charter. In the early 1930s, the Soviets never agreed in talks in Geneva or elsewhere even to a verbal definition of aggression that excluded the right of an international political movement, such as the Communists, to intrude itself into a foreign society as a revolutionary force for change. In the Soviet view, this was not a form of "aggressive" intervention.

Also, the Soviet attitude toward the world organization should be viewed in retrospect as having been simply part of Moscow's two-track policy (see chapter 5). As previously discussed, one road led to illegal subversion and establishment of Soviet-style states; the other, lesser road led to a game played out in the arena of conventional diplomatic intercourse. This latter, conventional course was largely confined to such mundane matters as setting up embassies (including its secret GRU or NKVD spy component); establishing official interstate recognition; regulating commerce; settling minor disputes between foreigners; regulating citizens' foreign travel; deciding extradition disputes; holding summits; signing treaties; etc.

Fundamental to Soviet thinking about international affairs and any institutionalization of international law in a world organization such as the league or the United Nations was that decisions (resolutions) passed by these bodies could have no lasting effect on the true, underlying, causative factors underlying world affairs: namely, the economic system of capitalism and its "inevitable," imperialistic expression in foreign policy and in causing wars. The capitalist system, said Soviet doctrine, its views voiced repeatedly by the leadership (even into the 1980s), inevitably bred imperialism, global class struggle, and war.

Lenin could even imagine proletarian states coming out and fighting major just, *offensive* liberating wars against capitalist states for global domination. In these conflicts it would not matter, said Lenin, which side initiated such wars. If they were of the "progressive" type, Soviet initiation of war was perfectly justified.[7]

While Stalin toned down, or at least on occasion concealed, these basic doctrines for the sake of trade or diplomatic intercourse designed aboveboard to further the interests of the Soviet state on the playing field of the world arena, he nevertheless gave every indication of hewing to the creed's basic premises—doing so, in fact, right up until his death and the publication of his final exegesis, *The Economic Problems of Socialism*, as well as in Stalin's references to international "shock brigades" alluded to in his main address to the Nineteenth Party Congress in October 1952. A contemporary Russian historian puts it this way:[8]

> [In the 1930s] the idea of "world revolution" was not entirely discarded. The question of how it would be brought about was simply taken off the agenda until more favorable conditions arrived for its realization.

In the context of peace campaigning and pacifism, Stalin spoke bluntly—that is, to comrades—about such pacifist verbiage in the West. Such talk, he said, was either a cover for aggression by capitalist nations or a case of sheer naiveté on the part of those who thought the world could have true peace as long as capitalist countries had not been overthrown and replaced with Soviet-style "socialist" ones. As he frankly told the Leningrad Party organization in July 1928:[9]

> Imperialist pacifism is an instrument for the preparation of war and for disguising this preparation by hypocritical talk of peace. Without this pacifism and its instrument, the League of Nations, preparations for war in the conditions of today would be impossible. There are naive people who think that since there is imperialist pacifism, there will be no war. That is quite untrue. On the contrary, whoever wishes to get at the truth must reverse this proposition and say: since imperialist pacifism and the League of Nations are flourishing, new imperialist wars and intervention are certain.

A wrinkle of *tactical* change in the Soviets' publicly stated attitude toward the league came with Stalin's policy shift toward "socialism in one country," which in turn was followed by a "nationalist" focus on domestic matters. In his comprehensive study of Soviet law, Elliot

R. Goodman described the somewhat novel Soviet acceptance of its invited membership into the league in 1934 as follows:[10]

"When the Soviet leadership began openly to encourage the use of national symbols, the aggressive long-range goal of a [Soviet-style] world state was played down since the Soviet turn toward nationalism was occasioned by the weak and defensive position of the Soviet Union in the face of the threats of aggression from Germany and Japan. In an effort to counteract these threats, Stalin tried to follow the rule of power politics as he thought bourgeois nationalist diplomats conceived them. Stalin's biting commentary on bourgeois diplomacy, which he had recorded in 1913, goes a long way toward explaining his behavior as the head of the Soviet state in the 1930s: 'For a diplomat,' Stalin observed, 'word must have no relation to actions—otherwise what sort of diplomat would he be? Words are one thing, actions absolutely another. Good words are a mask for the concealment of unprincipled acts. To speak of a sincere diplomat is the same thing as talking about dry water or wooden iron.'"

In an interview in December 1933, the year of U.S. recognition of the USSR and only months before the USSR became a league member, Stalin sounded a somewhat, but only that, positive note about the League of Nations:[11]

Notwithstanding the withdrawal of Germany and Japan from the League of Nations, or perhaps just because of this, the League may be something of a brake to retard the outbreak of military actions or to hinder them.

Put another way, Stalin intended to use the league forum as additional anti-Fascist "bait" accompanying his Popular Front line in the Western democracies to attract voters to leftist parties. This was the lure used to attempt to form a joint anti-Fascist crusade via a Communist-led bloc that was directly linked, as Comintern chief Georgi Dimitrov explained it, to the "struggle for socialism," Soviet-style.

At this point, the question might well have been asked: Was the Stalin party line against Fascism a mere plank in a Popular Front program aimed at wooing voters to support coalition cabinets that included Communists and for those Communists eventually to attain political power in Western countries (as they actually did maneuver into power in the half-dozen eastern, southeastern, and central European countries at the end of World War II)? People in France and elsewhere in the mid-1930s were certainly beginning to get alarmed over Adolf Hitler's militancy. Yet did Stalin think that these democratic countries, their governments, and populations or the league would actually do anything to block Hitler's patent aggressiveness? Did Stalin think, in fact, Nazi ideology per se was all that central in matters of state, i.e., in the diplomatic game in which he had positioned the USSR as a major player?

In truth, it appears that Stalin had serious doubts, and rightfully so, about the substantiality of any possible joint, anti-Fascist position forged by the Soviets with the rulers of France or Britain. He seems not to have expected any such strong anti-Hitler stand in the West. Quite the opposite. There were known to be top officials in London and Paris who favored using Hitler as a weapon against Communist Russia.

As to Soviet ideology, Hitler's system, after all, was merely the "advanced form" of capitalism, the result of an "inevitable," historically determined "process." Moreover, the populations in those Western countries were distinctly in a mood of "bourgeois pacifism." Moreover, the peoples of those nations, as reported back to Stalin by his ear-to-the-ground embassies and GRU/NKVD agents, were becoming increasingly pacifist in the late 1930s.

Still, historians continue to disagree among themselves on this score. Some allege that Stalin, fearing Hitler, genuinely sought throughout the 1930s to close ranks with potentially anti-Hitler capitalist countries. These writers, including many Russian authors in the post-Stalin as well as post-Soviet periods, claim that Stalin, or, that is, the "Soviet government," would have gladly cooperated with the Western powers even to the extent of waging an allied preventive war against Hitler to stop his aggression—as, say, in the case of German expansion into Czechoslovakia in 1938. This interpretation in the form of a virtual consensus held among a number of Western and Russian historians, however, appears to be unsupportable, especially when the military weakness of the USSR itself at that time is taken into consideration, as it certainly was perceived by Stalin, who in the purges had just decapitated the Soviet general staff and for whom the RKKA and even the "Russian nature" (congenital "laziness" and "drunkenness" being some of the negative factors singled out by Lenin, Stalin, Vyshinsky, et al.) were unsuited.

Stalin, need it be said, never ceased to take Soviet military weakness and overall vulnerability into account when, in fact, verbiage to the contrary, he refused to commit the Soviet armed forces to war via any such deals with Western states or to employ the Red Army for distant if not dubious missions. As the Soviet leader had frankly told the Eighteenth Party Congress in March 1938, the Soviets had no intention of "pulling chestnuts out of the fire" for any capitalist state no matter how small or large it might be. Nor, for that matter, did those Western states evidently have any serious intention to use their own, considerably weak militaries to stem Hitler. This was proved by their inaction during 1938–1939 when, thanks to Munich appeasement and its aftermath, Hitler extended his territorial annexations broadly to include not only "German" Sudetenland in western Czechoslovakia (given the Czechs by Versailles), but also the whole of Czechoslovakia, which Hitler converted into a German "protectorate." Moscow would not budge from this "neutral" position until the late spring of 1941, when the Soviet Union itself was on the verge of being invaded by the German armies poised along its western frontier.

These latter writers further note that Stalin, in any case, did not consider the USSR to be engaged in a genuine ideological war with the Nazis and Fascists, despite Soviet pretensions to this effect in its propaganda about the "anti-Fascist struggle." Stalin was always ready to put aside any ideological considerations in the name of the higher concern of realpolitik and *raison d'etat,* meaning the defense of Soviet *state* interests, regardless of swastikas, fasces, or eagles on the flags of states. As Stalin told the Seventeenth Party Congress in February 1934:[12]

> Fascism of the German type . . . is wrongly called national socialism [yet] there is not an atom of socialism in it. . . . We are far from enthusiastic about the Fascist regime in Germany. But Fascism is not the issue here, if only for the reason that Fascism in Italy has not prevented the USSR from establishing the best relations with that country.

By 1937, Stalin had studied information from his hundreds of well-placed foreign agents. He surveyed and had processed other information from abroad and on the whole was aware of two major trends in European politics at that time: (1) Hitler was on the march; also, Stalin was familiar with Hitler's expansionist plans as laid out plainly in *Mein Kampf,* stated aims by the fuehrer that the Soviet leader, for one, took seriously; and (2) the other European powers were not going in any concrete way to try to stop the German dictator; instead, they would attempt to appease him as well as to egg the German dictator into ventures farther to the east at Soviet expense.

STALIN'S CAUTIOUSNESS

Soviet propaganda about the "capitalist encirclement" and the reputed aims of Allied intervention in 1918 to unseat Lenin's regime were not entirely "imagined" by the suspicious Bolsheviks. For example, Churchill's remark that Bolshevism needed to be "strangled in its cradle" were not idle words to the ears of a regime that was in the violent process of consolidating its dictatorship and establishing some its shaky legitimacy, and, moreover that had fought off some "fronts" of the Allied intervention. For a time as World War I ended and the intervention enterprise began to run out of steam and Bolshevik armies seized more and more territory, the Allied intervention simply withered away. Its main purpose, in any case, had been initially to protect arms dumps and ports that figured in the war against the Central Powers (when Russia was a fighting Western Ally in the war). By 1918, the Whites and the Greens (Russian socialists) had taken on the Red Army but in the end lost out to the "Red horde." In the aftermath of World War I, Lenin, then Stalin after 1924 after Lenin died, surveyed the world as the new Soviet Republic was being established. Having sought in the preceding years of 1919 to 1920 to recover lost tsarist borderlands, "adventurous" attempts had been made by the Bolshevik leaders to carry the Soviet revolution into western territory. One of the first targets in 1920 had been Poland, another former tsarist duchy. But this adventure turned out to be foolhardy, a mission impossible for the new, fledgling Red Army, which was no match for the better trained and equipped Poles under Pilsudski, who wished to terminate the Soviet Republic altogether. Stalin, as political commissar at the time sitting on the authoritative Soviet war council (*Sovet Oborony*) headed by Lenin, with his work there mostly admired by Lenin and who tended to defer to him on military strategy, was among the first to realize the futility of trying to take Warsaw in 1920. In this undoubtedly wise restraint, the Gensek had shown signs of native cautiousness, of putting the priority on keeping the new Soviet Republic intact rather than building—at least at that time—a new empire to the west.[13] This high-level dispute over strategy during the Soviet civil war that had raged so bitterly between Stalin and Tukhachevsky and others in the 1920s remained a sore point, a festering grudge that was held by both officials toward each other. For Stalin and Marshal Klimenti Voroshilov, who was among those who sided with Stalin on this issue, it was a good reason one day to get rid of the adventurous, "Napoleonic" marshal.

The latter used to boast openly about exporting revolution abroad on a "bayonet tip." Tukhachevsky had succeeded with Trotsky, Zinoviev, and the other Cominternists in inserting that ambitious aim into the very protocols of the Communist Third International, Lenin's General Staff of World Revolution, established in 1919. Stalin, to say the least, was less than enthusiastic toward the organization. He preferred to use the Comintern for propaganda purposes as well as for recruiting agents in foreign countries.

Besides, many of Stalin's opponents in the tumultuous struggle to succeed Lenin after 1924 worked under the aegis of the Comintern. That most of these Cominternists were Jews, let alone former associates of the equally *ukharsky* Trotsky, was not lost on the anti-Semitic, Russia-first Stalin.

As early as the mid-1920s, Stalin, a budding nationalist bent on "building socialism in one country," had opted for blending in with the diplomats of Europe. He agreed that it was necessary to learn how to play their game. As the proverb goes, "A wise wolf scouts the prey." Getting deeply involved into the European diplomatic game—instead of allowing the Soviets to become alienated black sheep of the fold because of their red-colored, subversive, and revolutionary aims—was a better, more productive course economically (in terms of trade) as well as politically, in terms of realpolitik. Lenin tended to think along the same lines, as his latest writings indicated. Yet it was Stalin who made this involvement his mantra. Helping Stalin in this enterprise of "blending in" was Maxim Litvinov, the smooth-talking, multilingual old Comintern hand. Having exploited the cosmopolitan Litvinov's talents in disarmament and peace conferences in Geneva and elsewhere, which were staged in the West over a half-dozen years, Stalin finally in 1930 appointed Litvinov commissar of foreign affairs. The commissar thereupon became *the* Kremlin spokesperson for peace and collective security—much of it with obvious disingenuousness. Forgotten were Maksim Maksimovich's earlier expressed sentiments, such as, "[The Bolsheviks]," he once said, "regard as their highest aim to carry the torch of revolution to Berlin."[14]

The "siege mentality" of the Soviet leaders in their propaganda line about the "capitalist encirclement"—which, said, Lenin, will one day be replaced by a "socialist encirclement" of the capitalist world beginning just beyond the Soviet frontiers—whether or not exploited as a useful exaggeration or as a half truth, exercised a strong influence over the development of the Kremlin's foreign strategy. The constant refrain of the presence of a "foreign threat" was used as a pretext, but sometimes in the genuine sense of an excuse, for the ongoing, concerted Soviet arms buildup after 1929, the militarization of the economy, and, given the threat of "imperialism," the dictatorship's exercise of control over the population. By these means would be guaranteed the people's obedience under conditions of forced industrialization via the Five-Year Plans and the coerced collectivization of the peasant farmers. All of which were said by the Soviet leadership to be motivated by defense priorities and the demands of any administrative-command state.

As Stalin consolidated his personal power in—and by—carrying out his ambitious domestic program in the 1930s, his foreign policy line had to be one of cautiousness, of non-involvement in military clashes for which the Soviet Union clearly was not yet prepared. It was a policy that included the none-too-subtle wooing of industrially rich America (see chapter 8). The soft-treading policy of noninvolvement in war (whatever might be the wishes of those in the West plumping for substantive collective security) also became one of deflecting would-be aggressors, especially Nazi Germany, in other, safer directions in terms of Soviet state interests. This included a policy of Stalin's creation of getting into the diplomatic swim in Europe, talking disarmament and peace at relevant conferences, yet without entailing any military sacrifice or contribution of troops by the USSR itself. Least of all did it mean curtailment of the Soviets' own gigantic, partially concealed military buildup.

In other words, largely under Stalin's guidance, Soviet diplomatic strategy by the time of Hitler had become that of playing one hostile side off against the other. Above all, it meant staying altogether out of European armed conflicts. In this way any threat to Soviet security was kept as remote as possible by Soviet maneuvering and sidestepping. This gambit of watchful neutrality was accompanied by a refrain of peace and disarmament propaganda that, for insiders at least, rang hollow. They remembered the decade-long secret German-Soviet military collaboration and Stalin's all-out military buildup program, which hardly looked peaceful in their respective illegality and intentions. Also recalled were Lenin's essential ideological positions on the inevitability-of-war-as-long-as-capitalism-exists. This doctrine was coupled to Stalin's thinking and actions in the early 1930s. As Stalin had put it candidly in 1925 and on other occasions, when the inevitable big war breaks out, the Soviets would remain out of the struggle until the final end game. Then the Soviets would enter the conflict in order to "tip the scales," as he put it, in their own favor. As Stalin used to say, *razumeyetsya, yasno*—"clear, one would think." Yet some observers in the West tended to overlook these Stalinite theses. Still, Stalin the statesman and politician was always cultivating and tending to the Soviets' international image. He envisioned "Russia" as a great power that was to be both respected as well as emulated for its "socialist" system and ideals. Stalin never assumed an entirely go-it-alone autarchic posture for the Soviet Union in world affairs. As was proven by Stalin's sudden switch to a "democratic alliance" with the capitalist West in July 1941, Stalin's was not a policy of utter detachment and alienation from the rest of the world. Nor was it one of becoming the world's Bolshevik pariah. Far from it. The Stalinist way throughout his entire political career, when he wore the statesman's hat, was to place the accent on Soviet *respektabel'nost* ("respectability," a cognate in use in Russia then as now). This meant Russia's acceptance by the rest of the world as a basis for the Soviets to assume the status of a world power. It was a status that Russia's very geographical size, plentitude of natural resources, and for which its unique authoritarian/totalitarian political system (the Soviets having developed the first such system in the twentieth century) equipped it. Such respect and power among the world's collection of states would win for the USSR, the "citadel of socialism," the support of the "toiling urban and rural masses" and "progressive bourgeoisie" as well as anti-colonial, "national-liberation" fighters in the West's colonies throughout the Third World. Stalin political persona included the formula: "I am the state and the state is me." In this author's view, the idea held among some authors and commentators toward Stalin and Soviet politics that "the Kremlin" and the Soviet leader gave little or no thought to world opinion or to the reactions of the world public to its policies, foreign or domestic, is to misunderstand a key operating factor in Soviet foreign policy. Which was always, at least it seems to Stalin's mind, to win as much influence abroad as possible, and to do so by largely conventional means.

Stalin was perfectly aware of constitutional, democratic electoral, and governing practices that were solidly in place in the most industrially advanced foreign countries. He devoted much thought to influencing and working within these processes abroad—say, via "agents of influence," who were tasked with penetrating Western governing institutions and corporate industry and thereby influencing members of the "ruling circles" in ways that served Soviet national and international interests. The idea is mistaken, to this author, that Stalin cared little about the Soviet reputation abroad and, instead, "did whatever he wished"—as, say, even planning a preemptive war against Germany in 1941—just as other dictators did and as, indeed, Stalin had in his decision in December 1939 to invade Finland. But, like any good chess player, he later backtracked on the Finnish gambit and settled for capturing "some material."

The assumption concerning Stalin's alleged rashness stems essentially from the presupposition that since Stalin's rule was a dictatorship enjoying arbitrary powers, the Soviet dictator himself, therefore, needed to give no thought to foreign reactions to Soviet moves. How Soviet actions might be felt at the top or at the grassroots in democratic countries, it is alleged, did not matter to Stalin. In this view, the manner in which or the justification by which the USSR would go to war with Germany in the 1930s or 1940s also was irrelevant. But was it? If that were true, how does one explain, for example, the carefully worked-out propaganda about the Soviets' new-style "democracy" embodied in the Stalin constitution of 1936? Why would Moscow bother with a propaganda exercise like that, say, accompanying its extravagant Soviet pavilion at the New York World's Fair in 1939? The same goes for Stalin's many interviews over several decades with American newsmen and the countless treaties made with foreign countries. In them, the bottom line invariably was that the USSR is a well-meaning, peaceful state. No other friendly country need fear the "peace-loving" land of the Soviets. Why bother with such posturing if all Moscow had in mind was conquest and the forceful export of Communism?

It seems reasonable to conclude that such "adventurism," to use the Soviet epithet against this type of policy, was not Stalin's way of enhancing or spreading Soviet power throughout the world—with the exception of the borderlands and his post-World War II "windfall" of satellites that formed the new Red Entente after World War II. The Soviet dictator preferred a sneaky, stage-by-stage, inside country-by-country acquisition of power aided by secret Soviet funding of leftist forces and led by Moscow-appointed native Communists and fellow travelers. These "fifth columns" were to operate in their own lands, availing themselves of the instrumentalities of "bourgeois democracy." No wonder on Stalin's orders that the Comintern was disbanded in 1943. It had long outlived its ostensible purpose and had become a distraction in Moscow's diplomatic game. It will be objected that forcible occupation of Eastern Europe by the Soviet Army at the end of World War II in 1944–1948 and the prewar incorporation of the ex-tsarist borderlands into the USSR in 1940 were nothing less than brazen act of expansionism. No doubt they were. Yet even the Soviet army incursions during the war might be classed as "windfalls" or "war booty." They were not the usual Stalinist way of bringing about, i.e., subversively, intended socialization of polities in foreign countries. Moreover, Stalin's record shows a distinct restraint on his part in pursuing territorial expansion *worldwide* in this way. Restraint was the mantra, as in the cases of Iran, Greece, the Turkish Straits, Italy, and even Germany and elsewhere during and after World War II. After all, as to Eastern Europe, Churchill and Stalin between them had worked out a verbal agreement (the original documents are available) for making percentage divisions of influence, country-by-country in the region. By these agreements, a "Soviet sphere of influence" was largely guaranteed and approved by the British prime minister according to the agreed percentages, which later Stalin violated. As a result of this secret diplomacy, Stalin acquired a half-dozen "satellites" to the west of the USSR, creating his own little Red Entente. True, these lands were not converted into full-fledged Soviet republics as were the other forcibly annexed, 1940 Soviet territorial acquisitions at the expense of the Baltic countries, Poland, and Romania. What Stalin had needed by way of a buffer, as he indicated pre-1941 for defense of the USSR before the Germans attacked, the Soviet dictator now insisted disingenuously after World War II that he still needed with the defeat of "Fascism" for, as he claimed, the Soviets' "external security." This was an extension of Soviet power just over the Soviet border in lands abutting the USSR, that long-held Soviet strategy that Molotov boasted of in his retirement memoirs.

Stalin had shown his true colors by deceptively voicing democratic sentiments at wartime summits with the Allies. This was a bluff on his part. He wished to keep receiving valuable Lend-Lease supplies from the United States while evidently secretly contemplating the sovietization of "his" neighborhood in eastern, central, and southeastern Europe. He had long hinted that he expected the West to formally recognize his 1939–1940 acquisitions.

Continued Soviet expansionism became, in fact, one of the main igniters of the Cold War after 1945. Another fuse was Stalin's ominous, ideologically intoned, February 1946 electoral speech in Moscow. This was followed four months later by Churchill's response in his famous "Iron Curtain" speech in Fulton, Missouri, in June 1946. Oddly, some historians—in the East and West—recall Churchill's Fulton speech yet ignore the earlier, ominous Stalin speech that had actually helped give rise to Churchill's warnings about Stalin's postwar expansionism from Stettin on the Baltic to the Black Sea.

8

America in Stalin's Future

We are definitely in favor of economic deals with America, and with all countries but particularly with America. . . . We will need American industrial commodities such as locomotives, automobiles, and so on more than the commodities from any other country.
—*Lenin in October 1919 and February 1920*

Despite his being the leader of a capitalist nation, President Roosevelt is today one of the most popular men in the Soviet Union.
—*J. V. Stalin*

Stalin said he had good personal relations with Roosevelt.
—*N. S. Khrushchev*

In his own way, [Stalin] was an Americanophile. He considered the United States a determining factor in world politics at a time when Americans thought themselves . . . isolationists.
—*William Taubman, Stalin's American Policy*[1]

Stalin was a one-hundred-percent realist. [Moreover] even in his advanced years he possessed a phenomenal memory, never forgetting anything [or] anyone with whom he worked and respected. [As to Maxim Litvinov] in the entirely new international situation confronting the USSR after the German attack [June 22, 1941], Litvinov [who had been dismissed in favor of Molotov in 1939] was appointed Deputy Commissar of Foreign Affairs as well as Ambassador to the United States.
—*Robert Ivanov, Russian historian*[2]

By 1940, it became clear to both Stalin and Hitler that America was going to be the key "giant-that-came-last" participant in the global conflict. Whereas the Germans hoped the United States would stay out of any European conflict as long as possible, Stalin reasoned that sooner or later America would enter the war. And from his point of view, the sooner, the better. To Stalin, ideological differences would not be an inhibiting factor in assuring victory for the Soviet state with America's help.

Stalin's well-located NKVD and GRU "agents of influence" worked assiduously in this direction, especially in Washington, DC, and New York City. In 1940–1941, they attempted to manipulate public and official opinion in America in the direction of friendship toward the Soviet Union. Stalin had indicated—i.e., by late 1940—that the "Nazi-Soviet honeymoon" had run its course. The phony "friendship" was, in fact, fast evolving into outright hostility. The deterioration in German-Soviet relations in 1940 and the manner in which Stalin kept alive his relations with the United States are neglected in standard histories of the period. Some historians have failed to detect the early signs of Stalin's newfound wariness and disenchantment with his alliance with Hitler. Some authors have also tended to overlook the Soviet leader's attitude toward America, President Roosevelt, and the potential of the United States, its capitalist system aside, in a future anti-Axis coalition together with the Soviet Union.

STALIN WATCHES AMERICA'S SLIDE TOWARD WAR

Stalin knew that even before World War II began in September 1939, the Roosevelt administration had been taking various steps "short of war," to use the expression of that time, in order to help the Allied cause against the Axis. Such salient moves were attentively monitored by Stalin. In fact, he personally oversaw his several networks of agents operating in the United States. These included well-placed spies, moles, and agents of influence working in high places within the Roosevelt administration—in fact, in the White House, at the Treasury Department, and in the State Department, as well as in the grassroots in clubs, the media, America's defense plants, and research institutes involved in defense research and development.

Well before the Japanese attack on Pearl Harbor on December 7, 1941, pro-Allied administration-initiated measures, defying the country's isolationism, were leading by a red thread to U.S. involvement in World War II. The process of gradual American entry into the world-historical conflict was closely followed by the belligerents and potential belligerents of Europe, including, above all, Stalin in the USSR. His party-controlled press *Pravda* and *Izvestiya* never ceased to report on such developments in America.

The step-by-step process was unwinding in America as follows:

- FDR's "quarantine" speech of 1937 formally ended American isolationism (the sternness of which shocked the appeasement-minded Chamberlain Cabinet in Britain);
- The Roosevelt administration's sharp increase in defense expenditures, January 1939;
- Its circumvention and then the congressional amendment of the Neutrality Act (1939–1941);
- FDR's declaration of a "limited" national emergency and his establishment of the Liaison Committee to supervise assistance to the Allies, September–December 1939;
- The president's restoration of the U.S. Advisory Commission for the Council of National Defense, May 1939;
- His sale of surplus war materiel to Britain and the trade of U.S. warships for British bases in the Caribbean Sea and Newfoundland, June and September 1940, harbingers of Lend-Lease;
- The Roosevelt-backed, first peacetime draft in the nation's history passes by a single vote, September 1940;
- Introduction of the historic Lend-Lease bill to Congress, January 1941;
- Conducting of secret U.S.-UK British army staff talks in Washington, January–March, 1941;
- Lifting of the "moral embargo" on trade with the USSR, January 1941;
- The Lend-Lease Act is passed and signed by the president; it includes both Britain and Greece, March 1941;
- Establishing naval patrols for the purpose of reporting to British warships on locations of German submarines in the Atlantic Ocean, April 1941;
- U.S. army occupation of Greenland and Iceland, April–July 1941;
- Heavy Nazi U-boat damage to Lend-Lease convoys en route to Britain in the North Atlantic, April–June 1941;
- Establishment of America's "first CIA," known as the OSS (Office of Strategic Services), July 1941;

- Proclamation of the propitious Anglo-American Atlantic Charter by Roosevelt and Churchill, August 1941, with its tacit invitation to all nations victimized or to be victimized by aggression to join in an alliance in the name of collective security (this translated into the Declaration of the United Nations, January 1942);
- Orders to American warships to shoot on sight at German submarines, September 1941;
- Following the German invasion of the USSR, June 22, 1941, a trip by close FDR aide Harry Hopkins to Britain and Russia, June–July 1941;
- Extension of the Lend-Lease Act of March 1941 to the Soviet Union, June 1941;
- Beginning of the first U.S.-UK-Soviet Lend-Lease supply conference in Moscow, September 1941: "First Protocol" for aid signed October 1941; and
- Authorization to arm merchant ships and dispatch them into war zones, November 1941.

These and other moves by the Roosevelt administration—i.e., especially the ones made well before December 7—made Stalin realize the folly of totally alienating the powerful, so-called "imperialist" republic overseas. There were indications, in fact, that executing a demarche by Moscow toward the United States was precisely the Soviet leader's intention—how early, in what prewar years can only be surmised. The question for Stalin was only one of when and how this move should be made.

Stalin's maneuvering with respect to the United States struck a contrast with Hitler's tactic of writing off and alienating America altogether after pursuing in the 1930s a half-hearted attempt to win support, at least among Americans of German extraction. The German Pavilion at the New York World's Fair was poorly attended, created a controversy, and was prematurely shut down in 1939. This was an obvious contrast to the much-touted Soviet Pavilion across the way from the German Pavilion, the former towering over most of the other countries' concessions at the fair while attracting much favorable attention. Ironically, this big project of Soviet public relations had been launched just at the time of reputed Soviet pursuit of a viable agreement with France and Britain toward forming an anti-Hitler bloc via the talks held in Moscow in the summer of 1939. This was when Stalin's overtures to Germany were far more feasible, the Soviet leader thought, than would be establishing uncertain, unprofitable military ties with the two distant West European states, who in general were anti-Soviet.

In the first days of July 1941, i.e., about week after the German invasion, the Soviet dictator had finally executed his abrupt turn toward the Western Allies. This surfaced in his monumental address to the Soviet people and the world on July 3. Yet even before this final reorientation of Soviet policy in 1941, the long-held tactic of the Bolsheviks, and in particular of Stalin, had been to take advantage of and even provoke divisions within the "capitalist-imperialist" world. Above all, by this stratagem, the Soviets, Stalin said, must align themselves "with one section" of the bourgeois states through skillful diplomacy so as to avoid being overwhelmed by some other coalition of bourgeois states. This was exactly what the Soviet dictator was to do. We must assume that he had undoubtedly worked this out in his mind well before his July 3 address. That speech was too comprehensive and radically different in its contents to have been thought up merely at the spur of the moment just days after the German invasion.

STALIN'S AMERICAN AFFINITIES

Throughout 1940–1941, Stalin had been kept informed of U.S. intentions in the war by his ubiquitous GRU (military intelligence) and NKVD-NKGB (civilian intelligence) agents in Washington, DC. He was well aware of FDR's various actions against the Axis. He knew of the sympathies that FDR and others in the Roosevelt "brain trust" so often voiced toward the USSR, and specifically toward Stalin. This, despite traditional American anti-Communism and the president's own occasional anti-Communist statements (as at the time of the Nazi-Soviet pacts of August–September 1939 and the Soviet aggression against Finland in December of that year).

Not to be forgotten, either, was the significant U.S. economic aid rendered to Soviet Russia in the recent past under Stalin's vast industrialization program during the 1930s. The great Dnepropetrovsk hydroelectric station, for instance, was built with American equipment. American assistance was lent for the Gorky tractor plant that began to produce farm machines and later tanks. Many other U.S.-assisted breakthroughs occurred during the Soviet industrialization program under the Five-Year Plans. Stalin more than once referred to what he called the Americans' great "business acumen" (*delovitost'*).[3]

3

Did the Soviet leader perhaps not reckon that one day America must surely enter the war? Did he reason that when it did, this would tip the scales, to use Stalin's expression, in ways that could favor Soviet national interests and security—that is, via a joint U.S.-Soviet coalition fighting the Nazi-Fascist-Japanese Axis? Peter Niblo, author and former U.S. intelligence officer, surmises that this indeed was the case. He writes:[4]

> Could this Lend-Lease idea also have been received—possibly conceived—in Moscow just as a massive German buildup of forces along the borders of Eastern Europe [facing the USSR] was being reported to the Kremlin? Could a desperate need for military supplies by Moscow have been envisioned by Stalin by late 1940? One might answer that Stalin was still Hitler's ally. Why, then, would Lend-Lease be of any interest to him? . . . The Kremlin's main objective as war approached became immediate U.S. military aid without a need for compensation.

The Soviet leader certainly had no doubts about the strength and durability of the American economy. He recognized this even during the Great Depression. In his conversation with H. G. Wells in Moscow in July 1934, Stalin—America's stalled economy and growing unemployment aside—expressed strong confidence in America's speedy recovery. He specifically praised President Roosevelt's efforts in helping to bring this about. The Soviet leader described FDR as a leader with "initiative (*initsiativa*), courage (*muzhestvo*), and decisiveness (*reshitel'nost'*). There is no doubt," Stalin told Wells, "that of all the captains (*kapitany*) ruling in the contemporary capitalist world, Roosevelt is the strongest figure." Rare praise of a capitalist president by the leader of the "socialist citadel," the USSR! No other Western leader ever got such a eulogy from Stalin.

Although Stalin now and then said, no doubt disingenuously, during the Nazi-Soviet honeymoon that he admired the firm leadership of Hitler, he never once rated the fuehrer as highly as he did President Roosevelt either before June 22, 1941, or after. During World War II as well, Stalin made other flattering comments about America and FDR. No doubt the praise was in part motivated by the service via the Lend-Lease program that Washington was rendering. Yet Stalin also appreciated having the intimate relationship he thought he had forged with the president. There were even mutual Stalin-Roosevelt complaints (behind the PM's back) against Churchill in which FDR made negative remarks to Stalin about the British Empire and colonialism.

Still, beyond the fact that Stalin relished his mutual personal rapport with Roosevelt, he proceeded to exploit this relationship to the hilt. This was seen in the two wartime summits with the American leader and the British prime minister held in 1944–1945. By this time, Stalin perceived that FDR had a similarly favorable attitude toward him. Undoubtedly, the bugged conversations he overheard electronically between the president and other officials, including Churchill, kept Stalin well informed. For Roosevelt's part, his admiration for Stalin seemed genuinely motivated by respect, even affection for the man he called "Uncle Joe." There were friendly gestures, like FDR's grinding up some of his Chesterfield cigarette tobacco at one of the Big Three meetings for Stalin to tamp into his pipe.

It seems evident, in fact, that as early 1939, or nearly six months prior to the start of World War II, Stalin already appeared to have second thoughts about his obdurate anti-American stance and propaganda. The latter had been rigidly cast in the usual, dogmatic Marxist-Leninist manner. Official Soviet ideology had generally lumped the United States in with the other "imperialist" nation-states that included Nazi Germany and Fascist Italy together with, given some reservations in America's favor, Great Britain and France.

STALIN AT THE EIGHTEENTH PARTY CONGRESS

But Stalin was not always entirely consistent as to this traditional ideological treatment of America. One example of revision turned up as early as March 10, 1939. The occasion was the watershed Eighteenth Party Congress. In this much-observed speech by foreign eyes and ears, Stalin led off his main report by making some telltale distinctions among the "imperialist powers."

First, Stalin bluntly stated that a "new imperialist war has already become a fact." Then in a lengthy passage he proceeded to strike a contrast between what he called the "openly aggressive" capitalist states and the "non-aggressive" ones. The latter, he said, included not only France and Britain, but also the United States. Taken together, he said, these states *"possess enormous resources"*—an obvious hint that this might become a major factor in the coming war against the Axis. Stalin claimed that any weakness perceived in the West Europeans' "appeasement" policies toward Nazi Germany and Fascist Italy did not stem from the Western states' very considerable economic and military power. This strength, he said startlingly, makes them, in fact, *"undeniably stronger [than all the Axis countries] combined."*

If Stalin could think this about the Western democracies, could he not also imagine a "grand alliance" that would include these powerful states in opposing the Axis? Given his views toward these two and toward America, could not the Soviet leader also assume that a war between the democracies and Germany might not only be prolonged *but one the West would ultimately win?*

As to the democratic nations' appeasement policies culminating in the Munich Conference of 1938, Stalin alleged, perhaps disingenuously, that these policies merely reflected, as he said in his Eighteenth Party Congress speech, a "fear of revolution that would arise if they became involved in war and if the war became worldwide in scope." The implication here was that if their participation in the coming war were perceived as offensist instead of merely defensive, the Western powers would be depicted as traditional "imperialistic plunderers." Any such offensism, he hinted, would be a stigma of aggressiveness that those countries would surely wish to avoid.

It was also by implication a stigma that the USSR itself would likewise seek to avoid when the Soviet Union itself would become involved in the war.

STALIN'S DEFENSISM

Was Stalin perhaps revealing his own, future strategy for the Soviets? Namely, that Soviet entry into the future, "inevitable" war—i.e., against the aggressive Axis—*should be made to look purely defensive.* Indeed, during and after World War II, Stalin repeatedly emphasized the innocent "defensiveness" of the Soviet entry into that war.

In fact, in December 1939, this was the defensist line that was unfurled under Stalin in the Soviet aggression against Finland. Of course, the Finnish "artillery attack" against the outskirts of Leningrad had been feigned by the Soviets. The same ruse was employed on the Korean Peninsula in June 1950. This was when Soviet propaganda claimed that South Korea had first attacked North Korea. In the post-Stalin period under Brezhnev in 1968, the Soviet Army's invasion of Czechoslovakia in August was depicted by Soviet propaganda as a "defensive retaliation" against an imminent "imperialist attack." Again, in 1979 in the war against Afghanistan, the latter, a "hostile, anti-Soviet regime," said Soviet propaganda, was planning to attack the USSR. As their doctrinal statements always claimed, the Soviets, after all, "never waged aggressive war." The Red Army was a "deeply defensist" army.

After Hitler's armies attacked the USSR on June 22, 1941, and in subsequent speeches and references to the invasion, Stalin always stressed that the Soviet Union possessed a harmless, purely defensive strategy. The Soviet Union had been deceived and victimized by the Nazi aggressor. The enemy had not even issued a declaration of war, he complained. Here Stalin conveniently overlooked the fact that the Soviets in the past had never issued such declarations whenever they themselves had opened aggressive military hostilities. If, therefore, Stalin had been planning to wage offensive war against Germany— say, by the next year, 1942—this claim would have been regarded as totally disingenuous. In such an event Stalin, as usual, would have invented a pretext for launching *Grozá*, the alleged plan to preempt the German attack.

STALIN ON THE WEST'S PLANS

In his March 1939 report, Stalin accused the Western democracies "of hoping," he said accusingly, "to foment aggression [and] not to inter- fere with the aggressors' plans to involve the Soviet Union in war . . . so as to ultimately dictate terms to those powers who would be weak- ened by war." This line had been enunciated in so many words by Stalin on several earlier occasions. It was a foregone conclusion, he claimed, that the Western powers' strategy was one of "active neutral- ity." Or better, exploitative neutrality at Soviet expense, as many Rus- sian historians continue to maintain.

Stalin further stated at the 1939 Congress, significantly so, that the USSR "would never pull chestnuts out of the fire," as he put it, for any other countries victimized by aggression and war. Indeed, the Soviets never lifted a finger when Hitler occupied Czechoslovakia in 1938 fol- lowing the Munich conference "of appeasement."

For his part, Stalin had indicated in an earlier analysis, as noted above, that the USSR would enter the coming, "inevitable" war deliberately, at its own choosing, when the time was ripe for it to do so. When it did enter the war, the Soviets would be able, as Stalin phrased it in 1925, to "tip the scales" to their advantage. They would thereby reap the most benefit for themselves from the war. Part of that tipping of the scales was the added "weight" of America, which Stalin sought to exploit to Soviet advantage.

In these candid statements, a hard-nosed Stalin was indicating in no uncertain terms a Soviet policy of exploitative, opportunistic neutrality—the mirror image of the very policies he was attributing to the Western capitalist democracies. Recent books, such as those by Martirosyan, Mel'tyukhov, Verkhovsky-Tyrmos, and others implicitly or explicitly praise Stalin as the authoritarian head of state who with consummate political skill had saved the union and Russia from disaster by acquiring a buffer zone for defensive purposes.[5]

THE SIGNIFICANCE OF STALIN'S HINTS

In retrospect, what is pregnant about Stalin's observations in 1939–1940 was his candid admissions on various occasions of the power of the Western states, and particularly of America, in any future military showdown with Germany. Their power, he implied, would become the deciding factor in the survival of the USSR itself.

At the same time, how seriously should Stalin's references be taken to the likelihood of "revolution" breaking out in the Western capitalist countries should they become involved in war? Any such revolutionary fervor would depend on the justness of the war from the democratic peoples' perspective, about which moral—and morale—factor Stalin never lost sight as the USSR stood on the brink of a "just" war.

True, in his March 1939 speech to Congress, Stalin had added, it seems disingenuously, perhaps as a mete ideological feint, that such countries recalled well what had happened to their polities after World War I. This was when Soviet-inspired revolution and Cominternism was on the rise in Eastern and Central Europe and spilled over farther west. It was the time when the apparently forged, inflammatory "Zinoviev letter" of 1924, a scandal in Britain, had put a crimp in the new, evolving British-Soviet relations that were just unfurling at that time. Stalin's allusions to revolution had the ring of mere propaganda, as tom-tom thumping for party consumption.

Rather, what was remarkable and pregnant the Soviet leader's prewar remarks in terms of the immediate future was the fact that Stalin had made the distinction between "aggressive" and "non-aggressive" states in the capitalist West. Lenin had never made such a distinction whenever he described the "imperialist bloc" of nations, including especially America. The latter state, in fact, as Lenin claimed, was one of the principal "imperialist marauders" destined to play an even greater "plundering" role in the future. What Lenin apparently sought was to rally peace forces *within* capitalist states in order to weaken them. He contrasted the policies of their "bourgeois" governments with the peaceful, socialist programs of Communist parties and the Soviet Republic. In his 80 million published words, Lenin, unlike Stalin, never sorted out capitalist states according to their respective non-aggressiveness, let alone as to their possible service to the Soviets as allies.

Leaving aside the 21-month-long, tinsel-like "Nazi-Soviet honeymoon" with its extravagant, mutual eulogies and its propagandized condemnations of the Anglo-French "plutocrats"—a Nazi epithet politely mimicked by Soviet propaganda, which had never used that term previously in its ideology—here was Stalin occasionally voiced un-Bolshevik, revisionist views toward the United States. He seemed to regard America as a special case, a potential ally in the struggle against "Fascist" (that is, Axis) aggression. At same time, Stalin's focus on America was by no means entirely benign. His attitude toward the United States generally showed a mixture of respect and an almost compulsively stated wish to see it as a weakened and defeated capitalist state—that is, *in the long term*. However, in the *short* term—and Stalin was famous for making such temporal distinctions in the deliberate, stage-by-stage way he designed policy—he sought to exploit American friendship. This was, in fact, reflected in Lend-Lease during the four-year "strange alliance" of World War II with the capitalist West.

It should be noted that Lend-Lease had the effect of not only crucially helping the Soviet Union defeat the Germans and the East-West comradely alliance. It had also strengthened Stalin's regime, perhaps the unavoidable by-product of this major assistance. Of course, such strengthening was never acknowledged by Stalin and Soviet propaganda. On the contrary. In postwar speeches and propaganda, the Soviets invariably maintained, taking their cue from Stalin's Bolshevik Revolution anniversary addresses each year during the war, that the Soviet victory reflected the superiority of the Soviet system of one-party rule.

STALIN AND THE CPUSA

Specifically in terms of subversive Communist plans vis-à-vis the United States' social, economic, and political order, Stalin often showed that he personally resented the reluctance of American "progressive forces" to unite solidly around the Communist Party of the United States. He often gave the impression of thinking that such solidarity was futile given American political culture and tradition. Moreover, Stalin's security forces seemed to have had little faith in the CPUSA even as a contributor of spies for the NKVD-NKGB let alone as a truly revolutionary party and viable engine of subversion. In fact, the notorious political and personnel misfortunes of the CPUSA were assiduously followed by Stalin. While he never ceased to intrude in that party's affairs, he was clearly disillusioned with the results of his interference. This took the form of repeated purges of leading CPUSA party officials when they got out of line as viewed from Moscow, especially when it tried to dictate policies and strategy and tactics that it hoped would be followed by the American comrades.

Stalin's interest in the American Communist Party was also conditioned by its recruitment of spies, which, after all, was one of its principal tasks. But spies served the Soviet state, not the Informburo, or Information Bureau of the Central Committee, which replaced the former Comintern that was dissolved in 1943. Under Stalin, it had served mainly as an adjunct of two-track Soviet diplomacy. For his part, the exiled Trotsky, the ever-zealous world revolutionist, noted this cretinization of the Comintern and created his own Fourth International in defiance of Stalin.

The culmination of the unique Soviet attitude toward America as a strong, out-of-area power of potential assistance to the USSR saw the light of day when Stalin made his world-shaking address on July 3, 1941.

AMERICAN "COLOSSUS"

In his calculations, Stalin, no less than Hitler, obviously had taken into account what was then often known abroad in the interwar years as the "American colossus." The United States was like the "shotgun on the wall" that is bound go off by the last act of a three-act play. To be assured of victory, Stalin reasoned that the Soviet Union should be on the same side as America. This hope and trust were seen in many ways in the run-up to June 22, 1941, especially by the fact that the Stalin Kremlin always kept its lines open to Washington. U.S.-Soviet relations since 1933, various ticklish issues between them aside, were never seriously obstructed, let alone severed.

America's economic reach and power were well known worldwide. After World War I, Europeans became accustomed to the flow into their countries of advanced American commodities—their stunning importation of the great variety of American consumer goods. Most of Europe's washing machines, refrigerators, sewing machines, factory equipment, radios, cars, financial capital, and so on all bore the "Made-in-the-USA" label or the logos of American banks. The same was true of the flow of such American-made heavy-industrial producers' goods into Stalin's Russia in the 1930s.

Stalin likewise ordered a number of American consumer goods to be copied and produced in Soviet factories—which they eventually were. For example, the first Soviet official limousine was a carbon copy of an American Packard. It was used by the upper Nomenklatura, or party and state officialdom. Many other American designs, whether of Douglas civilian aircraft or Singer sewing machines and other textile machinery, were similarly adopted and imitated.

As a result, the United States was universally regarded as the vanguard among the industrialized nations or those planning to be such, as was the USSR. (Today, the tradition is continued by Japan and China, both of whom emulate American economic practices.)

American economic dominance was particularly visible during the immediate post-World War I and interwar periods. At that time, recovery from the extremely destructive, demoralizing Great War was followed in a decade by the Great Depression. The sharp downturn in the American economy seriously hobbled Europe's own economic performance and development since they were so dependent on the U.S. economy, as seen in the global downturn that began in 2008. In the whole post-World War I period, American capital had become a critical factor in the economic health, or ill-health, of Europe. The dynamism of the American economy, especially as it involved its military-industrial potential, and its recovery out of the Depression were as impressive as they were crucial. When viewed from abroad, U.S. economic prowess, above all its military-industrial potential, came to be widely seen as a factor that would come into play in a future war. Moreover, the country's economic success, the Depression (1933–1937) aside, was based significantly not on state-socialist command of the economy, as found in Soviet Russia, Fascist Italy, and Nazi Germany. Recovery took off on the basis of private enterprise. Capitalism's grassroots energy could not be easily dismissed by the totalitarian powers. Indeed, this was duly acknowledged and appreciated by them as an engine of progress.

As viewed from Nazi Germany, America was a country that Hitler preferred—as it turned out, up to 1941—to keep out of European affairs. He ordered his navy at all costs to avoid torpedoing American naval craft or any hostile acts that would precipitate war with the United States. Nazi propaganda efforts in the United States generally failed as did their undercover activities, in contrast to the success enjoyed in this regard by Stalin's Russia. This was a rather remarkable accomplishment by the Soviets given the large numbers of Americans of German extraction and the relative remoteness of "Russia." In contrast to Lenin's Cominternist tactics, Stalin's nuanced, more adroit tactics in winning influence in America paid dividends.

For obvious reasons, Moscow, in contrast to Berlin's attitude, seems to have had its eyes on America as a potential wartime ally—pro tem Soviet propaganda to the contrary. U.S. corporate and small business, organized labor, and able business-management teams with their legally trained executives—who in some cases in 1940–1941 began to leave private business to head the newly established government agencies in Washington, DC, to supervise the U.S. military buildup—got the American economic juggernaut off to an impressive start. This was especially true of arms production even before Pearl Harbor in December 1941. All of this was monitored by the Soviets.

The American economy soon began to meet the country's military necessities amid the crescendo of war abroad. Stalin did not need his *rezidentura* spies in the United States in order for him to be cognizant of this fact. Having by 1937–1938 already helped to tame the Depression, the Roosevelt administration and the New Deal Congress rose impressively to the new challenge of girding up the country's loins. This response was undeniably "world historical" in its implications at that time. As the world grew more dangerous almost by the hour, the economic feats performed by the "American miracle" did not go unnoticed in the capitals of London, Berlin, and Moscow, if not in Tokyo, except for the fanatical war party there.

During the two years after war broke out in Europe in September 1939 and around the time of Pearl Harbor, the U.S. economy was already turning out a staggering $181 billion worth of military aircraft, ships, and munitions alone. By 1942, American defense production equaled the combined total of Germany, Italy, and Japan. Two years later, even this figure doubled!

The Soviets, as did the Germans, watched closely as this upturn in American defense production took place, and most particularly as Lend-Lease after March 1941 began to flow to their main enemy, Britain. Hitler, in fact, had decided on his conquest of Soviet Russia when he did (i.e., even before defeating England) precisely because of his fear and loathing of eventual direct American involvement in the war. (This is documented in the memoirs and diaries of leading Nazi officials.)

STALIN'S HOPED-FOR LEND-LEASE

It was after U.S. President Franklin D. Roosevelt's homey analogy of "lending a neighbor a garden hose to put out a fire" that Americans came around to the concept of Lend-Lease. Though some agreed with Senator Burton K. Wheeler of Montana that the Lend-Lease agreement would "plow under every fourth American boy," Congress nevertheless passed the Lend-Lease bill by a sizable majority in March 1941.

As Stalin watched, the Lend-Lease Act became law on March 11, 1941. Ironically, the signing by FDR took place on the very day that NKGB chief, V. N. Merkulov, issued a secret report stating that there was solid evidence from "many reliable diplomatic sources in Berlin [that] Germany is planning an attack on the Soviet Union that very likely will take place in summer of this year."

Above all, Lend-Lease signified that the U.S. economic achievement would translate tangibly into many-sided aid to Britain. The legislation, which was by its scale all but unprecedented in the United States or, in fact, the history of any country, authorized the president to send an initial $7 billion in war materiel wherever and to whatever nation was assigned by the White House to be the recipient (the Democrat-controlled Congress, in any case, seldom let FDR down). Britain and Russia were the principal recipients among the two-dozen eventual ones.

The law gave the president exclusive power to sell, transfer, lend, or lease such war materials. The president was to set the terms for aid, repayment "in kind or property, or any other direct or indirect benefit which the president deemed satisfactory." Days after Lend-Lease was passed, Roosevelt appointed his close friend and adviser, Harry L. Hopkins, as the initial expediter of the war-aid program. A few months later, in July, probably for reasons of poor health, Hopkins yielded his job to Edward R. Stettinius, Jr. This official, another of Roosevelt's reputed "pro-Soviet" brain trusters, headed the new Office of Lend-Lease Administration, organized on October 28, 1941.

In its original form in the spring of 1941, the Lend-Lease program was intended for Great Britain, China, and countries of the British Empire. It was not until November 7, 1941, the twenty-fourth anniversary of the Bolshevik Revolution, that Soviet Russia was formally included under the program (although de facto, Lend-Lease aid had started to flow to the USSR in September).

Total Lend-Lease aid exceeded $50 billion, of which the British Commonwealth received some $31 billion and the USSR received over $11 billion, or an estimated $12.5 billion, in today's monetary values more than $60 billion. Within 15 years after the termination of Lend-Lease, settlements were made with most of the countries that had received aid, although a settlement with the USSR was not reached until 1972. Smaller countries received more than $1 billion in Lend Lease goods. Among these were Mexico, Central America, Iceland, South America, Africa, the Near East, countries in the Caribbean, and some of the smaller European countries.

In all, 38 countries and 19 American republics benefited from the program. It amounted to 14 cents out of every dollar the United States spent to fight the war. An agreement at the end of the conflict called for the British Empire to repay $650 million out of its $31 billion debt.

Ironically, one of the main drafters of the administration's side of the Lend-Lease particulars, especially as the aid was to be extended later to the Russians, was Assistant Treasury Secretary Harry Dexter White. In well-documented testimony at a congressional hearing in 1948, White was identified by Soviet spies as having acted as an agent for the NKGB. Only three days after these accusations were made against him amid his denials, White died allegedly of a heart attack. The *Venona* documents establish beyond any doubt his treason in the Silvermaster spy ring (named for another Treasury official) and as an agent in the secret Soviet Operation Snow (assigned to pushing the United States into war with Japan, a Soviet enemy).

Meantime, the warring powers observed how much-vaunted American neutrality and isolationism were fast becoming anachronisms. In any case, the Neutrality Law of 1935 had contained many convenient loopholes. These were duly exploited by the administration. Here was a government that in the mid-to late 1930s had already perceived the Axis as America's and the world's main enemy. Indeed, in his memoirs, ex-Foreign Minister Ribbentrop complained that the U.S. government, in taking the early, anti-German stand that it did, had exempted the USSR from its list of a potential enemies, despite, complained Ribbentrop, the Soviets' communism and obvious aggressiveness.

Early on, it was perceived in Moscow that Roosevelt and many, if not all, of his closest aides thought that the United States was far readier than the French or British (later, Churchill and Foreign Minister Anthony Eden being exceptions in London) to accept Stalin's Russia as a potential ally. This, despite misgivings among some top officials within FDR's administration itself. Some, for example, not only denounced the Communist regime of Stalin. They regarded it as a house of cards that would collapse with a German invasion. Some in the Roosevelt administration held out little hope for a Soviet victory in a war fought with Nazi Germany.

As to Soviet Russia as a civilized nation-state, FDR himself had once spoken some distinctly unflattering words about it. Did Stalin recall them? At the height of Soviet Russia's aggression against Finland, in February 1940, Roosevelt said:

"The Soviet Union, as everybody who has the courage to face the fact knows, is run by a dictatorship as absolute as any of the dictatorships in the world. It has allied itself with another dictatorship [with the Nazi-Soviet pacts—A. L. W.] and it has invaded a neighbor so infinitesimally small that it could do no conceivable possible harm to the Soviet Union, a neighbor which seeks only to live at peace as a democracy and a liberal, forward-looking democracy at that."

Moreover, U.S. public opinion, closely monitored by the NKVD and GRU and personally by Stalin, was much slower than the Roosevelt brain trust in accepting Russia in this friendly way—even after June 22, 1941. A poll taken on June 24 showed 35 percent in favor of aid to Soviet Russia, 54 percent opposed. A month later, however, the Gallup Poll indicated that 70 percent of the sample favored the "sale of war supplies" to Russia. In September of that year, a third poll showed that almost half of the sample approved extension of credits to the USSR to purchase American supplies. Even the American Federation of Labor, a strongly anti-Communist organization, expressed similar strong support for giving aid to the USSR.

On March 27, 1941, just after Lend-Lease became law, Roosevelt declared an unlimited national emergency. This unique action served to broaden the effect of the first, or "limited" emergency decreed in 1939. It served to provide further underpinning for the Lend-Lease policy. At that time, the president also broke off relations with Germany and Italy, freezing all of their assets in America. He proceeded to make other quasi-military moves. These included dispatching U.S. troops to Iceland to help that country bolster its military defenses. In April, Lend-Lease aid was extended to China, a country Roosevelt had long favored in its war against Japan. Interestingly, Stalin later joined in a limited way in this U.S. pro-China policy, Japan being a threat as well to the Soviet East, or rear, despite the Soviet-Japanese neutrality agreement of April 1941.

Already by the end of 1941, just two months after the German invasion of June, the USSR was receiving Lend-Lease aid.

Just as in World War I but to a greater degree in the 1940s, the weight of U.S. military participation in an anti-Axis war would become *the* deciding factor in the outcome of the global struggle. This was perceived quite clearly by the warring and neutral powers by March 1941. This was when the powerful United States, long appreciated as an industrial colossus by the Stalin Kremlin and not less so by the German leadership, became the self-declared and globally welcomed participant in the anti-Axis camp as the "arsenal of democracy." On December 7, 1941, when Japan attacked Pearl Harbor, America's entry into the war was consummated. This attack was followed the next day by the formal U.S. declaration of war on Japan. Then a few days later came Germany's declaration of war on the United States, followed by the latter's declaration of war against Germany.

In his postwar memoirs, Churchill described how elated and relieved he was over the chain of events that culminated on December 7. Stalin was also buoyed by the event. He, too, greeted the American entry into the big war with considerable fanfare in his state-controlled media in which, as the Soviet leader had apparently long calculated, his country and the United States would collaborate as "democratic" warring partners. This collaboration would be played out in ways that would be profitable to the Soviet Union by "tipping the scales" in its favor, as Stalin had put his long-term stratagem way back in 1925.

To conclude: In 1941 and before, Stalin had assured victory for his state and for his personal dictatorship by his adroit maneuvering in terms of securing future Allies, especially U.S. partnership, in the months preceding the German invasion of the USSR and the Pearl Harbor attack by the Japanese.

Stalin virtually allowed the Wehrmacht to attack on June 22, all but tricking and luring Hitler into inevitable defeat as some realistic German military staff officers themselves foresaw. (See chapter 10 for a full discussion of the pluses and minuses of the way in which Stalin and the Red Army coped under such extremely disadvantageous conditions with the German onslaught in Operation Barbarossa.)

Moreover, Stalin and his military strategists' defense-plus-offense—baffling and a losing proposition as it seemed and still seems to many observers in the West and in Russia—nevertheless proved to be a winning combination for the USSR and in particular for its supreme leader, who personally took the main credit for Germany's defeat. Ultimate victory was achieved despite the horrific losses in men, equipment, and territory in the grueling opening months of the war. After the war, Stalin admitted to war production tsar Eric Johnston that the United States had been a major factor in the Soviet victory in the East over the Axis. Marshal Zhukov was even more enthusiastic about American aid in the war, saying:[6]

> "When we entered the war, we were still a backward country in the industrial sense as compared to Germany. . . . Today [1963] some say the Allies really didn't help us. . . . But, listen, one cannot deny that the Americans shipped over to us materiel without which we could not have equipped our armies held in reserve or have been able to continue the war. . . . We did not have enough munitions, [and] how would we have been able to turn out all those tanks without the rolled steel sent us by the Americans? To believe what they say [in the USSR] today, you'd think we had had all this abundance!"

In effect on July 3, 1941, Stalin had declared the opening of a Popular Front war, the military analog of his 1930s Popular Front, "anti-Fascist" electoral tactic deployed in the Western democracies. He pulled out all of the stops in democratic terminology, which was duly echoed in U.S. propaganda about the USSR.[7]

A "STRANGE" U.S.-SOVIET ALLIANCE

Stalin dressed up his pro tem alliance with capitalist America in attractive ways. The smiling, mustachioed, pipe-smoking "Uncle Joe" succeeded in winning many millions of friends in the United States and in the West as a whole. His success far outdid any past feat of Stalin's peace-loving diplomacy. This winning of friends and influencing people strategy became a huge, metaphorical "Soviet Pavilion" and "Popular

Front." It was a favorable impression toward Stalin and the Soviet Union that would remain intact for the duration of World War II and even well into the postwar period. It extended well beyond the death in April 1945 of "Uncle Joe's" putative friend, Franklin D. Roosevelt.

This widespread friendship felt in the United States and the West toward the USSR prevailed in the postwar years (up to the Korean War in 1950), despite such jarring notes as the dictator's little-publicized remark made to the number two Yugoslav Communist official, Milovan Djilas, in 1946 to "have another go at it" (apparently meaning war with the capitalist West). Also ignored was Stalin's hard-line February 1946 electoral speech that was soon followed by Kremlin propaganda about the "two hostile camps" of Eastern socialism versus Eastern "capitalist imperialism" confronting each other in militant ways.

As already noted, Soviet foreign policy under Stalin and Vyacheslav Molotov's close supervision traveled a serpentine path. It was often described by Western observers as zigzagging between two extremes. At one pole seemed to be the traditional Soviet assertion of world revolution based on Marxist-Leninist ideology. This level of Soviet policy included the tactic of carrying out subversion in foreign lands. This intelligence in the West consisted mainly of industrial espionage but it also involved "agents of influence" Moscow would secretly or sometimes openly cultivate to support its policies in order to buttress its foreign diplomacy. As already noted, the other track was the traditional pursuit of national interest via the tools of diplomacy. In this kaleidoscope of tactics and strategy oscillating between the two poles, America always occupied a leading position in Stalin's calculus. Soviet relations with the United States became affected by this two-sided combination. Sometimes adversely so, as when the USSR proclaimed the goals of establishing a "World Republic of Soviets," although that line was distinctly soft-pedaled by Stalin but much emphasized in anti-Soviet circles in America, as represented by such officials as J. Edgar Hoover and later the House Un-American Activities Committee. The hostility was triggered by such actions as the Soviets' invasion of Finland when that nation's national anthem, "Finlandia," became a hit tune in America. At the time, Britain had threatened to bomb the oil wells in the Soviet Caucasus. In a major speech in December 1939, President Roosevelt railed against Soviet Communism. These were strong reactions that appeared to unnerve Stalin, who was always protective toward the Soviets' global reputation, causing him to reconsider such extreme actions, especially as the USSR was expelled from the

League of Nations. For the first time since 1917, the Soviet Union was becoming a universally perceived pariah-state. This was definitely not a development to Stalin's liking, i.e., to scrap the 20-year effort of the USSR to be a normal participant in world affairs.

Back in 1933, the Roosevelt administration's price for recognizing the USSR was in large part based on the Kremlin's promise to renounce pursuit of world revolution by means of subversion within the United States. However, despite Soviet promises to the contrary—and, ironically, as abetted by formal recognition itself with the opening of the bustling Soviet embassy in Washington and Soviet legations elsewhere in the country—Soviet espionage not only continued, but even increased in America.

Yet there was a twist to this activity. Soviet spying was mainly directed against the U.S. defense industry. Technical secrets that were assiduously gathered by Moscow in the long run, ironically, actually helped the Soviets develop weapon designs (of tanks, war planes, wheeled vehicles, naval ships, munitions, etc.) that were used effectively in their later defense against the German invaders. Thus, this egregious espionage not only paid off for the USSR, but ultimately also for the Allied effort as a whole! The same, however, cannot be said of notorious Soviet atomic spying during and after the war, which, of course, worked against U.S. interests, and in no uncertain terms.

Stalin never personally visited the United States, or for that matter any Western country after he became the Soviet leader. Yet as a Lenin co-conspirator in the early 1900s, Stalin had visited several Central and East European capitals, including Vienna, Prague, and Warsaw. (Nikita Khrushchev was the first Soviet leader ever to visit the United States, in 1959.).

Yet it is clear that Stalin had a great appreciation of the industrial and potential military power represented by the United States as well as by the resourcefulness of Americans. As canvassed earlier, it might almost be said that unlike Lenin, who had described the United States as the most evil, congenitally capitalist, and imperialist of all Western states, Stalin was a *declared*, at least, Americanophile, doctrinal dogmas aside.

Lend-Lease aid to Russia, beginning in the summer of 1941, became the capstone of the Soviet dictator's high regard for America. In July 1941, he even dared to plead to U.S. envoys in Moscow for America to send a division of U.S. Army troops to help defend the USSR.

It was also an integral part of Stalin's assured victory over the Axis that he knew he could count on American aid via an alliance he had seemingly anticipated with the overseas giant well before mid-1941.

STALIN DEFENDS STATE INTERESTS

Finally, when it came to foreign policy, Josef Stalin was a past master at making the needed combinations and readjustments.

First, largely for party consumption and in secret, he would allude to Soviet global designs that he said his diplomacy abetted. Then he would table this remote goal in favor of more immediate, attainable ones related to defending "Russian" state interests. Often this was accompanied in diplomacy by a trial and error procedure resembling the much-quoted (in Soviet military and civilian literature) Napoleonic formula of *S'engage et depuis on vôit*, or roughly translated, "Try it and see what happens."

Above all, Stalin knew how to exploit diplomacy in order to advance Soviet national interests. He employed flexible and pragmatic means in a process in which he showed impressive skill. In his maneuverings, Stalin was as cautious as he was deceptive. Perhaps the illegitimacy of the very regime he headed and its bad reputation abroad helped make him act in a deceptive way. He seemed to realize, with evident realism, that revolutionary, expansionistic ambitions always had to be tempered and placed at a lower level of priorities by the imperatives of space and time and by the power of rival nation-states, most of whom despised Communism.

Just as his ultimate, expansionistic goals had to be carefully concealed and/or camouflaged, the process of realizing basic, world-girdling Leninist aims often had to—by force of circumstances—be postponed. This prompted debate abroad as to how seriously Stalin really took Marxist-Leninist ideology.

Stalin conducted foreign policy like chess, Russia's national indoor sport. This brainy, multilayered game was known to have been a favorite of Stalin, as well as of Lenin. As in chess, Stalin would patiently study his opponent and make his moves accordingly in order to better his rival. He would keep his eye on the overall strategy, his own, and his opponent's. He would zero in on the other's big, backboard pieces. His zigzag tacking sometimes involved surrendering pieces and sometimes meant moving one step backward in order to advance two steps forward. In Stalin's way of conducting it, Soviet diplomacy, again like chess, went by discretely phased stages. His moves resembled openings, middle-, and end-games. As the overall game proceeded, plays had to be carefully calibrated in advance, crafted dynamically *in medias res* in accordance with the opponent's own dynamic strategy. Also, the moves had to be adjusted to the vagaries of unforeseeable events in the world arena.

As in chess, the diplomatic game was bound to have twists and turns, advances and losses ("sacrifices"), all in the hope of maneuvering Soviet power in the long run into a better, more commanding position on the board—i.e., in the global arena.

For his part, Winston Churchill likened Stalin's methods to the quite un-chess-like tactics of a burglar. "[He] will try every door in the house, enter all rooms which are not locked and when they come to one that is barred, if [he is] unsuccessful in breaking through, [he] will withdraw and invite you to dine that evening."

The burglar metaphor aside, the chess analogy seems more accurate in tracing Stalin's behavior toward the West, including the United States, as it played out in the 1920s, 1930s, and 1940s. The Soviet leader would maneuver in apparently baffling ways. Sometimes he was warmly ingratiating, other times brutally uncompromising. During the first talks in July 1941 leading up to the Lend-Lease shipments beginning in the autumn, Stalin would display this supposedly erratic, contradictory behavior within the space of 24 hours.

Yet in the final analysis, by using at times baffling tactics, the Soviet dictator always attempted and often succeeded in placing the Soviets into a better position "on the board" as a result of his zigzags and maneuvers. This in turn helped Moscow more closely approach its ultimate goal under Stalin's leadership of becoming a superpower. Even its joining of the League of Nations, as the Soviets did belatedly in 1934 after disowning it bitterly for 15 years, was one of those pregnant, if apparently contradictory, Soviet moves

As viewed by Stalin, many such proximate "goals," i.e., openings and middle-games, lay along the long path to eventual Soviet world domination—which became a retreating horizon that as one approaches it, draws farther away. Was this to Stalin's liking? Was he "ready" for it? Apparently so. Unlike Hitler, Stalin took no risks to make the elusive horizon come ever closer to being a concrete reality. In the welter of unpredictable and conflicting events, trends, and the vicissitudes worldwide of departing and arriving foreign leaders with their unique personalities, particularly in the democracies, retreat as opposed to offense sometimes seemed to Stalin to be the best policy. At other times, offense seemed possible, as against South Korea in June 1950 in the Korean war that was planned and backed if not originally conceived in Moscow. Even in this, Stalin displayed a certain caution.

The "world-historical" game of grand strategy and diplomacy was viewed by Stalin as a protracted, stage-by-stage process. He conducted it flexibly, advancing Soviet interests bit by bit. He also set about realizing the sacred "pledge" that he had made symbolically to the party in his funeral oration at Lenin's bier in January 1924 (to extend the borders of the USSR and carry out world revolution). As the former head of Soviet foreign intelligence in the 1940s, Gen. Pavel Sudoplatov, wrote:[8]

> "Stalin's . . . first priority was the fulfillment of their geopolitical aspirations to transform the Soviet Union into the largest super-power in the world."

Josef Vissarionovich (Djugashvili) Stalin ruled the Soviet empire almost as long as Queen Victoria reigned in Great Britain. Like the queen and all rulers who have held power for almost a generation—as well as those who held it for a shorter, eventful period, as did an extremely powerful Napoleon Bonaparte—Stalin cast a long shadow over the land and the globe. He left his mark on every facet of his country's society, which he sought to shape, even on the contours of buildings known as "Stalin wedding cake." If ever there was a tyrant of whom it could be said that he regarded himself as an "engineer of human souls"—including, as it turned out, the souls of foreign diplomats—that leader was Stalin.

In the initial 1941 Lend-Lease negotiations as well as in the wartime and postwar conferences with the other members of the Big Three, Roosevelt and Churchill and their emissaries, Stalin was always in command of the proceedings in the sense that the other two summiteers routinely deferred to him. This was an advantage that he knew how to skillfully exploit. Always chesting his cards, his true designs, Stalin's effect on these leaders, while not "hypnotic," was at least extremely potent in its persuasiveness and firmness.

Above all, it was part of Stalin's methods to rapidly shift tactically *in medias res* as though he were buffeted by objective, Newtonian forces while at the same time helping to direct the vectors of those forces to his own advantage. How else to explain his expansion into Eastern

Europe during and after World War II—i.e., his retention of the lands he had won during the short period of his collaboration with the Nazis (1939–1941) and Western toleration of violation of agreements made at Yalta? A chess master always keeps his eye on potential plays lying several moves ahead. As he does, he attempts to deceive the opponent by keeping him in the dark as to the master's basic strategy.

Memoirs written by lower-echelon Western participants in Big Three meetings always later expressed their awe mixed with dismay at the way Stalin would maneuver and tack and how he would wind up generally getting his way over his other Allied conferees. These cognomens indeed caught the essence of Stalin's nature and style. A true tyrant, like Ivan the Terrible in Russian fact and legend, Stalin was not satisfied unless he had penetrated and controlled tyrannically every facet of Soviet society, including especially the minds of his immediate aides. In this respect, Stalin left his colleague-dictator Adolf Hitler way behind. To Stalin's aides, loyalty to him, as with Tsar Ivan III and his obedient entourage, was a matter of life and death.

Stalin's curiosity about key foreign countries, their systems, leaders, and exploitable vulnerabilities knew no bounds. This was especially true in connection with his interest in America—as principal helper in Soviet industrialization, possibly as a future Soviet ally and donor of vital military aid in the "inevitable" war to come. That Stalin perceived this possibility, if not likelihood, by 1940–1941 now seems undeniable.

The Soviet dictator inserted himself into every possible field, a fact that U.S. Lend-Lease negotiators in Moscow immediately discovered to their surprise at the opening of Lend-Lease talks in July 1941. This included Stalin's command of every item to be shipped on his long, initial U.S. aid wish list. Once briefed on whatever matter, he considered himself to be an authority. This included everything from *belles-lettres* to linguistics, from military science, biology, and agronomy to constitutional law and the types of military equipment to be sent via Lend-Lease. His memory has been described as prodigious. True, he would arrive at his conclusions as a rule only after consulting specialists. But once he had immersed himself in the nitty-gritty of whatever endeavor or subject, Stalin would make the final decision absolutely on his own. He chose whichever plan, conclusion, tactic, strategy, work of art—or assassination and execution—that he thought best filled the bill of "socialism" or "socialist realism" as he interpreted it. This, of course, buttressed his own personal power. At the same time, whatever policy he and his aides crafted toward other countries had to advance the Soviet global cause of world revolution and domination.

It is said that his method of conducting Politburo sessions was to hear input from the other dozen-plus members of that highest body. Stalin would then follow Russian alphabetical order, duly placing himself near the end of the list of speakers. He would then sort out the views he had previously heard as he arrived at his own conclusion.

It is testified by Soviet army memoirists that this also was his procedure, as commander-in-chief, when conducting sessions within the councils of military high command, or Stavka, during the war. Unlike Hitler during the Russian campaign, Stalin—at least, by 1942—would carefully weigh what his commanders had to say before making the final decision. Poets and novelists, architects, economists, cinematographers, composers, scientists, marshals, admirals and generals, and diplomatic-service officials—anyone performing a public function in the society or for the state—knew that whatever party line or decision would be reached, it would be Stalin alone who would ultimately color it and approve it. And woe to those who did not take this into account. Perhaps this is what Hitler meant when he described his Soviet counterpart as an outstanding organizer and administrator.

Stalin would likewise keenly observe how policy, tactics, and strategy in the war were being carried into effect. This, too, directly affected Lend-Lease, sometimes in adverse ways, since lower officials feared to act unless they thought Stalin would approve. Decision making at lower levels was thus often hamstrung. Typical, totalitarian bureaucracy, developed to the nth degree in Soviet Russia, also complicated the execution of Lend-Lease assistance at the middle and grassroots levels.

During the war, everyone was expected to think and work as Stalin thought they should. The penalty for failing to understand Stalin's methods and the system could mean, and often did, prison, the gulag, or the firing squad. Unlike some of other dictators in history, Stalin set very high standards of *rabotosposobnost'* (capacity for work, diligence). Vacations for the boss were working vacations. He was an indomitable toiler at his job of Soviet leader (unlike Lenin, who was essentially lazy, spending little time at his desk). Any number of foreign diplomats, such as those discussing Lend-Lease and other sensitive matters with the Soviet leader in 1941 and throughout the war, noticed how shrewdly and intelligently Stalin conducted himself and the affairs of state.

STALIN AND FDR

"It is beyond all question that later on [Roosevelt] will be accessible to our influence."

—*Maxim Litvinov in a letter to Stalin*[9]

As mentioned earlier, Stalin had always shown a mixed attitude toward America. He would sometimes display flashes of apparently genuine admiration for the rich country. It seemed that he regarded the United States as a special case. Only rarely did he express the view—even privately—that America was actually ripe for Soviet-style revolution; he acted as if this were only a remote possibility. Yet his direct involvement in the subversive, espionage affairs of the GRU and NKVD-NKGB activities as well as the above-ground propaganda line of the CPUSA in America were anything but perfunctory.[10]

During preparations for Lend-Lease in 1941 and in wartime conferences, Stalin also seems to have understood that President Roosevelt's cabinet along with lower officials in the executive branch—the Department of State, the War Department, etc.—was relatively united around the head of state and government.

This unity in Washington at times contrasted with that of the British government. The government in London, operating under conditions of a less stable, virtual coalition parliamentary democracy, was shot through with officials who either wanted nothing to do with Stalin's Russia or who welcomed the mutual annihilation of Germany and Russia in war. Of course, there were partisans of this point of view within the American government as well. But there they were outnumbered by others of opposite persuasion. In any case, the strength and unity of the American presidential system of government as contrasted to the British parliamentary system, not to mention Roosevelt's own personal charisma, were positive factors adding to the contrast in policy-making and the difference between American and British attitudes toward the USSR. Churchill's own charismatic influence in England was to arise only later. (Roosevelt, after all, had been in office since 1933, Churchill since 1940.)

Some in high places in London also regarded Soviet Russia as a useful pawn in deflecting Hitler eastward. There were partisans of this view in Washington as well.

Yet Churchill was not far behind Roosevelt and his team in regarding Stalin and the USSR as a strong, potentially dependable co-combatant against Hitler. In some respects, Churchill's government led the way in paving a road to Moscow for extending U.S. Lend-Lease aid to the Soviets. Suspicions on one or the other side of the "strange alliance" during the war—namely, that either the eastern or western half might defect and at some juncture strike a deal with Hitler—was never too seriously entertained, it seems, either in Moscow or the Western capitals, at least not in the spring and summer of 1941. In any case, such suspicions, when they cropped up, came and went.

Stalin knew that Roosevelt's authority over his own governmental team was extremely strong. He knew the president had his will in most areas of domestic and foreign policy-making (e.g., he was even trying to pack the U.S. Supreme Court in violation of the U.S. Constitution). FDR's reelection to a third term in 1940 only buttressed the Soviet view of the president's nearly autocratic as well as popular rule. Therefore, from Stalin's point of view, working with any of FDR's several closest associates was the best way to influence American policy in preferred, Soviet directions. This became obvious at the very first Lend-Lease talks in Moscow in July 1941 in which Stalin personally took part.

While debunking the American boast of its being eminently if not uniquely the most democratic of all countries in the world, there were often hints from Stalin that he thought America and Americans to be industrious and relatively peace loving, imbued with a commendable "bourgeois-democratic" spirit and entrepreneurial initiative. He was also informed of Roosevelt's and the American public's long-standing, anti-Nazi posture. These characteristics, to Stalin's mind, evidently, were quite unlike those of any other capitalist state.

According to the Russian historian Yu. B. Basistov, as early as 1939 Stalin considered the United States to be a "pro-Soviet" country among only three so classified. Besides America, only Greece and Yugoslavia were so designated. American power, of course, helped make it preeminent over the others.

SPIES AND AGENTS OF INFLUENCE

"The task is to penetrate into those places where policy is born and developed, where discussions and debates take place, where policy is completed. Penetrating the surroundings of Roosevelt himself is the goal that we seek in our everyday work."[11]

The Soviet leader also appears to have thought that a certain naïve streak ran through the American people and its leaders. This was true of the Americans in ways that were quite unlike the traits found in the jaded, old-European states and their encrusted systems. If Churchill compared Stalin to a burglar, Stalin once compared Churchill to a common pickpocket. Nothing like these negative views was ever expressed by Stalin toward Roosevelt.

On the other hand, Soviet security chief Lavrenti Beria's son, Sergo, wrote in his memoirs that Stalin and the Soviet leadership regarded democratic countries as essentially hobbled by their "slow-moving" democratic political system.[12]

Unlike dictatorships, democracies must contend with public opinion, and leaders of totalitarian countries would have to take this into account as well, Sergo Beria pointed out, citing attitudes held by his father and Stalin. This put the democracies at a disadvantage with countries ruled by one-party dictatorships. The latter could expedite matters pretty much as they wished and whenever they chose. The so-called "parliaments" of dictatorships merely rubber-stamped the dictator's prior decisions.

The point is that democratic countries' openness and democratism allowed—indeed, invited—Stalin and the Moscow leadership to influence public opinion. This was especially the case with the United States. Here such influence was brought to bear by squads of Soviet "illegals" and "legals" and fellow travelers. These measures were carried out far more successfully in the United States than in any other leading capitalist country during the prewar and war periods.

As a result, it seems undeniable that Lend-Lease, as tenuously supported on the American side in Congress and among the people—as it had to be supported in order for it to be put into effect—probably would have been inconceivable without such influence and Soviet penetration in America.

It is therefore ironic in retrospect that Soviet spies and agents of influence operating in Washington, DC, New York City, and elsewhere in a sense actually paved the way to such closer approaches to the USSR. This was represented and symbolized by, and culminated in above all, Lend-Lease, which in turn helped save Russia from Nazi conquest and as a consequence prevented German control over Eurasia.

Such domination had been Hitler's ultimate goal. Under the influence of his reigning authority on geopolitics, Professor and General

Karl Haushofer, the fuehrer was convinced that dominating Eurasia would lead ultimately to victory across the oceans over to the United States. Precisely for that reason, Hitler was building long-range bombers and rockets while working earnestly in Norway on atomic fission in order to ultimately develop nuclear weapons. Having left the war against England unfinished, Hitler had sought to conquer Russia as a guarantee against an America that in entering the war would tip the scales against the Axis. Hitler calculated that he could preempt this likelihood by conquering the Russian giant to the east and thereby also inherit its rich resources. As Austrian historian Heinz Magenheimer points out:[13]

> "Hitler reckoned with the probability of the United States entering the war if it were prolonged, and this was to play an important role in his considerations how best to deal with the Soviet Union. That he clearly recognized the growing weight of the United States was revealed, in early July [1940], by the Z-plan—the temporary resumption of the Kriegsmarine's ship-building programme—and the discussions of the basic principles with leaders of the OKW and the branches of the Wehrmacht in summer and early autumn. [The plan to attack the USSR] was likewise designed to anticipate intervention by the United States on Britain's side. On the one hand, the issue was to establish an impregnable empire in continental Europe, on the other, to ensure that Japan kept its back free for a confrontation with Britain and the United States in eastern Asia and the Pacific."

STALIN AMONG THE BIG THREE

As noted earlier, the Soviet dictator held an unusually favorable opinion of the American president. How much of his reputed personal admiration for Roosevelt stemmed from purely exploitative motives is hard to say. He fulsomely described FDR as a skillful leader of his people. At the same time, Stalin regarded the American leader as a foxy character, a *politikan* (political operator) whom only he, Stalin, could outwit. After FDR's death in April 1945, Stalin lamented the fact that the "vulgar" anti-Soviet Truman, whom he disliked, had taken over in the White House. Also, there is evidence that Stalin had his suspicions regarding America's alliance with Britain. At times in the pre-June 1941 period, he seems to have entertained the notion that

America, like the British, was egging Soviet Russia into war with Germany. Both Western countries, he seems to have thought (and as many Russian historians still maintain), relished a coming fratricidal struggle between the two totalitarian states.

The Americans, through their Ambassador in Moscow, Lawrence Steinhardt, repeatedly and routinely vehemently denied such motives. Russian and Western historians of one school of thought maintain, on not entirely convincing evidence, that Stalin, right up to the cataclysm of June 22, 1941, sincerely sought continued long-term, peaceful relations with Nazi Germany.

As to Stalin's two other colleagues of the Big Three, it was clear to everyone that Stalin liked Roosevelt but disliked Churchill. How much of this reflected Stalin's pre-June 1941 attitudes is not known. Yet it could not have been lost on Stalin that Churchill had always been a dyed-in-the-wool anti-Communist, whereas Roosevelt seldom cast the USSR in an unfavorable light. Memoirists close to Stalin write that he actually heard Stalin make bitter criticism of Churchill. Before becoming prime minister, Churchill, indeed, had once exclaimed that Bolshevism should have been "strangled in its cradle."

Moreover, the British government as a whole was always an object of suspicion on Stalin's part. Within Moscow's Commissariat of Foreign Affairs, it was hard to find any Soviet official who thought, or who dared to think, highly of the British. Meanwhile, officials like ex-Foreign Minister Maxim Latino (who was returned by Stalin as a deputy minister in the Foreign Commissariat in late 1941 as well as being posted as ambassador to Washington), as with the Deputy Commissar of Foreign Affairs S. A. Lozovsky, an apparent Litvinovite, had obvious sympathies for America.

The latter, like Litvinov, a Jew, was executed in 1952 on false charges stemming from Stalin's then anti-Jewish campaign. Litvinov himself barely escaped such punishment in the later years. The Jewish aspect is interesting in that Stalin was convinced, not unlike Hitler, that Washington was run by "Jewish money."[14] When Harry S Truman replaced Roosevelt after FDR's death in April 1945, Stalin reasoned that, unfortunately to his mind, a new, "non-Jewish" group was now in charge in America.

Another sore point with Stalin vis-à-vis the British was the content of the information relayed secretly to the Kremlin by such agents as the "Cambridge Five" in London as well as from his alert ambassador there, Ivan Maisky.

   Namely, when the USSR invaded Finland in December 1939, Britain was seriously considering the military contingency of RAF bombing of the Caucasus oil fields, the main source of Soviet petroleum and gasoline. This unprovoked, naked Soviet aggression had caused an uproar of pro-Finnish sentiments in England. It did also in America but nowhere near as potently as it did in Europe. Finland, after all, was just around the bend to the north from the British Isles. Moreover, many of the military and civilian officials who were to oversee such dire measures against Soviet targets in the Caucasus remained in the British government after Churchill took over in May 1940, of which continuity Stalin was kept fully informed.

   Some historians, both Russian and Western, believe that Stalin never forgave the British for these and other "sins." He thus remained permanently suspicious of the British prime minister's motives despite other indications that Churchill's motives in 1940–1941 could have been interpreted differently. Namely, that the British leader merely hoped in all honesty that if Germany invaded the USSR, as he surely thought it would, his country would welcome Stalin into the Allied, later United Nations, fold as an ally and encourage U.S. Lend-Lease aid to the USSR's war effort. It is another piece of irony that the only country capable of giving such aid on a large scale was the United States, not the disliked (by Stalin) Great Britain (although the British, of course, contributed to Lend-Lease shipments to the USSR).

   The Russian historian Robert Ivanov writes of U.S.-Soviet relations in the immediate pre-June 1941 period as one, he says, in which the "two great powers, the USSR and the USA, though not yet participating in the second world war, realized that their positions were not all that different." He continues:[15]

> "The USA and the USSR were potential allies in the sense of their both opposing complete German domination on the European continent. Both the Soviet Union and the U.S., moreover, were mutually alarmed by Japan's aggressive policy in the Far East that threatened the national interests of both countries. To Stalin's mind, the ultimate authority in all matters, including foreign affairs, was Lenin. Soon after World War I, it was Lenin who had predicted that conflict between Japan and the U.S. was inevitable. This at once meant that by further analysis relations between America and the Soviet Union were bound to become closer. . . . Once they both did enter the

conflict, a vast reorientation of forces did, in fact, take place on a world scale. It would be one in which the USA would play the leading role. By taking all this into account, warnings sent by Washington to Moscow could not help but have alarmed Moscow. . . . Ideological and political factors between countries belonging to antagonistic social and economic systems do play a decisive role in their relations. Nevertheless this role need not be all-determining. Geopolitical factors operating in the relations between states do assert themselves. They can, in fact, assume the dominant position over ideological, political, and class factors. . . . Similarly, in World War I, geopolitical determinants of policy led to a reorientation of forces so that the main countries of the Entente—Russia, England, France, and the USA—all found themselves on the same side of the barricades."

Ivanov implies above that despite Stalin's miscalculations concerning the timing of German aggression against the USSR and his "stubborn refusal" to face that fact, he nonetheless surely did understand these geopolitical truisms. Stalin's singling out of America took various forms. At the wartime summits, Stalin not infrequently tried to pit FDR against Churchill. He knew FDR disagreed with the latter on various postwar issues, particularly those that might negatively affect the integrity of the British Empire. He also greatly admired FDR's number two man, Harry Hopkins, with whom he had gotten along so well in the pre-Lend-Lease talks in Moscow in mid-1941. Hopkins was the official who had smoothed the way to carrying out this vital assistance. Ex-foreign spy chief Gen. Pavel Sudoplatov has described Harry Hopkins as a "Soviet agent." Hopkins is so described in the Venona papers.

Soviet spy penetration within the upper echelons of the U.S. government was incredibly extensive. It was a strong factor in the Soviet realignment toward America. Agents and spies included among others Assistant Secretary of the Treasury Harry Dexter White, American diplomat and policy-making aid Alger Hiss, and Laughlin Currie, Roosevelt's economics assistant within the White House and a spy courier. Secret Soviet agents operating for the USSR as spies were at work in the War Department, the OSS, the Air Corps, the War Production Board, the Office of War Information, the Departments of Agriculture and Commerce, and the administration of Lend-Lease; Eleanor Roosevelt was said to have had a woman Soviet agent as a personal friend; and so on. In all, this activity made the administration look like

Swiss cheese. To appreciate the scale of this Soviet penetration, imagine that such a situation existed and was exposed today within the administrations of, say, Reagan, the Bushes, or Clinton. The shock and public outcry would be—justifiably—deadening. That such penetration could be occurring would seem unbelievable.

It is hard to deny that this widespread penetration by Soviet agents of influence, not to mention the many unnamed Soviet sympathizers in the American bureaucracy and at the highest levels in Washington, DC, all became potent factors that led Stalin, before World War II and Lend-Lease, in the direction of accommodation with the U.S. government, which he calculated he could influence so well. As, in fact, he did.

Hopkins was the top American official chosen by Roosevelt who had first approached Stalin in July 1941 with offers to ship large amounts of aid to the beleaguered USSR. That country was then fighting for its very life against Nazi Germany after only a month of war. The Soviet leader's expressed admiration for Hopkins might well have stemmed from the American official's known sympathies for Soviet Russia as well as his putative admiration for Stalin personally—and, of course, because of Hopkins' proximity to FDR.

Roosevelt once remarked to former U.S. ambassador to the USSR William C. Bullitt, after the latter had expressed strong doubts about the trustworthiness not to mention brutality of Stalin:

> "Bill, I don't dispute your facts, they are accurate. I don't dispute the logic of your reasoning. I just have a hunch that Stalin is not that kind of man. Harry [Hopkins] says he's not . . . and I think that if I give him everything I possibly can [by way of Lend-Lease aid] and ask nothing from him in return, noblesse oblige, he won't try to annex anything and will work with me for a world of democracy and peace."

Early in 1942, Roosevelt wrote to Churchill as follows:

> "I know you will not mind my being brutally frank when I tell you that I think I can personally handle Stalin better than either your Foreign Office or my State Department. . . . He thinks he likes me better, and I hope he will continue to do so."

Again, as in chess, Stalin tried to figure out Roosevelt's "game" as it was being played out before his eyes—as, for instance, in the pre-Lend-Lease negotiations of the summer and fall of 1941 and at the Big

Three wartime summits in Teheran and Yalta. He always applied to foreign leaders and their aides his considerable talents that he had put to such good use for 20 years as the Soviet Communist Party's general secretary in charge of vetting top party and government officials in the Soviet Union. He played this key role after his appointment to this post in 1922 by Lenin, amid the latter's extravagant praise of his talented Georgian, Stalin. Stalin's card-file memory concerning the party and government officials' personalities, the vulnerabilities and strengths of hundreds of his chosen, key nomenklaturists selected for top positions, was extraordinary.

In other words, sizing up people, including foreign diplomats and leaders, became Stalin's stock in trade and one at which he excelled. Stalin always insisted on having and reading ahead of time from his intelligence sources the bulging files on any and all officials and leaders with whom he was to come into contact.

As Robert Sherwood wrote in *Roosevelt and Hopkins*, Harry Hopkins described Stalin favorably this way after his first meeting with him in late July 1941:

> "There was no waste of word, gesture, nor mannerism. It was like talking to a perfectly coordinated machine, an intelligent machine. Joseph Stalin knew what he wanted, knew what Russia wanted and assumed that you knew. . . . He wore no armament, military or civilian. . . . His hands are huge, as hard as his mind."

When Stalin looked at America in the 1920s, he saw a country that was, relatively speaking, an industrial giant, and that was in general peace-minded. For instance, in diplomacy, such as at the London Disarmament Conference (1935–1936), it was the "out-of-area" Americans alone who favored virtually unlimited disarmament. By contrast, the British refused to negotiate serious reductions in naval armaments while the Germans and Japanese altogether boycotted the conference. Fascist Italy participated only as a nonvoting member.

Also, Stalin understood well the phenomenon of virulent American isolationism. At the same time, he perceived that business interests in America, especially after the financial crash on Wall Street of 1929, were eager to make deals with the USSR, regardless of ideological differences and Soviet revolutionist propaganda. Stalin, like Lenin, was well aware of the apolitical, non-ideological nature of profit-seeking

American businessmen. (The analogy today might be Fidel Castro's wooing of pacifists or certain ideologically numb, profit-minded American business interests, especially the wheat farmers and their lobbies in Washington, in his pursuit of lifting the U.S. embargo on American trade with Communist Cuba.)

Stalin, moreover, was reassured when FDR, in his first year in the White House, had decided as one of his first acts in foreign affairs to recognize the USSR (in 1933). America was the last Western country to do so some 10 years after most European countries had extended recognition. Roosevelt perceived, even that early in the pre-World War II years, that the USSR might one day join Great Britain, France, and the United States in opposition to any aggressor nations. Secretary of State Cordell Hull was convinced, notes an American scholar, that "only such a union could recall the jingoist nations to their senses. The serious deterioration in the prospects for world peace were uppermost in the president's mind as he prepared his approach to Russia [in 1933]."

What immediately followed during the 1930s were large and significant American business deals with the USSR. The result was that no less than two-thirds of all Soviet industrial enterprises were built with sizable U.S. aid in the form of machines and technical assistance by qualified personnel.

In his time, Lenin had set a precedent for capitalist aid to the Soviet Republic. He had allowed large Western capitalist concessions to exploit Russian oil, gold, and other natural resources. These at first were granted by Moscow to the British—exploiting to Soviet benefit resources in the Caucasus and in Siberia. Yet Lenin had spoken especially positively of potential American assistance. He was aware, of course, of the aid dispensed through the Hoover ARA food program that had saved the lives of some 4 million Soviet citizens in the early 1920s.

These earlier precedents of Western and especially American assistance in the form of the ARA and the help given Soviet industrialization in the 1930s by Ford, General Electric, et al., served as significant, tangible forerunners of Lend-Lease aid. They were also the prelude to post-World War II American relief aid to the Soviet Ukraine dispensed through UNRRA in 1945–1946. This U.S. aid tradition might even have been continued under the Marshall Plan after 1947 had Stalin not vetoed USSR and Soviet East European satellite participation in the large and effective American aid program for Europe.

Not to be forgotten either was the fact that Stalin the Georgian was an avid student of Russian history. He seemed to be a Russophile, i.e., in the romantic, nationalist sense. Yet he did not hesitate to complain, as Lenin did, about certain negative characteristics that he found in individual Russians. Stalin often touted "Great Russian" superiority and Russian expansionism of the tsarist past—i.e., Russia as a "civilizing force" over the "backward" borderlands to the south and east. During the war, he cut medals and awards with the visages of tsarist military heroes like Generals Kutuzov and Suvorov. He was flattered when writers like Alexei Tolstoy described him as a latter-day Ivan the Terrible or Peter the Great. Whether the Georgian bestowed such fulsome praise on *Rus'* and Russians for purely opportunistic reasons is difficult to confirm. Yet it appears his feelings along this line were in many cases genuine. Also authentic was his interest in Russian culture, toward which he was by no means indifferent. His attendance at performances of the Bolshoi opera and ballet seemed not to be merely perfunctory. Stalin ably played on these sentiments when in conference with Westerners. The latter were thus favorably impressed with Stalin's "Russian patriotism." Perhaps it is accurate to say that for Stalin, as King Louis XIV said of his relation to France, "the state is me." The close identification of Josef Stalin to the Russian state is defended even today by nationalist-minded Russian historians.

As a result of his consciousness of Russian history and his personal role as an updated tsar-turned-commissar, he therefore was aware of the long, positive tradition in cooperative American-Russian relations. This "nationalistic" awareness on Stalin's part seems to have in a sense abetted the Soviet leader in pursuing an alliance with America and the West, if an often-stressed one, before and during World War II. Of course, the factor of sheer desperation was primary in Stalin's mind after June 22, 1941.

By playing on Russo-American traditions of cooperation, Stalin was, above all, able to win American favor. This paid off in the dispensing of Lend-Lease aid and monetary credits to the USSR during and after the war. It could also be used as a diversionary tactic by the Soviet dictator to get his way when it came to the territorial giveaways—e.g., at the Yalta Conference of 1945. Playing upon FDR's sympathies was one example of this.

Did they also perhaps discuss extending such aid to the Hammer's favorite country, the USSR? Peter Niblo, author and former

9

Nazi-Soviet Pacts and Aftermath

"The ideological contradictions between National Socialist Germany and the Soviet Union were in past years the sole reason Germany and the USSR stood opposed to each other in two separate and hostile camps. The developments of the recent period seem to show that differing world outlooks do not prohibit a reasonable relationship between two states, and the restoration of cooperation of a new and friendly type."

—*German Foreign Minister Ribbentrop*

"The Reich government and the Soviet Government, judging from all experience, must count it as certain that the capitalistic Western Germany and of the USSR."

—*Ribbentrop*

With the partial opening of the archives of Soviet civilian, military, and security police authorities, the contents of the Orwellian memory hole, to which so many historical truths were committed in the Stalin period, began to be exhumed, with the result that wholesale revisionism has been sweeping through Russian historical science ever since. In this process, almost no stone has been left unturned. One of the great "white spots," as Russians call intentional omissions in the Soviet historical record, concerns Josef Stalin's intentions and plans during and after the signing of the crucial Nazi-Soviet agreements and secret protocols drawn up by Berlin and Moscow 70 years ago in August–September 2009.

CONTROVERSY OVER STALIN'S DEFENSE POLICIES

Despite the presence of documents, controversy still rages over the intent and meaning of the Ribbentrop-Molotov pacts of August–September 1939 and the two Berlin-Moscow trade deals that followed. Hitler's motives seem obvious: to put the USSR on hold and contented with receiving spheres of influence at its borders as Germany turned westward. Yet Stalin's motives are not all that clear.

One school of thought follows the conventional line that has dominated history books in the USSR and abroad, at least up until recently. This point of view, namely, is that Stalin's military policy from 1939 until the German invasion of the Soviet Union on June 22, 1941, was largely defensist. That is, Stalin had no aggressive or preemptive grand strategy in place vis-à-vis Germany or any other prospective capitalist enemy. The Soviet dictator intended merely to keep the USSR out of a world war, predicted as "inevitable" by Marxism-Leninism, as long as possible. In this way, the Soviets would have time to build up their defenses in the expectation of a coming global conflict that sooner or later would involve them as well.

Moreover, Stalin had also voiced the notion that it was "better to be attacked" than be perceived as the aggressor. This reflected Stalin's concern about the Soviet image abroad and the prospect of an eventual Soviet alliance with the "forces of good," the anti-Axis Western powers. To earn this status, obviously the Soviets would have to be perceived as being victims of German aggression, not the aggressors.

An alternative view is held today by some post-Soviet historians that seems related to evident nudging from the Putin-Medvedev government. This group of historians claims that Stalin is to be praised for having concluded a prewar "devil's pact" with Hitler, deceptive and immoral as it was. Only in this way could the USSR have time to prepare itself for the "inevitable": the coming war with Nazi Germany.[1]

Among such defensive moves, this school maintains, were the Soviet territorial acquisitions of 1939–1940. These included half of Poland, all of the Baltics, and geostrategic parts of Finland as well as northern Bukovina and Bessarabia bordering on the Romanian oil fields. Termed a "buffer zone" by some Russian and Western authors, these annexed territories were not the fruit, the writers maintain, of a deliberate Soviet expansionist policy. Rather, the annexations added up to protective measures "wisely" taken by Stalin against the day of a German invasion. That they remained parts of the USSR after 1945 is deemed irrelevant or is rationalized by some historians in two ways: (1) as security against some future invasion from a hostile West; (2) as territories rightfully integral parts of "Russia" and whose "legal" union with imperial Russia dates back centuries, were sanctioned by treaty, and are thus expressions of international law.[2]

The Molotov-Ribbentrop pacts were of course violated by the German invasion of June 22, 1941. Thus, critics of these deals of 1939 claim that Hitler had merely misled Stalin.

Soviet and post-Soviet historiography thus views the German invasion as an unforgivable "double-cross" (*perelom*) since by initiating war and taking the Soviets by surprise, Hitler had torn up the 1939 pacts. Against this are aligned a few Russian historians, whose numbers appear to be growing in the RF, who do not agree that that the invasion had taken Stalin by surprise or that he had been tricked or outsmarted by the deals with Hitler. Stalin had not placed any faith in the German dictator. Nor can Stalin personally be blamed for the disastrous opening of the war on the Eastern Front, in which Soviet defenses buckled under the blitzkrieg onslaught. The blame lay with the Red Army commanders, in particular Zhukov and Timoshenko.[3] This tragedy did not occur, as alleged by many Russian and Western historians, because the Soviet dictator had foolishly allowed Soviet Russia to become a "sitting duck," a "dupe." Nor did Stalin ignore such warnings of an attack from his own, highly informed foreign intelligence as well as warnings of an imminent attack proffered by Roosevelt and Churchill. At least two of Stalin's most reliable agents had predicted the precise date of the invasion. Stalin, it appears to many historians, simply distrusted any such warnings by the Western powers, those duplicitous "Munich appeasers" who, it is alleged in past and contemporary Russian historiography, had refused serious Soviet overtures to build collective security guarantees against Axis expansionism. The Soviet leader, independently processing his own intelligence inputs in his own way, distrusted much of what his own agents were telling him in spring 1941.[4] This argument is challenged by such historians as Martirosyan, Verkhovsky-Tyrmos, and Yuri Zhukov.

Having pursued a policy of joining the League of Nations and defining and touting the principle of nonaggression and "collective security," Stalin, who at this stage in the mid-1930s thrust forward Maxim Litvinov to instrument this putatively peace-minded policy, sought seriously, it is alleged by some authors, to curtail Hitler. However, Stalin was frustrated in this "sincere endeavor," alleges this school of historians, by the reluctance of England and France to join in establishing collective security.[5] As Alvin Z. Rubinstein phrased it, "Ideologically derived on the part of England and France shaped the behavior of the Western leaders to a greater extent than they did Soviet policy."[6] Because of Western suspicions, indicated Rubenstein, who perhaps reflected a consensus among historians, the Franco-British Munich appeasement policy evolved into abandonment of the Soviet's principal east European ally, Czechoslovakia, and with it the abandonment of the Soviet pursuit of collective security.

As noted earlier, Litvinov, a symbol of respectable collective security, was abandoned by Stalin as an outdated talisman in early 1939 when the rigid, orthodox close aide to Stalin, Molotov, took over foreign affairs. As Molotov purged the foreign ministry of Litvinovites, the formerly useful commissar went into political hibernation until his reappearance in the summer of 1941. This was when Stalin installed him as ambassador to the United States as the wartime "strange alliance" got under way.

With Molotov in charge, it was perceived by some observers that the Soviets would now look out for themselves and pursue bare-knuckled realpolitik, but always in the name of defense. Yet this appears to be what Stalin had been pursuing all along. In Marxist terms, the "content" of Soviet policy was the same, only the "form"—i.e., Litvinov to Molotov—had changed.

In contrast to the above lines of argument in its several versions, a second, or "offensist," school finds support among a small group of Russian as well as Western historians. This group claims that Stalin all along was plotting an offensive war of his own—above all, against Germany. Ultimately, Stalin was planning to extend his "preemptive" or "preventive" war against all of "capitalist-imperialist" Europe. As Molotov dictated to Chuev in his memoirs, referring to Stalin's view of three world wars: "Stalin looked at it this way. World War I has wrested one country from capitalist slavery. World War II has created a socialist system. A third world war will finish off imperialism forever."[7]

SPECIFICS OF NAZI-SOVIET PACTS AND PROTOCOLS

When the two sides got down to business in August, amid friendly toasts and extravagant ceremonies staged by the Soviets for the visiting German emissary, Joachim von Ribbentrop, two major agreements with their secret protocols followed.

The Treaty of Nonaggression, known as the Nonaggression Pact, was signed on August 23, 1939. By its terms, each side pledged not to attack or support an attack against and not to ally itself with any group of powers directed against the other contracting party. Each promised to consult the other on all questions of common interest. A secret protocol was attached to the pact that established the northern boundary for Lithuania, an independent, sovereign state, so that German and Soviet spheres of influence would be divvied up between the two powers. Likewise with sovereign, independent Poland, its boundary was redrawn so that its western half at the rivers Narew, Vistula, and San would fall to Germany while the eastern portion would fall to the Soviets—details of which were to be settled later "by friendly agreement." Germany declared her "disinterestedness" in the Soviet demand that Bessarabia fall under Soviet "influence" but had not intended that the Soviets would usurp Lithuania as they did in August 1940. (Between August 4 and 6, Lithuania, Latvia, and Estonia, respectively, became the fourteenth, fifteenth, and sixteenth union republics.)

By the Soviet-German trade agreement signed on August 19, then augmented and reaffirmed on August 29, two days later the Wehrmacht invaded Poland. Soon the Germans were receiving oil, phosphate, food, platinum, and other raw materials from the USSR in exchange for German machines, machine tools, and munitions. More than 50 percent of Soviet foreign trade at this time was with Nazi Germany.

By September 6, foreign observers noticed a diametrical shift in Soviet propaganda. It began to assume to a friendly, pro-German stance while the Western powers, England and France, Czechoslovakia, et al., were scorned in the Soviet press. Later, when the German army triumphantly entered the Polish capital of Warsaw, Moscow sent its hearty congratulations to Berlin.

On September 9, the Kremlin indicated that Soviet military action against Poland would begin in "several days." On September 14, Molotov asked Berlin to clarify when exactly they thought Warsaw would fall and Poland would collapse so that Moscow could say that Russian minorities would be "protected." Then on September 16, Molotov stated that Soviet military action in eastern Poland was "imminent."

On September 17, Stalin announced that the Red Army would cross the Polish frontier that day. It did, occupying its (larger) half of Poland, which boundary, as we noted, was jointly drawn to Soviet advantage west of the Curzon Line. On September 20, Molotov proposed that the Soviet Union and Germany should finalize their joint Soviet-German destruction and occupation of Poland, or the "Polish settlement," as they termed it euphemistically, respecting the former Polish state that was now moribund. On October 1, 1939, Stalin sent Hitler a congratulatory telegram in which he stated: "The friendship of Germany and the Soviet Union, sealed in blood, has the necessary foundation upon which to become long-term and solid." In remarks to members of the Comintern on September 7, 1939, and in his address to the Politburo on the same day, Stalin observed with typical *sang-froid:*[8]

> "The war that is going on between the two groups of capitalist countries—namely, the poor ones versus the rich ones for colonies, sources of raw materials, etc.—is for the redivision of the world, for world domination! We have no objection if they fight very hard and weaken one another.
>
> "It's not bad at all if at the hands of Germany the wealthiest capitalist countries are shattered and the capitalist system undermined. . . . We can maneuver and instigate one against the other so that they can fight against each other all the better. The nonaggression pact [with Germany] to a degree helps Germany. But at the next moment it instigates one against the other."

Thus followed on September 28 the second major Soviet-German agreement of 1939, the German-Soviet Boundary and Friendship Treaty. As with the first pact, this one was accompanied by a secret protocol respecting the status of Lithuania and other matters. The protocol also affirmed joint Soviet-German suppression of any hostile "agitation" within Polish society. This "suppression" took the usual harsh Soviet and German forms. The Katyn Forest massacre of Polish officers by the Soviet NKVD troops was one such example. Like the very existence of the secret Nazi-Soviet protocols, the Katyn massacre was vehemently denied by Soviet authorities (as well as by foreign fellow-travelers) right up to and including the Gorbachev period after 1984.

An apparently major spin-off for the Germans from the secret protocols was use of a northern naval base on Soviet territory near Murmansk. Known as Basis Nord, the Germans were given the right to use the base facilities for their surface naval ships and submarines. As a specialist on Hitler's northern war observed, "the securing of a Soviet base illustrated the ability of the Germans and Soviets to work together in accordance with the secret protocols and to labor toward the implementation of their cozy agreement—the division of Europe."[9]

Other cooperative Soviet-German talks and agreements followed in late 1939 and early 1940. The most important of these was the

German-Soviet Commercial Agreement signed in Moscow on February 11, 1940. By this deal, the Soviets were to ship billions of reichsmarks' worth of war-related materials and goods to the Germans. These were freighted to Brest-Litovsk- and then offloaded from the wide-gauge Soviet railroad cars to freight cars on the narrower-gauge tracks and hauled west to Germany. In the first 18 months following the signing of this important agreement, the following were shipped to the Germans:

- 1 million tons of grain for cattle plus legumes valued at 120 million reichsmarks
- 900,000 tons of mineral oil coasting about 115 million reichsmarks
- 200,000 tons of cotton costing approximately 90 million reichmarks
- 500,000 tons of phosphates
- 100,000 tons of chrome ore
- 500,000 tons of iron ores
- 300,000 tons of scrap metal and pig iron
- 2,000 kg of platinum
- Manganese ore, metals, lumber, rubber, and numerous other raw materials, including especially grain

In addition, the Russians granted Germany the right of transit for German traffic to and from Romania, Iran, Afghanistan, and other countries of the Near and Far East. Russian freight rates for any food-stuffs purchased by the Germans from Manchukuo (under Japanese occupation) were reduced by 50 percent.

The goods received in return by the USSR from Germany as part of the trade deal did not substantially enhance the Soviets' defense posture. One such example was the German "gift" of the unfinished German battle cruiser, the *Lutzow* (whose design resembled that of the *Bismarck*). It had been towed through the Baltic Sea and Gulf of Finland to Leningrad. The work on the cruiser by German engineers assigned to the project continued for more than a year until it was "interrupted" by the German attack of June 22, 1941. By the end of the war in 1945, the unfinished hulk of this German ship lay on the bottom of the gulf near Leningrad.

CARVING UP THE WORLD

One of the most intriguing but also exaggerated aspects of the Nazi-Soviet negotiations and discussions during 1940 concerned those that revolved about joint German-Soviet "dividing up of the world" between

Germany and the USSR into zones of influence. Such vast concepts became part of the "geopolitical" discussions that took place between Molotov and Ribbentrop in Berlin in November 1940. The deception in such talks on the German Foreign Minister's part only became known later. (For instance, on November 12, 1940, Hitler had issued his secret Instruction No. 18 to prepare for war in the east "irrespective of the results yielded by these discussions [with Molotov in Berlin].")

After the war, the secret documents showed that Hitler had made a decision already in July 1940 to plan an attack on the USSR (originally scheduled for May 1941). Ribbentrop himself had been let in on this decision. Yet here was the deceptive former wine salesman presenting Molotov with a spurious invitation to join the Axis that by then also included Japan. Upon the German invitation, the Soviets, seemingly to "cooperate" with Hitler, proceeded to proffer a draft of a proposal for such a joint Soviet-Nazi redivision of the world. By its terms, the USSR would become a formal ally of the three other Axis powers (i.e., the concept of Quadpartite Axis); Moscow proposed that this could become an additional "secret protocol."

In the Soviet draft of this protocol that was—allegedly—to become part of a large Nazi-Soviet global carve-up—at least as Hitler disingenuously presented it and as Stalin, equally disingenuously, received it—stated that Soviet "territorial aspirations center south of the national territory of the Soviet Union in the direction of the Indian Ocean." Later this was refined by both the sides to read in the concluding phrase ". . . south of Batum and Baku in the general direction of the Persian Gulf."

Alas, as he sat down for discussions with the German dictator, Molotov blithely ignored the idea of such an alliance with the Axis. Instead, in somber Berlin in mid-November 1940, with British bombing raids being carried out over Berlin, the Soviet commissar of foreign affairs, acting on orders from Stalin, ignored all talk of Soviet membership in the Axis and, instead, bluntly made demands on Hitler that the fuehrer had no intention of yielding to. But at least Molotov had got his point across. Namely, Russia was now making fresh demands to convert the whole of southeastern Europe, into which the Germans had been making inroads towards the end of 1940, into a Soviet sphere of influence! Molotov also queried Hitler on Berlin's growing amity with Finland, the old war fighting enemy of the Soviets and a potentially full-fledged ally of Germany.

The Germans were stunned by Molotov's candor. The visit had been bumpy.

NEW TENSIONS

Of course, an agreement for forming a Quadpartite Pact that would include the Axis powers and Soviet Russia never materialized. Again, "chestnuts"; Stalin had no intention of hitching the Soviet wagon to the Wehrmacht's panzerwaggens. Instead of deepening the August 1939 Nazi-Soviet friendship, Stalin's new, barbed Soviet demands and show of suspicion via Molotov only strengthened Hitler's resolve to go ahead and refine Operation Barbarossa. Molotov's demands especially concerned the Balkans and his stipulation that Bulgaria should be part of the Soviet security sphere despite Hitler's plans to convert that geostrategic country into a German satellite. Molotov had added that a Soviet military base should be built at the Dardanelles. Both Italy and Germany, Molotov had demanded, should assist the Soviet Union in realizing its goals in the Balkans and at the Straits, especially if Turkey should resist Soviet pressures toward the latter. Hitler had every reason to expect that as soon as their present wishes were granted by Berlin, which in any case was out of the question, Stalin would likely make even more demands that would interfere with the fuehrer's expansionist plans, not to mention his plans to attack the USSR. Molotov's further extravagant claims amounted to a virtual encircling movement extending from Poland south to the Balkans.

Meantime, Georgi Dimitrov had recorded in his diary on November 25 that Molotov had revealingly remarked to him, upon the latter's return from Berlin: "Our relations with the Germans look lively but there exist serious differences between us. . . . We are pursuing a course of demoralizing the German troops that are occupying the various countries. But we're going about this without shouting about it."

To which Dimitrov responded, "But won't this interfere with Soviet policy [toward Germany]?" Molotov replied: "Of course. But it must be done anyway. We wouldn't be Communists if we didn't follow such a course. It's only that it must be done quietly."

In aggravating relations in this way with Nazi Germany, Stalin may have also perceived that his potential enemy had entered a difficult phase in the post-May 1940 period by occupying part of France and coping with British military pressure in North Africa, the Balkans, and the Mediterranean, and the advent of U.S. military aid to Britain in the form of Lend-Lease. It appeared that by the autumn of 1940, Nazi Germany for all intents and purposes had reached the pinnacle of its expansionist power. As perceived by Moscow, Hitler now had to face a downhill peril in the form of a strengthened Britain and the looming danger from America. "Interventionist" Roosevelt's reelection in November 1940 and the defeat of the putative "peace monger," Wendell Willie, only underlined this ominous future facing Germany—but notably not the Soviet Union.

In retrospect, it appears that by 1940, both sides were aware of the other's ultimate war plans and the potential for a head-on clash between the two powers. As the new archival documents in Russia now show, Stalin, perhaps by mid-1940, was already onto Hitler's *Drang nach Osten* war plans. Yet he may have thought, at least in 1940 but not by early 1941, that the Germans would not launch their attack against the USSR until they had defeated England in the ongoing air battle and possible landing assault against it (Operation Sea Lion).

Stalin apparently became aware that Sea Lion had been canceled despite German disinformation that the plans for the cross-Channel invasion were going ahead. German actions in Finland, moreover, were alarming to Moscow. When the Soviets exerted political pressure to gain control of Finland's nickel production (the Germans had contracted to purchase 75 percent of the yield), Hitler then deployed elite mountain troops to the nickel mines at Petsamo. After the Red Army occupied Bessarabia, Hitler signed a treaty with Bucharest in August that promised protection of Romania (headed at that time by the pro-Nazi Antonescu regime) "from aggression." Some Soviet-German "friendship"!

On the German side, plans proceeded on Barbarossa. However, because of faulty military intelligence and its overestimation of the debilitating effects of the military purges in the USSR of 1937–1938, Hitler and his military-intelligence services had grossly underestimated overall Soviet strength, especially the Soviets' capacity to produce large numbers of reserves so as to accelerate production of advanced weaponry such as the T-74 and KV tanks and the Katyusha rocket-firing artillery.

One of the first history textbooks to appear in the post-Soviet period again harped on the more conventional line on the run-up to the signing of the Nazi-Soviet pacts of the spring and summer of 1939 and anticipated the new line that appeared at the end of 2009. The collegium of authors of this particular text, in fact, placed the blame on those two Western countries for the failure to reach common ground with England and France on collective security arrangements with the USSR to oppose Hitler's expansionism. This interpretation in turn suggested that Stalin had no other choice but to unite pro tem with Germany since the USSR would be left alone to face an armed-to-the-teeth Nazi Germany as the West looked the other way or even relished the Soviets' predicament.[10]

This textbook introduces events of this period in somewhat non-Soviet fashion as follows:

> The prospect of a future war led the Soviet leadership to mobilize domestic resources for the rapid building of heavy industry and a well-developed military-industrial complex, which in turn further led to a harsher regime in the country. . . . As a result of the Bolshevik victory in Russia stabilizing the post-World War I correlation of forces in the international arena could not take place. . . . The rise of totalitarianism in both Russia and Germany signified their joint rejection of universal human values. . . . They became "genetically" united.

Continuing in this vein, the authors allege that the 1938 Munich appeasement policy of France and England, the passive "wait-and-see attitude" toward Hitler's Germany assumed by both countries, and "above all, their attempt to use Germany against the Bolshevik threat merely increased Hitler's appetite. . . . Munich was a gigantic miscalculation on the part of Western diplomacy and opened the door to military expansion of fascism, bringing nearer the beginning of a 'big war' in Europe."

The Russian historians, writing in the early 1990s, then claim that, given the appeasement policy and the West's rejection of Soviet proposals for collective security, "a great change" in Soviet policy perforce resulted "as Maxim Litvinov was dismissed in favor of V. M. Molotov as Commissar of Foreign Affairs." (Note that Stalin is not mentioned.)

Another textbook reviews, in objective fashion and without editorial comment, the contents, including the secret protocols, of the Nazi-Soviet agreements of late 1939.[11] The book makes no value judgment; it simply reports the seizure of territory by the USSR (Poland, the Baltic countries, et al.) under terms of the agreements and their protocols. Nor does the text make any reference to Soviet-German discussions of 1940 for dividing up regions of the world into zones of influence, German and Soviet. Instead, it mentions only that the *Axis* powers sought to "carve up the world."

* * *

Although the Nazi-Soviet agreements shook the world, a few astute observers were taken by surprise at the time. Some officials in Britain actually worried over the likelihood of such an alliance. Perhaps they were aware of that long tradition of Russian and particularly Lenin's own admiration of Germany.

In retrospect, it seems that London (and certainly not Washington, which had no leverage at all with the Kremlin) could not have prevented this Moscow-Berlin alliance—to be activated in war, present, and future—no matter how forthcoming and accommodating the British were toward the Soviets in the spring and summer of 1939. In any case, there was precious little of that given democratic Britain's and its establishment's scorn for Soviet Communism.

Moreover, it seems to this author to be untenable to allege meta-historically that if London had been more accommodating toward the Kremlin during the negotiations in 1939 prior to the first Soviet-German pact of August, Stalin could have been "enticed" away from his tilt toward Nazi Germany. There were too many impediments for that to happen, not the least being Stalin's own scorn for and suspicions toward the British.

It is even possible to argue, as some Russian and Western researchers and historians have, that Soviet talks with British envoys in Moscow were a mere Soviet game, a ploy or "inducement" to goad Hitler into coming to terms with Moscow in ways, as we saw, that were extremely favorable to the latter—at least in the short term. Even in the long term, by these agreements Stalin had won large amounts of territory from the Baltic south to the borders of Romania that were to become part of the large bloc of post-World War II captive nations known as the central, east, and southeast European "People's Democracies" along with the permanently established Soviet republics of Estonia, Latvia, and Lithuania.

It could be said that Stalin had, indeed, honored the famous "behest" made in his funeral oration over Lenin's bier in January 1924 to carry Soviet-style revolution abroad. In his memoirs, Stalin's number one aide, Molotov, remarked to his interviewer, Feliks Chuev, that Stalin, to be sure, hadn't done too badly in this respect.

Statements, secret or open, made by leading officials and the Soviets' own military planning all point in this offensist direction, or so it is claimed by these historians. This offensism allegedly includes Stalin's secret speech to military graduates on May 5, 1941, that rattled with offensive sabers; two successive, pre-June 1941 Red Army field manuals that contained mainly offensist principles rather than defensive ones; and a significant military strategy paper addressed to Stalin on May 15, 1941, by the Red Army's topmost senior officers (Vasilievsky, Timoshenko, and Zhukov) that advocated preemptive war (see chapter 10).

The defensists counter that there is no proof Stalin ever saw this document. Such plans were often drawn up by staff officers, such as the one of May 15 roughed out in pen and ink and that wound up among the private papers of Vasilievsky. The document may, in fact, never have reached Stalin's desk. At least, there is no record that it had.

On the ideological front, the revisionists of the "preventive war" persuasion refer back to Lenin's "Report on Peace" of November 8, 1917. The Soviet leader had then called on the Western "laboring and exploited masses" to end their nations' participation in war (World War I) and, following the Soviet example, "emancipate" themselves "from all forms of slavery and exploitation." The socialist "new order," Lenin continued, "will not be bound by treaties." We have "lit the torch of world revolution," he wrote in the draft of the first post-1917 Program of the Russian Communist Party (Bolsheviks). The Soviets will "carry the revolution into the most advanced countries and in general into all countries." In a speech on March 7, 1918, Lenin declared: "History marches forward on the basis of liberation wars." The revisionists claim that such Leninist principles were never abandoned, especially not by the allegedly "true Leninist" Stalin.

All this is denied, of course, by Martirosyan and other historians. They defend Stalin as a nationalist-minded leader who had, in fact, broken with the Comintern tradition of hurrah-revolutionism in favor of defending Soviet—that is, Russian—*state* interests.

By contrast, the offensist revisionists further note that with the establishment of the Comintern in 1919, Lenin's long-nurtured dream of fostering global sovietization was finally realized. Soon Soviet diplomacy was running, as we have noted above, on its "two tracks." Perhaps a better analogy for the twofold, if not duplicitous nature of Soviet foreign policy and behavior in the international arena, according to the anti-Stalin/preventive war revisionists, would be an iceberg. The visible portion consisted of "legalistic" diplomacy, talk of "peaceful cohabitation" (later termed "peaceful coexistence") for the purpose of gaining time and misleading the "deaf, dumb, and blind" enemy and enhancing Soviet power worldwide while also, tangentially, abetting the global revolutionary cause of sovietization. The larger, submerged portion of the iceberg consisted of global subversion via legal and/or illegal Communist parties organized within countries throughout the world. These fifth-column forces infiltrated all layers of society in the given capitalist or Third World countries and served, to use Stalin's later phrase of 1952, as international "shock brigades."

As to the mid-1930s collective security gambit assigned by Stalin to the allegedly moderate Foreign Affairs Commissar Maxim Litvinov, the offensist revisionists claim that this was merely a diversion on the dictator's part to frighten Germany into striking a deal with Moscow. The latter was at all times only pretending to be closing ranks with the Western capitalist states. Indeed, Stalin aborted all such discussions with Western diplomats (during the talks with them, he had secretly passed on transcriptions of the negotiations to Berlin) as soon as a deal with Nazis was in the works. It should be added that the 10-year experience in Soviet-German military collaboration from the 1920s to the early 1930s was followed by a period of abundant bilateral trade between Germany and the USSR. German economic assistance to the industrialization of Soviet Russia under Stalin, in fact, was in some respects more significant than that of the United States, despite the latter's help in building railroads, the Dnepropetrovsk dam, Soviet tractor and textile factories, and so on. Between 1921 and 1938, Germany exported to Russia more than $2 billion in commodities; the United States, $1.4 billion.

Later, of course, by the August–September 1939 secret protocols and other agreements, Soviet raw materials—oil, grain, cotton, chrome, iron, etc., that by the special agreement of 1940 were to total more than 3 million tons—were shipped to Germany on schedule. Supposedly, they were "used in the war" against the Western Allies.

However, the true importance of this Soviet trade with Germany is questionable. Germany, on its own and by exploiting conquered countries, proved that it was quite self-sufficient in producing the types of goods necessary for maintaining total war. These goods included war-related fuel. Note that the Germans amply imported synthetic gasoline or oil from Romania as well as from some Western countries, neglecting what was imported from the USSR under the post-August 1939 trade deals. Moreover, these agreements were one-sided in the way they were fulfilled. For their part, the Germans failed to live up to their half of the bargain by neglecting to deliver finished aircraft and other weapons for Soviet study. Stalin, of course, was aware of this shortfall but continued with ostentatious trade relations with Nazi Germany anyway. Also, the Soviets appeared to be exporting certain raw materials that were expendable (to them as well as to Germany) largely for show in the knowledge that these exports were not really all that essential to the German war machine. As Moscow knew, the latter was well supplied with what it needed from occupied countries in *Festung Europa* as well as by imports from Latin America and elsewhere. Even

U.S. oil companies were still doing business with Germany into 1941. Note, too, that Germany fought three more critical years of intense war in Russia without once suffering a shortage of fuel, food grains, strategic metals, etc., although all such shipments from Soviet Russia, of course, ceased after the end of June 1941.

For their part, the traditional defensists insist that Germany notwithstanding, Stalin was serious about collective security. However, he suspected that the British and French were not. Moreover, he seems to have believed that an appeasement policy, perhaps eventually becoming an anti-Soviet alliance with the Axis, was a more likely decision to be made by London and Paris than agreeing to serious collective security arrangements with the USSR. Hence, Stalin's resort to a deal with Berlin.

On the other hand, Sudoplatov, a top aide to Beria of the NKVD, wrote in his memoirs, *Special Tasks*, of the crucial importance of the Stalin deal with Hitler against the background of Soviet achievement of the status of the Soviet Union as a great power. "Although originally this [expansionist] concept was ideological in nature, it acquired the dimensions of Realpolitik. This possibility arose for the Soviet Union only after the Molotov-Ribbentrop Pact was signed [in August 1939]. In the secret protocols, the Soviet Union's geopolitical interests and natural desires for the enlargement of its frontiers were for the first time formally accepted by one of the leading powers of the world."

This clutch of offensist historians further maintains that Stalin made his pacts with Hitler in the hope that war would be encouraged and with it revolution. Stalin, it is alleged, relished—indeed, encouraged—German expansionism westward against France, the Lowlands, and Britain. The Soviet leader, it is claimed, hoped to see all of the capitalist combatants self-destruct, as he indeed indicated to Comintern chief Georgi Dimitrov in September 1939. Meanwhile, it is alleged by some writers of this school that Stalin planned to launch a preemptive war against Germany that was to begin either by July 1941 (a minority view) or at the latest by mid-1942. The Red Army would sweep clear through Europe, meeting the rebellious masses as it carried the red banner westward. In 1939 and in 1940–1941, these Russian historians note that several of Stalin's closest hard-line aides—Molotov, Zhdanov, Mekhlis, and Shcherbakov—spoke assuredly of "extending the frontiers of socialism" on the wings of the "inevitable" coming war. Wilhelm Pieck, the German Communist leader, predicted the following in his notes from an information meeting in Moscow on February 21, 1941:[12]

On the other hand, defensists and a majority of Western and Russian historians respond to the above arguments by insisting that such revolutionary-sounding phrases from the top Soviet leaders were little more than braggadocio, or as Russians say, *vranyo*. Purported sovietization of all of Europe was pie-in-the-sky mumbo-jumbo intended as grist for party zealots. Were this pan-European sovietization on the tips of bayonets actually true of Soviet designs, it is claimed, the Soviet Army in 1945 would simply have continued marching west beyond Berlin and Prague in 1945. Why not? Stalin, after all, was aware of the pledge by the Western Allies, particularly by the Americans, that they would withdraw their troops from the European theater as soon as possible. Defensists further contend that this offensist-revisionist line is in essence "pro-Nazi" and a favored argument by those who tend to believe Hitler was partly right in attacking the USSR, the far "more evil" entity. Nor is the offensist position supported by hard, convincing evidence. Interestingly, putative Soviet offensism and an imminent Soviet-launched preemptive war is the same argument that was employed by Hitler—namely, that Operation Barbarossa was necessary because Stalin was planning an imminent attack.

With the above in mind, these questions arise: What about the immediate pre-June 22, 1941, period? What kinds of military defensive—or offensive—measures did Stalin actually undertake? These could be tangible hints of what the Soviet dictator was planning vis-à-vis Germany.

It may be asked of the offensist school how far was Stalin prepared to go, and how soon, in order to wink at or least of all assume the initiative in unleashing a second world war, assuming that that was his plan to gain in the early 1940s world domination.

As seen in the discussion in the next chapter, arguing against the offensist interpretation is evidence that Stalin, on the contrary, appeared to have worried over the Red Army's lack of preparedness to wage such a war, *even defensively*, right up until June 1941. Defensists of various stripes dismiss this offensist interpretation by claiming that Stalin harbored no such vast plans, that there is no convincing proof that he did. In fact, Stalin had placed Cominternism at a very low rung of Soviet priorities and was too realistic to engage in reckless adventurism. In the epilogue in chapter 12, we canvas Stalin's post-World War II policies and actions against the backdrop of the Cold War and what looked to many analysts and Western policymakers like a serious Stalin plan to keep expanding Soviet power, even to the extent of risking if not unleashing World War III.

GAINING TERRITORY BY THE PACTS

Meanwhile, the defensist school does not subscribe to the theory that Stalin wished, as some of his aides frankly stated, that the capitalist-imperialist Western powers, whether democratic or Fascist, would mutually destroy themselves. Nor do the defensists canvas or dismiss as fact the tactic explicitly advocated by Lenin and Stalin that the Soviets should encourage as much as possible tensions and "contradictions" between rival capitalist-imperialist powers, even to the point of egging them into fratricidal wars.

By the terms of the Nazi-Soviet pacts and the protocols of August–September 1939, plus the unilateral Soviet moves to gain territory for itself in 1940, the Soviets acquired a buffer zone in the Baltic countries, northern Bukovina, and Bessarabia. This was intended, it is argued, merely to provide a quantum of space and time for the Soviets to continue their defensive buildup. Moreover, by means of the Soviet-Finnish War, in the winter of 1939–1940, the Soviets acquired additional "protection" in the form of acquiring geostrategic territory at Finland's expense on the Soviet northern frontier—but resorting to war only after protracted diplomatic negotiations with Helsinki failed to budge the Finnish leadership, which in any case seemed to lean more toward Berlin than Moscow. Later Stalin demanded all of Bukovina but in discussions with the Germans he had agreed to Soviet incorporation only of the northern portion, which had once been part of the tsarist empire.

To the defensist historians as well as to the new crop of Stalin apologists, these acquisitions of 1940 are not viewed as outright expansion by Soviet Russia. For his part, Martirosyan argues that Finland was only disputably an independent country, that by treaty it had been part of the Russian Empire. The intransigence shown by the leader in Helsinki to prolonged, "patient" Soviet requests for grants of rights to leased use of Finnish bases and small amounts of its territory to defend itself in a coming war were summarily dismissed by the Finns. To gain these geostrategic bases (allowing direct Soviet naval access to the Baltic Sea), the historian argues, Moscow was "obliged" to use force in December 1939 that started the three-month Finno-Soviet Winter War.

The debate over just what Stalin was planning in 1939–1941 is more than an academic exercise. A new generation of Russian youth now has new secondary school textbooks in their hands. This writer has examined several of these histories and finds that, for the most part, Communist propaganda about events and domestic and foreign policy under Lenin and Stalin and their successors from 1917 to 1991 has been purged. Yet some lingers on. In the name of historical truth as well as the therapeutic uses of exposing and condemning past Communist behavior, it is crucial to fill the "white spots" in the Soviet record.

The Communists are still extremely active in today's Russia. And, ominously, they still refuse in many ways to recognize their party's past mistakes, lies, and inhumanity. Even Mikhail Gorbachev, in the heyday of glasnost, stubbornly refused to acknowledge the very existence of the 1939 secret protocols

When this war ended amid the usual postwar calls for "no more wars," Stalin and the Soviet Union resumed the pursuit of Soviet expansionism approximately where it had left off before June 1941. The "buffer" territory that had been seized by the Soviets to the west of its frontiers in 1940—deemed by Moscow and fellow-travelers abroad merely as insurance in order to absorb any future German attack— was incorporated into the USSR. It became permanently sovietized as a part of the ever-expanding Soviet empire. Then began a period of additional expansion and determined sovietization in eastern, central, and southeastern Europe as the Soviets created a half-dozen client states, or "satellites," immediately to its west.

In other words, another "struggle," to use the Soviet term, had begun. This one was a cold one but a Cold War with very hot overtones and violent episodes, such as the Soviet-supported proxy conflicts fought on the Korean and Vietnamese peninsulas in the 1950s and 1960s. More than 100 other conflicts, as tabulated in the 1970s by the Yugoslav paper, *Polytika*, were also part of the post-World War II landscape. All of these wars, the paper said, had a Marxist-Leninist edge to them.

To some observers, it seemed in retrospect that, as far as Stalin and the "lodestar" of Marxism-Leninism were concerned, World War II and the "strange alliance" in it of East and West against the common Axis foe had only been a passing interlude. It appeared that the Soviet dictator was serious when he remarked to the Yugoslav Communist aide, Milovan Djilas, in Moscow in 1946 that soon, as he put it, "we'll have another go at it." Meaning another "big war"—World War III—a war that, as Molotov said of the preceding big war in an interview in the 1980s, would further "extend socialism" worldwide.

10

Pre-Barbarossa War Plans

"Understanding the country's lack of preparation for war, Soviet leadership made efforts to give Germany no pretext for opening hostilities against the USSR and at any cost avoid war or at least delay it until 1942."

—A. I. Yurev, Newest History of Russia: February 1917
to the Beginning of the 21st Century (school textbook),
Giperborea, Moscow, 2010, p. 254.

"No, Stalin saw through it all. Stalin trusted Hitler? He didn't trust his own people! . . . He had a main goal—not to give Hitler a pretext for [starting the war]."

—V. M. Molotov, Molotov Remembers, pp. 23, 25.

June 22, 1941—Russia's December 7, 1941—is a day for Russians that will forever "live in infamy."

Sixty years ago, the Nazi armies, following Gens. Mannstein and Guderian's battle-tested blitzkrieg tactics and strategy applied so successfully against Poland in the autumn of 1939 and the Western Allies in 1940, juggernauted into the Soviet Union in massive strength before the first light of dawn. Within hours, the German and their allies' armies had advanced 30, 40, and 50 miles in various sectors along Russia's 1,800–2,000-mile western frontier.

How could it have happened that more than 160 Soviet divisions—infantry, cavalry, tank, and motorized—deployed for weeks along the USSR's long western border could be caught totally unawares by a huge invasion force?

On June 13, 1941, Soviet agent Richard Sorge, who was having an intimate affair with the wife of a top Japanese official through whom he gleaned a good deal of top secret information, informed the Kremlin that a German attack would be launched on June 22.

Sorge, to the NKVD in Moscow on May 19, 1941: "I repeat, 10 armies combined in 150 divisions will launch an offensive across a broad front."

Yet Stalin chose not to believe these and other such reports, some of which also reached him from London and Washington. The Soviets were even getting information from inside the German general staff close to which the Soviets had a mole named Starshina. Moreover, with the Enigma machine and the Ultra Deciphering machine, the British at Bletchley Hall were able to read German general staff communications traffic. They knew all about Operation Barbarossa. Yet Stalin reputedly thought that the British and Americans were only trying embroil the Soviets in a war with Nazi Germany. His own agents, he wished to believe, were being duped or were simply imagining things.

STALIN'S FIRST REACTIONS

Under Stalin's nose, some ominous things were happening. For instance, crates of diplomatic-staff members' personal belongings, including their pet hounds, were observed at the German embassy in Moscow being readied for air shipment out of the Soviet Union. This, too, was mentioned in Soviet intelligence reports passed to the top Soviet leadership. Trains carrying German military equipment, such as tanks and other vehicles, were observed rumbling east at various rail hubs in Eastern Europe.

Stalin, it is said, ignoring or ridiculing some of these intelligence reports, contented himself with thinking that the Germans would not attack. He based his assumptions on what appeared to him to be, it is claimed by some traditional historians, the general Soviet military advantage over any prospective enemy, in the west or the east, in the form of the mighty Soviet "deterrent"—as it existed, at any rate, on paper. Above all, the Soviet leader, it is claimed, continued to nurse the idea that Germany would not and could not prepare such an attack any time before 1942. Would the Germans fight a two-front war of the type Germany lost in World War I? They surely would not invade the USSR while still fighting England and planning on going with the German Operation Sea Lion of invading the island. Was Hitler so mad and adventurous that he thought he could take on a laterally extended country of 11 time zones, a military potentially capable of mobilizing upward of 10 million soldiers, and an economy capable of converting rapidly to a war footing?

Yet if this was Stalin's reasoning—and not all historians today go with this rather boiler plated interpretation—Stalin had obviously exaggerated Soviet military strength. Indeed, on the eve of the Nazi attack in mid-1941, Soviet Russia's military strength in some respects did look impressive. According to statistics published in Russia in 1995, the Soviets had 6 million soldiers under arms (not including a backup reserve of millions of conscripts of all ages), with an estimated all-told actual or potential 300 divisions of armed men with 120,000 artillery pieces and mines, 23,300 tanks, and 22,400 aircraft. Its planes outnumbered the Germans' two to one—10,000 to 11,000 Soviet military aircraft to 5,000 of the Luftwaffe, about half of which were deployed on the Eastern Front on the eve of the war.

Yet much of this equipment was obsolete, particularly the tanks. Impressive new weapons like the T-34 medium tank was not yet deployed in sufficient numbers to give the RKKA an advantage over the German panzers. Moreover, other new equipment, such as the heavy KV tank, was spread around the frontier too thinly as well as illogically by leaving gaps between the RKKA frontier-covering forces. Most units were left with arms of at least a decade-old vintage. True, by late spring, these forces had been augmented by an additional deployment of 800,000 Red Army troops brought up from rear positions to the western frontier. About two-thirds of this imposing force were positioned in several military districts (Kiev, Carpathian, and the southern fronts) directly abutting—dangerously, that is—the western frontier opposite the Wehrmacht formations. (We further examine this deployment in this chapter.)

Only 100,000 Soviet troops were directly on the border, most of whom were NKVD border guards. The rest of the troops covering the frontier, some 170 RKKA divisions, were mostly deployed at a distance of approximately 5 to 12 miles from the border (i.e., the first covering echelon with 56 divisions) while the second echelon, consisting of 52 divisions, was on line at a distance of from 30 to 60 miles from the border. Sixty-two divisions were deployed at a distance of some 250 miles.

EARLY GERMAN SUCCESSES

On their part, for Operation Barbarossa the Germans had assembled on their eastern front 19 German panzer and 15 motorized infantry divisions, some 3,350 tanks, 7,230 artillery pieces, and 2,770 combat aircraft. On the first day alone of the invasion, with such forces the Germans had destroyed 1,200 Soviet aircraft, 800 of which were destroyed on the ground. By the end of the first month of the war, of the 170 Soviet divisions by then deployed on the western front, 28 were destroyed while 70 more had lost half of their complement of soldiers and equipment. Considerable damage, nonetheless, was done to the Wehrmacht by the outclassed yet brave Red Army soldiers, who were caught in a German *kessel* (cauldron), or pocket in which RKKA units were surrounded. But the resistance and in some cases escape from the pockets were not enough to seriously blunt the German attack overall as the Wehrmacht drove east at a rapid rate.

The war, in fact, did not begin gradually to turn in the Soviet favor to any significant degree until after the successful defeat of the German assault on Moscow, or Operation Typhoon, during the period of December 1941 to January 1942. Some writers in the West single out the Battle of Stalingrad in early 1943 as the turning point in the war. Yet the above, earlier date is more accurate, and is acknowledged, for example, in the diary of German Army Gen. Franz Halder.

In the following four months since June 1941, the Germans had occupied more than 500,000 square miles of territory with a population of 74.5 million. By December 1941, killed or taken captive was a total of 7 million Soviet soldiers of which 4 million were POWs; desertions on the Soviet side numbered upward of a million men.

On the Soviet side, total losses in equipment during the six-month period were staggering: i.e., 22,000 Soviet tanks and upward of 25,000 aircraft were destroyed.

STALIN'S BEHAVIOR ON THE DRAMATIC DAY

According to the conventional version of the catastrophic events of that early Sunday morning, the zero hour itself of Operation Barbarossa had caught Stalin asleep in his dacha in Kuntsevo just outside Moscow.[1] The Soviet leader had returned to his "nearby" dacha, it is claimed, after an unusually tense, late-night session of Politburo in the Kremlin. The discussions that took place that fateful Saturday night, June 21–22, remain secret, although impending war was surely the main item on its agenda.

It was around 3 am on June 22 when Stalin, it is alleged, in his dacha, was awakened by his bodyguard, Lt.-Gen. Nikolai Vlasik (Stalin's

"Bormann") to answer an urgent telephone call. On the *Vertushka* (official phone line) was his right-hand man, Aleksandr Poskrebyshev, who broke to him the terrible news of extended armed conflict along the western frontier, including the bombing of major Soviet towns and cities.

Minutes later, Zhukov, then chief of the general staff, telephoned Stalin. According to Zhukov, who seems unclear as to exactly where Stalin was located, Stalin became nearly speechless over the line as Zhukov related briefly what was happening—to the best of Zhukov's knowledge under prevailing conditions of primitive communications—on Russia's exploding western front. Then Stalin, so continues this version of the story, immediately got on the phone to summon the Politburo to meet with him in immediate emergency session in the Kremlin. Vlasik drove him at top speed to the Kremlin in the leader's black, Packardlike ZIL limousine with its bulletproof windows along the widened highway specially used for official vehicles (and, as planned in the 1930s, broad enough to accommodate Soviet tanks).

As he sped along, writes the late Stalin biographer ex-Gen. Dmitri Volkogonov, who loathed the dictator, Stalin gazed out of the limousine windows "at the empty streets, unaware that German aircraft were already on their way to bomb Soviet towns and aerodromes." When he arrived at the Kremlin and was driven through the main Borovitsky Gate, ex-Gen. Volkogonov relates, Stalin went up to his office by the entrance reserved for him alone. Silent and somewhat cautiously, the members of the Politburo filed into Stalin's office. They were followed by Timoshenko and Zhukov. Without a word of greeting, Stalin said to no one in particular, "Get the German consul on the phone."

Molotov left the room. A tense silence descended. When he returned, all eyes were fixed on him. He went to his place at the table and with his speech impediment stammered out: "The ambassador [Schulenburg] reported that the German government has declared war on us." (Actually, no formal declaration of war was made, as Stalin and historians noted later.) He glanced at the piece of paper in his hand. "The formal reason is a standard one [reading]: 'Nationalist Germany had decided to forestall an attack by the Russians'" (Molotov omitted the word "Socialist" in the official German title). Ironically, this was similar to the pretext given by the Soviets when they attacked Finland on a Sunday in December 1939.

"Stalin sat down and looked at Molotov with angry eyes," Volkogonov continues, "as if he were remembering his [Stalin's] confident prediction six months earlier that Hitler would 'never wage war on two fronts," and that the USSR had plenty of time to strengthen its western defenses. Then some of the general officers were asked to report what they knew about the invasion. They did not have much to report; communications were inadequate, to say the least. But what they did report stunned everyone, above all Stalin.

According to Volkogonov, whose version is now doubted by historians such as Verkhovsky-Tyrmos and Martirosyan: "Stalin had never had so great a shock in his life. His confusion was obvious, as was his anger at having been so misled, and his fear before the unknown. The Politburo members remained with him in his office all day [on the 22nd], waiting for news from the border. They left the room only to make a phone call, have a cup of tea, or stretch their legs. They said little, hoping that the failures were only temporary. No one doubted that Hitler would receive a resounding rebuff."

Eventually, as more grim news poured in, Stalin certainly did begin to "understand." The first, cautious order sent to the commanders along the western border and to the Baltic fleet already engaging the enemy—Directive No. 1—was itself limited in the type of Red Army response it permitted. Still laboring under the notion that the Germans were not truly unleashing a war in the full, strategic sense along the whole frontier or was he being extra cautious in affirming for world public consumption that it was the Germans who attacked first,[2] Stalin directed: "Undertake no actions that could cause political complications [with Germany]." Some histories maintain, but without any convincing supporting evidence, that Stalin apparently thought that the conflict, even though already under way, could be settled peacefully. It was in any case a limited one allowing Germany only to gain some momentary advantage.

In spring 2000 on the fifty-fifth anniversary of the Soviet capture of Berlin, Gens. Kvashnin and Gareyev commented on this in an article published in the *Nezavisimaya Gazeta* weekly supplement, *Independent Military Review*: [This directive (of June 22, 1941)] disoriented the troops. If in actual fact the supreme commander himself did not know whether the country was in war or not, how would a regiment commander be able to conduct operations if he did not know what political consequences would follow?

Then began a period in which, for almost two weeks, Stalin kept himself out of view, or so the story goes and there is reason to doubt this version. Still, the visitor's log to Stalin's office, which was recently released from the archives, shows the Soviet leader in his office day after day after June 22, missing only about a couple of days, and then reemerging in the first days of July, his reappearance culminating in his major radio address of July 3 (see Appendix I for text).

For its part, the Politburo hoped Stalin would address the people, it is said in traditional summaries of Stalin's behavior at this time. Instead, the dictator, it is claimed, was "too stunned" or protective of his image to go before the public himself. In his place, he gave Vice Premier Vyacheslav Molotov the thankless task of explaining the disaster to the people and of spurring them into retaliation. In the Verkhovsky-Tyrmos version and as suggested by Sergo Beria, Stalin was very much in command of himself in those trying days, kept his cool, and was away from his office only briefly as he drafted his speech at his dacha on the Wehrmacht attack and the proposal for an East-West alliance to fight a popular-front war. In this adroitly cast speech, the Soviet leader addressed the whole Soviet people with an opening that unprecedentedly contained the address, ". . . brothers and sisters." Apparently, during the days of his being out of the public eye, Stalin pondered as to the best way to rally the people. Addressing them merely as "comrades" was not the way, although "comrades" did remain in part of his opening address. Adding the religious sounding *brat'ya i sestry*, "brothers and sisters," was a harbinger of further concessions to the citizens' religiosity that were to come (among them, the ringing of church bells, the refurbishing of the Orthodox Patriarchate, and the reopening of some churches).

Indeed, here the Soviet leader showed that he was not lacking in flexibility and political acumen. In a sense, his partly non-ideological form of address to his people at this crucial time provides a microscopic sample of Stalin's overall "strategic" elasticity of a type that can table ideology in favor of higher priorities. Stalin was capable of such "ideological suspensions" when the dire need to do so arose—as it indeed did on several occasions during his quarter-century reign.

By November 1941, Stalin was ready to give a newsreel appearance—reviewing a military parade, as was his custom, from atop the Lenin Mausoleum. The occasion was the twenty-fourth anniversary of the October Revolution accompanied by a military parade in Red Square, November 7, 1941. On that same day, the Red Army was battling the German Army less than 50 miles to the west and south of the Soviet capital. Under such dangerous circumstances, would the heavily protected Stalin take such a risk? What if a German Heinkel bomber . . . ?

As disclosed only recently, the ultra-security-conscious Stalin did not actually speak in Red Square as depicted in a newsreel at the time of the parade. Although he had appeared on Revolution Day even in the Moscow subway to deliver his annual address, his speech the next day, November 7, allegedly in Red Square was, in fact, later dubbed onto the footage shot of the parade in Red Square on that bitter-cold day. According to this story, the security-conscious Stalin had ordered the cameras to be set up later inside the Kremlin in order to stage the speech. Audiences watching the newsreel presumably did not notice that on this cold day the leader's breath did not show up on the screen as he stood reading his address—as it turned out, indoors.

Thus, on the preceding June 23, the stuttering (ironically, England's World War II monarch, King George VI, had the same speech defect) Molotov did what he could in his brittle, tenor voice to broadcast the address. Nearly everyone heard his shocking words. In those days, the Communist authorities had rigged up at almost every main intersection or meeting places in towns and villages across the USSR's ubiquitous indoor and outdoor loudspeakers. The address was aired several times.

As for Stalin himself, so the story goes (see the next section for the evolution of Russian historiography on Stalin's behavior), he continued to remain "secluded" for weeks. He would venture only haphazardly to the Kremlin, or he would stay in a house on Kirov Street in the capital, or sometimes he would stop over at general staff headquarters a few blocks away. Although there were as yet no air-raid shelters in Moscow—except for the intentionally deeply dug subways, of course—all official buildings were very closely guarded.

However, as exploding shells near the outskirts of the capital began to be audible (some detonating in Moscow itself) later in the summer of 1941, extensive protective measures were adopted. A special shelter was built for Stalin near his dacha. Also, evacuation measures were ready, if the need arose, to move Stalin and his entourage to safely distant Kuibyshev located 600 miles to the southeast of Moscow on a large loop of the Volga River.

So ran the standard version of Stalin's behavior and actions during those first hours, days, and weeks of the German invasion.

DEVELOPMENT OF HISTORIOGRAPHY ON STALIN'S REACTIONS

Before Nikita Khrushchev's secret speech to the Twentieth Communist Party Congress in Moscow in February 1956, Stalin's war preparations were officially described as having been "fully adequate" and to have been "exclusively defensive" (*sugubo oboronitel'niye*), not offensist. Soviet declaratory military doctrine and strategy, it was averred, was one merely of "active defense" (*aktivnaya oborona*). The party line was that Stalin had wanted peace as long as possible. At the same time, he built up the country's industries and defense capability for a war that he "wisely knew" would eventually—as he said, "inevitably"—come. It would be a war that would be foisted upon the USSR, certainly not an aggressive one launched on Soviet initiative.

In similar fashion immediately after World War II, Stalin was to order his civilian and military propagandists to describe what he called the long-standing Soviet defense policy's recognition of "permanently operating factors" in war. These boiled down to a Soviet policy of overt defensism based on the USSR's 11-time-zone-wide territory and its "peaceful aims" and intentions. Was this mere disingenuous hindsight?

Likewise, in this earlier, pre-1956 version, it was claimed in retrospect that by the Nazi-Soviet agreements of August–September 1939, Stalin and the military had wanted merely to "delay" the inevitable "big war" for as long as possible so as to be fully prepared when it finally did come. As it turned out, it *was* "postponed"—by a year and 10 months, as Stalin boasted in his first war speech on July 3, 1941. By the Germans' "perfidious" attack on June 22, Hitler had torn up these agreements, double-crossing Stalin by unexpectedly putting into action Operation Barbarossa—which had been first conceived by Hitler back in June 1940 if not foreshadowed in Hitler's 1920 "bible," *Mein Kampf*.

However, three years after Stalin's death in 1953, much of this boilerplated version of the events of 1941 began to be scrapped in part by the Communist Party and its corps of historians. With this came Khrushchev's secret "de-Stalinization" speech at the Twentieth Communist Party Congress in February 1956. He brought to light many alleged new facts (including, it should be noted, a number of Khrushchev distortions) about Stalin.

The late dictator was depicted by Khrushchev—one of whose aims was to tar some of his rival comrades with Stalinism, thus exonerating his own deep involvement in Stalin's crimes (especially in the purges of 1937–1939 in the Ukraine)—as not only genocidal and paranoic, but also as a self-glorifier who covered up his many costly policy mistakes before and during the war that had cost the lives of millions of soldiers and civilians. Many of the dictator's military decisions were fatally flawed, Khrushchev alleged. They were the product of a disordered mind. For instance, according to Khrushchev, to the horror of his top military commanders Stalin used a large globe instead of large-scale military maps to plot Red Army counteroffensives. (The suggestion here was that Stalin acted like Ivan the Terrible, as in Sergei Eisenstein's famous film of the late 1930s of the same name, in which the half-mad, bearded tsar is seen running his acquisitive fingers over an outsized globe as he planned his next conquests.)

However, by contrast, more credible information, based on later memoirs by retired soldiers and others, proposes that while Stalin interfered in battlefield decisions made in the first months of the war, by the later war years, he began gradually to defer more to the professional military—Zhukov, Shaposhnikov, Timoshenko, Vasilievsky, Rokossovsky, Vatutin, Yeremenko, et al. Their input was crucial when the commander in chief, Stalin, approved the soldiers' detailed combat decisions. However, in the earlier period of the war, many of the reckless, offensive operations, like many of Hitler's after 1941, were ill-conceived and needlessly costly in casualties. Stalin was largely responsible for approving if not himself initiating these ill-conceived early offensive operations.

According to Khrushchev, one of the Stalin-fostered fantasies grossly covered up the late dictator's utter lack of military acumen as well as his "actual" behavior on the eve of and after the German invasion on that fateful morning. In his narrative delivered at the Twentieth Party Congress in 1956 and in his taped memoirs after 1964, Khrushchev ridiculed the notion that Stalin had been a "genius" strategist. That after the Wehrmacht's surprise attack, he had risen bravely to the Nazi challenge, firmly taking the helm, ably leading the Soviet armed forces and people to ultimate victory. The truth, claimed Khrushchev, was just the opposite. There was no surprise at all—that is to say, not to Khrushchev and a few others—about an imminent German invasion. Only Stalin was duped, by himself. As Khrushchev put it, "Sparrows were chirping about it at every crossroad." Yet, he complained, Stalin had stubbornly refused to believe many of his own intelligence agents' reports that had crossed his Kremlin office desk prior to the attack. These reports, dozens of them, had warned of an approaching, full-scale Nazi invasion. Some warnings had come from Stalin's best foreign agents. Other reports came from official sources in the West, including a personal, secret message from Prime Minister Winston Churchill (who did not reveal his source of information—namely, the

Enigma machine that by means of the Ultra operation decoded messages of the German high command).

Stalin's highest military intelligence (GRU) officer, Lt.-Gen. Filipp I. Golikov (1900–1980), helped water down or otherwise discredit the most ominous reports before they reached Stalin. (Stalin, who centralized all sensitive functions within himself, had set up no "intelligence assessment" department—a department that was instituted in the Soviet Ministry of Defense only after his death.) Lavrenti Beria, head of the NKVD, also participated, it is said, in the discrediting of such reports. Most of this behavior by Golikov and Beria was motivated by sycophancy. On June 21, the day before the German invasion, Beria personally assured Stalin: ". . . I and my people [in the NKVD], Iosif Vissarionovich, firmly remember your wise instruction: Hitler will not attack us in 1941!"

When the attack occurred on June 22, Khrushchev had snarled, Stalin "fell to pieces." He was paralyzed by "nervousness and hysteria." He retreated in confusion to his dacha at Kuntsevo, claims Khrushchev, where, as some others claimed, he began drinking heavily. Hours after the invasion, he cowered when some Politburo members came to visit him at his suburban retreat. Stalin thought they were going to "arrest him," Khrushchev claimed. But Molotov, Malenkov, Beria, et al., had come to visit the dictator in order merely to plead with him to rise to leadership.

But Stalin was inconsolable. "We f***** up, all is lost," Stalin reportedly growled sullenly to the astonished Politburo squad.

Moreover, in these first days and weeks, Stalin immediately started wheels turning, according to ex-Gen. Dmitri Volkogonov, the post-Soviet biographer of Stalin, to work out a cowardly compromise with Hitler. This claim has never been convincingly verified and appears to be part of the de-Stalinization effort, according to this story, or fantasy, Stalin tried with this gimmick to halt the German invasion. In return in his suit for peace, Stalin would agree to hand over to the Germans all three Baltic Soviet republics, plus Moldavia as well as a large share of Ukrainian and Byelorussian territory already occupied by the invading Wehrmacht. Recent Russian sources vehemently deny the veracity of this "cave-in" story. A similar version of Stalin's "collapse" was put out in the officially cleansed and emasculated (under Brezhnev in the 1960s and 1970s) memoirs of Marshal Georgi Zhukov as well as by post-1956 Communist historians—at least up to the mid-1990s. The noted post-Soviet military historian, Volkogonov, hewed to this version in his 1991 biography of Stalin. However, present-day Communist and pro-Communist newspapers in Russia as well as some independent historians claim that Stalin was a dedicated Russophile and leader of the "Russian state" who would never have made such deals with Hitler after June 22. Stalin's domestic policies in "building socialism" were mostly justifiable.

NEW VERSIONS OF STALIN'S BEHAVIOR ON JUNE 22

Today, however, the long-held anti-Stalin version is being challenged in several ways. As they reexamine the newly opened documents, some Russian historians now are recasting their investigations in terms of answering several big questions:

If Stalin was totally unaware of a German military threat and therefore was "caught utterly by surprise" by the German attack—as official Soviet histories of the period claim—then why had he started actively mobilizing for war the way he did and as documents show that he did in the opening months of 1941? Why would he plan, if indeed he had, to preempt a German attack, as some Russian military writers today insist that he did, if he didn't expect a sudden attack from the other side? The same documents, some of them new, show that he was fully aware of the German buildup opposite Russia's western front.

On the other hand, assuming that Stalin was preparing his own preemptive attack for a later, secret date or, alternatively, was actively preparing for war of whatever type against the Wehrmacht to be launched at some proximate date, is it possible that he was simply misled as to the exact day and time of Hitler's attack (as Molotov said)? As a result, he was preempted by Hitler.

The overriding questions can be put as follows:

- Had Stalin poorly prepared Soviet Russia for a German invasion?
- Was he, in fact, taken totally unaware when the Germans crossed Soviet borders in force in the early morning hours of June 22, 1941, or did the catastrophe ensue because of other reasons?
- As a result of the surprise attack, did Stalin virtually collapse, secluding himself for weeks in his dacha outside Moscow, leaving others, the military, and his closest aides in the Politburo to cope on their own with Hitler's "double-cross"?

Until recently, the answer to each of the above was a nearly unqualified "yes." However, the evidence has been reexamined in terms of

Stalin's behavior on June 22 and during the days immediately following the debacle on that fateful Sunday morning. Testimonies by memoirists cast some doubt on the assumptions of the conventional view—namely, that Stalin was "paralyzed," hysterical, etc., that he removed himself from the scene in total confusion, wallowing in alcohol, as it is claimed, for several weeks.

One of the most telling recent pieces of evidence that this may not be true is Stalin's very busy Kremlin office log during those trying days and weeks from the end of June to the first week of July. Recently disclosed documents show that instead of the leader's seclusion, Stalin was constantly present in his office on all the days following the German attack, working, as usual, past midnight. Without evidently missing a single day, at least until the very end of June, Stalin was holding important meetings in his office in Moscow with all of his top military, party, and government officials. Documents found in newly opened archives disclose that the Soviet leader engaged in daily, many-hour sessions with his top military and civilian officials. Among the most frequent regular visitors among a dozen or so such top officials in Stalin's office on a daily basis in late June were party and government officials Molotov, Beria, and Kaganovich and military staff officers Zhukov, Shaposhnikov, Timoshenko, and Vatutin.

Stalin always tried to keep his vilest deeds—and mistakes—off the record. He ordered almost all top-secret documents and stenographic transcripts (that is, when they were kept) to be destroyed. What he didn't destroy, his closest aides destroyed, either to protect the leader or themselves. Yet the ultra-secretive dictator could not erase all the evidence. Some formerly hidden facts have been discovered in civilian and military archives in Russia in recent months and years. Since the demise of communism in Russia, certain memoirists have begun to speak out in ways that clash with the formerly accepted versions of events.

As to preparations—as was seen from his address and remarks at the reception to the graduating military cadets in the Grand Kremlin Palace on May 5—Stalin had said outright that the principal, near-term enemy was Germany, for which threat, he said, stepped-up military offensive (his word) preparations should be made, including, it seemed, planning of a Soviet preemptive attack. From documents released in recent years, it has been learned that Stalin was already sending out feelers to a number of states in search of future wartime allies— allies in a common war against Germany. Among those governments approached were France, the United States, England, Czechoslovakia,

Romania, and Poland—the latter three being approached through their governments-in-exile.

Stalin's war preparations for the country and his own actions in mid-1941 during the first days of the German penetration into the USSR was analyzed from anew approximately beginning in 1997 in such Russian publications as *Voprosy istorii* (*Problems of History*), *Vtoraya Mirovaya Voina* (*The Second World War*), *Istoriya Sovetskovo Obshchestva v Novom Osveshchenii* (*The History of Soviet Society in a New Light*), *Voenno-Istoricheskiy Zhurnal* (*Military-Historical Journal*), *Prepodavaniye Istorii v Shkolye* (*The Teaching of History in the Schools*), and other journals.

Together with these a small number of books published in Russia since the mid-1990s likewise elucidate the controversy, among them in particular the volume by Russian academician Yuri N. Afanas'iev, ed., *Rossiya XX Vek Drugaya Voina 1939–1945* (*Russia in the 20th Century: The Other War, 1939–1945*), published in 1996, as well as in Edvard Radzinsky's biography of Stalin that came out the same year. Added to these titles is the 600-page study of the period from 1939 to 1941, written by military historian Mikhail I. Mel'tukhov, published in 12,000 auspices of Films for the Humanities and Sciences in Princeton, New Jersey. This film's French and Russian historian-consultants hewed to an "offensist" line on Stalin military strategy.

The latest picture that emerges of Stalin's behavior and actions in the immediate aftermath of June 22 differs in significant respects from Khrushchev's and other traditional treatments found in Soviet and Western histories. It also radically differs from the offensist line of some historians. The new version is to a degree embodied in the very latest favorable treatment of Stalin (as notably by Arsen Martirosyan and historians of his persuasion) in the sense of alleging that Stalin was not taken by surprise. But in Martirosyan's case at least, top RKKA commanders, not Stalin, are blamed for the collapse of the western front as the Wehrmacht drove in.

As will be discussed in chapter 11, for their part, historians Verkhovsky and Tyrmos claim that Stalin had no other choice but to allow the Germans to invade. Above all, it was necessary that the Soviet Union be attacked as a victim and not be accused of launching a preemptive war against Germany. Following from this was Stalin's emphasis upon Hitler's betrayal and double-cross in breaking the German-Soviet agreements.

In their memoirs published after the demise of communism, Molotov, Sergo Beria, Sudoplatov, and Andrei Malenkov make these positive points as do some authors in the historical journals mentioned above (in particular, in *The Teaching of History in the Schools*, Issue No. 1, 1998), the line taken here is: Stalin did not "collapse" upon hearing from his aides and military commanders of the German invasion on the morning of June 22. Though he was angry and cursing, he retained his composure. Molotov put it this way in his edited memoirs, *Sto Sorok Besed s Molotovym* (*140 Conversations with Molotov*), edited by Felix Chuev (1993):

> "Stalin seldom lost his temper . . . I wouldn't say he 'lost his head' [in the days following the invasion]. He suffered, but he didn't show any signs of that. He is not portrayed as he really was. They depict him as a repentant sinner! Well, that is plainly absurd. [In that period] he worked as usual, day and night, never losing his head or his gift of speech."

Molotov further noted that Stalin had edited the speech that he, Molotov, delivered the day of the invasion.

Molotov's version sounds quite believable if for no other reason that this close aide of Stalin nevertheless is critical of Stalin here and there in his frank conversations with the interviewer, Felix Chuev. (Although Molotov dissembles occasionally in claiming, for instance, there were no secret protocols to the 1939 Nazi-Soviet agreements.)

Sudoplatov, in his book *Special Tasks*, states:

> "In his memoirs, Khrushchev portrays Stalin's 'panic' and 'confusion' in the first days of the war and later. I saw no such behavior. Stalin did not isolate himself in his dacha until June 30, 1941. The Kremlin diary [office log] shows that he was regularly receiving visitors and monitoring the deteriorating situation. From the very beginning of the war, Stalin received Beria and [his deputy] Merkulov in the Kremlin two or three times a day. . . . It appeared to me that the administrative mechanism of command and control was functioning without interruption. In fact . . . I maintained a deep belief in our ultimate victory because of the calm, clear, businesslike issuance of these orders."

For his part, Sergo Beria notes in his book that Khrushchev was a notoriously poor witness (Georgi Malenkov's son, Andrei, says the same) as to Stalin's behavior in Moscow in late June 1941. Khrushchev, he insisted, was a habitual liar and loved to flatter himself while embarrassing and overpowering his Politburo rivals and enemies with tales of their own "Stalin taint" (while overlooking Khrushchev's own deep involvement in the bloody purges in the Ukraine in the late 1930s). Martirosyan[3] uses stronger language by calling Khrushchev a "Trotsky-ist." Beria's son points out that Nikita Khrushchev was not witness to Stalin's behavior at the time of the German invasion. On June 22 and in the following days, Khrushchev was posted in far-off Kiev, Ukraine. Indeed, his name does not appear on Stalin's late-June office log, mentioned above. His last appearance in Stalin's office is recorded as having taken place on June 16. So how could he have possibly known what Stalin was doing after that date? Sergo Beria claims that he himself, however, was near Stalin during those days, that he held private conversations about the fateful events with his father, Lavrenti Pavlovich, a top member of Stalin's inner circle in charge of the secret police and other sensitive, central affairs of state, and who witnessed everything in those days. Sergo Beria writes, notably attacking Zhukov inter alia:

"Not a single book [including Zhukov's memoirs] does justice to the facts. . . . What Khrushchev and Zhukov had to say [about Stalin's behavior and actions at that time] has no relation to historical accuracy. A fact is a fact, after all. [The facts are that] on the [Saturday] night of the invasion it is not true that military commanders were sleeping peacefully or were partying. On the contrary. [As to Stalin] he was, to be sure, upset about how things were going at the front. When it is suggested that Stalin never expected Hitler to strike, that he had faith in Hitler, or that the latter had deceived him is just another myth. . . . Stalin was not so much upset by the so-called 'surprise attack' as he was by the fact that the Army was incapable of holding back the first onslaught of the attacking forces. [Various] commanders, including Commissar of Defense Timoshenko and Chief of the General Staff Zhukov before and during the first hours and days of the attack . . . had many times assured Stalin and the Politburo that the Red Army could withstand an attack. [Earlier] they had always said, 'The Army possesses all that is needed.' But when Stalin heard that the army was retreating toward the east, he was quite naturally shaken. . . . It is true that our Army was not yet sufficiently prepared to fight against mechanized forces such as the Wehrmacht [Sergo Beria, like some of today's Russian historians, blames the military for this lack of preparation.— A. L. W.]. Stalin knew about the invasion plan 'Barbarossa' before June 22 from intelligence officers. . . . In his first speech of

July 3, Stalin himself spoke about how Hitler, by his 'perfidious attack,' had violated the Nazi-Soviet Pact, 'ignoring the fact that the whole world would regard her as the aggressor.'"

Then Stalin added significantly as though implicitly to answer the question, why didn't the Soviets strike first? "Naturally," argued Stalin, "our peace-loving country, not wishing to take the initiative in breaking a pact, could not itself resort to perfidy."

Leaving aside here the question of whether Stalin and the Soviets actually may have been developing a military strategy for waging their own preventive war against Germany, the political-declaratory side of this doctrine—as opposed to the unpublished, operational part of the doctrine and strategy—did not allude to offensism. If it had included such aggressive statements—made declaratively to a broad domestic and foreign audience—it would damage the Soviets' global reputation. Above all, it would also have precluded any possible aid that might eventually come to the USSR from the as-yet noncombatants or potential "coalition" partners, such as the United States. Indoctrination of Soviet soldiers is also a factor here. Soldiers are not motivated to fight by declarations of aggressive intent. Many military writers, Western and Soviet, have made that point.

As it was, the USSR was able to win the support of the Western Allies and the invaluable Lend-Lease aid mainly because the USSR was seen as the hapless victim, not the initiator of an aggressive attack. There is even some evidence that Stalin was prepared to fall back on Allied aid in case other scenarios failed. In other words, he did not entirely burn his bridges with the West despite the Nazi-Soviet agreements of 1939–1940. The fact that he kept the "Westerner" Litvinov in limbo rather than in purgatory. He was later to be exploited toward the West once again as deputy commissar of foreign affairs and Soviet ambassador to the United States (during World War II). Anastas Mikoyan, the Armenian "Teflon" perennial in the Stalin Politburo, is another example of a useful emissary. He flaunted the air of a debonair, flexible negotiator. Yet his own political loyalties and affinities were rigidly Stalinist—at least while Stalin was alive. In the post-Stalin period, a similarly accommodationist role was played by another hardy perennial in the Politburo, Premier Alexei Kosygin. Like Mikoyan, he too was an orthodox party-liner on foreign affairs, though relatively less rigid than other top Soviet officials on domestic policy.

One of the Russian journals points out that the problem with Stalin's assessment of the intelligence reports that warned of the invasion (coming from such agents as Richard Sorge in Tokyo) was their often contradictory nature. One author points out that the contradictions even extended to inside the Nazi leadership itself, where invasion dates were repeatedly shuffled and changed, and that Soviet partial knowledge of this also confused the picture. Hitler's decisions, as we saw, were kept secret even from top Wehrmacht commanders, let alone from the amicable German ambassador to Moscow, Count von Schulenburg. The latter strongly opposed a German war against Russia. Schulenburg was later executed in Germany because of his alleged involvement in the 1944 plot to kill Hitler, and possibly also for his earlier pessimism about Barbarossa and evident friendliness toward the Soviets.

Nor, as it is alleged in both new and old Russian literature on the subject, did Stalin trust what Churchill had told him. Stalin was convinced, not without some basis, that the Western powers kept hoping that Germany would attack the USSR, not only because it was a Communist dictatorship, but also because the Germans would thereby become bogged down in a self-destructive, two-front war. The new "generation" of Russian historians also nearly unanimously adheres to this point of view. In some instances, Soviet agents also made this point—as they said, based on secret information—in their messages to the top Kremlin leadership. Meantime, English officials, particularly within the military, it is true, erred profoundly, as Hitler himself had, in thinking that the Soviets could not withstand a German onslaught whether it were made in the short or long run.

Half-joking at a postwar Big Three summit, Winston Churchill brought up this sensitive subject personally to Stalin—namely, the latter's show of incredulity toward the prime minister's warnings. Stalin punted back that, after all, it was hard for him to believe "everything" that he was told, even by his own agents.

One Russian journal author points out that the well-known story of Sorge's pinpointing of the date of the Nazi invasion is itself suspect (Yu. P. Bokarev, *The Teaching of History in the Schools*, No. 1, 1998). Bokarev notes that Sorge reputedly made his prediction *even before Hitler and the German High Command had themselves fixed the date!* In any case, Stalin, it is revealed in new documents, had a copy of Wehrmacht planning embodied in part in Operation Barbarossa. This is also claimed by Sergo Beria.

In the matter of Stalin's preparations for meeting what he and everyone had expected would be a German attack sooner or later, evidence that, indeed, defensive preparations were speeded up, on Stalin's orders, during the spring of 1941 and right up until the invasion. Half of all the Soviet armed forces were deployed on the front facing the Germans after massive mobilization and redeployments were under way in late spring. Many emergency preventive measures, it turns out, had been taken—yet not completed—to meet the invasion threat or to prepare to wage a preemptive attack from the Soviet side.

Meanwhile, Stalin realized that the Soviets possibly would not be ready for full-scale war of whatever type, defensive or offensive. Some analysts say that he thought the Red Army would be prepared, however, by July 1941. Yet in his interview with Chuev Molotov, Stalin claimed that it would be ready for battle only "by 1943." In any case, the Soviet leader evidently calculated that on their part, the Germans would likely not attack before 1942. As a result of these surmises, Stalin relied on the diplomatic ploy of stalling and misleading Hitler by means of several ruses that he thought would work.

For example, he had ordered the news agency Tass and the party newspaper *Pravda* on June 14, 1941, to publish vehement denials that the Soviets were building up forces along their western frontier. They were, the item suggested, doing nothing extraordinary there, nor was German-Soviet friendship weakening in any way. Nor were Red Army scouts—ground or airborne—positioned along the frontier permitted to shoot at straying German planes or in any way create a rumpus that would "provoke" the Germans. The boss himself explicitly conveyed such warnings to the Red Army leadership. He once remarked to Zhukov (according to Zhukov) that, "you must be out of your mind" in thinking the Red Army was prepared (in late spring 1941) to wage a preemptive strike. This was Zhukov's denial that Stalin had ever accepted the thinking contained, for example, in the notorious offensist Timoshenko-Zhukov memorandum of May 15 (see the discussion in the next chapter).

Besides making these verbal assurances through his controlled press—that he knew would be read and duly assimilated to Soviet advantage in Berlin—Stalin made sure that the deliveries of raw materials by rail to Hitler continued on schedule, which they were right up until June 22. Yet whether this diplomatic gambit reflected gross negligence and inattention on Stalin's part or whether, on the contrary, it was a last-ditch effort to "postpone the inevitable" remains a matter of contention among Russian historians. At the same time in early 1941, it seems true that Stalin was resentful as he made his vehement denials of the veracity of some of the reports he was receiving from his intelligence agents. On one occasion, he told the messenger of such information to go tell the agent to go "f*** his mother." Others he accused outright of being agents of Germany.

At any rate, according to Molotov, all that Stalin really cared about was preserving and strengthening the Soviet Union and, most important, he says, establishing Soviet innocence as to which side, Germany or the USSR, started the war on the Eastern Front.[4]

Another factor that may have affected Stalin was the flight of the top Nazi aide to Hitler, Rudolf Hess, to England in May 1941. This factor is still debated among historians, some of whom deny that Stalin reacted in any extreme, suspicious way. Many Russian historians note that the Cambridge spies—Burgess, Maclean, Philby, and Blunt—had led Stalin to believe that England might well one day close a deal with Germany. Only then would Germany turn on the USSR. In this version, Hess, an emissary of Hitler, had flown to England to help bring about a closing of ranks between the British and the Germans and end their war with each other. Similar information—or was it disinformation?—seems to have reached Stalin from his ambassador in London, Ivan Maisky. All this, so runs one version of the Hess flight, must in turn have influenced the "paranoid" Soviet dictator into thinking that Britain (and the United States) were involved in a plot to deceive him. Namely, that British warnings of an imminent German attack were intended merely to provoke a Soviet-German war. Some of these informers seemed to be motivated as much by sycophancy toward (or fear of) Stalin as much as by any hard information in their possession. Pleasing or placating the Khozain was often uppermost.

Another factor was the reluctance of Stalin's sycophantic chief of GRU Golikov to relay to Stalin the grim truth about the imminent execution of Operation Barbarossa. It also possible that Stalin was misleading Golikov and kept his bluff tactic secret, camouflaging it with denials of German intentions as laid out so clearly in the intelligence he himself was privy to and reading. Although Sergo Beria denies it, other historians believe that NKVD chief Lavrenti Beria himself may have also misled Stalin. He is said to have assured Stalin with the prediction that Hitler would not attack if it meant a two-front war for Germany. Yet here, too, Stalin may have been playing a game with Beria.

Yet there is evidence that suggests that intensive preparations for meeting an imminent German invasion were actually under way in late spring and in June (see the next chapter). The problem concerned inadequate preparations: completing movements of troops by rail from Siberia to the western military districts; securing signals and communications among units along the front (this lack of communications, control, and coordination was a major RKKA weakness—e.g., Soviet tanks even lacked radios); getting arms and fortifications in place; securing air bases with anti-aircraft batteries; building new defenses at the forward "Molotov Line"; and much else. None of this had been completed in time—amid assurances to Stalin from the Red Army high command that the army was on the ready and invincible.

In any case, it was expected—by RKKA strategists and perhaps by Stalin—that a forewarning of upward to two weeks would precede any actual invasion as the Wehrmacht actually deployed forces for such a vast undertaking. There would be a period of creeping up to war, as some Soviet military thinkers had suggested over the years and that may have become standard thinking in the military. There would thus be time enough, it was assumed, for both Red Army echelons—the first on the frontier and the "covering" second echelon and succeeding echelons—to deploy and rally to the defense of the country.

In other words, the blame for the surprise may not rest solely on Stalin's shoulders, and the pro-Stalin historians would agree, since they accuse the military of misleading Stalin. After all, the Soviet leader, who was not yet de facto commander in chief of the armed forces, had been assured by his military commanders that there was no worry. Still, at the very last minute, Admiral Nikolai G. Kuznetsov (1902–1974), on duty in the Baltic and who was one of the rare commanding officers to admit in his memoirs to have been be thoroughly cognizant of the imminence of the German danger.

Also, to some of the new Russian historians, it was not a case of Stalin's personal miscalculations or of his cowardice after the German juggernaut started rolling. More likely, it was the suddenness and sheer boldness and strength of the Wehrmacht blitzkrieg, the application to Russia of tactics that had worked so well against an entirely different type of enemy—in troop numbers and in terms of the smaller size of the targeted countries in the West in 1940. These blitzkrieg tactics were not supposed to be applicable against a country the size of the USSR, given its ultimate preponderance of troops and territorial space in which to retreat before counterattacking. The perception that such tactics would not work or be applied against Soviet Russia might to some extent have lulled the Russian military into unexpectancy concerning the nature a German attack. The RKKA my well have expected a degree of creeping into war rather than the sudden, all-out blitzkrieg the Germans inflicted on the Russians.

In any case, in June 1941, Soviet Russia had "on paper" 303 infantry, tank, motorized, and cavalry divisions, of which one quarter, however, were still in the process of being formed. Nor was the Red Navy unimpressive with, for example, 212 submarines and many surface ships. Equipped forces deployed along the western frontier numbered 163 infantry, cavalry, tank, and motorized divisions consisting of 2,743,000 men with 57,000 guns and mortars, 12,762 tanks, 8,696 military aircraft in good condition, and 545 naval ships. All of these composed the first strategic echelon of the Soviet military forces in the west. To cover them, the Red Army had deployed along the frontier 13 general-forces armies.

One may still wonder exactly what Stalin meant when, in his victory speech at a Kremlin reception in honor of Red Army commanders on May 24, 1945, he seemingly "repented" as follows:

> Our government committed no few mistakes; at times our situation was desperate, as in 1941–1942, when our army was retreating, abandoning our native villages and towns. . . . Another people might have said to the government: You have not come up to our expectations. Get out. We shall appoint another government, which will conclude peace with Germany and ensure tranquility for us. But the Russian people did not do that, for they were confident that the policy their government was pursuing was correct. . . . I thank the Russian people for this confidence! To the health of the Russian people!

ADDITIONAL OBSERVATIONS AND ISSUES

Adolf Hitler's decision to invade the Soviet Union in June 1941 was motivated, some historians believe, by the Fuehrer's fear of a two-front war that would be fought in future on the European continent. He imagined that the war would widen and that, for example, America, a crucial prospective combatant, would sooner or later enter the fray. Thus, by waging and winning a "preventive war" against the USSR in 1941—even before he had defeated England throughout 1940—the German dictator sought to preclude a repeat of that crucial German predicament of World War I: augmented forces of the Western Allies fighting Germany on one side, their Russian ally fighting Germany, and the Central Powers in the east.

Hitler had America on his mind, as did apparently Stalin. Sooner or later this large, crucial country with its impressive economy and defense-producing potential would surely enter the global fray. Hitler sought to preempt this likelihood by defeating Russia ahead of time, thereby dominating the Eurasian continent as proposed by his "official geographer," Gen. Karl Haushofer.

Stalin, by contrast, appears to have relished American entry into the war even before the USSR was attacked, at which time, by early July, he immediately sought Western aid against the "common foe," Germany. In his speech to the Eighteenth Party Congress in March 1939, Stalin had referred to the United States, along with Britain and France, as a "non-aggressive" capitalist country. Later, as we noted, he had sent friendly feelers in the direction of Washington. The Yakovlev-edited second volume of *Dokumenty* reproduces a revealing conversation that was held in Moscow on June 5, 1941, 17 days before the German attack, between U.S. Ambassador Lawrence Steinhardt and Deputy Commissar of Foreign Affairs S. A. Lozovsky. Both made significant concessions on various trade and other issues. It obvious that Lozovsky had been given orders from above in the Kremlin to be forthcoming to the American. The new Soviet attitude was quite perceptible.

But whether he looked forward to the likelihood of American involvement in hostilities with a diabolical aim in mind (viz., seeing the United States weakened and revolutionized by a global war that was to include Japan) or by a more realistic expectation that America might thence become a future Soviet ally must remain a subject for future investigation. At present, no documents support one or the other view.

The decision to attack Soviet Russia ran absolutely counter to Hitler's earlier, explicitly expressed tactic of seriously courting that state on a long-term basis. Indeed, both dictators had described their emerging interstate friendship as "long lasting." His and Stalin's joint initiatives in 1939–1940 in signing various sweeping agreements, including the Nazi-Soviet pact of August 1939 (see chapter 4), was, to Hitler's mind, a safe way of avoiding—short of war—the pincers of a two-front vice.

Still, it might be asked, if forestalling a two-front war by diplomatic means was indeed Hitler's principal motive in establishing "lasting friendship" with Soviet Russia, thus waiving Nazism's condemnation of "Jewish Bolshevism," why did the fuehrer suddenly decide to turn against his newfound Soviet ally in June 1941? Was, in fact, such an invasion nested in Hitler's plans all along? Likewise, Stalin is known to have confided to intimates that sooner or later Germany and then the USSR would be at each other's throats. As far as Germany was concerned, Propaganda Minister Josef Goebbels indicated the same prediction in his diary. So it would appear that stated sentiments of long-lasting friendship were disingenuous on both sides.

Or, on the contrary, did Stalin's own new show of westward aggressiveness, his large-scale territorial annexations in 1939–1940 against German interests in Central and Balkan Europe, and his various demands proffered in late 1940 so profoundly alarm the Germans that Hitler was "forced" to preempt Soviet Russia's own aggressive plans vis-à-vis Germany?

While historians—especially those in Germany and Russia today—do not agree on the answers to these questions, on one thing they unanimously concur: Germany's invasion of Soviet Russia in mid-1941 turned out to be Hitler's fatal mistake, dooming him to defeat against the Allies in World War II. His rout in Russia, like Napoleon's 125 years before, paved the way to the Allied victory, not only over the European Axis, but also over Japan, the new Asian ally of Hitler and Mussolini.

Significantly, too, Operation Barbarossa had precluded Soviet Russia's own joining, as seriously anticipated in Moscow and Berlin, a projected Four-Power Alliance, an expanded Axis, that was to include the USSR, Nazi Germany, Fascist Italy, and militarist Japan. This monumental scheme was seriously discussed in secrecy between the Germans and Soviets in 1940 and is now part of the public record. However, because of Operation Barbarossa, this potential grand alliance, embracing three continents (Europe, Asia, and Africa), obviously could never see the light of day. However, had it materialized, without doubt the outcome of World War II would have been vastly different.

Today, two groups of historians—some Russian, some German, others American or British—take opposing views on the question of the Nazi-Soviet alliance and the German attack together with its consequences.

One school insists that Hitler, as early as mid-1940, defying doubts in the minds of trusted aides (among them, it appears, Air Marshal Hermann Goering, Foreign Minister Joachim von Ribbentrop, Propaganda Minister Goebbels, and Nazi philosopher Alfred Rosenberg), had decided to invade Russia and terminate Nazi-Soviet friendship and collaboration—a scheme that he had in general long nurtured. The timing of the attack was not a badly calculated one. Having failed to subdue England in the air blitz of 1940–1941 and fearing eventual U.S. participation in the war, possibly alongside Soviet Russia, Hitler decided to act decisively before it was too late. He would settle scores with Bolshevik Russia once and for all and return, in a sense, to what he had preached so vehemently in *Mein Kampf.* Whatever Stalin was up to at that time by way of aggression was irrelevant. So runs one conventional interpretation.

On its part, a second group of historians—among whom are some contemporary Russian authors and scholars together with some Russian, German, and British ex-officials, memoirists, and other writers who in part rely in their research on newly opened Russian archives—insists that by their aggressive actions, Stalin and Molotov by mid-1940 had profoundly alarmed and infuriated Hitler.

At that time, Moscow had begun making brazen demands on the Germans, such as insisting on giving the USSR a unilateral free hand in the oil-rich Middle East, the Balkans, Finland, and the Turkish straits while threatening to seize the Romanian oil fields. In starting to gobble up large swatches of territory in the Baltic and East European regions, the Soviets did not bother to inform Berlin, Moscow's putatively sworn ally, of the dates and details as warranted by their agreements of 1939.

According to Ribbentrop, Hitler's pro-Russian, anti-British foreign minister, Hitler thus was forced into making a decision to stop Stalin, a conclusion he had reached, Ribbentrop and others claimed after World War II, only in late 1940. Hitler had not made the Operation Barbarossa decision, as alleged by some, Ribbentrop claimed, as early as June or July 1940.

As indicated above, one of the most intriguing, controversial questions haunting historians of World War II concerns Soviet—or rather, Stalin's—behavior in the aftermath of the signing of the several Nazi-Soviet agreements in Moscow beginning in August 1939.

As we have seen, in the conventional interpretation of the run-up to the German invasion of June 21, 1941, the Stalin regime was and still is depicted as being terrified at the prospect of any ensuing deterioration of Nazi-Soviet relations, let alone all-out war. After all, since the autumn of 1939, the Soviet leader had ordered his government-controlled media not to criticize Hitler and Nazism. Not even the word "fascism" was allowed to appear in print in Soviet media. Moreover, besides shipping him vital raw materials used in the war against the Western democracies, Stalin did all he could in other ways to help or even placate Hitler. For example, he ordered Communist fifth-column agents to sabotage Western defense plants (i.e., up until mid-1941), while sending congratulations to Hitler when the Wehrmacht took Paris in May 1940.

On several occasions and via various memoranda, Stalin and Molotov indicated fulsomely to Berlin that Moscow was on Germany's side in fighting the so-called "bourgeois," "plutocratic," and "colonialist" regimes of Western Europe. Both dictators relished the prospect of an utterly destroyed British Empire that together they would help bring about.

To this hypothesis, other authors respond: Yes, Stalin did all these things to placate, but also in order eventually to *mislead* Hitler. The Soviet dictator, it is alleged, greatly feared Hitler. He did all he could to demonstrate his friendship with his totalitarian German counterpart as well as showing loyalty to the Nazi-Soviet agreements. Stalin had drunk toasts to Hitler, whom, he said, he knew the German people admired and whose "iron rule" in Germany he sincerely respected no less than Hitler appreciated Stalin's new order. Stalin had made sure that the billions of dollars' worth of deliveries of war-related raw materials—rubber, oil, food, textiles, rolled steel, and other goods under the economic-aid terms of the Nazi-Soviet agreements—were made punctually. They were, in fact, kept strictly on schedule, reaching Brest-Litovsk in the former Poland and then downloaded from the wider-gauge Soviet railroad cars onto the narrower-gauge tracks to ship them on to Germany.

Meanwhile, some Russian historians allege today, Stalin, who was stalling for time during this "breathing space," was secretly planning his own offensive war against Germany and, in fact, the rest of Europe (see chapter 5). Historians who think this way find themselves in agreement with, for example, the British ambassador to Berlin in the late 1930s, Sir Neville Henderson. According to Henderson, Stalin's true motive in joining forces with the Nazis and helping them defeat the West was so that the USSR could stay out of the fray while watching the Allies and Axis destroy one another. The Soviets would help along this process of self-destruction by aiding Germany and by sharing the spoils of aggression with them, as described above. The ambassador perhaps had been reading Stalin's *Works*. At the conclusion of this collaboration and ultimate German defeat and/or mutual exhaustion of the belligerents, Henderson insisted, the Soviets would thereupon march west for the kill, sovietizing all of Europe as openly stated by their own ideologists as well as by the Comintern. Henderson, it seems, had taken seriously Stalin's statements along these very lines in 1925.

However, once Hitler perceived that this was Stalin's game, some argue, Hitler decided to act. Operation Barbarossa was formally approved by Hitler for active preparation and implementation by

December 18, 1940, just as disagreements with their Soviet "partner" over Romania, Finland, etc., were reaching a head. When they were informed of Hitler's final decision to go ahead with Barbarossa, Mussolini and many Nazi aides were left in a nervous state. In his diaries, Goebbels made fun of such "cowards."

As we now know, the British got wind of Barbarossa through their reading of German signal traffic via their captured (in Poland) Enigma machine and Ultra deciphering program at Bletchley. Not wishing in any way to reveal that they had this machine and remarkable program for reading general staff orders, the British nevertheless discreetly "leaked" to Soviet intelligence only bits of what they carefully chose from the closely guarded information lest it be known that the British had such a system. (Apparently, not even the ubiquitous Soviet agents in Britain were able to penetrate the premises where Enigma and Ultra were secretly ensconced.) Among these pieces of information, as we saw, were details of German planning for the invasion of the USSR.

Yet Stalin apparently remained unpersuaded by the British information, the secret source of which he did not, of course, know. He calculated that London was merely trying to break up the Soviet-German romance. Nor did some informed warnings by certain Red Army commanders in the spring and summer of 1941 impress Stalin, since in these early times he mistrusted his generals. He had brutally purged many of them in previous years, from 1937 onward, and continued to badger and threaten them. Even the warnings of his top spy, Richard Sorge, posted in Tokyo and who predicted within days the exact date of the German attack, did not convince Stalin that a Nazi double-cross was in the making.

At his post in Japan, Sorge, in fact, was abandoned and left defenseless by Stalin when the Japanese government learned of his espionage activities, for which he was executed in Tokyo in late 1941 when no attempt was made by the Soviets to get him out. (Sorge had also tipped off Stalin on Japanese planning for the Pearl Harbor attack—a bit of information that Stalin did not share with Washington.) Shortly before this, Sorge had informed Moscow that Ribbentrop was trying to get the Japanese to break their neutrality treaty with the USSR that had been signed in spring 1941. (His yeoman service to the boss was left mainly to the annals of history, although he was given posthumous recognition in the Brezhnev period of the 1970s.)

In articles appearing in the stateside Russian weekly *Panorama* in the late 1990s, Russian military historian Vladimir Lyulechnik demonstrated by references to archival documents how Stalin considered without reservation an eventual war with Germany to be "inevitable." He perceived that a short period of collaboration with Germany would delay the inevitable conflict while permitting Soviet Russia to further build up its own offensive and defensive military forces, a process that dramatically accelerated at this time. So Lyulechnik claimed.

Meanwhile, the allegation in old-style Soviet propaganda (still encountered today in Russia and in many Western history texts) that Stalin had seized the Baltic states and made other territorial annexations in 1939–1940 to create a "buffer" against a near-term German invasion of Russia is not borne out by the facts, Lyulechnik continued. His view is shared by a few Western-based historians (Raack, Tolstoy, Topitsch, and Suvorov, among others, cited in the bibliography) and a number of contemporary Russian historians (such as Bobylev, Nevezhin, and Radzinsky).

Moreover, the notion of delaying a German invasion as the motive for these annexations is canceled out by the fact that Stalin, by virtue of his seizures of the western lands, succeeded in further endangering the USSR by moving Soviet borders nearer to those of German-occupied Europe. The Germans could then proceed, as they did, to mobilize along that extended, largely unprotected front. Still, the "buffer" argument continues to be dominant in standard American world history textbooks and many books on World War II. Today, however, some Russian historians question the argument. As proved by what occurred in the early weeks of the war, the Soviets needed all of this territory to absorb the Wehrmacht's attack. In fact, an argument may be made that any defense that relied on some degree of tactical or even strategic retreat, as RKKA strategy appeared to embody by the spring of 1941 (see chapter 11), depended for its success on room to withdraw forces.

How had Stalin managed to be caught so ignominiously by Operation Barbarossa? From what has so far come to light from the partially opened archives in Moscow, it is clear that it was a case of Stalin's own offensive strategy blinding him to the Germans' corresponding offensive plans.

Ironically, the Soviet-German offensive strategy had been jointly worked out in the proto-blitzkrieg war games played out on the Russian steppe in the 1920s up to 1933. This was when the German general staff sent representatives—Guderian, Manstein, Keitel, Brauchitsch, Model, Horn, et al.—to Soviet Russia in the years and months preceding Barbarossa for waging offensive war (see chapter 3). The offensive strategy, ironically, had been the brainchild of Marshal Mikhail Tukhachevsky and his associates, whom Stalin had purged in 1937–1938 and who had previously been participants in the Soviet-German military collaboration of the 1920s. (There is some new documentation for the possibility that Tukhachevsky actually was involved in a germinating plot to do away with Stalin. At the same time, there were many utterly ridiculous trumped-up charges made against the marshal at the purge trial in 1937, among which was that he was "Trotskyite" and that he was collaborating with the Germans.)

Indeed, the German generals' familiarity with and appreciation of the talents of their Soviet counterparts of the 1920s indirectly contributed to Hitler's perception of an enfeebled, "decapitated" Red Army due to the bloody repressions of those top Soviet officers that had taken place 10 years later in 1937–1939. Three out of 54 marshals were bloodily purged. Similarly liquidated were 13 of 15 Army commanders; 8 out of 8 fleet admirals; 50 of the 57 corps commanders; and so on. Some of the best Red Army military brains were purged, including all 11 vice commissars of defense. A total of 43,000 officers were liquidated! This left inexperienced "lieutenants" in charge. Two years later, the Soviets' debacle in the early, disastrous phase of their Winter War against Finland merely confirmed Hitler's impressions of a paper tiger Red Army. British intelligence got the same impression, which dovetailed with London's apparent disinterest in collective security arrangements with such a weakened power as Soviet Russia.

In Moscow in the spring of 1941, Zhukov and Timoshenko, respectively chief of the general staff and commissar of defense, urged Stalin to sharply boost preparedness on the western front and to take other measures *kak vozmozhno skoreye*, or as soon as Zhukov even called for a preemptive strike against the Wehrmacht. He continued to urge a counteroffensive strategy that became the theme of Stalin's secret speech to the graduating cadets in May 1941.

In the opening weeks of the "Great Fatherland War," Stalin would issue urgent orders to commanders to wage counteroffensives, or at the very least "partial counteroffensives." And he called for the arrests of a number of frontline commanders, many of whom were in due course tried and shot on Stalin's orders. These included such officers as his commander of the entire western front, Gen. Dmitri G. Pavlov, his chief of staff, Gen. Vladimir E. Klimovskikh, together with his signals and artillery commanders. The commander in chief of the Fourth Army, Andrei A. Korobskov, likewise was shot, as were the commanders of an aviation division on the western front and of the Kiev Military District Air Force.

Stalin's occasional erratic behavior in this period anticipated Hitler's in the concluding phase of the war in Europe. At that time, the German dictator sometimes gave frantic orders that were unrealistic to the frontline commanders ordered to carry them out.

During this initial period in Moscow, Stalin did not assume the post of supreme commander in chief, although he quickly ordered the formation of a combat high command headquarters, or Stavka. Stalin's self-appointment to the post of commander in chief came later in the year 1941.

As to his later, vainglorious rank of Generalissimus, Stalin did not appropriate that supreme title for himself until the end of the war in 1945. The latest previous holder of this highest rank was Gen. Alexei V. Suvorov (1730–1800), awarded to him in 1799, the year before his death. Besides Suvorov, there were only three other holders of this title in Russia.

PART THREE

The War and Its Aftermath

Stalin Bluffs and Defeats Wehrmacht

Was Stalin, as alleged by many historians, "taken by surprise" by the German attack on June 22, 1941?

Given the failure to complete the Red Army's full, defensive preparations and the fact that the RKKA could not and, in fact, actually did not block the Wehrmacht's onslaught in Operation Barbarossa, can Stalin, then, rightfully be blamed for the catastrophe that occurred in the weeks and months following the invasion?

From the available literature published in Russia and in the West over the years, it would appear that the answers to all of the above questions is a resounding yes. Yet today a number of Russian historians, some of them specialists on the Soviet military, take issue with what they consider to be a one-sided, erroneous consensus that has been built up for many years concerning Operation Barbarossa and how Stalin and the Red Army coped with the German attack.

REASSESSING STALIN

As scholars debate over Stalin's actions in the spring of 1941, well over 50 percent of the population of the RF today, the great majority of whom are by no means sympathetic toward Communism, and defying the negative portrayals of Stalin that are found in many books, nevertheless regard the Soviet leader as having been a "great" (*velikiy*) leader.

This may puzzle some readers in the West. They are accustomed to largely one-dimensional biographies of Stalin, including those published in recent years. Readers throughout the world have long assimilated conventional histories of the USSR and World War II and of Stalin. In them, the Soviet dictator is depicted as a ruthless despot—which indeed he was—whose immoral, allegedly dysfunctional authoritarian leadership essentially weakened the Soviet Union by leaving it in a vulnerable, defenseless state on the very eve of the German attack in June 1941.

In other words, such books have nothing positive whatever to say about the Soviet dictator's stern, authoritarian leadership. Authors even skirt Stalin's decade-long, intense military buildup of the USSR together with the virtual militarization of Soviet society that he undertook beginning in the early 1930s and without which the Soviets would have been left hopelessly defenseless against both Germany and Japan.

In the prevalent literature about Stalin over the years, many readers moreover may have gotten the impression that he can best be summed up as a rigid ideologue. At any given time, the dictator was out to sovietize the entire world. Such authors, whether in the West or in Russia, emphasize Stalin's anti-Western propaganda, his draconic domestic and opportunistic foreign policies on the eve of Hitler's aggression in Europe, and especially the way the USSR became stigmatized and isolated from the rest of the world. They scorn Stalin infamous "honeymoon" with Hitler under the terms of the Nazi-Soviet pacts, secret protocols, and trade agreements of 1939–1940. These notorious "dealings with the devil," it is alleged, only succeeded in leaving the USSR all but defenseless and without allies in the face of looming German aggression by 1940–1941.

Such writers further claim that Stalin, by his hostile anti-Western propaganda and his "friendship" with Nazi Germany, merely succeeded in alienating the democratic Western powers as potential allies. Stalin thus needlessly and dangerously isolated the USSR. The latter therefore became a pariah State that was expelled from the League of Nations in 1939 after Stalin ordered the invasion of little Finland in the Winter War of December 1939 to March 1940. The Soviet Union was depicted as a menace to the independence of neighboring countries. In 1939–1940, the Kremlin had forcibly annexed former tsarist territories in the Baltics by sovietizing Estonia, Latvia, Lithuania, and parts of Finland and eastern Poland—all with Hitler's reluctant accession.

Thanks to Stalin, it is claimed, the Soviets were duly "double-crossed" by Hitler on June 22, 1941, and were taken by surprise as the Germans revved up the Wehrmacht engines of their panzers, motorized infantry, and the Luftwaffe that were poised menacingly—and ostentatiously—along the 1,800-plus mile western border of the USSR in the late spring of 1941.

However, this widely disseminated interpretation of Stalin and the events of 1939–1941 are now being disputed by some Russian historians, not all of whom may be considered outright Stalin apologists. In some cases as largely non-Communist observers and as strong critics of Stalin's tyranny, these authors, along with most of the Russian population, are tending now to reject the boiler plated, conventional depiction of Stalin as a dumbfounded bungler who was "caught off-guard" by the Wehrmacht or, as some earlier revisionist historians claim, the world leader who was even responsible for World War II.

As reviewed in the preceding chapter, the old view toward Stalin was essentially a holdover from the Khrushchev-inspired de-Stalinization campaign inaugurated in 1956. It was continued more or less unabated up to the present. Another motivating factor is some historians' deeply held, personal contempt for Stalin, a hatred that is in many respects, of course, understandable. Yet such hostility can lead to the attitude that "nothing positive" can or should be attributed to a tyrant's leadership.

Countering this wholesale anti-Stalin mantra are two contemporary, widely read, non-Communist, and, in fact, generally anti-Stalin Russian historians, Yakov Verkhovsky and Valentina Tyrmos.[1] These authors claim that Stalin was really never hoodwinked by the Nazi dictator. This is proved, among other evidence, by what he said to intimates confidentially just after the signing of the August–September 1939 Molotov-Ribbentrop pacts: "We outsmarted them," he told them.

Moreover, the authors claim that Stalin "bluffed" Hitler in the spring of 1941 by the Soviet leader's deliberate posturing of his "being in denial" about Hitler's Operation Barbarossa and the heavy German deployments along the frontier. This research points to a strong possibility that Stalin may have indeed been bluffing and letting Hitler show himself as the aggressor by invading the Soviet Union and making it the "victim of Fascist aggression." As Stalin had earlier said, "It's better to be attacked" in any given war than to be perceived as the aggressor. In his speech of July 3, 1941 (see Appendix I), Stalin, pointing the finger of aggression at Germany, said (my emphases—A. L. W.):

> "Of no little importance in this respect is the fact that fascist Germany suddenly and treacherously violated the non-aggression

pact she concluded in 1939 with the USSR, disregarding the fact that she would be regarded as the aggressor by the whole world."

Stalin, moreover, seems to have been perfectly cognizant, through his impressive network of foreign intelligence agents, of Hitler's Soviet invasion plans formulated from mid-1940 through May 1941. Yet the Soviet leader also realized that the Red Army was not prepared to defend itself—and unable to mount an adequate defense in mid-1941 and certainly not achieve a victory at the start of war by means of alleg- edly "traditional," Soviet *offensist* strategy and tactics.

On the contrary, as now seems quite evident, Stalin by the spring of 1941 was resigned to the inevitability of the German invasion. The fact is that he had no other choice but be resigned to that eventuality and cope as best as possible with the consequences. At the same time, the Soviet leadership had no doubt of the ultimate failure of Hitler's plan to conquer and occupy the huge Soviet Union, either up to the Ural Mountains let alone beyond that geographical boundary separating European Russia from Asia.

A close cohort of Stalin, Soviet President Mikhail Kalinin, expressed Stalin's view, which was his wont, as did others in the entourage when the head of state said in so many words of the imminent Weh- rmacht invasion, "Let them come on! We'll crush them!" Stalin him- self exclaimed in April 1941: "Let them try it!"[2] Others voiced similar sentiments as if to say, "So let them invade. Their ultimate defeat is assured." This was an opinion that contained a good deal of substance. It was a realistic assessment. In their and Stalin's view, the German invaders in the long run would be swallowed up by Russia's vastness, by its unfriendly weather (Hitler had disastrously delayed the inva- sion), and, above all, by the Soviet deployments of its constantly aug- mented Red Army (RKKA) ranks via continuously deployed reserve forces. Throughout the spring of 1941, RKKA combat units were being secretly deployed in depth in successive echelons resembling the type of defense that the Russian Army had deployed under General Mikhail Kutuzov in the successful defense against Napoleon's Grande Armée in 1812. (Ironically, this was just 129 years, almost to the day, before the German invasion on that Sunday morning the day after the Summer Solstice in 1941).

Recall that on the seventieth anniversary of the start of World War II, just weeks after the signing of the Nazi-Soviet Nonaggression Pact in August 1939, Prime Minister Vladimir Putin, speaking in somber tones in Poland on September 1, 2009, described the pact with its secret protocols as "immoral." Yet, he added significantly, historians should develop a "balanced" perspective toward Stalin's policies in the ominous, perilous era of 1939–1941. This presumably meant to give some weight to the claim of Stalin's greatness in the several respects that this relates to saving Soviet Russia, or the "Russian state," and, therefore, the Russia of the future from the utter destruction that Hitler had planned for it in the 1940s.

Such a new perspective on Stalin is reflected to one degree or another in currently published editions of Russian histories now being used in classrooms by students in Russian secondary schools. These government-endorsed textbooks cast Stalin as "one of the most successful leaders of the USSR."[3] Or, more often, they speak in positive terms of the "Soviet government," which of course Stalin headed. At the time of the seventieth anniversary commemorations (of the pact and of the start of World War II), several issues of the popular Russian weekly news magazine, *Itogi*, the Russian *Newsweek*, were devoted to discussion of the meanings of the double anniversaries. Several interviewed historians described what they called the "positive contributions" made by Stalin before and during the Great Patriotic War and that led to the Soviet victory over the German invaders in 1941–1945. One historian argued in *Itogi* that the 1939 nonaggression and friendship pacts of late 1939 were Stalin's "only choice," given the threat to the security of an isolated, vulnerable Soviet Union posed by Hitler's aggressive Nazi Germany. Stalin, he wrote, had by his deals with Hitler shrewdly won time to prepare for his country for what the Soviet dictator regarded as early as the 1920s as an inevitable war and since 1938 as a war with Nazi Germany: Stalin took seriously Hitler's plan, as predicted in *Mein Kampf*, with which Stalin was all too familiar, to invade and occupy Russia for German *Lebensraum* and enslavement. This coming war moreover was anticipated in Marxist-Leninist Soviet dogma, which repeatedly warned against the "imperialism" imbedded in "rapacious" forms of contorted capitalism.

Thus, in a curious way, an ideology—Marxism-Leninism—that was widely and correctly reputed in many respects to be dogmatically farfetched had produced a mindset in the Soviet leadership that led it to be prepared for war emanating from west of its frontiers. When by 1939 the USSR was likewise menaced by militaristic Japan along the Soviet far eastern frontier bordering Japanese-occupied Manchuria, Stalin, the Politburo, and his military were all too aware of the tangible, imminent military threat that confronted them on not one but two widely separated fronts, west and east. Not an enviable situation!

How Stalin handled this ticklish situation—and he handled it with political acumen crossed with brutality—actually saved Soviet Russia and the Russian state. In a sense, the autocrat's success reverberates to the present day by having made the post-Soviet Russian Federation possible. Moreover, if with the defeat of the USSR by the Axis all of Eurasia had fallen into the enemies' hands, the very security of the United States would have been catastrophically endangered.

So if Stalin is deservedly *velikiy* to most Russians, maybe American and other Western readers should also reconsider their totally hostile attitude toward "the worst tyrant in world history," as Stalin surely was.

STALIN BLUFFS IN THE "GREAT GAME"

Prior to the German invasion of the USSR in late June 1941, Premier Stalin single-handedly dismissed crucial information supplied to him by his best foreign agents. Historians claim the Soviet dictator chose to ignore and even ostentatiously ridicule the intelligence data of his well-placed spies concerning Hitler's clear intention to invade the Soviet Union.

Yet Stalin's alleged "denial" of and dumbfoundedness over Operation Barbarossa, Hitler's attack plan for conquering the USSR, is now being questioned by some Russian historians. It appears the Soviet dictator may have intentionally allowed the German attack to occur. Above all, he was not going to allow Hitler to depict the Soviet Union as the aggressor. This, after all, was the deception the Nazis had perpetrated against the Poles and world opinion in late August 1939—the aggression that triggered World War II. Stalin remembered how the Germans had contrived the phony "Gleiwitz raid" by so-called "Poles" (that is, Germans dressed in Polish uniforms) against a German outpost on the German side of the Polish frontier. Hitler used this ersatz "raid" as a pretext for launching a war against the Polish "aggressor." It was thus uppermost to Stalin not to allow the Germans to pull this trick on the USSR in the coming big war. Russia must be seen as the victim in the world-historical war with Germany.

Russia also needed allies, the British and above all the Americans, who could lend the Soviet Union valuable aid (Lend-Lease) and moral support. In his May 5 speeches to the graduating cadets, Stalin had actually spoken of the importance of having allies in a major war as well as holding the moral high ground, which, as he told the cadets, the Germans had lost as a result of their perfidy and plundering. He contrasted Napoleon to Hitler in this respect by pointing out that whereas Napoleon had once been perceived as a liberator, he had become an oppressor. Hitler was always and remained an oppressor.

As of the spring of 1941, everyone could have guessed who those Soviet "allies" might well turn out to be, especially after the Soviet leader had spoken so negatively of the Germans at the Kremlin reception for the graduates.

In the spring of 1941, Hitler and his so-called allies were actively deploying upward of 190 divisions along the 1,800-plus-mile Soviet western border, which included the so-called Molotov Line drawn after the Soviet annexations of 1939–1940, when the Soviet border was shifted westward by at least 200 miles.

It is claimed conventionally that Stalin chose to ignore this obvious buildup. He recklessly dismissed the warnings of his agents and military commanders. He did so, it is alleged, because he feared he might encourage a German attack. Stalin, it is claimed, thus mindlessly left Russia unprepared for Hitler's onslaught. The Soviet dictator chose instead irrationally to appease Hitler with the famous editorial in *Pravda* on June 14, 1941, and repeated efforts to renew Moscow-Berlin talks—amid snubbing by Hitler and Ribbentrop. In this groveling way, it is claimed, Stalin thought he could postpone a German invasion. In any case, the Soviet leader is said to have reasoned that Hitler would not be so foolish as to fight a war on two fronts, west and east, as long as the British held out and were not defeated. So runs the prevalent explanation for Stalin's virtual inaction in the spring of 1941. It is found in many Western as well as Russian history books.

Meanwhile, however, some contemporary Russian historians dispute this version. Some authors, like Verkhovsky and Tyrmos, question this conventional view (and who can scarcely be accused of being "pro-Stalin"). Verkhovsky and Tyrmos note that the very contents of the German invasion plan had been known to Stalin since the autumn of 1940. By late winter 1940–1941, the precise date of the invasion, June 22, 1941, had been pinpointed by several Soviet agents in Germany and elsewhere. This date was reconfirmed by numerous Soviet intelligence sources in the spring of 1941. Relying on Enigma/Ultra code decryption of German general staff messages, London and Washington likewise weighed in by warning Stalin several times of the imminent danger of a Wehrmacht invasion. To quote an old Russian proverb, "One cannot hide an awl in one's pocket."

BARBAROSSA MATERIALIZES

On that fateful spring Sunday morning at 3:30, the Wehrmacht's S (*Stunde*)-hour attack signal, *Dortmund*, was transmitted to the well-equipped German forces numbering over 5 million amassed along Russia's serpentine western frontier. The German blitzkrieg jumped off and stormed eastward with all its destructive fury. The massive attack had devastating consequences for the thinly spread defending Red Army and Red Air Force, who were taken by surprise. RKKA strength along the enemy's main axes of attack was in many sectors five times weaker than those of the invaders. Over the following months, the Red Army found itself fighting largely losing battles on 12 operational fronts in the newly formed three main western fronts—the northwestern, western, and southwestern and their vulnerable border districts.

During the first two weeks alone, the enemy had penetrated more than 300 miles into Soviet territory. The Germans and their allies bombed and occupied the key industrialized parts of European Russia comprising 40 percent of the population, half of its entire quantity of artillery munitions, 63 percent of coal mining, well over half of steel and aluminum production, and the largest portion of the Soviet grain and meat breadbasket. By the autumn of 1941, they had crossed several rivers and defense lines, taken Minsk, Kiev, Dnepropetrovsk, Smolensk, and many other major towns and industrial centers in Byelorussia, Ukraine, and the RSFSR. As the German invasion proceeded, the Politburo in Moscow weakly ordered the Red Army to stay out of German-occupied territory. It confined Red Air Force missions from encroaching more than 90 miles inside enemy territory.

In the midsummer of that first calamitous year, the Wehrmacht and its allies stood at the gates of Moscow, Leningrad, and in the south at Rostov-on-Don and Odessa. In those months, 103,000 Soviet aircraft were destroyed. On the first day alone, 1,200 planes were destroyed, mostly on the ground, 20,500 tanks and vehicles, and more than 6 million small arms were lost. In 18 months of the "Great Patriotic War" (as Stalin chose to call it in memory of the war against Napoleon in 1812), the Germans had taken some 3 million Red Army POWs, 65 percent of the total defending forces. The Soviets had incurred a crippling loss of civilian and military lives and material destruction. One-third of the country's blast furnaces lay in ruins; steel production fell by almost 75 percent; the Donbas coal mines and the General-Electric equipped Dnepropetrovsk Dam were destroyed. The much-touted plan for mobilizing industrial output (1941–1942) was thrown totally out of kilter. Is it believable that Stalin could have been so "blind" and/or so brutal as to "allow" this to happen?

According to some younger Russian historians and memoirists who date back to the war and prewar years and who had insider experience (trusted agents like *shpionka* Zoya Rybkina [Voskresenskaya]), this disastrous opening phase of the war, she says, was the result of Stalin's "grand bluff."

STALIN'S NOT-SO-BLIND EYE

Such historians and witnesses as these dispute the conventional belief about Stalin's allegedly stubborn "state of denial" about Barbarossa, his supposed turning a blind eye to the enormous German buildup on Russia's western frontier.

These historians present a different rationale for Stalin's seemingly odd behavior. They claim during the first quarter of 1941 that Stalin, in fact, did *not* "ignore" the intelligence inputs of his own agents. Far from it; he knew perfectly well about the presence of the massive deployments of enemy troops and aircraft. How could he not be aware of them or deny what so patently was going on? The historians ask if it is really credible to imagine the well-informed, always suspicious, and involved Stalin would not be cognizant of the impending invasion.

Moreover, his sources included his most tested, reliable senior military commanders together with the world's best spy rings and agents. These agents included the *Rote Kapelle* (Red Orchestra) and key informants like double agent Richard Sorge, posted in Tokyo, who transmitted hundreds of well-documented pieces of intelligence concerning German invasion plans. Another such agent was a mole working deep inside the German general staff itself. Significantly, Stalin never purged any of these well-informed agents because of their ominous information. Ostensibly, yes, the Soviet dictator did bitterly criticize them, alleging the British were "instigating war" between the USSR and Germany. But that appears to have been blather, a form of Stalin disinformation (in Russian, *dez*).

Yet, as some Russian historians and ex-Soviet agents now argue, this was simply part of Stalin's game of bluff. Under no circumstances, Stalin reasoned, should the Soviet Union be accused of "inciting" the Germans, of giving them any excuse ("provocation" is the Russian term) for attacking.

In his memoir-interview shortly before he died in 1986, Molotov admitted: "We knew that war was coming, that we were weaker than Germany, that we would have to retreat. . . . The only question was how far would we have to withdraw? To Smolensk, to Moscow?"[4] As Molotov also disclosed: "[Our message in *Pravda*, June 14, 1941, that denied Soviet-German hostility] was justifiable. This was directed at giving the Germans no pretext for justifying their attack." (Goebbels, incidentally, appears to have been on to this Stalin ploy. He claimed in his diary at the time that the Soviet leader was attempting to place any guilt for war on Germany's shoulders.)

THE "BLUFF"

This was part of the bluff. Stalin calculated that in a war with the powerful, experienced Wehrmacht and its several armed allies, the relatively weak Soviets would need an alliance with the Western powers. Under no circumstances, therefore, should the USSR be perceived as an aggressor. This is how the USSR was perceived in the Winter War with Finland, 1939–1940. During this three-month conflict, Britain had actually threatened to bomb the Soviet Caucasus. Next time, in a much larger war, Stalin reasoned, Soviet Russia must be cast as the *victim* of attack, not the aggressor, and must close ranks with anti-Axis allies.

Actually, there were signs in late 1940 that Stalin was making overtures to Britain, and Prime Minister Winston Churchill, to do just that—close ranks against the common enemy.

On her part, Stalin's super-spy, Zoya Rybkina, an extremely intelligent and resourceful secret agent (who once waltzed with German Ambassador Schulenburg during an NKVD spy mission within the German embassy in Moscow), clearly perceived the bluff aspect of Stalin's public policy. She was careful, however, not to reveal that she knew what Stalin was up to. Recalling in a postwar memoir a meeting that her supervisor, Gen. Pavel Fitin, had with Stalin in the Kremlin, she writes that the dictator's posture in questioning the intelligence about the German threat "was part of Stalin's attempt to legitimize his own 'strategic plan.' By not deploying the necessary numbers of troops on our frontier, Stalin was letting the whole world know who really started the war. Although the Hitlerites regularly violated our air space and coastal areas, thereby trying to provoke us into retaliating, we did not succumb to this trick. Instead, we sought to receive aid from our allies, the U.S. and Britain, and thus gain the support of world public opinion." (Incidentally, Voskresenskaya was no Stalin apologist. She welcomed the dictator's death in March of 1953.)

There indeed is evidence that in the months preceding Barbarossa, Stalin put Marxist-Leninist ideology. He none too subtly courted London and Washington. He appeared, in fact, to have been paving the way toward a future alliance with the Western capitalist states, and especially with the well-heeled, anti-Axis "Arsenal of Democracy," America. As it turned out, U.S. Lend-Lease aid was indeed slated to include the Soviet Union as was indicated even *before* the German invasion. Stalin more than welcomed this proffered aid. In his remarkable "un-Communist" turnabout speech, broadcast on July 3, 1941, just 10 days after the German invasion, the Soviet dictator described the Western powers unprecedentedly as democratic "allies" (*soyuzniki*). He thereupon requested that the British send *troops* (!) to the USSR to help bolster Soviet defenses. Stalin and Marshal Zhukov appreciated this Lend-Lease aid that began reaching the Soviet armed forces by the autumn of 1941. Both of these leaders are on the record as describing Lend-Lease aid as crucial and indispensable in the Soviet victory over Germany.

Why had Stalin found it necessary to play this dangerous game of apparent denial that all but seemed to welcome the German "surprise" onslaught, a game leading to the disaster of the opening months of the 1,418-day long "Great Patriotic War"?

Writing in their recent, widely read, well-researched book (in Russian), *Stalin: Secret "Scenario" at the Beginning of the War*, Verkhovsky and Tyrmos show with rather convincing evidence that Stalin fully realized—as he many times complained to his own commanders and ministerial bureaucrats—how weak and unprepared his armies were as the threat of the German invasion loomed by the spring of 1941. The authors argue, given the fact that Soviet military preemption of the enemy invasion was out of the question (and was in any event rejected by Stalin), what other option did the Soviet leader have but to absorb the initial attacks and later launch counterattacks?

Stalin, in fact, appeared to be relying on the advent of a protracted war, a possibly short "creeping up to war" (*vpolzaniye v voinu*) as the RKKA covering forces engaged the invaders. Over days and weeks, the Soviets, it was assumed, would have time to stop or at least slow down the Wehrmacht's advance deep into Soviet territory. However, just what Stalin expected or planned in detail is still a closely guarded secret in Russia. This secrecy continues to trigger controversy among military historians in Russia as well as abroad. Yet it appears the Soviet dictator calculated by deploying echelon-by-echelon millions of reserve forces as the Germans advanced. In the end, the RKKA would ultimately surround and swamp the enemy.

In what appears to be the overall Soviet strategy as of the spring of 1941, the Soviets would employ tactics of "active defense" and powerful counterattacks mounted in a timely fashion by successive, well-armed, in-depth echelons (which, incidentally, resembled General Kutuzov's strategy in 1812). Employing such "fluid battle" tactics and tiered "tactical mobility," the war would in turn escalate—gradually, as Stalin imagined—into a "protracted war," which the Soviets, given their expanse of territory and advantage in manpower, were bound sooner or later to win.

Stalin's notorious inhumanity would allow for a likely massive loss of life among the Soviet defenders at the very beginning of hostilities because of his bluff of playing victimized sitting duck instead of meeting the German threat head-on preventively. To prepare for these probable initial losses, the Soviets had already begun in early 1941 moving production facilities (whole factories and assembly lines) from vulnerable western areas to safer locations eastward to the Ural Mountains.

They also secretly deployed additional RKKA divisions to the border districts.

Above all, the Soviet dictator did not intend to satisfy that cherished German hope of fighting a frontier *Hauptschlacht*—i.e., decisive, initial battles at the frontier, described by the eminent von Clausewitz and contemporary German strategists, which would determine the ultimate outcome of the war. This was supposed to resemble the Hitler-Guderian blitzkrieg tactics of 1940 updated in the spring of 1941 to utterly destroy the Soviets' frontline defensive forces. For decisive frontier battles to materialize, the German general staff had counted on large numbers of RKKA troops being deployed along the frontier (as resembled the case in the German attack on France in 1940).

Stalin, however, planned to prevent this German hope from being realized despite the fact that his military had committed large numbers of RKKA troops to guard the long frontier. Yet, instead of allowing a *Hauptschlacht* to decimate Soviet defenses, only half of the Soviet forces committed to defense in the initial stages of the conflict were deployed at the frontier. Stalin and his commanders had now contemplated a tiered, deep-echelon defense (which was based on the conclusions drawn from the secret February 1941 Soviet war games). However, too little time remained to flesh out this apparently sensible strategy.

STALIN'S COSTLY ERRORS

As Stalin and his commanders, including Zhukov, later admitted, the leaders had placed too much confidence in the underequipped NKVD and RKKA covering forces deployed in the first echelons along the frontier. The German blitzkrieg easily smashed through this line with its many gaps. Nor had they counted on the factor of surprise as being so crucial. Some authors also maintain that Stalin's overall offensive strategy contributed to the disaster. "The fault," wrote Fugate and Dvoretsky, "was not in ignoring the threats of war and 'being caught off guard' by the German onslaught. The fault was Stalin's adherence too long on a first-strike or offensive war strategy for the Red Army plus his failure to allow the February 1941 defense plan to be implemented fully to the extent demanded by his ablest leaders."

The frontline forces had been assigned to blocking and at least to slowing down the advancing Wehrmacht—at least until the RKKA could retaliate with massive, offensive counterattacks. According to the Soviet plan, these were to be executed by the numerous well-armed Soviet reserve forces that would augment the defending echelons westward toward the rear. However, the lack of preparation as well as of past experience (among new commanders) in organizing this complex, dynamic type of mobile defense led to the disaster in the opening days, weeks, and months of the war.

Unfortunately for the Soviets, the Germans, by maximizing the factor of surprise and mastering "tempo" (the pace of attack), had succeeded in disrupting this evolution of the battle—or "operational pace"—as envisioned by the Soviet commanders. As a result, the Soviet failure to stop the onslaught reached a catastrophic point. The RKKA command, control, and communications and the Soviet capacity to maneuver and carry out deployments of additional troops were utterly disrupted.

SOVIET WEAKNESSES

To cite some of the glaring, underlying weaknesses on the Soviet side as evidently perceived by Stalin himself in 1941, as tacitly admitted by Stalin's number one confidante, Molotov, and as documented by military historians:

- The defending Soviet forces were poorly led. Stalin's purges of 1937 and later had decapitated the RKKA of its most competent, experienced line and staff officer corps. Stalin, as usual, hounded his professional military, threatening them with repression, which was known as "having tea in the basement of Lyubyanka," that is, with Lavrenti Beria, "Stalin's Himmler."
- While some deployed Soviet equipment was state-of-the-art, much of it was not or was not of the highest quality nor in sufficient numbers in the hands of troops. The newest, best machines were still in production or on the drawing board and were otherwise not deployed. In many cases, as with the diesel-powered, heavily armored T-34 and KV tanks—and, in fact, with vehicles within the entire RKKA vehicle park—were in large numbers under repair and/or otherwise out of service. Nor in numerous cases did recruits know how to operate the new vehicles. The Red Air Force had not yet fully deployed the new Yak-1 and Pe-2 light bombers. Of the total Red Air Force park of 18,000 aircraft, only about 3,700 were of the latest models.

- A major weakness of the RKKA defense was the chaos associated with the Soviet employment of mechanized forces. Stalin had earlier vacillated on the usefulness of mechanized corps. Until 1940, he had left disbanded the formation of the Soviet version of the German panzers. By June 1941, he had changed his mind and endorsed such mechanized corps. But there had not been time to create and integrate such formations into the RKKA's order of battle. By the time of Barbarossa, many Soviet mechanized units were understrength and equipped with obsolete vehicles. Horses and a motorized infantry were the main Soviet forces facing the highly mobile Wehrmacht. Only one such mechanized RKKA corps, the VI attached to the 10th Army, was up to full combat strength. It took the Soviets, in fact, two years to perfect full exploitation of mechanized corps and the tactics associated with them. This accounted in large part for the German victories in battle, including those in which the Wehrmacht was outnumbered by the RKKA, up to mid-1943 and the Battle of Kursk.

- The western frontier could not be fully covered because of lack of trained, equipped troops to fill in the many gaps. The reputed Moscow military research group, *Strategiya KM*, recently presented data showing how weak were the 182 RKKA divisions eventually deployed along the western frontier, 80 percent making up the first strategic echelon. These were the soldiers, including NKVD border troops, who took the brunt of the Wehrmacht's juggernaut. As Stalin and others calculated, most of these forces would be in the beginning—as they actually were—outnumbered by the enemy in some sectors by as much as from four to six times. In the largely inexpert hands of these frontier forces were 47,000 infantry weapons, including mortars, 5,000 aircraft, and more than 4,000 tanks. Most of this equipment was lost in the very opening days. Moreover, Stalin insisted on concentrating his best-equipped defending forces to the south bordering Romania and Ukraine. He thought the main German thrust would be through that oil-rich region. Yet the German strategists outfoxed the Soviet commanders. They opted for their main offensive to be centered north, not south of the Pripet marshes. This choice of main axis of attack at the center enormously enhanced the factor of surprise for the Wehrmacht. It exposed the error of Stalin's fixation on the southern axis.

- The western portions of the USSR, moreover, contained the most untrustworthy populations. These were the millions of discontented Poles, Ukrainians, Balts, and Romanians who had been forcibly sovietized in 1939–1940 under Nazi-Soviet collaboration. These forcible annexations by the Soviets allowed Stalin to pick up territory—as the retired Molotov boasted to an interviewer in the 1980s—that "extended the frontiers of socialism." But it also meant inheriting less trustworthy populations as well as challenging Soviet ability to arm and defend these territorial acquisitions.

• Prewar Five-Year Plan targets, as usual, were not met, despite Stalin's draconic measures in June 1940 that penalized minor worker tardiness, let alone absenteeism, with dockings of pay and even imprisonment.

STALIN APPROVES A MODIFIED KUTUZOV STRATEGY

Given these and other unfavorable circumstances, by the early spring of 1941, the Soviet dictator appears perforce to have opted for a modified "Kutuzov"-like defense-in-depth strategy.[5] His idea evidently was to combine defensive as well as offensive tactics. It was the strategy adopted by the great Russian hero-general who had led his country's defense against Napoleon's Grande Armée. Kutuzov had defeated the enemy by swallowing up his armies within the Russian expanse and later overwhelming the French in numbers of troops. (Stalin, well aware of this tradition, even cast a soldier-hero's medal in the name of tsarist General Kutuzov.)

Some Russian historians now claim that Stalin, instead of planning an unthinkable preemptive attack against the poised enemy, chose to bluff. He began to act publicly and among his aides as if nothing untoward were happening in German-Soviet relations. By means of Aesopian language, published in unsigned articles in *Pravda* (such as the notorious, unsigned editorial of June 14, 1941), in open and/ or secret diplomatic messages relayed by Stalin to Berlin (including a bizarre proposal for a Hitler-Stalin summit to be held in the spring of 1941 (a proposal that was intentionally leaked to the world), Stalin continued to demonstrate ostentatiously that he stood for peace with the German-led Axis. He made sure such peaceful intentions and signals were widely publicized for the consumption of world public opinion.

Despite, or better, because of the looming German threat to the west, Stalin ordered his own Red Army line and staff officers to make absolutely no response, let alone execute any aggressive move against Germany. These were Stalin's orders even when Luftwaffe recon aircraft, in some cases even German ground troops, periodically violated Soviet borders. Even after the initial German attacks of June 22, 1941, Stalin acted as though this "incursion" might have been a mere "provocation" hatched by certain" irresponsible" German commanders who had not been so ordered by Hitler to attack the USSR. Instead of making any plans to disrupt the impending invasion, the Soviet dictator chose demonstratively to "placate" the enemy. For instance, NKVD operative Ambassador Dekanozov was instructed to continue tirelessly (Stalin evidently used this as bluff appeasement) to propose Soviet German negotiations to German Foreign Minister Ribbentrop. This ploy was duly continued for many hours even *after* the German attack, with Ribbentrop simply ignoring ostentatious Dekanozov's entreaties.

Throughout the spring of 1941, Stalin indicated that the Soviets for their part would continue to honor peace and remain loyal to the "everlasting friendship and cooperation" embodied in the Nazi-Soviet agreements of 1939 and 1940. These landmarks included the nonaggression and friendship pacts, secret protocols, and trade agreements of those years that the Soviet media incessantly harped on the Stalin party line about the "enduring" Soviet-German friendship for months prior to the invasion. (This posture of appeasement amused Nazi propaganda chief Goebbels. In his diary, he ridiculed the Soviets for their "cowardice," suggesting Stalin's game was to try to put the onus of war on Hitler's shoulders.) Moreover, the Soviets kept on sending the large-scale shipments of Soviet strategic material to Germany right up to late June 1941. Sent by rail without interruption to Germany for over one-and-a-half years, they were valued at some $65 million (in today's prices, nearly $500 million). These Soviet supplies consisted of food, petroleum, tin, copper, nickel, tungsten, molybdenum, rolled steel, and other strategic manufactured and raw materials. There was nothing secret about these shipments. The Soviets advertised them as peaceful gestures.

DID THE BLUFF PAY OFF?

By appearing to delay the obvious, thereby supposedly gaining time to build up Soviet defenses, what was the ultimate rationale behind Stalin's bluff? Some researchers say Stalin, under no circumstances, was going to give Hitler the pretext to claim that the

Wehrmacht's invasion had been "forced" on the Germans by Soviet aggression—as, in fact, Hitler actually did claim the day after the German invasion. As noted above, the Soviet leader reasoned that the USSR must by all means prevent Germany from perpetrating another fraudulent "provocation," as the Nazis had done with their phony Gleiwitz raid of August 1939. Ironically, this was the same ploy that Stalin himself used in December 1939 as a pretext for *his* aggressive war against Finland by claiming that Finland had dropped artillery salvos on the Russian village of Mainila on the outskirts of Leningrad. This pretext was later exposed by the League of Nations' Lytton Commission, embarrassingly for Moscow, as a fraud. The exposure led to the expulsion of the Soviet Union from the league, a humiliation that severely sullied Stalin's much-cultivated Soviet image of a "peace-loving nation." This also contributed to the further isolation of the USSR at a time when it desperately needed allies.

PREVENTING A RUSSIAN "GLEIWITZ"

Days before Barbarossa was unleashed, Stalin ordered all available NKVD border guard agents to thoroughly police the frontier to make sure no such German "provocation" of the Gleiwitz type was being hatched as a pretext given world public opinion to excuse the German aggression.

Throughout June 1941, Stalin continued publicly to "ignore" the warnings sent to him from London and Washington on the imminence of the German invasion. Items appeared for foreign and domestic consumption in the Soviet media that stressed the appeasement line toward Germany. Stalin was protecting the moral high ground. Yet at the same time, Stalin and his military continued fleshing out the western frontier with RKKA deployments, movements by truck and rail carried out at night and explained deceptively as "training exercises."

As pointed out earlier, Stalin knew the invasion threat was real and was based on absolutely hard intelligence as reported to him by his very able spy rings, and which in some cases was derived from Enigma/Ultra Western intelligence. (It appears that Stalin knew that Enigma was the source of this intelligence as shared with him by Churchill from London.) Under such dire, threatening circumstances, what did Stalin's own military defense plan look like?

STALIN'S MILITARY DEFENSE PLAN

According to several Russian historians and such experts as the British author John Erickson, Fugate and Dvoretsky, and others, Stalin aimed to defeat the Germans by means of absorbing the initial attacks and then by a "proactive defense" to destroy the enemy. What Stalin's actual plans were is still a closely guarded secret in Russia.

As Russian émigré military specialist Col. Robert Savushkin explained, "Stalin evidenced anxiety [about the German threat]. . . . He gave permission to bring troops to combat readiness, but once again reminded them of behaving so as not to yield to provocation or allow themselves to be drawn into war. But it was already too late."[6]

If the depiction of the USSR as the victim of aggression was a Stalin motivation for his policy of appeasement of Hitler in the immediate pre-attack period, his tactic had worked. The Soviet Union had become entitled to Lend-Lease aid and its life-saving, if "strange," alliance with the Western powers.

HOW "UNPREPARED" WAS THE RKKA?

As Joseph W. Kipp, noted Russian-reading specialist on the Red Army at the Foreign Military Studies Office at Fort Leavenworth, Kansas, has written, it is an exaggeration to contend that the RKKA, with Stalin's acceptance, was taken utterly by surprise on June 22 or that, thanks to Stalin and others, the military was "totally" unprepared and that it could have risen to the Wehrmacht challenge.[7] That a better defense was impossible was not Stalin's or even the RKKA leadership's fault.

The fact is that there was simply not enough time or the equipment and other factors by which an adequate defense could have been mounted. The civilian and military leadership from Stalin on down did the best they could under the adverse circumstances. As other military writers have suggested, if Stalin and the military had committed more troops directly to defense at the frontier, the debacle might have been even worse, the loss of men and equipment that much greater. The debacle in the opening weeks of the war thus might have spelled the utter defeat for the USSR if Stalin and RKKA leadership had met the Germans for a decisive *Hauptschlacht,* or border showdown, with the Germans, as some of the latter strategists had hoped—but in vain since Stalin did not oblige. The author deems "nonsensical" the widely held notion among Western historians that the Soviets in their operations theory and actual combat neglected the study and application of tactics for strategic or tactical defense. Kipp points out that in the summer of 1939 in their border war with the Japanese at Khalkin-Gol, Soviet forces under Zhukov had, in fact, adopted prolonged defensive tactics until sufficient forces were brought into the theater of military action in order for the RKKA to conduct offensive operations. As he notes, "Reading of the 1936 RKKA Field Regulations beyond the first chapter's general principles, must lead to the conclusion that the Red Army accepted defense as a means to an end."

Kipp further explains that the question of whether the Soviets can be accused of failing to appreciate the full dimensions of the German threat and particularly the potential decisiveness of blitzkrieg is a salient one. The issue concerning decisiveness of initial operations had always been a topic of debate within the RKKA whenever discussion turned to the "future war" and the "initial period of war." Some thinkers had warned that there would be no creeping up to war and no time to prepare for an enemy blitzkrieg. Instead, there would be a "leap into war."

In the pre-June 1941 period of discussion and war planning, a consensus seemed to develop among the Soviet war planners that the best option for meeting such a threat would be to carry out its concentration and deployment of defending forces in echelons still further from the frontier so as to avoid the dreaded *Hauptschlacht.* This danger would increase, of course, as the enemy's forces, in planning blitzkrieg, enjoyed a number of key advantages, e.g., in combat experience, coordinated use of combined mobile forces, superior communications, and so on.

The unresolved issue was how might the Soviet Union deal with that threat as Nazi-Soviet relations deteriorated from the late fall of 1940 to the spring of 1941. As Kipp writes:

> [By the spring of 1941] the Soviet military and political elites undertook a series of prudent measures to improve the Soviet

defensive posture during those last months of peace. . . . Soviet military doctrine emphasized intensive actions during the initial period of war, but it still saw those actions in terms of covering force engagements, in which the forward elements of the first strategic echelon would disrupt enemy deployments, while protecting the deployment of the rest of the first strategic echelon and provide the time for the mobilization, concentration, and deployment of the second strategic echelon.

This author together with military specialists Fugate and Dvoretsky notes that the commanders' conference of December 1940 and the war games of January 1941 together with the February game, however, pointed out a number of dilemmas associated with this posture. The reports, including by Zhukov, indicated that the stubborn fact of the spring of 1941 was that the western borderlands posed a new and different set of problems relating directly to the conduct of operations in the initial phase of the war. This meant that the Soviets, not having had time to fortify the new regions it had annexed in 1940, would be vulnerable to German attack. The construction of fortifications along the Molotov Line had been very slow. Even with this effort, the pace of construction was painfully slow. Kipp continues:

> "The Soviets continued their own practice of creeping up on war by engaging in covert mobilization which would allow them to improve substantially their defensive posture without provoking a preemptive move by Hitler's Germany. Overt mobilization was, as Marshal Shaposhnikov described it in *Mozg armii [Brain of the Army]*, an act of war, which would impose the onus for starting hostilities upon the USSR [my emphases—A. L. W.].

As to where the RKKA would undertake its counteroffensives as the Wehrmacht predictably drove forward, Stalin had opposed placing the main effort in the Western Special Military District, or central front on a beeline on the uplands leading toward Moscow. Instead, Stalin opted for a concentration in the Kiev Special Military District. In terms of where and how the Germans actually struck at the USSR in late June with the greatest force, Stalin was proved wrong. German strategists put the emphasis on the central, not the southern direction (*napravleniye*). Yet Stalin's rationale suggested, Kipp continues, that the Soviet leader had opted for the strategy of a "prolonged war" (*zatyaznaya voina*), or war of attrition. He showed that defending the Ukraine and the vital, resource-rich southwestern regions of the USSR would be the key to victory. Given the size of the Soviet Union and its retention of forces of production as well as sources of raw materials safely in the country's interior, and the assistance it expected to receive as an ally of the West, and above all of the United States, Soviet Russia could be assured of defeating the enemy. Under the circumstances, prolonged war would be the best defense for the USSR. "Stalin believed," writes Kipp, "that in the case of a prolonged struggle the industrial wealth, agricultural products, and raw materials [would prove vital]."

12

Epilogue: Winning the War, Losing the Peace

When World War II ended amid the usual postwar calls for "no more wars," Stalin unwisely resumed the pursuit of ideological antagonism and Soviet expansionism approximately where it had left off before June 1941.

If under Stalin's leadership in the face of Axis aggression Soviet acquisition of geostrategic positions of strength prior to June 1941 made some sense. After the end of the war following the four-year period of East-West wartime collaboration, Soviet expansionism became an anachronism. The "buffer" territory seized by the Soviets to the west of its frontiers in 1940—deemed by Moscow, fellow-travelers, and current historian-eulogists of Stalin as territory seized merely in order to absorb any future German attack—was permanently absorbed into the USSR. It remained so after 1945.

These independent lands became sovietized as integral parts of an ever-expanding Soviet empire. With the Soviet Army's occupation of some half-dozen countries of central, southeastern, and Eastern Europe under Generalissimus/Gensek/Premier Stalin's dictatorial guidance, there began a period of additional Soviet expansion and determined "satellitization" of countries in a region (one of the world's oldest seats of civilization, in fact) of formerly independent countries commonly known as Eastern Europe. The whole world watched as these occupied nations (Austria was an exception when the Soviets withdrew their occupation forces in 1954, a year after Stalin's death) essentially remained captive, oppressed nations until the demise of the USSR in 1991.

Stalin had thus unfurled another "anti-imperialist struggle," to use the Soviet term, that he decided to resume after World War II. With this policy came the establishment of the Cominform and the Party Central Committee's Information Bureau. Both of these bodies served as surrogates of the old Comintern, which Stalin had ostentatiously disbanded in 1943, an event which some optimistic observers had taken as symptomatic of a Soviet shift away from Communist "internationalism."

The ensuing Cold War, clearly started from the Soviet side in 1946, lasted some 40 years. Costing each side from $4–10 trillion, it was crossed with violent episodes and proxy wars that were encouraged and supplied by the Soviets and their newly become quasi-ally, Maoist China. Besides the Korean and Vietnam wars, more than 100 other conflicts, as tabulated in the 1970s by the official Yugoslav Communist newspaper, *Borba,* became part of the violent, post-World War II global landscape. All these wars and local conflicts, the Yugoslav Communist paper said, were Marxist-Leninist inspired.

In the UN Security Council, Stalin and the Soviet Union further displayed their postwar antagonism by issuing more than 100 vetoes in the five postwar years. This helped isolate the USSR from the other four permanent members of the council. The obstreperous Soviet blockade of Berlin in 1948 was simply one of several episodes in which Stalin single-handedly all but destroyed whatever comity had existed in the East-West wartime alliance.

Needless to say, the Soviet media rattled with Cold War rhetoric. It was returned with equal rancor and suspiciousness from the Western side. This was a struggle in which, among others, many institutions and objective scholars in the West were groundlessly attacked (this author included, as in a long *Izvestiya* article written by this government daily's foreign editor, M. Mikhailov). Other victims of Soviet media attacks included George Kennan, Frederick Barghoorn of Yale, Zbigniew Brzezinski, and other scholars. In addition, there were dangerous "brushes" at sea and in the air between armed forces units of the United States and the USSR. These encounters at times threatened to ignite a hot war between the two well-armed powers.

HINTS OF A COMING COLD WAR, 1946

A month *before* Winston Churchill delivered his famous "iron curtain" speech at Fulton, Missouri, on March 5, 1946, Stalin, on February 9, had already indicated that by then he had begun designing that curtain, and even earlier. It seemed that the Soviet dictator, not satisfied with relishing the Allied victory over the enemy as well as his own timely preparations for war in the 1930s and his leadership in the Great Patriotic War on the eastern front, turned his attention to strengthening his dictatorship as well as laying plans for further expansion of Soviet power abroad. The same brutality that had accompanied his rule before the war again cropped up soon after 1945.

Stalin's electoral speech of early February sounded ominous notes. In this address, the Soviet leader declared that World War II had been no "accident" but had been quite predictable.[1] It was not an ad hoc product of an adventurous Nazi leadership, Stalin suggested; it had not been caused by any such "subjective" factors. In Stalin's view, war had flowed necessarily from the capitalist system.

In this ominous speech, the Soviet leader proceeded to sketch out a postwar economic program in which, as before the war, heavy industry linked to defense production would be emphasized over the lower, "Group B" inputs and outputs of consumer goods. The Soviet dictator appeared to be serious when he remarked to the Yugoslav Communist official, Milovan Djilas, in Moscow in that same year that soon, as Stalin put it, "We'll have another go at it." He also told Djilas that the Soviets would impose their Communist system as far as the Soviet Army would reach.[2] Presumably, this meant another "big war"—World War III—a war that, as Molotov said of the preceding big war in his interviews with Chuev in the 1980s, might further "extend socialism" worldwide. The Soviet ambassador to the UN, Yakov Malik, went so far in 1952 as to remark that "World War III has already begun."

Throughout the whole postwar period, traditional Marxist-Leninist ideological pronouncements again cropped up in the political literature. Soviet-inspired vitriol about "capitalist imperialism" again took center stage on the diplomatic level as well as in Soviet-controlled media as Soviet foreign policy veered toward ever-increasing anti-Western hostility.

The opening of a new, dangerous era of East-West tensions and outright armed conflicts—with Stalin's support and evident initiative—was a shock to all those, whether in Russia or in the West, who had entertained the notion of a new, live-and-let-live relationship between the Western democracies, in particular the United States, and the Soviet Union under Stalin's—"Uncle Joe's"—continuing leadership. Evidence that Stalin and his Politburo colleagues were declaring a postwar Cold War against the capitalist states severely disillusioned many people, particularly among Soviet sympathizers in the West. Still, in some cases, being unable or unwilling to impute the hostility mainly to Stalin and the Soviets, such fellow-travelers instead blamed Washington and the Truman administration that succeeded Roosevelt's in April 1945 for the demise of U.S.-Soviet comradeship-in-arms.[3]

For other more objective observers, it seemed incomprehensible that Stalin would pick up the mantra and cudgels of "anti-imperialism" and scorn for capitalism and "liberal democracy" exactly where Soviet propaganda had left off before 1941. Added to this Stalin's intractability and reactionism was stepped up NKVD/GRU espionage against the United States. This spying was mainly directed at obtaining know-how for designing and manufacturing a Soviet A-bomb. The Soviet effort, which was under Lavrenti Beria's direction, merged with Stalin's overall postwar defense plans to modernize the Soviet armed forces. In particular, this meant upgrading the Soviet air force with long-range bombers with ranges that would allow them to reach targets in America and return to bases in the Soviet Union. The Soviets also began doing research and development on rockets as carriers of nuclear warheads.

Observers recalled that tensions between Stalin and Washington—that is, between Stalin and FDR in the latter's final months before he died on April 12, 1945—had already set in late in the war. Earlier East-West differences had arisen over numerous issues ranging from accusations concerning delayed Allied opening of a second front in Europe. Its postponement until June 1944 was attributed by Stalin in his media and in correspondence with Allied leaders to Western stubbornness and/or a deliberate attempt on the part of the West to see the Soviet Union bear the burden of war against Nazi Germany. Another omen of approaching East-West discord was Stalin's betrayal of East-West agreements concluded at the Big Three Yalta summit in 1944. These concerned promised establishment of free, democratic political systems in the countries of Eastern Europe under Soviet army occupation.

Another antagonistic factor during the war was Stalin's bitter allegations that the Western powers would likely make a separate peace with Germany and leave the USSR out of the picture altogether as co-victor. Another Soviet propaganda ploy was to claim that the United States was even planning to invade the USSR. An obligato to this yarn was supplied by Soviet sources concerning Hitler's fate after the spring of 1945. The Soviet propaganda machine bandied it about that Hitler might still be alive, hiding in the West and about to once again perform services for "Western imperialism." The truth was that Stalin's NKVD had recovered Hitler's remains in Berlin in May 1945. They knew that the fuehrer had committed suicide in his bunker. Today Hitler's bones, including part of his bullet-ridden skull, are held under lock and key in the Russian Federation.

These and other such accusations were upsetting to most Western officials and the public. Soviet propaganda and actions suggested to them the persistence of tensions between East and West that would likely continue and even deepen after the war.

COLD WAR CHRONOLOGY

The timing of the train of events and signs of this postwar East-West conflict are often obscured in books about the period. The question of when and to whom to assign the initiation of the Cold War has often been addressed.[4] It was later notably tackled, for example, in "Letters" in the liberal *New York Review of Books* issues of September 8 and October 20, 1966. The correspondence was published in response to controversial articles for *NYRB* written by Arthur Schlesinger Jr. and Gar Alperovitz. Both had debated as to where the responsibility had lain for initiating the Cold War.

For his part, Schlesinger had referred to French Communist leader Jacques Duclos's militant, "Cominternist" article published in April 1945 in *Cahiers du Communisme.* Schlesinger demonstrated to Alperovitz that the Cold War did *not* begin with Allen Dulles's falsely alleged, "secret 1945 negotiations with the Nazis." Soviet-American Cold War antagonism, he wrote, clearly stemmed from actions undertaken by the Stalin regime, not by the United States.

This author commented in two published letters noted above that both historians were engaging in futile pinpointing of the exact start of the Cold War. I suggested that in any case Soviet-American animosity went back a good deal farther than April 1945, perhaps even as far back as the Bolshevik seizure of power in Russia in November 1917. Yet, as I wrote, if one were to single out an obvious, more recent event for the beginning of the Cold War, the Yalta conference of February 1945 might be a convincing starting point. This conference saw the first signs of a downhill course in Soviet-American relations (we omit here an analysis of this conference while referring any interested readers to the studies cited in the following discussion).

Moreover, the downturn was the culmination of a process of East-West alienation that had actually set in during World War II itself. Early, nuanced evidence of this was Stalin's decision in the mid-1940s to remove the moderate Earl Browder from leadership of the CPUSA (he was eventually expelled from membership in the CPUSA). Browder was purged after Duclos had attacked him. Significantly, in Browder's place, the hard-line William Z. Foster was made general secretary of the CPUSA. It was an important signal of the gist of Stalin's emergent postwar policy particularly as it applied to America.[5] Also, this indication came, notably, just at the time of Yalta. What transpired at Yalta clearly demonstrated the beginning of the freeze in Soviet-American relations.

The details of this crucial conference of February 4–11, 1945, have been canvassed many times by reputed historians and assorted writers. In this author's opinion, perhaps the best overall summary may be found in *Soviet Diplomacy and Negotiating Behavior: Emerging New Context for U.S. Diplomacy*, Vol. 1, a special study prepared by a team of scholars for the House of Representatives Committee on Foreign Affairs in 1979. The contents of the voluminous study were perhaps best summed up by George Kennan in his monumental 8,000-word response to a U.S. State Department request in 1946 for an explanation of the then-puzzling hostile Soviet behavior. Kennan's report was in turn summarized in his famous "X" article published in *Foreign Affairs* in that publication's June issue of 1947. Former U.S. Ambassador to the Soviet Union John R. Deane had described this behavior in similar terms in his book, *The Strange Alliance*, as follows:[6]

> "In my opinion there can no longer be any doubt that that Soviet leadership has always been motivated by the belief that communism and capitalism cannot coexist. Nor is there any doubt in my mind that present-day Soviet leaders have determined upon a program pointed toward imposing communism on those countries under their control and, elsewhere, creating conditions favorable to the triumph of communism in the war against capitalism, which they consider to be inevitable."

The pent-up hostility between the United States and the USSR, shelved "for the duration," floated to the surface as soon as victory loomed on the horizon. As the defeat of Nazi Germany approached, the whole postwar settlement of Europe clearly lay before these two most militarily powerful powers in the world, the United States and the USSR. Their bipolarity was thrown in relief by the weakness of both France and Britain by the end of the war. Of course, long before Yalta, Stalin and his associates had made it clear, and not only via pontifical ideological pronouncements, that the Soviets considered all of Eastern Europe their exclusive bailiwick, a region to be "liberated" by the Red Army and subject to sovietization.

Rereading chapter XXXII of Robert E. Sherwood's *Roosevelt and Hopkins—An Intimate History* is instructive. In this chapter, entitled "Beginnings of Dissension," Sherwood, a playwright and part-time historian, details the degree to which the Soviet-American "strange alliance" had deteriorated by the winter of 1944–1945. Singling out March 1945, Sherwood reports in his chapter on the Yalta conference that by the middle of that month, a situation had developed in Romania that strongly indicated that the Russians were determined to set up governments in Eastern Europe in conformance with their own interpretation of the word "friendly" and without regard for the principles of the Atlantic Charter of 1941, to which Moscow had given at least verbal support. Soviet machinations in Poland in 1944–1945 had also become a sore point.

It was beginning to appear evident that a complete deadlock had developed among the British, Russian, and American conferees, as Sherwood noted. There was now a growing feeling of uneasiness born of the unknown and the inexplicable regarding the true relationship between the Soviet Union and the United States, Great Britain, and the other members of the United Nations. It was beginning to be feared that a monstrous fraud had been perpetrated at Yalta, with Roosevelt and Churchill as the unwitting dupes. A similar description and dating at Yalta of the manifest worsening of Soviet-American relations may be found in George F. Kennan's classic *Russia and the West Under Lenin and Stalin*.

The East-West freeze process had clearly accelerated toward the end of the European phase of World War II. While it is also clear that the Western Allies are not entirely blameless for the East-West disagreements that arose, it is clearer that Stalin's Russia played the crucial role in initiating what came to be called the Cold War. The Soviet leader did this mainly by supporting or instigating political, economic, and military aggression in the 1940s and 1950s. Stalin's policy of Communist expansionism led to the formation of NATO and the Warsaw Pact Alliance, two armed fortresses facing each other. Stalin's rejection of the Marshall Plan in 1947 was especially symptomatic of the Soviet leader's postwar, anti-West posture. So was his promotion of a new ideological war that was outlined and led by the party by his favored party secretary of that immediate postwar era, the notorious hard-line West-baiter, Andrei A. Zhdanov.

A "NEW" STALIN?

During his maneuvering in the troubling, dangerous times of the late 1930s, Stalin showed himself to be a skillful if amoral leader. His speech of July 3, 1941, might have been considered a favorable harbinger of imminent, positive change in the Soviet leader's overall attitude toward the West. Yet it was a call for East-West comity that was pegged merely to the war.

Having "saved the Russian state," as pro-Stalin historians today like to put it, the Soviet dictator had the opportunity to show even more flexibility and statesmanship toward the West in the postwar environment. He refused. Why did he sully the chance of becoming the leader of a totalitarian state who would act as a reformer at home while adopting a new course abroad toward his wartime Allies now that the "Fascist menace" that had appeared in the international arena in 1933 had been liquidated? Instead, Stalin brought back to life in his policies at home and abroad all of the worst features of his dictatorship and methods of ruling the party and state. These included the rejuvenated Lazarus of class struggle ideology; hatred of capitalism; and concern over the legitimacy of his own, one-party regime. Did Stalin resort to this reactionism because his sole motivation had always been merely to protect and increase his own personal autocratic power?

He had spoken so often of democracy and harmonious East-West relations in interviews (even before the war) and at the summits with the two other members of the Big Three. At home as well, Stalin could have carried forward the democratic-sounding promises made at the time of the 1936 "Stalin" constitution and made real the propaganda promises that accompanied the constitution's appearance. However, after 1945 instead of reform, he hardened the domestic as well as foreign policies of the state.

TODAY'S RUSSIAN HISTORIANS ON THE COLD WAR

In the preceding chapters of this book, we have examined the work of the prolific historian Arsen B. Martirosyan. Recall that this was the historian whom Putin's Ministry of Justice had singled out to deliver a significant lecture on Russian historiography to a group of criminal law students at a prestigious law institute in Tula in 2009. This may not necessarily imply that the Russian government approves in its entirety Martirosyan's recasting of Soviet and Russian history. However, it seems doubtful that the most important "power" ministry, as police-related offices are known in Russia, the central Ministry of Justice headed by a Putin appointee, would sanction a major speech directly under ministry auspices if Martirosyan's overall treatment of Russian history were anything less than acceptable to the top authorities. This is especially true in the light of President Medvedev's earlier decree of that year on education, specifically on the teaching and writing of Russian history.

What are this prolific historian's views toward Stalin's postwar policies?[7] Perhaps not surprisingly, the professor endorses all of Stalin's hard-line postwar policies and actions. He claims that these measures, especially in foreign policy and Soviet rearmament, were absolutely necessary because of aggressive "Western Anglo-Saxon designs against the USSR."

He begins his discussion by alluding to Churchill's Fulton, Missouri, speech but ignores Stalin's monumental electoral speech of the month before. As he discusses Churchill's address of March 5, 1946 (the Russian historians gives an incorrect date of Churchill's speech), inter alia, Martirosyan laces in comments on the theoretical British contingency plan of 1945, "unthinkable" to militarily oppose any Soviet army attempt to impose its will forcibly further into Europe in 1945. The Russian historian casts this contingency document of the British Armed Forces Joint Planning Staff as an actual, concrete plan to invade the USSR by July 1945! He claims that Stalin got wind of this "attack plan" through the well-known NKVD agent and Deputy Chief of Covert Intelligence (*nelegal' naya razvedka*) Iskhak Abdulovich Akhmerov (the name is Tartar). Akhmerov had been transferred in 1932 to NKVD foreign intelligencer and first served under diplomatic cover in Turkey and other countries in the 1930s, including China. During World War II, Akhmerov operated in the United States by posing as a clothier and using such cover names William Grienke, Michael Green, and Michael Adamec. He was one of Moscow's most productive agents and used code names in intercepted Venona decrypts of Soviet intelligence messages like "Mayor" and "Albert." In late 1945 or early 1946, Akhmerov was returned to the USSR and was promoted to NKVD Deputy Chief of Covert Intelligence Section with the rank of colonel. He received the Order of Red Banner twice and other awards, including that of Honored Chekist. One of his closest contacts in the United States had been with Roosevelt aide Harry Hopkins, who had been the key figure establishing the contents of Lend-Lease aid to the USSR in Hopkins' extended talks with Stalin in July 1941. Hopkins was regarded by the NKVD as a "quasi"-agent, not as a deliberate one. Martirosyan also cites alleged U.S. plans to invade the USSR.[8] In summation, the historian states that, "it was not Stalin who was planning World War II but the West, and especially the United States that hoped to subject the Soviet Union to barbarous nuclear bombardment. Nor was it Stalin who had declared the Cold War or lowered an Iron Curtain. All this was the work of the West. Such is the historical truth" (pp. 22–23).

Holding a diametrically opposed position from Martirosyan and, in fact, to most historians in Russia or the West on the postwar Stalin is the writer (apparently of Ukrainian descent) Keistut Aleksandrovich Zakoretskiy. This author presents himself on several promotion-type Russian Web sites as the right hand of Viktor Suvorov (Vladimir Rezun), author of *Ice-Breaker* and other books describing Stalin's alleged plans to wage a preemptive war against the USSR in the summer of 1941. Suvorov wrote the preface for Zakoretskiy's current volume, *Tret' ya mirovaya voina Stalina* (*Stalin's World War III*).[9]

In this 540-page volume, the author alleges that stage by stage in the postwar years Stalin was actively planning a third world war against the West. His 18 chapters bear such titles as: "The Theory and Practice of Provocations"; "The 'Peaceful' Policy of the USSR in Eastern Europe"; "Who Began the 'Cold War'?"; "A Red Army Stronger Than Any Other"; and "The Nuclear War That Never Happened." In the chapter about the start of the Cold War, Zakoretskiy accuses several Russian mainline historians and memoirists of distorting the truth as he engages in his own form of "demythologizing" Russian historiography. It is erroneous, he writes, to ascribe the beginning of the Cold War to Churchill's speech in Fulton. Citing the 1988 Soviet *Political Dictionary*, which alleges that it was this speech that set off the Cold War, the author retorts that Stalin's electoral speech of February 9 was hardly

"peace-loving." He notes that in this address Stalin blamed capitalism for the war. "Could anyone call Stalin's postwar plan to increase
defense spending three times over as an indicator of a 'peace-loving'
state? . . . Stalin could scarcely wait to create a basis for increasing tensions, whether in Iran or Korea."[10]

Another view toward worsening East-West relations after 1945
assumes the plague-on-both-houses position. This theme is presented
in V. V. Sogrin's *Istoriya SShA (History of the USA)*. In this 2003 school
text, the Russian historian writes:[11]

> "After acknowledging [in the 1930s] Stalin's relegation of world
> Communist revolution to a lower priority given his national pro-
> gram of 'building socialism in one country,' both sides [the West
> and the USSR] nevertheless continued to distrust one another. . . .
> In the 1930s the West counted on not being attacked by the Fascist
> aggressor while hoping that such an attack on the USSR would
> lead to mutual destruction. . . . In the final analysis the choice of
> concluding a military-political alliance with the USSR was made
> only on the basis of the countries' national interest. . . .
>
> "During the war relations between the USSR and America
> showed two faces. On the one hand, there was mutual sympathy
> and solidarity. . . . On the other, each country's postwar plans pos-
> sessed its own characteristics. For the USA, it was liberal capital-
> ism; for the USSR, socialism. This led to discord and discussion
> in the course of which compromises were made that in turn led
> to division of the world into spheres of influence [in which each
> side became defensive about its own sphere]. . . . Today heated
> controversy among historians and politicians continues over the
> origins of the Cold War. The most convincing conclusion about
> this is the one that puts the blame on both sides."

ASSESSING STALIN'S ALLEGED GREATNESS

Stalin's putative statesmanship and his *nachruhm* as a "great" leader
could have been fully realized had he taken an entirely new stance
after World War II.

It may be objected that any such thing is "impossible" for an autocratic
leader to manage. Yet history is replete with examples of powerful leaders who did make profound changes in the direction of moderation. In

the Communist world, there is the example of Czechoslovak Communist Party First Secretary Alexander Dubcek, a Slovak and radical reformer of the late 1960s who became an ardent reformer. Aleksandr Yakovlev, party secretary in charge of ideology under Mikhail Gorbachev, was another example of a high-ranking Communist official whose change of heart in democratic directions was radical, although surfacing only with the demise of Communist rule in the USSR. Yet Yakovlev had long hoped for fundamental political reform in his country. Gensek/President Gorbachev himself was another example of a reformist top leader in the Communist world. In China, one or two leading Beijing officials, one the party general secretary, have come forward as potential reformers. But they were rapidly swept aside by more orthodox officials of the Chinese Communist Party Politburo. In the West, there was Nelson Mandela, former head of the militant, pro-Communist National African Congress (ANC) of the Republic of South Africa. Mandela discarded his former Soviet, quasi-Marxist-Leninist formulas and was later elected RSA's president, whose term did not show any of his former ideological beliefs.

To those Russians, intellectuals, war veterans, and others who never had any faith or trust in Stalin, it was no surprise that this *palach* ("butcher") never changed when the war ended. Yet, in a sense it is tragic, especially for the people of the USSR, that Josef Stalin, with his enhanced popularity at home after the war, did not avail himself of the opportunity that his alliance and apparent camaraderie with leaders of the West together with the favorable postwar political landscape that had presented him with the possibility of casting East-West relations in new, progressive ways.

Some Western observers were, in fact, so stunned and disappointed by the "postwar Stalin" that they speculated that the Soviet leader might have become a "prisoner in the Kremlin," a tool of hard-liners. Of course, that ridiculous notion was dispelled by what the *Khozain* himself said and did as the war wound down, and as he evidently planned his aggressive postwar moves while tightening controls at home in ways that in some respects were as harsh than his prewar measures. This severity became especially evident in 1950–1953 and seemed to reach a crescendo shortly before the dictator's death in March 1953 with the notorious Jewish doctor's plot together with hints of a purge of his closest associates within the ruling Politburo, including even Molotov.

Recalling the discussion in the introduction to this book, we might agree that whatever greatness Stalin had earned as a preparer of his country for war and as a defender of the state as "warlord" at a time of the Soviet Union's and its peoples' greatest peril, that he could not bring himself to earn the highest form of fame by a show of flexibility and humanity after the big war. Stalin's detractors say that the Soviet leader was simply incapable of any such feelings or willingness to change. If not a prisoner of the Kremlin, Stalin nevertheless was the captive of the very system he himself had built up and perfected since the early 1930s. Some writers attribute Stalin's behavior to paranoia. These observations may contain some truth.

The rigidity on Stalin's part is perhaps a lesson for all contemporary dictators or would-be autocrats, however "benevolent" they may occasionally appear to be. They had once shown the capacity to adapt and maneuver that such autocrats at times had to display in their own political life as they adapted themselves under trying political circumstances. Once in power, especially after a long duration, they should likewise be willing to adapt themselves to new circumstances within their own polities, especially in their relations with other nation-states against whom it had been "useful," in their earlier view, for the preservation of their power to maintain hostile relations—say, as scapegoats for the autocrat's hard-line policies at home.

Tendencies on the part of a single or collective dictatorship to harden, to become self-protective and resistant to change, will only lead to stresses and strains in the system in the long run, as much history of such regimes clearly shows. This in turn may lead to the demise of the very system that the autocrat and his oligarchy attempt to prop up in shortsighted ways.

Stalin's system certainly began to degenerate in this way even while he was alive. Dogmatism and the Cold War mentality only led to more alienation among states and to renewed isolation and endangerment of the Soviet Union. Such harsh, autocratic measures only plague the oppressively ruled nation itself with the onus of being the world's pariah that is further burdened with the expense of building up their militaries in excessive, threatening ways. This is demonstrated starkly today in the cases of North Korea and Iran, and potentially even by the oligarchy ruling the People's Republic of China, if it is not careful to avoid Stalin's mistakes. The same danger, in fact, faces Venezuela under Hugo Chavez's emerging autocracy and his concentration on military expansion. Cuba is another autocratically ruled state that is in the throes of internal tension and potential collapse.

Stalin's policies, domestic and foreign, had assured victory. Perhaps another, less draconic regime ruling a largely agrarian society could not have met the Nazi challenge. Perhaps Russia's industrialization (which actually got under way in tsarist Russia at the turn of the century) would have proceeded too gradually under a non-autocratic regime in order to meet the challenge of a militarized Nazi Germany of the 1930s. All this, of course, is debatable, a meta-historical "if." That the Western democracies hardly measured up to the Axis challenge, most of whom were defeated in war, may or may not be a case in point, assuming a gradualist (in its industrialization), democratic, multiparty Russia had faced Hitler—perhaps perilously. Stalin's measures had assured victory.

Yet it is certain that a potentially peaceful world that could have emerged after 1945 was not assured mainly because of the nature of the regime ruling in the Kremlin. Instead, after 1945, the worst features of traditional Stalinism reappeared in the world's largest nation-state poised geostrategically atop the "crown" of the Eurasian continent.

When the present Russian leaders become satisfied with the history rewrite program they undertook in 2009, it is hoped that the "demythologization" of Russian historiography that the authorities are now demanding will include a clear focus on the counterproductive rigidity and inhumanity of Stalin. This Russian telling of the state's past should disclose what was lost to the people of that country as well as to the world because of Stalin's lack of courageous, creative, postwar leadership.

This might be a useful lesson for other nation-states in the world. Unfortunately, there are today several Stalinesque leaders who are ruling in many areas of the globe. With exorbitant offensive-oriented defense programs, self-centered foreign policies, censorship, draconic criminal codes, and gulags, all by-products of one-party rule, they appear to be ignoring the negative lessons of Stalinism.

Perhaps at their peril.

Appendix I: Stalin, Soviet Premier, Broadcast to the People of the Soviet Union

July 3, 1941

[*Soviet Russia Today*, August 1941]

Comrades! Citizens! Brothers and sisters! Men of our army and navy! I am addressing you, my friends!

The perfidious military attack on our Fatherland, begun on June 22nd by Hitler's Germany, is continuing.

In spite of the heroic resistance of the Red Army, and although the enemy's finest divisions and finest airforce units have already been smashed and have met their doom on the field of battle, the enemy continues to push forward, hurling fresh forces into the attack.

Hitler's troops have succeeded in capturing Lithuania, a considerable part of Latvia, the western part of Byelo-Russia, part of Western Ukraine. The Fascist air force is extending the range of operations of its bombers, and is bombing Murmansk, Orsha, Mogilev, Smolensk, Kiev, Odessa, and Sebastopol.

A grave danger hangs over our country.

How could it have happened that our glorious Red Army surrendered a number of our cities and districts to Fascist armies? Is it really true that German Fascist troops are invincible, as is ceaselessly trumpeted by the boastful Fascist propagandists? Of course not!

History shows that there are no invincible armies and never have been. Napoleon's army was considered invincible, but it was beaten successively by Russian, English, and German armies. Kaiser Wilhelm's German Army in the period of the first imperialist war was also considered invincible, but it was beaten several times by the Russian and Anglo-French forces and was finally smashed by the Anglo-French forces.

The same must be said of Hitler's German Fascist army today. This army had not yet met with serious resistance on the continent of Europe. Only on our territory has it met serious resistance. And if, as a result of this resistance, the finest divisions of Hitler's German Fascist army have been defeated by our Red Army, it means that this army too can be smashed and will be smashed as were the armies of Napoleon and Wilhelm.

As to part of our territory having nevertheless been seized by Germany's Fascist troops, this is chiefly due to the fact that the war of Fascist Germany on the USSR began under conditions favorable for the German forces and unfavorable for Soviet forces. The fact of the matter is that the troops of Germany, as a country at war, were already fully mobilized, and the 170 divisions hurled by Germany against the USSR and brought up to the Soviet frontiers, were in a state of complete readiness, only awaiting the signal to move into action, whereas Soviet troops had still to effect mobilization and move up to the frontier.

Of no little importance in this respect is the fact that Fascist Germany suddenly and treacherously violated the non-aggression pact she concluded in 1939 with the USSR, disregarding the fact that she would be regarded as the aggressor by the whole world.

Naturally, our peace-loving country, not wishing to take the initiative of breaking the pact, could not resort to perfidy.

It may be asked how could the Soviet government have consented to conclude a non-aggression pact with such treacherous fiends as Hitler and Ribbentrop? Was this not an error on the part of the Soviet government? Of course not. Non-aggression pacts are pacts of peace between states. It was such a pact that Germany proposed to us in 1939.

Could the Soviet government have declined such a proposal? I think that not a single peace-loving state could decline a peace treaty with a neighboring state, even though the latter was headed by such fiends and cannibals as Hitler and Ribbentrop. Of course only on one indispensable condition, namely, that this peace treaty does not infringe either directly or indirectly on the territorial integrity, independence, and honor of the peace-loving state. As is well known, the non-aggression pact between Germany and the USSR is precisely such a pact.

What did we gain by concluding the non-aggression pact with Germany? We secured our country peace for a year and a half, and the opportunity of preparing its forces to repulse Fascist Germany should she risk an attack on our country despite the pact. This was a definite advantage for us and a disadvantage for Fascist Germany.

What has Fascist Germany gained and what has she lost by treacherously tearing up the pact and attacking the USSR?

She has gained a certain advantageous position for her troops for a short period, but she has lost politically by exposing herself in the eyes of the entire world as a bloodthirsty aggressor.

There can be no doubt that this short-lived military gain for Germany is only an episode, while the tremendous political gain of the USSR is a serious lasting factor that is bound to form the basis for development of decisive military successes of the Red Army in the war with Fascist Germany.

That is why our whole valiant Red Army, our whole valiant navy, all our falcons of the air, all the peoples of our country, all the finest men and women of Europe, America, and Asia, finally all the finest men and women of Germany—condemn the treacherous acts of German fascists and sympathize with the Soviet government, approve the conduct of the Soviet government, and see that ours is a just cause, that the enemy will be defeated, that we are bound to win.

By virtue of this war which has been forced upon us, our country has come to death-grips with its most malicious and most perfidious enemy—German Fascist. Our troops are fighting heroically against an enemy armed to the teeth with tanks and aircraft.

Overcoming innumerable difficulties, the Red Army and Red Navy are self-sacrificingly disputing every inch of Soviet soil. The main forces of the Red Army are coming into action armed with thousands of tanks and airplanes. The men of the Red Army are displaying unexampled valor. Our resistance to the enemy is growing in strength and power.

Side by side with the Red Army, the entire Soviet people are rising in defense of our native land.

What is required to put an end to the danger hovering over our country, and what measures must be taken to smash the enemy?

Above all, it is essential that our people, the Soviet people, should understand the full immensity of the danger that threatens our country and should abandon all complacency, all heedlessness, all those moods of peaceful constructive work which were so natural before the war, but which are fatal today when war has fundamentally changed everything.

The enemy is cruel and implacable. He is out to seize our lands, watered with our sweat, to seize our grain and oil secured by our labor. He is out to restore the rule of landlords, to restore Tsarism, to destroy national culture and the national state existence of the Russians, Ukrainians, Byelo-Russians, Lithuanians, Letts, Esthonians, Uzbeks, Tatars, Moldavians, Georgians, Armenians, Azerbaidzhanians, and the other free people of the Soviet Union, to Germanize them, to convert them into the slaves of German princes and barons.

Thus the issue is one of life or death for the Soviet state, for the peoples of the USSR; the issue is whether the peoples of the Soviet Union shall remain free or fall into slavery.

The Soviet people must realize this and abandon all heedlessness, they must mobilize themselves and reorganize all their work on new, wartime bases, when there can be no mercy to the enemy.

Further, there must be no room in our ranks for whimperers and cowards, for panic-mongers and deserters. Our people must know no fear in fight and must selflessly join our patriotic war of liberation, our war against the Fascist enslavers.

Lenin, the great founder of our state, used to say that the chief virtue of the Bolshevik must be courage, valor, fearlessness in struggle, readiness to fight, together with the people, against the enemies of our country.

This splendid virtue of the Bolshevik must become the virtue of the millions of the Red Army, of the Red Navy, of all peoples of the Soviet Union.

All our work must be immediately reconstructed on a war footing, everything must be subordinated to the interests of the front and the task of organizing the demolition of the enemy.

The people of the Soviet Union now see that there is no taming of German Fascism in its savage fury and hatred of our country, which has ensured all working people labor in freedom and prosperity.

The peoples of the Soviet Union must rise against the enemy and defend their rights and their land. The Red Army, Red Navy, and all citizens of the Soviet Union must defend every inch of Soviet soil, must fight to the last drop of blood for our towns and villages, must display the daring initiative and intelligence that are inherent in our people.

We must organize all-round assistance for the Red Army, ensure powerful reinforcements for its ranks and the supply of everything it requires, we must organize the rapid transport of troops and military freight and extensive aid to the wounded.

We must strengthen the Red Army's rear, subordinating all our work to this cause. All our industries must be got to work with greater intensity to produce more rifles, machine guns, artillery, bullets, shells, airplanes; we must organize the guarding of factories, power stations, telephonic, and telegraphic communications and arrange effective air raid precautions in all localities.

We must wage a ruthless fight against all disorganizers of the rear, deserters, panic-mongers, rumor-mongers; we must exterminate spies, diversionists, and enemy parachutists, rendering rapid aid in all this to our destroyer battalions.

We must bear in mind that the enemy is crafty, unscrupulous, experienced in deception and the dissemination of false rumors. We must reckon with all this and not fall victim to provocation.

All who by their panic-mongering and cowardice hinder the work of defense, no matter who they are, must be immediately haled before the military tribunal. In case of forced retreat of Red Army units, all rolling stock must be evacuated, the enemy must not be left a single engine, a single railway car, not a single pound of grain or a gallon of fuel.

The collective farmers must drive off all their cattle, and turn over their grain to the safe-keeping of state authorities for transportation to the rear. All valuable property, including non-ferrous metals, grain, and fuel that cannot be withdrawn, must without fail be destroyed.

In areas occupied by the enemy, guerrilla units, mounted and on foot, must be formed, diversionist groups must be organized to combat the enemy troops, to foment guerrilla warfare everywhere, to blow up bridges and roads, damage telephone and telegraph lines, set fire to forests, stores, transports.

In the occupied regions, conditions must be made unbearable for the enemy and all his accomplices. They must be hounded and annihilated at every step, and all their measures frustrated.

This war with Fascist Germany cannot be considered an ordinary war. It is not only a war between two armies, it is also a great war of the entire Soviet people against the German Fascist forces.

The aim of this national war in defense of our country against the fascist oppressors is not only elimination of the danger hanging over our country, but also aid to all European peoples groaning under the yoke of German Fascism.

In this war of liberation we shall not be alone. In this great war we shall have loyal allies in the peoples of Europe and America, including the German people who are enslaved by the Hitlerite despots.

Our war for the freedom of our country will merge with the struggle of the peoples of Europe and America for their independence, for democratic liberties.

It will be a united front of peoples standing for freedom and against enslavement and threats of enslavement by Hitler's Fascist armies.

In this connection the historic utterance of the British Prime Minister Churchill regarding aid to the Soviet Union and the declaration of the United States government signifying its readiness to render aid to our country, which can only evoke a feeling of gratitude in the hearts of the peoples of the Soviet Union, are fully comprehensible and symptomatic.

Comrades, our forces are numberless. The overweening enemy will soon learn this to his cost. Side by side with the Red Army, many thousands of workers, collective farmers, and intellectuals are rising to fight the enemy aggressor. The masses of our people will rise up in their millions.

The working people of Moscow and Leningrad have already commenced to form vast popular levies in support of the Red Army. Such popular levies must be raised in every city that is in danger of enemy invasion, all working people must be roused to defend our freedom, our honor, our country—in our patriotic war against German fascism.

In order to ensure the rapid mobilization of all forces of the peoples of the USSR and to repulse the enemy who treacherously attacked our country, a state committee of defense has been formed in whose hands the entire power of the state has been vested.

The state committee of defense has entered upon its functions and calls upon all people to rally around the party of Lenin-Stalin and around the Soviet government, so as to self-denyingly support the Red Army and Navy, demolish the enemy, and secure victory.

All our forces for support of our heroic Red Army and our glorious Red Navy! All forces of the people—for the demolition of the enemy!

Forward to our victory!

Appendix II: Stalin's Biography in Current Russian Military Encyclopedia

From the post-Soviet *Voyenniy Entsiklopedicheskiy Slovar'* (*Military Encyclopedia Dictionary*), Izdatel'stvo Ripol Klassik, Moscow, 2001, 2 vols. Below is the complete entry in the encyclopedia for Stalin, Vol. 2, p. 593 (translated by Albert L. Weeks).

"Stalin (Dzhugashvili), Iosif Vissarionovich (1879, or by other data, 1878–1953). Soviet party, state, and military official; commander and Generalissimus of the Soviet Union (1945). Hero of the Soviet Union (1943); Hero of Soviet Labor (1939).

"Completed studies in a seminary (1894). Participated in the execution of the October Revolution in 1917. From 1917–1922, he served as People's Commissar of Nationalities while for a time in 1919 serving as People's Commissar of State Control. During the Civil War, he was on the staff of the Council of Workers and Peasants Defense; was a member of the Revolutionary Military Council of the Republic (RVC) and of the RVC of the southern, western, and southwestern fronts. After 1922, General Secretary of the Central Committee (Ts.K) of the All-Union Communist Party (Bolsheviks) (after 1952, CPSU). Led the construction of socialism in the USSR. Stalin retained the post of secretary of the Ts.K of the party while after May 1941 served as Chairman (Premier) of the Council of People's Commissars (or Council of Ministers) of the USSR.

"During the Great Patriotic War (VOV), 1941–1945, he served as Chairman of the State Committee of Defense (GKO) and of Stavka of the Supreme Command as well as People's Commissar of Defense and Commander-in-Chief of the Armed Forces of the USSR. Stalin was one of the organizers of the anti-Hitler Coalition. Despite making a number of strategic miscalculations and errors, Stalin played a positive role in organizing the victory of the Soviet people in the VOV.

"The Stalin cult of the person played a negative role in the life of the Soviet people and brought a train of illegality, did immense harm to society, and led to the abuse of power and to the unleashing of repression and widespread physical destruction of Soviet people."

Appendix III: Stalin's Speech at the Reception in the Kremlin in Honor of the Commanders of the Red Army

Moscow, May 24, 1945

(Note: Generalissimus Stalin admits to having made mistakes.—ALW)

Comrades, permit me to propose another toast, the last one.

I would like to propose that we drink to the health of the Soviet people, and primarily of the Russian people. *(Loud and prolonged applause and cheers.)*

I drink primarily to the health of the Russian people because it is the most outstanding of all the nations that constitute the Soviet Union.

I drink to the health of the Russian people, because, during this war, it has earned universal recognition as the guiding force of the Soviet Union among all the peoples of our country.

I drink to the health of the Russian people, not only because it is the leading people, but also because it is gifted with a clear mind, a staunch character and patience.

Our government committed no few mistakes; at times our position was desperate, as in 1941–1942, when our army was retreating, abandoning our native villages and towns in the Ukraine, Byelorussia, Moldavia, the Leningrad region, the Baltic region, and the Karelo-Finnish Republic, abandoning them because there was no other alternative. Another people might have said to the government: "You have not come up to our expectations. Get out. We shall appoint another government, which will conclude peace with Germany and ensure tranquility for us."

But the Russian people did not do that, for they were confident that the policy their government was pursuing was correct; and they made sacrifices in order to ensure the defeat of Germany. And this confidence which the Russian people displayed in the Soviet government proved to be the decisive factor which ensured our historic victory over the enemy of mankind, over Fascism.

I thank the Russian people for this confidence!

To the health of the Russian people! *(Loud and prolonged applause.)*

Bibliography

Afanas'iev, Yu. N. (ed), *Drugaya voina* (*The Other War*), Rossiiskii Gosudarstvenniy Universitet, Moscow, 1996.

Andrew, Christopher, and Mitrokhin, Vasili. *The Sword and the Shield: The Mitrokhin Archive and the Secret History of the KGB*, Basic Books, New York, 1999.

Anfilov, V. A. *Proval 'blitskriga'* (*The Downfall of Blitzkrieg*), Nauka, Moscow, 1974.

Anisimov, Yevgeniy. *Istoriya, Rossii ot Riurika do Putina, lyudi, sobytiya, daty* (*History of Russia from Rurik to Putin: People, Events, Dates*), Piter Press, St. Petersburg, 2008

Antonov-Ovseyenko, A. *Portret tirana* (*Portrait of a Tyrant*), Peidg, Moscow, 1994.

Antonov-Ovseyenko, A. *The Time of Stalin: Portrait of Tyranny*, Harper & Row, New York, 1980.

Azovstev, N. N. V. I. *Lenin i sovetskaya voyennaya nauka* (*V. I. Lenin and Soviet Military Science*), Nauka, Moscow, 1981.

Baldwin, Hanson W. *The Crucial Years 1939–1941: The World at War*, Harper & Row Publishers, New York, 1970.

Basistov, Yu. V. *Stalin—Hitler: Ot Pakta do Voiny* (*Stalin and Hitler: From the Pact to War*), Blitz Publishers, St. Petersburg, 2001. (Basistov served as a colonel in the RKKA and fought in the war against Germany.)

Becker, Fritz. *Stalin's Blutspur durch Europa Partner des Westens 1933–45* (*Stalin's Bloody Tracks Across Europe: The West's Partner 1933–45*), Arndt, Kiel, 1995.

Bellamy, Chris. *Absolute War: Soviet Russia in the Second World War*, Alfred A. Knopf, New York, 2007.

Berezhkov, Valentin M. *At Stalin's Side: His Interpreter's Memoirs from the October Revolution to the Fall of the Dictator's Empire*, Birch Lane Press, New York, 1994.

Beriya, Sergo. *Moi otets Lavrentii Beriya* (*My Father, Lavrenty Beria*), Sovremennik, Moscow, 1994.

Blank, Stephen J., and Jacob W. Kipp. *The Soviet Military and the Future*, Greenwood Press, Westport, 1992.

Brandt, M. Yu., et al. *Rossiya i mir Uchebnaya kniga po istorii* (*Russia and the World Textbook on History*), Vlados, Moscow, 1994.

Carr, E. H. *What Is History?*, Vintage Books, New York, 1962.

Carr, E. H. *German-Soviet Relations Between the Two World Wars, 1919–1939*, Arno Press, New York, 1979.

Chamberlin, William Henry (ed). "Blueprint for World Conquest," *Human Events*, Washington, DC-Chicago, 1946.

Chaney, Otto Preston. *Zhukov*, University of Oklahoma Press, Norman, 1971.

Chubaryan, A. O. *V. I Lenin i formirovaniye sovetskoi vneshnei politiki* (*V. I. Lenin and the Formulation of Soviet Foreign Policy*), Nauka, Moscow, 1972.

Chuyev, Felix. *Sto sorok besed s Molotovym* (*140 Conversations with Molotov*), Terra, Moscow, 1991.

Claasen, Adam A. *Hitler's Northern War: The Luftwaffe's Ill-Fated Campaign 1940–1945*, University Press of Kansas, Lawrence, 2001.

Clausewitz, Carl. *On War*, Princeton University Press, Princeton, 1976.

Conquest, Robert. *The Great Terror: A Reassessment*, Oxford University Press, New York, 1990.

Conquest, Robert. *Stalin: Breaker of Nations*, Penguin Books, New York, 1991.

Crozier, Brian. *The Rise and Fall of the Soviet Empire*, Forum, Rockland, CA, 1999.

Davies, Sarah, and Harris, James (eds), *Stalin: A New History*, Cambridge University Press, New York, 2006.

Deane, John R. *The Strange Alliance: The Story of Our Efforts at Wartime Co-operation with Russia*, The Viking Press, New York, 1947.

Degras, Jane (ed). *The Communist International Documents, 1919–1943*, Oxford University Press, London, 1956–1960, Vols. 1–2.

Deighton, Len. *Blood, Tears, and Folly: An Objective Look at World War II*, HarperCollins, New York, 1993.

Deriabin, Peter S. *Inside Stalin's Kremlin*, Brassey's, Washington, DC, 1998.

Donnelly, Christopher. *Red Banner: The Soviet Military System in Peace and War*, Jane's Information Group Ltd, London, 1988.

Dunne, Walter S., Jr. *Stalin's Keys to Victory: The Rebirth of the Red Army in WWII*, Stackpole Books, Mechanicsburg, 2006.

Dvoretsky, Lev. *Alien Wars: The Soviet Union's Aggressions Against the West*, Presidio Press, Novato, CA, 1996.

Dyakov, Yuri, and Bushuyeva, Tatyana. *Red Army and the Wehrmacht: How the Soviet Militarized Germany, 1922–1933, and Paved the Way for Fascism*, Prometheus Books, 1995.

Eissenstat, Bernard W. *Lenin and Leninism: State, Law, and Society*, Lexington Books, Lanham, MD, 1971.

Erickson, John. *The Road to Stalingrad: Stalin's War with Germany, Vol. 1,* Yale University Press, New Haven, 1975.

Erickson, John, and Dilks, David. *Barbarossa: The Axis and the Allies,* Edinburgh University Press, Edinburgh, 1994.

Ericson, Edward E. *Feeding the German Eagle: Soviet Economic Aid to Nazi Germany, 1933–1941,* Prager Publishers, Westport, CT, 1999.

Fest, Joachim. *Hitler,* Random House, New York, 1975.

Folly, Martin. *The United States and World War II: The Awakening Giant,* Edinburgh University Press, Edinburgh, 2002.

Fortunatov, V. V. *Otechestvennaya istoria dya gumanitarnikh institutov; Rekomendano nauchno-metodicheskim sovetom (Fatherland History for Institutes of the Humanities, recommended by the Scientific-Methodological Council),* Piter Press, St. Petersburg, 2009.

Fortunatov, V. V. *Noveishaya istoriya Rossii v litsakh 1917–2008 (Newest History of Russia as Seen Through Persons, 1917–2008),* Piter Press, St. Petersburg, 2009.

Fugate, Bryan, and Dvoretsky, Lev. *Thunder on the Dnepr: Zhukov-Stalin and the Defeat of Hitler's Blitzkrieg,* Presidio, Novato, 2001.

Fugate, Bryan, and Dvoretsky, Lev. *Operation Barbarossa: Strategy and Tactics on the Eastern Front, 1941.* Presidio, Novato, 1984.

Gaddis, John Lewis. *We Now Know: Rethinking Cold War History,* Clarendon Press, New York, 1998.

Gaddis, John Lewis. *We Now Know: Rethinking Cold War History,* Clarendon Press, New York, 1998.

Gafencu, Grigore. *Prelude to the Russian Campaign,* Hyperion Press, Westport, CT, 1981.

Gareyev, M. A. *M. V. Frunze—Voyenniy teoretik (M. V. Frunze—Military Theoretician),* Voyenizdat, Moscow, 1986.

Gellman, Barton D. *Contending with Kennan,* Praeger Publishers, New York, 1985.

Gellman, Irwin F. *Secret Affairs: Franklin Roosevelt, Cordell Hull, and Sumner Welles,* Johns Hopkins University Press, Baltimore, 1995.

Getty, J. Arch, and Oleg V. Naumov, *The Road to Terror: Stalin and the Self-Destruction of the Bolsheviks, 1932–1939,* Yale University Press, New Haven, 2010.

Glantz, David M., and House, Jonathan. *When Titans Clash,* University Press of Kansas, Lawrence, 1995.

Glantz, David M. *Stumbling Colossus: The Red Army on the Eve of World War,* University Press of Kansas, Lawrence, 1998.

Goebbels, Josef. *The Early Goebbels Diaries, 1925–1926,* Praeger, New York, 1962.

Goebbels, Josef. *The Goebbels Diaries, 1939–1941,* G. P. Putnam's Sons, New York, 1982.

Goodman, Elliot R. *The Soviet Design for a World State,* Columbia University Press, New York, 1960.

Gor'kov, Yuri, Kreml', Stavka, Genshtab (*Kremlin, High Command, and General Staff*), RIF Ltd, Tver, 1999.

Gorodetsky, Gabriel. *Mif "Ledokola": Nakanunye voiny (The Myth of the "Ice-breaker" on the Eve of War*), Progress Akademii, Moscow, 1995.

Gorodetsky, Gabriel. *Stafford Cripps' Mission to Moscow, 1940–42*, Cambridge University Press, Cambridge, 1984.

Gorodetsky, Gabriel (ed). *Soviet Foreign Policy 1917–1991: A Retrospective*, Frank Cass, London, 1994.

Gorodetsky, Gabriel. *Grand Delusion Stalin and the German Invasion of Russia*, Yale University Press, New Haven, 1999.

Guglya, Yuri. *Dvukhmotorniye Istrebiteli, 1930–1945 (Two-Engined Fighters, 1930–1945)*, Arkhiv-Press, Kiev, 2000.

Hallas, Duncan. *The Comintern: A History of the Third International*, Haymarket Books, Chicago, 1985.

Harbutt, Fraser J. *The Iron Curtain: Churchill, America, and the Origins of the Cold War*, Oxford University Press, New York, 1986.

Hart, B. H. Liddell. *Strategy*, 2nd ed, Meridian Book, London, 1967.

Haynes, John Earl, and Klehr, Harvey (eds). *Venona: Decoding Soviet Espionage in America*, Yale University Press, New Haven, 1999.

Hillgruber, Andreas. *Germany and the Two World Wars*, Harvard University Press, Cambridge, MA, 1981.

Hitler, Adolf. *Hitler's Table Talk, 1941–1944*, Enigma Books, New York, 2000.

Kalugin, Oleg. *The First Directorate*, St. Martin's Press, New York, 1994.

Khrushchev, N. S. "The Crimes of the Stalin Era Special Report to the 20th Congress of the Communist Party of the Soviet Union," *New Leader Magazine*, New York, 1962.

Khrushchev, N. S. *Khrushchev Remembers the Glasnost Tapes*, Little, Brown and Company, Boston, 1990.

Kokoshin, Andrei A. *Armiya I politika Sovetskaya voenno-politicheskaya i voyenno-strategicheskaya mysl', 1918–1991 gody (Army and Policy: Soviet Military-Political and Military-Strategic Thought, 1918–1991)*, Mezhdunarodniye Otnosheniya, Moscow, 1995.

Kokoshin, Andrei A. *Soviet Strategic Thought, 1917–91*, MIT Press, Cambridge, MA, 1995.

Krasnov, Valeriy. *Neizvestniy Zhukov (The Unknown Zhukov)*, Olma Press, Moscow, 2000.

Krivitsky, Walter. *In Stalin's Secret Service*, Hyperion Press, Inc., Westport, CT, 1939.

Kuznetsov, N. G. *Kursom k pobede (On Course to Victory)*, Olma Press, Moscow, 2003

Laqueur, Walter. *Stalin Glasnost Revelations*, Charles Scribner's Sons, New York, 1990.

Latimer, Jon. *Deception in War: The Art of Bluff, the Value of Deceit*, Overlook Press, New York, 2001.

Leites, Nathan. *The Operational Code of the Politburo*, McGraw-Hill, New York, 1951.

Leites, Nathan. *The Soviet Style in War*, Crane Russak, New York, 1982.

Lenin, V. I. *Sochineniya*.

Librach, Jan. *The Rise of the Soviet Empire: A Study of Soviet Foreign Policy*, Praeger Publishers, New York, 1964.

Lukacs, John. *June 1941: Hitler and Stalin*, Yale University Press, New Haven, 2006.

Lukes, Igor. *Czechoslovakia Between Stalin and Hitler: The Diplomacy of Eduard Benes in the 1930s*, Oxford University Press, New York, 1996.

Malenkov, Andrei. *O moem otse George Malenkove* (*About My Father, Georgy Malenkov*), NTTs, Tekhnoekos, Moscow, 1992.

Martirosyan, A. B. *Tragediya 1941 goda* (*The Tragedy of 1941*), Veche, 2008.

Martirosyan, A. B. *Tragediya 22 iyunya: blitskrig ili izmena?* (*The Trasgedy of June 22: Blitzkrieg or Betrayal?*), Yauza, Moscow, 2006.

Martirosyan, A. B. *Na puti k mirovoi voine* (*On the Road to World War*), Veche, Moscow, 2008.

Martirosyan, A. B. *Stalin: biografiya vozhdya* (*Stalin: Biography of the Leader*), Veche, Moscow, 2008.

Martirosyan, A. B. *Stalin posle voiny, 1945–1953* (*Stalin After the War, 1945–1953*), Veche, Moscow, 2008.

Martirosyan, A. B. *Stalin i velikaya otechestvennaya voina* (*Stalin and the Great Patriotic War*), Veche, Moscow, 2008.

Sto mifov o Berii: Vdokhnovitel' repressiy ili talantliviy organizator? 1917–1941 (Instigator of the Repressions or Talented Organizer? 1917–1953), Veche, Moscow, 2010.

Mastny, Vojtech. *Russia's Road to the Cold War*, Columbia University Press, New York, 1979.

Mawdsley, Evan. *Thunder in the East: The Nazi-Soviet War, 1941–1945*, Hodder Arnold, New York, 2007.

McCarthy, Peter, and Syrin, Mike. *Panzerkrieg: The Rise and Fall of Hitler's Tank Divisions*, Constable, London, 2002.

Mel'tyukhov, Mikhail, Osokin, Aleksandr, and Pykhalov, Igor. *Tragediya 1941: Prichiny katastrofa* (*The Tragedy of 1941: Reasons for the Catastrophe*), Eksmo, Moscow, 2008.

Menaul, Stewart, and Dornan, James E., et al. *Russian Military Power*, St. Martin's Press, Inc., New York, 1980.

Molotov, Vyacheslav. *Molotov Remembers Conversations with Felix Chuev*, Ivan R. Dee, Chicago, 1993.

Montefiore, Simon Sebag. *Stalin: The Court of the Red Tsar*, Weidenfeld & Nicolson, London, 2003.

Mosier, John. *Deathride: Hitler vs. Stalin on the Eastern Front, 1941–1945*, Simon & Schuster, New York, 2010.

Mukhin, Yuri. *Kto na camom dele razvyazal vtoruyu mirovuyu voinu? (Who Actually Started World War II?)*, Yayuza-Press, Moscow, 2009.

Müller, Rolf-Dieter, and Ueberschäar, Gerd R. *Hitler's War in the East 1941–1945*, Berghahn Books, New York, 1997.

Murphy, David E. *What Stalin Knew: The Enigma of Barbarossa*, Yale University Press, New Haven, 2005.

Narinskiy, N. M., and S. Dembski. *Mezhdunarodniy krizis 1939 goda v traktovkakh rossiiskikh i pol'skih istorikov (The International Crisis of 1939 Through the Treatises of Russian and Polish Historians)*, Aspect Press, Moscow, 2009.

Nazi-Soviet Relations 1939–1941, U.S. Department of State, Washington, DC, 1948.

Nekrich, Aleksandr. *Pariahs, Predators, Partners German-Soviet Relations 1922–1941*, Columbia University Press, New York, 1997.

Newman, Randall. *Deutsche Mark Diplomacy: Positive Economic Sanctions in German-Russian Relations*, Pennsylvania State University Press, University Park, 2002.

Ogarkov, N. V. (ed), et al. *Sovetskaya voyennaya entsiklopediya (Soviet Military Entsiklopediya)*, Voyenizdat, Moscow, 1978–80, Vols. 1–8.

Orenstein, Harold S., and David M. Glantz. *Soviet Documents on the Use of War Experience, Vol. 1, The Initial Period of war 1941*, Frank Cass, London, 1991.

Ostrovskiy, V. P., and. A. I. Utkin. *Istoriya Rossii XX vek (A History of Russia in the 20th Century)*, Drofa, Moscow, 1997.

Page, Stanley. *The Geopolitics of Leninism*, Columbia University Press, New York, 1982.

Paperno, A. *Tainy istorii (History's Secrets)*, Terra-Knizhniy Klub, Moscow, 1998.

Pauwell, Jaques R. *The Myth of the Good War: America in the Second World War*, Lorimer & Co, Toronto, 2002.

Petrov, Vladimir. *June 22, 1941: Soviet Historians and the German Invasion*, University of South Carolina Press, Columbia, 1968.

Pikhoya, Rudolf. *SSSR: Istoriya velikoi imperii, pod znakom Stalina (USSR: History of the Great Empire, Under the Sign of Stalin)*, Piter Press, St. Petersburg, 2009.

Pleshakov, *Constantine: The Secret Histoiry of the German Invasion of Russia, June 1941*, Weidenfeld & Nicolson, London, 2005.

Pomogaibo, Alesandr. *Psevdoistorilk Suvorov i zagadki vtori mirovoi voiny (Pseudo-Historian Suvorov and the Enigmas of the Second World War)*, Veche, Moscow, 2002.

Pons, Silvio. *Stalin and the Inevitable War, 1936–1941*, Frank Cass, Portland, 2002.

Possony, Stefan T. *Lenin: The Compulsive Revolutionary*, George Allen & Unwin, London, 1966.

Raack, R. C. *Stalin's Drive to the West*, Stanford University Press, Stanford, CA, 1995.

Radzinsky, Edvard. *Stalin*, Doubleday Publishing Co, New York, 1996.

Rauschning, Hermann. *The Voice of Destruction*, G. P. Putnam's Sons, New York, 1949.

Rauschning, Hermann. *Govorit Gitler: Zver' iz bezdni* (*Hitler Speaks: A Beast Out of the Abyss*), Mif, Moscow, 1993.

Raymond, Ellsworth. *The Soviet State*, New York University Press, New York, 1978.

Roberts, Geoffrey. *The Soviet Union and the Origins of the Second World War Russo-German Relations and the Road to War, 1933–1941*, St. Martin's Press, New York, 1995.

Roberts, Geoffrey. *Stalin's Wars: From World War to Cold War, 1939–1953*, Yale University Press, New Haven 2006.

Rogovin, Vadim. *Stalinskiy neonep* (*Stalin's Neo-NEP*), BBK, Moscow, 1994.

Rossi, A. *The Russo-German Alliance August 1939–June 1941*, Beacon Press, Boston, 1951.

Rudzinski, Aleksander. *Soviet Peace Offensives*, Carnegie Endowment for International Peace, New York, 1953.

Sakharov, A. N. (ed), *Sovetsko-pol'skiye otnosheniya v politicheskikh usloviyakh 30-kh godov XX stoletiya* (*Soviet-Polish Relations Under the Political Conditions of the 1930s in the Twentieth Century*), Nauka, Moscow, 2001.

Sarin, Oleg, and Dvoretsky, Lev. *Alien Wars: The Soviet Union's Aggressions Against the World, 1919–1939*, Presidio Press, Novato, CA, 1996.

Savkin, V. Ye. *Osnovniye printsipy operativnovo iskusstva i taktiki* (*Basic Principles of Operational Art and Tactics*), Voyennoye Izdatel'stvoi Ministerstva Oborony SSSR, Moscow, 1972.

Schuman, Frederick L. *Russia Since 1917: Four Decades of Soviet Politics*, Alfred A. Knopf, New York, 1962.

Scott, H. F., and William F. Scott. *The Armed Forces of the USSR*, 2nd ed., Westview Press, Boulder, CO, 1981.

Scott, H. F., and William F. Scott. (eds). *The Soviet Art of War Doctrine, Strategy, and Tactics*, Westview Press, Boulder, CO, 1982.

Scott, H. F., and William F. Scott *Soviet Military Doctrine Continuity, Formulation, and Dissemination*, Westview Press, Boulder, CO, 1988.

Seaton, Albert. *Stalin as Military Commander*, Praeger, New York, 1975.

Sekrety Gitlera na stole Stalina (*Hitler's Secrets in Stalin's Desk*), Mostoarkhiv, Moscow, 1995.

Service, Robert. *Stalin: A Biography*, Belknap Press, Cambridge, MA, 2005.

Shirer, William L. *The Rise and Fall of the Third Reich*, Simon & Schuster, New York, 1959.

Shtemenko, S. M. *The Soviet General Staff at War, 1941–1945, Book One*, Voenizdat, Moscow, 1981.

Shukman, Harold. *Stalin's Generals*, Grove Press, New York, 1993.

Simonov, Konstantin. *Glazami cheloveka moyego pokoleniya* (*Through the Eyes of a Man of My Generation*). APN, Moscow, 1988.

Sogrin,V. V. *Istoriya SShA Uchebnoye po sobiye* (*History of the USA School Textbook*), Piter Print, St. Petersburg, 2003.

Sokolovsky, V. D. *Voyennaya strategiya* (*Soviet Strategy*), Izdatel'stvo Ministerstva Oborony SSSR, Moscow, 1st–2nd eds, 1962–1963.

Soroko-Tsyupi, O. S., et al. *Mir v XX veke* (*The World in the 20th Century*), Proveshcheniye, Moscow, 1997.

Soviet Diplomacy and Negotiating Behavior, Committee on Foreign Affairs, 98th Congress, Vol. 1, Government Printing Office, Washington, DC, 1979.

Soviet Documents on the Use of War Experience, Vol. 1, Frank Cass, London, 1991.

Soviet Peace Efforts on the Eve of World War II (*Parts 1 and 2*), Novosti, Moscow, 1973.

Spahr, William J. *Stalin's Lieutenants: A Study of Command Under Duress*, Presidio Press, Novato, CA, 1997.

Stalin, I. V. *Works*, The Hoover Institution, Stanford, 1967, 16 vols.

Stalin, I. V. *Sochineniya* (*Works*), Ogiz, Moscow, 1947, 13 vols.

Stalin, J. *On the Great Patriotic War of the Soviet Union*, Suren Dutt, Calcutta, 1975.

Stevenson, William. *A Man Called Intrepid*, Harcourt Brace Jovanovich, New York, 1976.

Sudoplatov, Pavel, and Sudoplatov, Anatoli. *Special Tasks*, Little, Brown & Company, New York, 1994.

Sul'yanov, Anatoli. *Arestovat' v Kremlye O zhizne I smerti Marshala Berii* (*Arrested in the Kremlin: On the Life and Death of Marshal Beriya*), MP Slavyanye, Minsk, 1993.

Sun Tzu. *The Art of War*, Oxford University Press, New York, 1963.

Suvorov, Viktor. *Ledokol* (*Ice-breaker*), Act, Moscow, 1997.

Suvorov, Viktor. *Den' "M"* (*M-Day*), Act, Moscow, 1997.

Suvorov, Viktor. *Samoubiistvo* (*Suicide*), Act, Moscow, 2000.

Suvorov, Viktor. Vybor (*The Choice*), Act, Moscow, 2000.

Tarle, Eugene. *Napoleon's Invasion of Russia, 1812*, Oxford University Press, New York, 1942.

Taubman, William, *Stalin's American Policy: From Entente to Detente to Cold War*, W. W. Norton & Co., New York, 1982.

Tokaev, G. A. *Stalin's War*, George Weidenfeld & Nicolson, London, 1951.

Tolstoy, Lev. *Voina i mir* (*War and Peace*), 2 vols., Act Izdatel'stvo, Moscow, 2000.

Tolstoy, Nikolai. *Stalin's Secret War*, Holt, Rinehart and Winston, New York, 1981.

Topitsch, Ernst. *Stalin's War A Radical New Theory on the Origins of the Second World War*, St. Martin's Press, New York, 1987.

Tucker, Robert C. *Stalin in Power: The Revolution from Above, 1928–1941*, W. W. Norton & Co., New York, 1992.

Utkin, A. I. *Rossiya i zapad* (*Russia and the West*), Gadariki, Moscow, 2000.

Utkin, A. I. *Mirovaya kholodnaya voina* (*Global Cold War*), Eksmo, Moscow, 2005.

Verkhovsky, Yakov, and Valentina, Tyrmos. *Stalin: Tainiy 'tsenariy' nachala voiny* (*Secret 'Scenario' of the Start of the War*), Olma-Press, Moscow, 2006.

Vigor, P. J. *The Soviet View of War, Peace, and Neutrality*, Routledge & Kegan Paul, London, 1975.

Voenniy entsiklopedicheskiy slovar' (*Military Encyclopedia Dictionary*), Voennoye Izdatel'stvo, Moscow, 1986.

Vigor, P. J. 2 vols. Izdatel'stvo Ripol Klassik, Moscow, 2001.

Volkogonov, Dmitri. *Stalin: Triumph and Tragedy*, Prima Publishing, Rocklin, CA, 1991.

Volkogonov, Dmitri. *Autopsy for an Empire: The Seven Leaders Who Built the Soviet Regime*, The Free Press, New York, 1998.

Volkogonov, Dmitri. *Lenin: A New Biography*, The Free Press, New York, 1994.

Vyshinsky, Andrei A. *The Law of the Soviet State*, Macmillan Company, New York, 1948.

Vyshlev, O. V. *Hakanunye 22 iyuniya 1941 goda* (*On the Eve of June 22, 1941*), Hauka, Moscow, 2001.

Walker, Martin. *The Cold War: A History*, Henry Holt and Co., New York, 1993.

Weeks, Albert L. *The Other Side of Coexistence: An Analysis of Russian Foreign Policy*, Pitman, New York, 1970.

Weeks, Albert L. *The Troubled Détente*, New York University Press, New York, 1976.

Weeks, Albert L. *Soviet and Communist Quotations*, Pergamon-Brassey's, New York, 1987.

Weeks, Albert L. *Stalin's Other War: Soviet Grand Strategy, 1939–1941*, Rowman & Littlefield, Lanham, MD, 2002.

Weeks, Albert L. *Russia's Life-Saver: Lend-Lease Aid to the U.S.S.R. in World War II*, Lexington Books, Lanham, MD, 2004.

Weeks, Albert L. *The Choice of War: Iraq and the Just War Tradition*, Praeger, New York, 2009.

Weinberg, Gerhard L. *A World at Arms*, Cambridge University Press, Cambridge, MA, 1994.

Weeks, Albert L. *Germany and the Soviet Union, 1939–1941*, E. J. Brill, Leiden, 1954.

Werth, Alexander. *Russia at War, 1941–1945*, Dutton, New York, 1964.

Whaley, Barton. *Codeword Barbarossa*, MIT Press, Boston, 1975

Woodward, Llewelllyn. *British Foreign Policy in the Second World War: Her Majesty's Stationery Office*, London, 1962.

Yakovlev, A. N. (ed). Rossiya. *XX vek 1941 god Dokumenty v 2-kh knigakh* (*Russia 20th Century the Year 1941; Documents in Two Books*), Mezhdunarodniy Fond Demokratiya, Moscow, 1998.

Yur'ev, A.I. *Noveishaya istoriya Rossii, Fevral' 1917 g. - nachalo XXI* (*Newest History of Russia, February 1917 to the Beginning of the 21st Century*), School Textbook, Giperboreya, Moscow, 2010, p. 254.

Zakoretskiy, Keistut. *Tret' ya mirovaya voina Stalina* (*Stalin's Third World War*), Yauza Press, Moscow, 2009.

Zhilin, P. A. *Istoriya voyennovo iskusstva* (*History of Military Art*), Officer's Library Series, Voyenizdat, Moscow, 1986.

Zhukov, Georgi K. *Vospominaniya i razmyshleniya* (*Reminiscences and Reflections*), Novosti Publishers, Moscow, 1990.

Ziemke, Earl F. *The Red Army, 1918–1941: From Vanguard of World Revolution to U.S. Ally*, Frank Cass, New York, 2004.

Zolotarev, V. A. (ed). *Istoriya Voyennoi Strategii Rossii* (*A History of Russian Strategy*), Poligrafresursi, Moscow, 2000. (General Zolotarev is academician of the Russian Academy of Sciences.)

ARTICLES

Batayeva, T. V. "*Uchebnik po istorii: orientiry i adresati*" ("Textbook on History: Guides and Addressees"), *Prepodavaniye istorii v shkole*, No. 4, 1998, pp. 46–56.

Bezymenskii, Lev A. "*Sovetskaya razvedka pered voinoi* (Soviet Intelligence Bobylev, Pavel N.) *Tochku v diskussii stavit' rano. K voprosu o planirovanii v general'nom shtabe RKKA vozmozhnoi voiny s Germaniyei v 1940–1941 godakh*" ("Calling an Early Halt to the Discussion About the Problem in the General Staff of the RKKA on Planning a Possible War with Germany from the Years 1940–1941"), *Otechesvennaya istoriya*, No. 1, 2000, pp. 41–64.

Chernyak, Aleksandr. "*O nashei velikoi pobede*" ("About Our Great Victory"), *Pravda*, April 12, 1995.

Dmitriev, V. "*Diplomatiya i voyennaya strategiya*" ("Diplomacy and Military Strategy"), *Voyennaya mysl'*, No. 7, July 1971, p. 51.

Dziak, John. "Soviet Perceptions of Military Power: The Interaction of Theory and Practice," National Strategy Information Center, Inc., Crane, Rusaak & Company, Inc., New York, 1981.

V.V. Farsobin, *U. Cherchiill', Muskuly mira* (*W. Churchill, Muscles of Peace*), book review of Churchill's writings, *Voprosy Istorrii*, No. 1, 2004, pp. 171–173.

Gilensen, V. M., "*Fatal'naya oshibka*" ("The Fatal Mistake"), *Voyenno-istoricheskii zhurnal*, No. 4, 1998, pp. 25–35.

Goffman, Ioakhim (Hoffman, Joachim). "*Podgotovka Sovetskovo Soyuza k nastupatel'noi voine*" ("Preparation by the Soviet Union for Offensive War"), *Otechestvennaya istoriya*, No. 47, 1993, pp. 19–31.

Gor'kov, Yu. A. "*Gotovil li Stalin uprezhdayushchii udar protiv Gitlera v 1941 g.?*" ("Did Stalin Plan a Preemptive Strike Against Hitler in 1941?"), *Novaya I noveishaya istoriya*, 1993, No. 3, pp. 29–45.

Gurkin, V. V., and Golovnin, M. I. "*Kvoprosu o strategicheskikh operatsiyakh velikoi oteshestvennoi voine, 1941–1945*" ("About the Problem of Strategic

Operations During the Great Fatherland War, 1941–1945"), *Voyenno-istoricheskii zhurnal,* No. 10, 1985, pp. 10–33.

Historicus. "Stalin on Revolution," *Foreign Affairs,* January 1949, pp. 175–214.

Kells, Robert E. Capt. U.S. Army, "Intelligence, Doctrine and Decision-making," *Military Intelligence,* July–September 1985.

Jacob W. Kipp, "Barbarossa, Soviet Covering Forces and the Initial Period of War: Military History and Airland Battle," http://fmso.leavenworth.army.mil/documents/barbaros.htm.

Jacob W. Kipp, "Lenin and Clausewitz: The Militarization of Marxism," *Military Affairs,* XLIX, No. 4 (December 1985), 184–191.

Jacob W. Kipp, "Barbarossa, Soviet Covering Forces and the Initial Period of War: Military History and Air Land Battle," *The Journal of Soviet Military Studies,* I, No. 2 (June 1988), 188–212. The article originally appeared here. There is a great deal of useful material on GPW in this journal, now called *The Journal of Slavic Military Studies.*

Jacob W. Kipp, "Blitzkrieg in Crisis: Barbarossa and the Battle of Smolensk," *Soviet and Post-Soviet Review,* 19, No. 1–3 (1992), 91–136. (Special number edited by David Holloway.)

Jacob. W/.Kipp, "Mass, Mobility and the Origins of Soviet Operational Art" in Karl Reddel, ed., *Transformation in Russian and Soviet Military History: Proceedings of the Twelfth Military History Symposium,* USAF Academy, 1986. Washington, DC: United States Air Force Office of Air Force History, 1990, 87–116.

Jacob. W/.Kipp, "General-Major A. A. Svechin and Modern War: Military History and Military Theory," Introductory essay for: Kent Lee, editor, A. A. Svechin, *Strategy.* Minneapolis: East View Publications, 1992, 21–60.

Jacob. W/.Kipp, "Two Views of Warsaw: The Russian Civil War and Soviet Operational Art, 1920–1930," in B. J. C. McKercher and Michael A. Hennessy, eds., *The Operational Art: Developments in the Theories of War.* Westport, CT: Praeger, 1996, 51–86.

Kumanev, G. A. "*Voina glazami nachal'nika genshtaba. K stoletiyu so Dnya pozhdeniya A. M. Vasilevskovo*" ("The War Through the Eyes of the Chief of the Genertal Staff. On the 100th Anniversary of the Birth of A. M. Vasilevsky"), *Pravda,* September 28, 1995.

Kunitskii, P. T. Maj.-Gen. "*Dostizheniye vnezapnosti po opytu velikoi otechestvennoi voiny*" ("Achievement of Surprise Based on the Experience of the Great Fatherland War"), *Voyenno-istoricheskii zhurnal,* No. 10, 1985, pp. 24–30.

Lenin, V. I. "*Ya proshu zapisyvat' menshe; eto ne dol'zhno popadat' v pechat'*" ("I Propose Writing Less and Not Reproducing This in the Press"), *Istoricheskii Arkhiv,* No. 1, 1992, pp. 12–30.

Lyulechnik, V. "*A k voine my gotovilis' I byli gotovy . . .*" ("Yes, We Were Prepared and Were Prepared for War . . ."), *Panorama,* May 8–14, 1996.

Lyulechnik, V. *"Nakanune i v gody voiny"* ("On the Eve and During the Years of the War"), *Panorama*, June 18–24, 1997.

Mar'ina, Valentin B. *"Dnevnik G. Dimitrova"* ("G. Dimitrov's Diary"), *Voprosy istorii*, No. 7, 2000, pp. 32–54.

Markoff, Alexei Gen. "Stalin's War Plans," *Saturday Evening Post*, September 20, 1952.

Mel'tyukhov, Mikhail I. *"Narashchivaniye sovetskovo voyennovo prisutstviya v Pribaltike v 1939–1941 godakh"* ("The Growing Soviet Military Presence in the Baltic Region in the Years 1939–1941"), *Otechestvennaya istoriya*, No. 4, 1999, pp. 46–70.

Nevezhin, V. A. *"1941 god: v 2 kn. Sost. L. Ye. Reshin Pod red. V. P. Naumova; vstupit. St. Akad. A. N. Yakovleva. Mezhdunarodnii Fond 'Demokratiya,' Moscow, 1998"* ("The Year 1941." In 2 volumes compiled by L. Ye. Reshin under the editorship of V. P. Naumov; Introduction by A. N. Yakovlev. International Fund, Moscow, 1998), book review in *Otechestvennaya istoriya*, No. 4, 1999, pp. 212–215.

Odnokolenko, Oleg. *"Val's s Shulenburgom"* ("Waltz with Schulenburg"), *Itogi*, No. 18, 2001, pp. 26–28.

Ogarkov, N. V. "History Teaches Vigilance," Foreign Broadcast Information Service, August 30, 1985.

Ogarkov, N. V. "The Defense of Socialism: Experience of History and the Contemporary World," *Red Star*, May 9, 1984.

Plimak, Yevgenii, and Antonov, Vadim. *"Stalin znal, shto delal"* ("Stalin Knew What He Was Doing"), *Moskovskiye novosti*, March 10–17, 1996.

Raack, R. C. "Stalin's Plans for World War II," *Journal of Contemporary History*, No. 26, 1991, pp. 215–227.

Raack, R. C. "Stalin's Role in the Coming of World War II," *World Affairs*, Spring 1996, Washington, DC, 1996, pp. 1–18.

Rabiner, Boris. *"Samiy perviy den' voiny"* ("The Very First Day of the War"), *Panorama*, June 12–18, 1996.

Roberts, Cynthia A. "Planning for War: The Red Army and the Catastrophe of 1941," *Europe-Asia Studies*, Vol. 47, No. 8, 1995, pp. 1293–1326.

Rogovin, Vadim, *"Stalinskiy neonep"* ("Stalin's Neo-NEP"), *BBK*, Moscow, 1994.

Savushkin, Robert Col. "In the Tracks of Tragedy: On the 50th Anniversary of the Start of the Great Patriotic War," *Journal of Slavic Military History*, No. 2, 1991, pp. 213–251.

Schwarz, Benjamin. "Rethinking Negotiation with Hitler," *New York Times*, November 25, 2000.

Sejna, Jan. *We Will Bury You*, Sidgwick & Jackson, London, 1982.

Shevelev, Lev. "Stalin and the Nuremberg Trial," Interview with Historian Natalya Lebedeva, *Moscow News*, No. 11, March 24–30, 1995.

Sluch, Sergei Z. *"Sovetsko-Germanskiye otnosheniya v Sentyabre-Dekyabre 1939 goda I vopros o vystupolenii SSSR vo vtoruyu mirovuyu voinu"* ("Soviet-German Relations in September 1939 and the Question of the Entry of the USSR into the Second World War"), Two parts, *Otechestvennaya istoriya*, Nos. 5 and 6, 2000.

Spadkov, Semyon., *Forum.msk.ru "Vinovat Stalina v katastrofe leta 1941 goda?"* ("Whether Stalin Is Guilty of the Catastrophe of the Summer of 1941") http://forum-msk.org/material/power/642721.html?pf=2.

Stanyshnev, Boris. *"Stalin, Gitler i Suvorov"* ("Stalin, Hitler, and Suvorov"), *Argumenty i fakty*, No. 15, 1995.

Volkogonov, Dmitri. *"Mir—eto tsel', kotoraya dostigayetsya lish' soobshcha"* ("Peace Was a Goal Achieved Only Jointly"), *Rossiiskiye vesti*, January 12, 1995.

Weeks, Albert L. "The Garthoff-Pipes Debate on Soviet Doctrine: Another Perspective," *Strategic Review*, Winter 1983, pp. 57–64.

Weeks, Albert L. "The Soviet View Toward Prognostication," *Military Review*, September 1983, pp. 49–57.

Weeks, Albert L. "Soviet Military Doctrine," *Global Affairs*, Winter, 1988, pp. 170–187.

Weeks, Albert L. "The Soviet Defense Council," *Defense & Diplomacy*, May 1990, pp. 42–47.

Weeks, Albert L. "Russia Unfurls Its New/Old Military Doctrine," *The Officer*, ROA National Security Report, January 1994, pp. 30, 35.

X. "The Sources of Soviet Conduct," *Foreign Affairs*, January 1949, pp. 566–582.

PERIODICALS

Journal of Contemporary History
Kommunist Vooruzhennikh Sil
Krasnaya Zvezda
Oteshestvennaya istoriya
Panorama
Pravda
Prepodavaniye istorii v shkolye
Reason
SshaA Ekonomika Politika Ideologiya
Voennaya mysl'
Voenniy istoricheskiy zhurnal
Voprosy istorii

GOVERNMENT DOCUMENTS

Nazi-Soviet Relations 1939–1941, U.S. Department of State, 1948.
Soviet Political Agreements and Results, Staff Study, Committee on the Judiciary, U.S. Senate, 86th Congress, 1959.
Soviet Diplomacy and Negotiating Behavior, Committee on Foreign Relations, U.S. House of Representatives, 96th Congress, Vol. 1, 1979.

Notes

INTRODUCTION

1. Chris Bellamy, *Absolute War: Soviet Russia in the Second World War*, Alfred A. Knopf, New York, 2007, p. 687. Bellamy's inserted quote about Stalin is from a book by Russian historian Viktor Cherepanov, published in Moscow in 2006.

2. Discussed in Albert L. Weeks, *Russia's Life-Saver: Lend-Lease Aid to the U.S.S.R. in World War II*, Lexington Books, Lanham, MD, 2004.

3. Consecutive issues of the Russian weekly news magazine *Itogi* carried a discussion of history rewrite. *Viz., Itogi*, August 10, 17, and 31, 2009. Quotes from this discussion are reproduced in chapters that follow.

4. As we will see later, Martirosyan's all but 100 percent endorsement of Stalin's leadership is found in his recent book *Stalin: Biografiya Vozhdya (Stalin: Biography of the Leader)*, Veche, Moscow, 2008, and others of his titles that are cited in the chapters to come. In *Stalin Biografiya*, the historian comments on what he terms "132 Myths About Stalin." In his phrasing, among them are the myths "that Stalin planned to annihilate the church in Russia"; "that Stalin could not stand criticism of himself"; "that Stalin personally created the leadership cult about himself"; "that Stalin decided all questions on his own and refused to listen to the opinions of others"; "that Stalin believed in world revolution and planned a 'German October Revolution' in 1923"; and "that Stalin liquidated the 'Lenin Old Guard.'" Martirosyan's other volumes in a series called 200 Myths About Stalin bear such titles (in English) as *On the Road to World War*; *Stalin and the Great Patriotic War*; *Stalin After the War, 1943–1953*; and *Deal of the Dictators or Peaceful Breathing Space?* Other contemporary Russian writers and historians who share Martirosyan's point of view to one degree or another include Vladimir Petrov, I. Mukhin, Yu. H. Zhukov, Ye. A.

Prudnikova, A. I. Koplakidi, A. Bushkov, M. Kalashnikov, D. Verkhoturev, S. Mironin, A. Sever, S. G. Kara-Murza, Yu. V. Yemel'yanov, V. V. Sukhodeyev, and M. Yu. Morukov. Recent, more mainline histories that present rather positively, if in subtle ways, descriptions of the Stalin period's industrialization and preparations for war as well as the Nazi-Soviet pacts in a not entirely negative light while also critical of Stalin's use of terror and Gulag camps, the "Stalin" Constitution of 1936, the gulag, purges, etc., include Rudol'f Pikhoya, *USSR: Istoriya velikoi imperii, pod znakom Stalina* (*USSR: History of the Great Empire, Under the Sign of Stalin*), Piter Press, St. Petersburg, 2009; Yevgeniy Anisimov, *Istoriya Rossii ot Riurika do Putina, lyudi, sobytiya, daty* (*History of Russia from Rurik to Putin: People, Events, Dates*), Piter Press, St. Petersburg, 2008; V. V. Fortunatov, *Otechestvennaya istoriya dlya gumanitarnikh institutov; Rekomendano nauchno-metodicheskim sovetom* (*Fatherland History for Institutes of the Humanities, Recommended by the Scientific-Methodological Council*), Piter Press, St. Petersburg, 2009; V. V. Fortunatov, *Noveishaya istoriya Rossii v litsakh 1917–2008* (*Newest History of Russia as Seen Through Persons, 1917–2008*), Piter Press, St. Petersburg, 2009.

5. Besides Vladimir Rezun (aka Viktor Suvorov) in his book, *Ice-Breaker: Who Started the Second World War*, a writer who supports this view is Brian Crozier in *The Rise and Fall of the Soviet Empire*, Forum, New York, 1999, pp. 61–62. Crozier quotes from Lev Dvoretsky's *Alien Wars: The Soviet Union's Aggressions Against the World, 1919 to 1989*, Presidio Press, Novato, CA, 1996.

6. Ivo Banac (ed.), *The Diary of Georgi Dimitrov*, Yale University Press, New Haven, 2003, entry for September 7, 1939, pp. 155–156.

7. Quoted in Valeriy Petrov, *Neizvestniy Zhukov* (*The Unknown Zhukov*), Olma Press, Moscow, 2000, p. 147. Some writers overlook Stalin's involvement in the state's military affairs. For instance, Gabriel Gorodetsky oddly claims that Stalin took "scant interest" in military affairs (Gabriel Gorodetsky in *Grand Delusion: Stalin and the German Invasion*, Yale University Press, New Haven, 1999, p. 227, quoted in Weeks, *Stalin's Other War*, p. 104). People who were close to Stalin knew that he took "an interest" in everything!

8. *Confessions of Saint Augustine*, Sheed & Ward, New York, 1951, Book Eleven, Section XXI.

9. Siegfried Kracauer, *History: The Last Things Before the First*, Marcus Wiener Publishers, Princeton, NJ, 1995, p. 194.

CHAPTER 1

1. When he was an artillery captain in the Red Army in 1942, Aleksandr Solzhenitsyn had been awarded the Order of the Red Star and the Order of the Patriotic War for bravery under combat, was arrested by SMERSH (acronym for "death to spies"), and became a "political prisoner." His crime: criticizing

Stalin in a letter to a friend, which had been opened by the prying eyes of the NKVD. Solzhenitsyn was beaten and first sent to a *psikhushka*, or psychiatric clinic. Four years later, he was dispatched to the Gulag in Siberia. He recounted his experiences in his novel *Cancer Ward* as well as in *One Day in the Life of Ivan Denisovich.* Albert L. Weeks, *Alexander Solzhenitsyn's One Day in the Life of Ivan Denisovich: A Critical Commentary*, Monarch Press, New York, 1976.

2. Aristotle, *Politics*, Book V, Chapter 11, p. 1,314a for discussion of how to preserve tyranny.

3. Arsen B. Martirosyan, *Stalin: Biografiya Vozhdya*, pp. 209–210, and *passim*.

4. *Soviet Diplomacy and Negotiating Behavior: Emerging New Context for U.S. Diplomacy*, Congressional Research Service, Government Printing Office, Washington, DC, 1979, p. 57.

5. Stalin's physical whereabouts were always a tightly kept secret. When chauffeured in his black, bulletproof Zil, his limo, shades drawn, would be "secluded" in a long line of other cars so that it was impossible to know which automobile contained the leader. Stalin nearly always traveled long distances by train, not by aircraft. All precautions were undertaken by NKVD railroad security guards to guarantee safe passage (i.e., to insure against sabotaged tracks or unfriendly citizens in towns and villages en route). Even Politburo members were often kept uninformed as to the *Khozain's* exact locations as well as his daily itinerary. It is also said that Stalin on occasion employed a double to mislead any would-be assassins. As far as is known, unlike Lenin and, for example, Leonid Brezhnev, Stalin was never once immediately threatened by assassination. Some authors may attribute such precautions on Stalin's part to his "paranoia." Yet, the fact is that Stalin had many enemies.

6. "Stalin's plans [in 1940] were simple: to gain a large slice of the European pie with Hitler's help; and later to confront the Germans with Western aid dictating terms to nations exhausted by war." Gen. Oleg Sarin and Col. Lev Dvoretsky, *Alien Wars: The Soviet Union's Aggressions Against the World 1919–1989*, Presidio, Novato, CA, 1996, p. xi.

7. This was one of the reasons why Stalin declined Berlin's "gracious" invitation for the USSR to join the Axis, a gambit attempted in Berlin by Hitler and Ribbentrop during Molotov's visit there in November 1940. However, Stalin and Molotov rejected the offer altogether as untenable but did so amidst bluffing about "considering the offer."

8. See Molotov's memoirs about the "great game," *Molotov Remembers*, pp. 24–5. The bluff tactic is discussed in chapters 11 and 12. For a discussion on the use of deception and bluff in war and diplomacy, see Jon Latimer, *Deception in War: The Art of Bluff, the Value of Deceit*, Overlook Press, New York, 2001.

9. G. K. Zhukov, *Vospominaniya i razmyshleniya: Novoye dopolnenoye izdaniye* (*Memoirs and Thoughts: New, Expanded Edition*), Novosti, Moscow, 1990, Vol. 1, p. 25 and pp. 173–174 and *passim*. Zhukov's memoirs are henceforth cited as

ViR, 1990. It is stunning to observe how the marshal by turns both criticized and praised Stalin, who in many ways treated this Soviet army hero badly after the war. Yet Zhukov could praise Stalin for what Zhukov described as the Soviet leader's many years' preparation of the USSR for war, the commander-in-chief's wartime leadership, and even Stalin's defense measures taken just before the Germans invaded in June 1941 (see discussion in chapters 10 and 11). In his recollections, Zhukov displays a certain sangfroid, even tacit understanding toward Stalin's purges of top Red Army officers in 1937–1938 and beyond for their failures to respond adequately to the Wehrmacht invaders. One gets the impression that Marshal Zhukov, despite the dictator's faults, which he also cites, considered Stalin to be a soldier's ideal, authoritarian leader as well as capable civilian commander-in-chief because of the leader's constant prewar attention to the nation's defenses and the way he increasingly listened to his professional military in wartime in the later phases of the Great Patriotic War.

CHAPTER 2

1. New, latter-day historians like Martirosyan claim that this cult was not Stalin's doing but that of his comrades. Martirosyan, *Stalin: Biografiya*, pp. 237–43; see historians' discussions in *Itogi*, July 13, August 10, August 17, August 31, 2009. Similar themes appeared on the 130th anniversary of Stalin's birth, December 21, 2009 ("Russia's Communists Mark Stalin's Birthday," AP, *Boston Globe*, December 21, 2009). A teacher in Kazakhstan, Lev Balayan, who described himself as an adherent of the teachings of Marx-Engels-Lenin-Stalin, posted on his Russian Web site, Stalin.ru: "Stalin resorted to extreme measures when it came to cowards, deserters, and traitors. Everyone knows today how necessary it was for Stalin to adopt such measures and put a stop to the panic that was shown in 1941 and into 1942. The Stalin leadership remained true to its country, to its people and the ideals of communism. Its warranted firmness brought about the turning point in the war by instilling fighting spirit into the army" (http://www.stalin.su/book.php?action=header&id+19).

2. Dora Shturman, *Mertviye khvatayet zhivykh* (*The Living Envy the Dead*), Leksikon, Jerusalem, 1982, p. 112. In *Social Contract*, Rousseau suggests that the government should shame any wrongdoers in the most public way possible, and that that form of punishment is to be desired in the type of Calvinist-like society he idealizes. It is one that reflects the Hobbesian idea that law must be the public conscience.

3. Arsen B. Martirosyan, *Biografiya*, p. 94.

4. The story of how Trotsky was murdered in Mexico with a blow of an ax to his skull in August 1940 by the NKVD-hired hit man, Ramon Mercader, is told firsthand by the man who was in charge of that "wet" operation that was

ordered from Moscow personally by Stalin: NKVD Gen. Pavel Sudoplatov, Deputy Chief of Foreign Intelligence, related in his book, *Special Tasks: The Memoirs of an Unwanted Witness—A Soviet Spymaster*, Little, Brown and Co., New York, 1994, chapter 4.

5. Josef Goebbels, *Early Goebbels Diaries, 1925–1926*, Praeger, New York, 1962. See pp. 62, 63, 67, 75, and 86, from which it becomes clear how much Goebbels, and Hitler as well, were influenced by or co-opted from Bolshevism. Mussolini once described Stalin as a "crypto-Fascist." Hitler's copying and favorable references to Marxist tactics, even the color on their banners, may be found in several places in *Mein Kampf*, notably on pp. 51–56, 224, 476, 711–712; 721–722, 726 ("We have indeed learned from studying the Marxist techniques . . ."), and 783 ("What once gave Marxism its success was the perfect playing together of political will and effective brutality"), Houghton Mifflin, New York, 1939.

6. *Molotov Remembers*, p. 254.

CHAPTER 3

1. Arsen B. Martirosyan, *Stalin Biografiya*, p. 96, *passim*. The Russian historian, implicitly favored by the current Russian government, claims that Stalin did not support the "Leninist-Trotskyite" idea of world revolution. Stalin rejected such ideology, the author asserts, as "utopian" and counterproductive to the Soviet state's progress toward becoming a major international power. The master practitioner of realpolitik, he claims, was Stalin, who, he says, always put the best interests of the Soviet (Russian) state above all other considerations. The author even accuses the Cominternists (where applicable, Martirosyan repeatedly reproduces their Jewish family names or Masonic connections) as being in the service of Western financial interests, mainly Jewish ones, who sought to embarrass the USSR for its revolutionism. Thus, he alleges, the Cominternists, backed by the Invoices, Radix, Bukharins, et al., and Lenin himself actually abetted the long-standing Western effort, he claims, to weaken "Russia" (aka, the USSR). The Versailles Peace Treaty exemplified this program, he says, by establishing a new little entente of Western lap dogs in Eastern Europe bordering on Soviet Russia. The recreation of Poland and Czechoslovakia and the three independent Baltic countries was an essential part of this "anti-Russian" Western enterprise.

2. Martirosyan, op. cit., pp. 141–154.

3. Robert Conquest, *The Great Terror: A Reassessment*, Oxford University Press, New York, 1990. Among those largely believing in the official version, notes Conquest, were such well-known writers and VIPs as Sir Bernard Pares, Romain Rolland, Theodore Dreiser, Harold Laski, Granville Hicks, Corless Lamont, et al., as well as members of Trotskyite groups and such publications

as the *Manchester Guardian* and *New Statesman*. Conquest cites the findings of the U.S.-based Dewey Commission, which investigated the trials and found the prosecution's evidence to be bogus. At the same time, Conquest asserts that the "vulnerability" existed in the USSR of a "military coup. [Yet] there is no evidence that any [military] conspiracy existed. Isaac Deutscher [widely read biographer of Stalin] has indeed written that 'all non-Stalinist versions concur in the following: the generals did indeed plan a coup d'etat'" (p. 186). Those generals and marshals who were accused and punished, among them Tukhachevsky, were rehabilitated by the Soviet government early in the post-Stalin period at the time of Khrushchev's de-Stalinization campaign after February 1956. William J. Chase, *The Comintern and the Stalinist Repression, 1934–1939*, Yale University Press, New Haven, 2002.

4. Conquest, op. cit., pp. 471–472.

CHAPTER 4

1. One of the best descriptions of this collaboration may be found in Yuri Dyakov and Tatyana Bushuyeva's *The Red Army and the Wehrmacht: How the Soviets Militarized Germany, 1922–1933*, Prometheus Books, Amherst, NY, 1995. I have mainly used the authors' well-sourced study for my discussion of this cooperation between Berlin and Moscow. A number of new Russian history textbooks, published in the Yeltsin-Putin-Medvedev period, also describe this collaboration.

2. One of the best accounts of Stalin's use of collective security slogans unsupported by Soviet action may be found in Jiri Hochman's *The Soviet Union and the Failure of Collective Security, 1934–1938*, Cornell University Press, Ithaca, NY, 1984. Opposing Hochman's view is a standard Soviet period work, *Soviet Peace Efforts on the Eve of World War (September 1938–August 1939)*, Vols. 1 and 2, Novosti, Moscow, 1973, and a contemporary history textbook used in the RF, Nikita V. Zagladin's *Vsemirnaya istoriya: XX vek (World History: 20th Century)*, Russkoye Slovo, Moscow, 2004, pp. 144–147, in which the Russian historian disputes the potion that Moscow was not seriously interested in establishing a workable East-West system of collective security to oppose Hitler. The author shies away from giving Stalin credit for such initiatives. Instead, the Zagladin repeatedly uses the expression the "Soviet government" (as on pp. 145–146) when discussing as well as endorsing such policies.

CHAPTER 5

1. *Soviet Diplomacy and Negotiating Behavior*, U.S. House of Representatives Committee on Foreign Affairs, 96th Congress, 1979, Vol. 1, p. 56. Dimitrov, later chairman of the Comintern, referring to treaties like that signed at

Brest-Litovsk between Germany and the Soviet Republic in March 1918 that provide for momentary truces, remarked: "We should use breathing spaces so obtained in order to gather our strength." Theodore J. Ultrix, specialist on the Soviet Commissariat of Foreign Affairs, wrote: "In the early days of the Soviet regime, the conception of 'Bolshevik diplomacy' seemed impossible to both friend and foe of the revolution. Could bomb-throwing revolutionaries suddenly don striped pants and sit down to tea with representatives of imperialism?" According to Ultrix, this they did with consummate ease since, in his view, ideology was no imperative to them or later to Stalin. Ibid., p. 47.

2. Among these Russian textbook titles are M. Yu. Brandt et al., *Rossiya i mir, Uchebnaya kniga* (*Russian and the World, Textbook*), Parts 1 and 2, Vlados, Moscow, 1994; V. P. Ostrovskiy and A. I. Utkin, *Istoriya Rossii: XX vek* (*History Russia: 20th Century*), Drofa, 1997; Ye. V. Lapteva, *Istoriya Rossii, Uchebnoye posobiye dlya vuzov* (*History of Russia, Teaching Guide for Technical Schools*), Akademicheskiy Proyekt, Moscow, 2009; V. E. Vagdasaryan et al., *Shkol'niy uchebnik istorii i gosudarstvennaya politika* (*School Textbooks on History and State Policy*), Nauchniy Ekspert, Moscow, 2009; I. I. Dolutskiy, *Otechestvennaya istoriya XX vek; rekomendovano Ministerstva obrazovaniya RF* (*Fatherland History in the 20th Century; Recommended by the RF Ministry of Education*), 2 Parts, Mnemozina, Moscow, 2002; and A. V. Filippov, *Noveishaya istoriya Rossii 1945–2006 gg; Kniga dlya uchitelya* (*New History of Russia, 1945–2006; Teacher's Book*), Prosveshcheniye, Moscow, 2007.

3. Albert L. Weeks, *Stalin's Other War; Soviet Grand Strategy 1939–1941*, Rowman & Littlefield, Lanham, MD, 2002, p. 27, and http://thinkexist.com/quotation/sincere_diplomacy_is-no_more possible_than_dry/1921. Aleksandr Yakovlev, *Omut Pamyati*, Fonda, Moscow, 2000, p. 83. Yakovlev, former member of the Soviet Communist Party Politburo, describes the "new" Soviet diplomacy as follows: "The post-October 1917 Soviet pose of renouncing secret diplomacy and going over to above-board diplomacy quickly changed. Deceit, lying, and dissimulation, so much a part of the history of diplomacy, were wholly adopted by Soviet foreign policy" (p. 110).

4. Quoted in Weeks, *The Other Side of Coexistence: A History of Russian Foreign Policy*, Pitman, New York, p. 54.

5. Nathan Leites, *The Operational Code of the Politburo*, McGraw-Hill, New York, 1961.

6. David Irving, "Crusade Into Russia, Part 3," http://www.fpp.co.uk/books/Hitler/1977/html_chapter/17.html. As Operation Barbarossa began to bog down by 1942, Hitler exclaimed to Ribbentrop that he felt like the legendary horseman who having unwittingly ridden across the frozen Lake Constance died of horror when he learned what he had done: "If I had had the slightest inkling of this gigantic Red Army assemblage, I would never have taken the decision to attack."

7. Stephen Koch, *Double Lives*, Free Press, New York, p. 54.

8. V. Stalin, *Sochineniya*, Ogiz, Moscow, 1947, Vol. 7, p. 86. Arsen Martirosyan vigorously denies that Stalin ordered in the 1930s a split in the working-class movement in Germany between the SDs and the Communists. Martirosyan, *Stalin Biografiya*, pp. 295–298. This well-known "mistake" by Stalin, now denied by some latter-day Russian historians, was even cited in the Brezhnev period in the 1970s by party ideologist Mikhail Suslov as a fundamental Stalin error that helped bring Hitler to power in 1933 by weakening the anti-Fascist unity of the proletariat and the lower middle class.

CHAPTER 6

1. For a discussion of this linkage, see Stanley W. Page, *The Geopolitics of Leninism*, Columbia University Press, New York, 1982, and Stanley W. Page, *Lenin and World Revolution*, McGraw-Hill, New York, 1959.

2. V. A. Zolotarev et al., *Miroviye voiny XX veka; Kniga 3; Vtoraya mirovaya voina: Istoricheskiy ocherk* (*World Wars of the 20th Century: Historical Outline, Book 3; World War II*), Nauka, Moscow, 2002. For the quoted excerpts, see pp. 25, 27, and 35.

3. Albert L. Weeks, *Stalin's Other War: Soviet Grand Strategy, 1939–1942*, pp. 61–62.

4. Arsen B. Martirosyan, *Stalin Biografiya*, pp. 157–160.

5. Domenico Settembrini, "Mussolini and Lenin," *Survey* (UK), Vol. 23, No. 3, 1977–1978.

6. Trotsky quoted in *Vozhd' i spodvizhniki* (*The Leader and Comrades-in-Arms*), Vol. 5, Olma, Moscow, 2004, p. 522, as asserting on August 5, 1919: "The road to London lies through cities in Afghanistan, Punjab, and Bengal."

CHAPTER 7

1. Frederick L. Schuman, *Soviet Politics at Home and Abroad*, Alfred A. Knopf, New York, 1946, pp. 229–230. This was one of the earliest appearances of the old Soviet diplomatic standby by which a Western proposal (say, as in later years for controlling the production of nuclear weapons and establishing a system of inspection) was shot down by a Kremlin counterproposal that simply precluded any further discussion or negotiation by posing sweeping, unrealistic demands. In the above case, imagine Stalin's "immediately" shutting down Moscow's secret collaboration with the German military, which included designing, building, and testing new lethal weapons, including prison gas, and playing war games on Soviet soil—all in the name of honoring a disarmament treaty that stipulated "abolition of all military training . . . etc." This was, to quote the Russian proverb, "raking water."

2. Ye. V. Lapteva, *Istoriya Rossii (A History of Russia)*, Akademicheskiy proyekt, Moscow, 2009, pp. 252–253. Note the historian's reticence to use Stalin's name. Instead, throughout she attributes what sound like reasonable policies to the "USSR," "Soviet government," etc., as though the state were leaderless.

3. Willard N. Hogan, "What Does the National Interest Require?" in Marina and Lawrence Finkelstein's *Collective Security*, Chandler Publishing Company, San Francisco, 1966, p. 68.

4. Stalin: "A new war cannot but impinge on us." To Stalin's mind, a new war was becoming inevitable. "The question cannot but arise before us being ready for anything." In 1925, he said: "But if war begins, we will not be able to sit with folded hands—we shall have to take action but we will take action last. And we will act so as to the decisive weight on the scales, the weight could be preponderant." Also: "The question of the army, of its might and pre-paredness, will certainly be for us the burning question in the event of com-plications in countries surrounding us." Quoted in Robert C. Tucker's *Stalin in Power: The Revolution from Above, 1928–1941*, W.W. Norton & Co., New York, 1992, p. 49.

In a *Pravda* editorial of July 1927, which Stalin authored, the Soviet leader wrote: "It is scarcely open to doubt that the basic question for the pres-ent is the threat of a new imperialist war. This is not a matter of some unde-fined and intangible 'danger' of a new war. It is a matter of a real, genuine threat of a new war in general and of a *war against the USSR in particular*" (my emphases—ALW). J. V. Stalin, *Sochineniya*, Robert H. McNeal (ed.), Politizdat, Moscow, 1967, Vol. 9, p. 322.

In Tucker's book, the author claims that "Stalin's collective security diplomacy was a calculated effort at coalition-building in Europe. He ear-nestly sought to bring about a strong politico-military anti-German group-ing based on France and Britain. *But it was not a coalition in which he wanted the Soviet Union to participate when war came.*" It is my contention (ALW) that Stalin had no such idea of forming an East-West coalition to stop Hitler. How-ever, Tucker's last sentence, I believe, is an accurate assessment of Stalin's reticence to involve his military in an anti-Axis war at that time (late 1930s) and pull "bourgeois chestnuts" out of the fire for the Western capitalist states. Just when Stalin began to calculate on a mutually destructive war of this type between Germany and the other Western capitalist states is unknown. That the Soviet leader voiced to Comintern chief Dimitrov this idea of such a use-ful, from the Soviet perspective, fratricidal war in the West is supported by the latter's diary and other evidence.

5. Lenin had said to the Moscow Party *aktiv* on December 6, 1920, "Until the final victory of socialism throughout the whole world, we must apply the principle of exploiting contradictions and opposition between two imperial-ist power groups . . . inciting them to attack each other. . . . If it should prove

Notes

impossible to defeat them both, then one must know how to rally one's forces so that the two begin to fight each other. For when two thieves quarrel, honest men have the last laugh. . . . As soon as we are strong enough to defeat capitalism [worldwide], we will seize it at once by the scruff of the neck." See a discussion of this Soviet tactic in Albert L. Weeks, *Stalin's Other War: Soviet Grand Strategy, 1939–1941,* Chapter 1, pp. 26–31. In 1939–1940, Stalin updated Lenin's tactic as Stalin counted on such "contradictions" in the form of all-out war in the West to afford the USSR much-needed time to prepare to meet the Germans in Hitler's coming, "inevitable" war against Soviet Russia. One such ploy was Operation White, an NKVD plan of using agents of influence in high places in Washington, DC, to worsen U.S.-Japan relations (read: "contradictions") in 1940–1941 so as to help bring on war between the two powers, which would be to Soviet advantage.

6. A congressional study by the U.S. Senate Judiciary Committee, published in 1959, found that the "thousand treaties and agreements . . . both bilateral and multilateral, which the Soviets have entered into not only with the United States, but with countries over the world [in the 38 years since the Soviet Union came into existence], its government had broken its word to virtually every country to which it ever gave a signed promise. It signed treaties of nonaggression with neighboring states and then absorbed these states. It signed promises to refrain from revolutionary activity inside the countries with which it sought 'friendship,' and then cynically broke those promises." "Soviet Political Agreements and Results," Staff Study, Committee on the Judiciary, U.S. Senate, Government Printing Office, 1959, p. viii. The study includes all of the treaties and the manner in which they were broken by the USSR.

7. Lenin's views on war—how a war might begin legitimately when started by a socialist state, how future wars would be fought between "proletarian" and capitalist states—all may be found in various places in the following basic Lenin writings about war written in 1916–1917: *Military Programme of Proletarian Revolution; The 'Disarmament' Slogan; Tasks of the Left Zimmerwaldists; Theses on the Attitude of the Swiss Social-Democratic Party Towards War; Principles Involved in the War Issue;* and *Bourgeois Pacifism and Socialist Pacifism* in V. I. Lenin, *Collected Works,* Vol. 25, Progress Publishers, Moscow, 1977. Lenin wrote in *Bourgeois Pacifism and Socialist Pacifism:* "In order to obtain a democratic and just peace, the bourgeois governments of all the belligerent countries must be overthrown, and that for this purpose advantage must be taken of the fact that millions of workers are armed and that . . . imperialist war has roused the anger of the masses" (p. 190). War, said Lenin, is the "locomotive of history" (p. 330). These and many more statements about war that were made by Lenin and Stalin and their successors may be found in Albert L. Weeks (ed.), *Soviet and Communist Quotations,* Pergamon-Brassey's, Washington/ New York, 1987.

8. Nikita V. Zagladin, *Vsemirnaya istoria XX vek* (*World History of the 20th Century*), *Uchebnik dlya 11 klassa* (*Textbook for the 11th Grade*, 6th ed.), Russkoye Slovo, Moscow, 2004, p. 115.

9. Stalin's address to Leningrad Party workers, July 23, 1928, as quoted in Jiri Hochman, *The Soviet Union and the Failure of Collective Security, 1934–1938*, Cornell University Press, Ithaca, NY, 1984, p. 29.

10. Elliot R. Goodman, *The Soviet Design for a World State*, Columbia University Press, New York, 1960, p. 81. The United States recognized the USSR and opened formal diplomatic relations with Stalin's state in 1933.

11. Supra, p. 81.

12. Quoted by Mikhail Heller and Aleksandr Nekrich in *Utopia and Power: The History of the Soviet Union from 1917 to the Present*, Summit Books, New York, 1986, p. 324.

13. Stalin, a Georgian from the Caucasus, favored extending Soviet rule southward into the resource-rich and vulnerable region. Yet many of his civilian and military comrades, including Red Army hotheads like field commander Mikhail Tukhachevsky, strongly favored (i.e., were gung-ho, *ukharskiy*) carrying the offensive westward to the Polish capital itself. In this respect, Tukhachevsky and others appeared to agree with Lenin, at least when the latter was in a revolutionary mood and would describe Poland as the gateway to Germany and beyond.

14. Librach, p. 51.

CHAPTER 8

1. William Taubman. *Stalin's American Policy From Entente to Detente to Cold War*, W. W. Norton & Company, New York, 1982, p. 18.

2. Robert Ivanov, *Stalin i Soyuzniki, 1941–1945 gg.* (*Stalin and the Allies, 1941–1945*), Rusich, Smolensk, 2000, p. 122. Ivanov notes that the "USA and the Soviet Union were potential allies since both countries sought to prevent Germany from dominating Europe" (p. 92). Post-Soviet Russian authors also note that both Lenin and Stalin said that they regarded the United States as relatively peace-minded compared to other capitalist countries. Radical U.S. disarmament proposals at European conferences after World War I are examples of such peace-mindedness. So was its own domestic disarmament.

3. Albert L. Weeks, *The Other Side of Coexistence: A Study of Russian Foreign Policy*, Pitman, New York, 1970, chapter 4.

4. Peter Niblo, *Influence*, Elderberry Press, Oakland, OR, 2002, p. 86.

5. Besides the several books by Martirosyan, an earlier, widely read volume by a Russian historian helped set the tone for later books. This book was Mikhail Mel'tyukhov's *Upushchenniy shans Stalina: Sovetskiy Soyuz i bor'ba za Yevropu, 1939–1941* (*Stalin's Lost Opportunity: The Soviet Union and the Struggle for Europe, 1939–1941*), Veche, Moscow, 2000. Its contents are canvassed in

Albert L. Weeks' *Stalin's Other War: Soviet Grand Strategy, 1939–1941*, Rowman & Littlefield, Lanham, MD, 2002, chapter 5, *passim*. It is noted in these readings that Stalin was perfectly aware of the political disloyalty to his regime lurking within the newly acquired, sovietized western territories. Hence, the resettlements of hundreds of thousands of native residents of these areas into the interior of the USSR and Stalin's increase in police surveillance within the territories that was followed by deployment of Soviet "partisans" during the Nazi occupation after June 1941.

6. Zhukov quoted in B. V. Sokolov, *Tainy vtoroi mirovoi (Secrets of the Second World War)*, Veche, Moscow, 2001, pp. 199–200. During the 45 postwar years, Soviet media and histories ignored or played down Lend-Lease aid. For the whole story about Lend-Lease and the Soviet propaganda treatment of it, see Albert L. Weeks, *Russia's Life-Saver: Lend Lease Aid to the USSR in World War II*, Lexington Books, Lanham, MD, 2004.

7. *The USSR Institutions and People: A Brief Handbook for the Use of Officers of the Armed Forces of the United States*, U.S. Government Printing Office, Washington, DC, 1945. This book, designed for U.S. Orientation Officers (i.e., U.S. Armed Forces indoctrinators), praises Stalin as a democratically "elected" leader. In general, the War Department/OWI handbook paints a rosy picture of a comradely ally whose politics resemble those of the United States but whose social customs, as among Soviet army enlisted personnel, differ from those of American GIs. The latter are instructed on how to "approach" such comrades-in-arms when they encounter them.

8. Pavel Sudoplatov, *Special Tasks*, Little, Brown and Company, New York, 1994, p. 96.

9. Amos Perlmutter, *FDR & Stalin: A Not So Grand Alliance, 1943–1945*, University of Missouri Press, Columbia, 1993, p. 90.

10. Herbert Romerstein and Eric Breindel, *The Venona Secrets: Exposing Soviet Espionage and America's Traitors*, Regnery Publishing, Inc., New York, 2000, pp. 100–101.

11. Perlmutter, ibid.

12. Sergo Beria, op. cit., pp. 119–120.

13. Heinz Megenheimer, *Hitler's War: Germany's Key Strategic Decisions, 1940–1945*, Cassell, London, 1999, p. 40.

14. Niblo, op. cit., p. 88.

15. Robert Ivanov, *Stalin i soyuzniki (Stalin and the Allies)*, 1941–1945, Rusich, Smolensk, 2000.

CHAPTER 9

1. *Itogi*, September and October 2009.

2. Arsen B. Martirosyan, *Na puti k mirovoi voine (On the Road to World War)*, p. 374; pp. 451–452.

3. Arsen B. Martirosyan, *22 iyunya: Pravda Generalissimusa (June 22nd: Truth of the Generalissimus)*, Veche, Moscow, 2005, pp. 423–428 and *passim*.

4. The defensist argument about Soviet Russia's stance just prior to the German attack was incorporated in instructions on how to lecture about the USSR top GIs given by the U.S. Army to its orientation officers in World War II. In their orientation, these junior officers referred to such manuals as *The USSR Institutions and People: A Brief Handbook for the Use of Officers of the Armed Forces of the United States.* "The Nazi-Soviet Pact," says the handbook, "was accepted by the Soviet people as an act of wisdom [gaining time] for them . . . in which to prepare for the Nazi attack which came in June 1941. . . . Soviet-advocated measures failed largely because the democratic powers mistrusted the Soviet Union. [The Soviet people felt] that the overtures made to the Soviet Union by Great Britain and France in the summer of 1939 lacked a basis for realistic and effective measures against Germany."

5. Arsen B. Martirosyan, *Na puti k mirovoi voine (On the Road to World War)*, Veche, Moscow, 2008, pp. 175–179. The Russian history professor, who addressed the RF Ministry of Justice school in late 2009, goes so far as to allege that Winston Churchill was in cahoots with "world Jewry" ("Zionism"), which had sought the downfall of the tsar in World War I. In the interwar period, the historian claims, Russian Jews within the Comintern, aided and abetted by Trotsky-Bronshtein (Martirosyan frequently inserts the Jewish family names of Soviet officials he scorns, such as Litvinov-Wallach), developed into an anti-Stalin cabal that became genuine "anti-Stalin plots" disclosed at the purge trials of 1937 and 1938. According to Martirosyan, Tukhachevsky and Yegor-evich, the latter chief of the Soviet general staff in the mid-1930s, were also implicated in anti-Stalin and anti-"Russian" plotting. The historian claims that the offensive Soviet war plans were developed with subversive intent by Tukhachevsky. They were carried forward "disastrously" by Marshals Timoshenko and Zhukov in spring 1941. In fact, the "Tukhachevsky-Trotsky" strategy, he claims, caused the Red Army's debacle in the opening months of the war. This appears today to be the view held in the RF among some of those who attribute extraordinary wisdom and greatness to Josef Stalin.

6. Alvin Z. Rubinstein, *Soviet Foreign Policy Since World War II: Imperial and Global*, 2nd ed., Little, Brown and Company, Boston, 1985, p. 19.

7. *Molotov Remembers: Inside Kremlin Politics: Conversations with Felix Chuev*, Ivan R. Dee, Chicago, 1993, p. 63.

8. Edvard Radzinsky, *Stalin*, Doubleday Publishing Co., New York, 1996, p. 440.

9. Adam A. Claasen, *Hitler's Northern War: The Luftwaffe's Ill-Fated Campaign, 1940–1945*, University Press of Kansas, Lawrence, 2001, p. 11. The Soviets were rather uncooperative with the Germans over access to this short-lived northern base. The base had little or no military significance and was, again, more for a show of bilateral German-Soviet "friendship" than substantial.

10. M. Yu. Brant et al., *Rossiya i mir. Uchebnaya kniga po istorii* (*Russia and the World. Textbook on History*), Vlados, Moscow, 1994, pp. 174–175.

11. O. S. Soroko-Tsyupi, ed., *Mir v XX veke* (*Peace in the 20th Century*), Proveshcheniye, Moscow, 1997, pp. 168–172.

12. Weeks, *Stalin's Other War*, pp. 21–22. Authors who hold this view essentially accuse Stalin of starting World War II, which may strike some readers as preposterous. The same notion might also include the dubious claim that Stalin was likewise solely responsible for Hitler's rise to power. An equally dubious allegation since the German Communists at times actively collaborated with the German Social Democrats against the Nazis.

CHAPTER 10

1. This version largely stems from the description of Stalin's whereabouts in the early morning hours of June 22 from Nikita Khrushchev's de-Stalinization speech and the anti-Stalin campaign that followed in similar versions in published history texts, such as that by Volkogonov, or in some memoirs. However, a later version (see the discussion below) puts Stalin not in one of his dachas but in his Kremlin apartment that night. At that location, it is said, Stalin received various phone calls, including Zhukov's. He immediately arose and called Politburo members and military officers to his office. For Verkhovslky-Tyrmos' version, which contrasts to the original by placing Stalin in his Kremlin apartment on the eve of the German attack, see their op. cit., pp. 494–497.

2. Verkhovsky-Tyrmos, op. cit., *The Great Game Goes On*, pp. 495–499.

3. Historian Martirosyan claims (*Stalin Biografiya*, pp. 273–282) that Stalin did not seek to destroy the Russian Orthodox Church in Soviet Russia. On the contrary, he alleges, Stalin ordered that religious landmarks in the USSR be preserved. Militant atheism, he says, was largely the work of officials like Yemelyan Yaroslavsky, a Lenin cohort, who died in 1943 and whose real name, the writer notes, was Minei Gubel'man. Stalin himself "had nothing against the church." The author suggests that the dictator himself did not order the destruction of the Moscow cathedral. Just before the war, the author says, Stalin encouraged religious belief via "39,000 religious organizations" and since 1936 had supported introducing democratic inroads into the Soviet political system—reforms that were marked, he continues, by the 1936 "Stalin Constitution." According to the historian, this charter's stipulated civil rights were often violated without Stalin's permission and against his preferences by local party organizations. The constitution promised the right to practice religion. At the same time, Martirosyan notes that anti-Soviet elements working within various religious groups, such as the Muslims, had to be purged, and church ranks were penetrated by frocked NKVD informers to root out such elements. The historian makes no mention of the destruction of the main Moscow church, the

Cathedral of Christ the Blessed Savior, on December 5, 1931, on orders, it is said, of deputy premier and Politburo member Lazar Moiseyevich Kaganovich. During World War II, Stalin particularly tolerated religious worship as part of his "nationalistic"-patriotic campaign to rally popular support for the war effort.

4. Molotov several times, for emphasis, tells Chuev that Stalin was careful to get the point across for world opinion that the Soviets were the *victims of attack*. As Molotov indicates, Hitler was not to be given any pretext for launching a preventive war against the Soviets, as Hitler indeed claimed in his address after the first day of the invasion. As Stalin had hoped, the fuehrer's claim did fall flat. It might not have had Stalin chosen to attack first in a preemptive war. The Soviet leader would then have wound up with the serious threat of defeat in the hands of the better-armed and better-prepared Wehrmacht, plus bearing the stigma of having committed aggression, with the result that the USSR would have had to face the Axis powers alone in war on two fronts.

CHAPTER 11

1. Yakov Verkhovsky; Valentina Tyrmos, *Stalin: Tainiy 'tsenarii' nachala voiny* (*Secret "Scenario" of the Start of the War*), Olma Press, Moscow, 2006.

2. Telegram from Ambassador Steinhardt in Moscow to Cordell Hull, April 6, 1941. Quoted in Barton Whaley, *Codeword Barbarossa*, MIT Press, Boston, 1975, pp. 52 and 278. Sergo Beria overheard similar remarks. President Kalinin on June 5, 1941: "The Germans are getting ready to attack us. . . . The sooner they come, the better; we will wring their necks" (quoted by Zastavyenko of the Institute of Marxism-Leninism to historian Petrov in Vladimir Petrov, *June 22, 1941: Soviet Historians and the German Invasion*, University of South Carolina Press, Columbia, 1968, p. 253.

3. A. B. Filippov, *Noveishaya istoriya Rossii, 1945–2006 gg; kniga dlya uchitelya* (*Newest History of Russia, 1945–2006; Textbook for the Teacher*), Prosveshcheniye, Moscow, 2007, p. 93. Another current textbook, N. V. Zagladin, *Vsemirnaya istiriya XX vek* (*World History 20th Century*), Russkoye Slovo, Moscow, 2004, states outright that Stalin "had no other choice" but to sign agreement with Germany in August 1939 and which showed farsightedness "on the part of the leaders of the USSR," p. 146. "Leaders of the USSR," "Soviet government," etc., are often-used euphemisms in school textbooks for what was in fact Stalin's autocratic rule.

4. *Molotov Remembers*, p. 22, 24, *passim*. Molotov insisted that Stalin knew Hitler would attack the USSR in 1941 and ridicules those civilian and military memoirists and historians who claim otherwise. The former alter ego to Stalin claims that Stalin never for a moment trusted Hitler and suggests that Stalin was only playing a game of bluff in the spring of 1941.

5. Just weeks before the German attack, as Stalin was deploying his quasi-Kutuzov defense, the dictator called into his Kremlin office Soviet historian

Yegeniy Tarle (1875–1955), well known for his history of Napoleon's war against Russia, *Nashestvie Napoleona na Rossiyu, 1812* (*Napoleon's Campaign Against Russia, 1812*). He talked with his favored historian for several hours. No transcript of the Stalin-Tarle discussions is known to exist, but it can be safely presumed that they revolved about Kutuzov's successful strategy against Napoleon, since that is the crux of Tarle's popular book. This assumption is illustrated by two additional facts: Stalin had recently set up a large exhibit at the historical museum in Red Square on Russia's successful defense against Napoleon. As the war got under way, Stalin ordered the minting of a "Kutuzov medal" to be awarded RKKA soldiers for valor in combat. This was a radical departure from the usual Soviet attitude toward the tsarist past, which Stalin had earlier begun embracing, as with Sergei Eisenstein's "docudrama" historical films, such as *Alexander Nevsky*, shown in Soviet cinemas several years earlier. For further discussion of the above, see Verkhovsky-Tyrmos, op. cit., pp. 331–332; 372; 378–379.

   6. Savushkin, Robert Col. "In the Tracks of Tragedy: On the 50th Anniversary of the Start of the Great Patriotic War," *Journal of Slavic Military History*, No. 2, 1991, pp. 213–251. Cf. pp. 222, 236. In general, Savushkin generally follows the anti-Stalin line on the leader's failure to "reduce the scale of the tragedy" by his having failed, Savushkin writes, to bring RKKA troops "to combat readiness and implementing a whole set of preparatory measures." At the same time, contradictorily, it seems, Savushkin recognizes the sense of Stalin's tactic of concealed mobilization and of constrained preparations, implying that this was a bluff in order to put the onus of starting the war clearly in Germany's lap. The question is, then, was Stalin's a "bad" strategy under the conditions, given the fact that the Soviet leader seemed determined that the USSR be seen as the victim of aggression? Moreover, subsequent events at the start of the war obviously proved that the RKKA was in no condition to mount an all-out, preemptive offensive against Germany of the type occasionally alluded to in their writings by Tukhachevsky and others. It is doubtful that the RKKA and Soviet society generally would have been ready in this sense of waging total war, least of all to wage a preventive war against Germany, even by 1942.

   7. Joseph W. Kipp, "Barbarossa, Soviet Covering Forces and the Initial Period of War: Military History and Airland Battle," http://www.rand.org/pubs/monograph_reports/MR880/MR880.ch3.pdf.

CHAPTER 12

   1. *Pravda*, February 10, 1946, p. 1. Deputy Premier Vyacheslav Molotov's electoral speech, February 6, carried the same ominous note (*Pravda*, February 7, 1946, p. 1). Stalin claimed that World War II stemmed from the "second

crisis of capitalism." This reference to capitalism was regarded as ominous as reported in foreign coverage of Stalin's speech. No war, Stalin continued, *"can ever arise accidentally."* The Soviet system had saved the USSR he said: "The Soviet social order is better than any non-Soviet system in the world." The past war was won by Soviet *"active defense."* Without heavy industry, Soviet defenses cannot be built up: "To lag in this emphasis on heavy industry means to lose and bring about the destruction of the Soviet system. [Such a buildup] will guarantee the safety of our country from any future contingencies." For his part, Molotov noted that the postwar Five-Year Plan would result in the Soviets' "overtaking and surpassing economically the most highly developed European capitalist countries as well as the United States of America . . . and which will be accomplished in the nearest future." Soviet foreign policy will keep the *"aggressor pack chained,"* he said. "This is why the Soviet Union is vigilant when it comes to possible *centers of violating the peace and international security or to any intrigues along those lines.* . . . The government and the leadership of the Soviet Army *are doing everything to ensure that as regards the very latest types of armaments, our Army will not be inferior to that of any other country." Soviet participation in the United Nations "is aimed at preventing fresh wars and curbing all and every imperialist aggressor."* He boasted that the Soviet victory in the East had guaranteed that the USSR would be ranked "among the world powers. Important problems in international relations henceforth cannot be settled without the participation of the Soviet Union. . . . The participation of Comrade Stalin [in such affairs] is regarded as the best guarantee of a successful resolution of complicated international problems." He noted that the strategy used in the war "was under the immediate guidance of Comrade Stalin, our great Army leader." [My emphases in the above quotations.—A. L. W.]

2. Milovan Djilas, *Conversations with Stalin*, Harcourt, Brace & World, New York, 1963, p. 114.

3. This was seen among such stances as Soviet refusal to admit or rectify Soviet reneging on Yalta agreements on democratization of Soviet-occupied East European nations; Soviet rejection of East European states' participation in the Marshall Plan of 1947; hostile coverage of the West in Soviet media; Soviet rumor-mongering over Hitler's being alive and "hiding out" in the West; and Soviet reticence to agree to a viable, mutual inspection regimen for East-West atomic research and development.

4. Of the many books on the Cold War, and they run in the many dozens, perhaps the best and most objective among the most recent is John Gaddis, *The Cold War: A New History*, Penguin Books, New York, 2005. Lamentably, however, these books ignore the Duclos letter as well as the symptomatic purging in early 1945 of Browder as Gensek of the world's most important Communist Party. For a discussion of the downturn in U.S.-Soviet relations immediately after the war, see Albert L. Weeks, *The Other Side of Coexistence: An Analysis of Russian Foreign Policy*. The transition from cold to hot war with

North Korea's invasion of the south in June 1950 is analyzed in Geoffrey Roberts, *Stalin's War: From World War to Cold War, 1939–1953*, Yale University Press, New Haven, 2006, pp. 264–371. Roberts, as other scholars have done, reproduces parts of texts of secret cables and other documents pertaining to the run-up to the Korean War (1950–1953). In these materials, Stalin is found declaring that the Far East is the "new center of revolution." As to the danger of a Third World possibly stemming from a war in Korea, the Soviet leader states frankly: "If war is inevitable, let it be waged now, and not in a few years when Japanese militarism will be restored as an ally of the USA and when the USA and Japan have a ready-made bridgehead in the form of the entire Korea run by Syngman Rhee." Mao had offered the opinion in early 1950 that the United States was "afraid of war" and would not intervene in Korea, while Stalin later declared that the Korean War showed "America's weakness" (Roberts, ibid., p. 369).

5. In the Venona transcripts, Browder is described by the NKVD as a Moscow tool who has become a liability to Moscow by 1944–1945. For one thing, his ambitious plan to create a left-wing arm of the Democratic Party in the form of a so-called Communist-run "political association" was vetoed in Moscow, probably at the highest level. It appears that Stalin wished to retain the purity of the Communist Party, not see it morphed into a putatively non-Communist entity. Browder had also been involved in some embarrassing incidents (for the NKVD) that might have exposed other agents, including some Browder himself had recruited for the NKVD via the CPUSA. Browder as CPUSA general secretary had been bitterly criticized by Jacques Duclos in his famous 1945 letter. Venona reveals that Browder enjoyed friendly, personal ties with President Roosevelt, which in turn may have been viewed in Moscow as a liability. See *Venona: Decoding Soviet Espionage in America*, pp. 215–216.

6. Cited in U.S. government document, p. 208. Kennan made similar observations, if somewhat more nuanced than Deane's and without reference to a Soviet "war" against capitalism, in Kennan's famous *Foreign Affairs* essay. For discussion, see Weeks, *Stalin's Other War*, pp. 16, 18, and 19–20. The 1979 House study on U.S.-Soviet relations after the war concluded: "Clearly, the signs were ominous [after World War II] for the future conduct of diplomacy and negotiations with the Soviet Union." At least, it might be added, as long as the USSR was led by Josef Stalin.

7. A. B. Martirosyan, *Stalin: posle voiny 1945–1953 gody* (*Stalin: After the War, 1945–1953*), Veche, Moscow, 2008. Quotations that follow are from chapters 1–30 of this book by Martirosyan.

8. Contingency war planning is, of course, the commonly used prerogative of any state but was especially true of the two atomic powers, the USSR and the United States. Moscow as well as Washington did such planning. The former's own plans have been detailed in various sources. One popular account was reported in the British newspaper *Telegraph* on September 20, 2007, "Soviet

Plan for World War III Unearthed." Russian defectors, especially those with a police background, have disclosed details of such Soviet war plans. U.S. plans against the Soviet Union bore such names as "Dropshot." Strategic Air Command General Curtis LeMay, wartime recipient of the Soviet "Great Patriotic War" medal, was often accused of planning a nuclear attack against the USSR. Martirosyan accuses Gen. Dwight D. Eisenhower of supporting the "Anglo-Saxon elite" in their plan to attack the USSR under the alleged code name "Totality." Other less extreme Russian historians have written about such U.S. war plans, accusing the United States of aggressiveness. These Russian authors are some of the most widely read in their own country and abroad and include mainline historians or memoirists like Lev Bezymensky, Oleg Rzheshevsky, Valentin Falin, and Yuri Zhukov.

9. Keistut Zakoretskiy, *Tret' ya mirovaya voina Stalina* (*Stalin's World War III*), Yauza Press, Moscow, 2009.

10. Ibid., pp. 303, 309.

11. V. V. Sogrin, *Istoriya SShA* (*History of the USA*), Piter, Moscow-St. Petersburg, 2003, pp. 169–170. Sogrin's book, appearing during the Putin period in Russia (2000–2008), displays a more or less middle-of-the-road aspect as concerns Stalin's foreign policy while in large part defending the Soviet position. This is also particularly true also of the major Russian work on the Cold War, Anatoliy Utkin, *Mirovaya knolodnaya voina* (*The Global Cold War*), Eksmo, Moscow, 2005. Namely for Sogrin, that Soviet foreign policy was largely determined by external forces that disposed the Soviet "government" to tack and maneuver accordingly—especially in the 1930s. In this interpretation, the Cold War after 1945 likewise is viewed as having been a case of two-sided, mutual folly and misunderstanding and not the result of Stalinist ideology or Soviet postwar expansionism. It stemmed largely from competing "spheres of influence" in which, given the differing political systems on both sides, both sides were guilty of adopting extreme measures of defense of their own sphere of influence. This pattern of historical interpretation is followed for the most part in other current, "mainstream" history texts in which the downplaying of the negative aspects of Stalinism is evident. Utkin's lengthy 2005 version of world politics largely blames the United States for postwar tensions. He accuses the United States of "imperial" designs.

Index

NOTE: *Page numbers followed by an* n *and a second number indicate that the reference is to a numbered note on the indicated page. For example, 178n109 refers to note 109 on page 178.*

Abyssinia, 6
Adamec, Michael, 224
Air Corps, 137
Akhmerov, Iskhak
    Abdulovich, 223
Alexander, Tsar I, 13
alien world organization, 93
All-Union Communist Party, 235
Alperovitz, Gar, 219
America, in Stalin's future, 105–142;
    affinities, of Stalin, 109–111;
    "American colossus," 116–119;
    Big Three, 134–142;
    CPUSA, 115–116;
    defensism of Stalin, 112–113;
    Eighteenth Party Congress, Stalin
    at, 111–112; and FDR, 131–132;
    Lend-Lease, 119–123; move
    toward war, 106–109; spies
    and agents of influence, 132–134;
    Stalin's deal with, 11–12; Stalin's
    hints, significance of, 114–115;
    state interests, 126–130;
    U.S.–Soviet alliance, 123–126;
    West's plans, 113–114
"American colossus," 116
American Communist Party, 116

American Expeditionary
    Force, 37, 55, 74
American Federation
    of Labor, 121
American Veterans
    Committee (AVC), 67
"anti-Fascist" line, xx
"anti-imperialism," 216, 218
"anti-Party elements," 28
"anti-Stalin plots," 265n5
"April Theses," 39
Armenia, 52
Astakhov, Georgi, 34
Atlantic Charter, 221
Austria, 40, 71, 78, 215

Baathist Party, 26
Balayan, Lev, 256n1
Baltic Sea, 159
Barbarossa, 200–201. *See also*
    Operation Barbarossa
Barghoorn, Frederick, 216
"base of world revolution," 45
Basis Nord, 148
Basistov, Yu B., 132
Battle of Kursk, 207
Battle of Stalingrad, 164

Beria, Lavrenti, 29, 133, 171, 206, 218
Beria, Sergo, 133, 167, 174–176, 178,
    180, 264n12, 267n2
Bessonov, Sergei, 76
Bezymensky, Lev, 271n8
"Big Three": Stalin among, 134–142;
    summits, 11
"Blackshirts," 46, 79
Bolshevik propaganda, 54
Bolshevik Revolution, 115, 120
Bolshevism, 17, 39, 44, 74–75, 99,
    135, 257n5
Bonaparte, Napoleon, 128
Borodin, Mikhail, 83
bourgeois democracy, 47, 64, 80, 103
"bourgeois pacifism," 93
"breathing space" (peredyshka), 55, 186
Brezhnev, Leonid, 255n5, 260n8
Britain, 12, 40, 55, 57, 60, 65, 71, 97,
    107–108, 111, 114, 119, 124, 134, 136,
    202–203
Brzezinski, Zbigniew, 216
"buffer" territory, 160
Bulgaria, 151
Bullitt, William C., 138

"Cambridge Five," 135
Castro, Fidel, 140
Cathedral of Christ the
    Blessed Savior, 267n3
Central Powers, 55, 99, 182
Chamberlain, Sir Neville, 6
Chavez, Hugo, 227
Chicherin, Georgi V., 43
China, 82–83, 93, 117, 120, 122, 226
Chinese Communist Party, 83
Chuev, Feliks, 154
Churchill, Winston, 8, 13, 45, 79,
    99, 104, 108, 110, 121–122,
    127–128, 131–133, 135–138,
    145, 178, 223, 248
Civil War, 54
Cold War, xxi, 104, 158, 160, 227, 242–
    243, 247, 269n4, 271n11; chronology
    of, 219–222; coming of, 216–219;
    contemporary Russian historians
    on, 223–225

collective security, 87–104; league
    weaknesses, 90–91; Soviet view
    toward league, 91–98; Stalin's
    cautiousness, 99–104
"Colonial Comintern," 82
Comintern, 26, 27, 43, 55, 64–66, 68,
    70, 75, 83, 92, 100, 103, 116, 148,
    155, 157, 258n1, 265n5
Cominternism, 114
Commissar of Nationalities, 8, 37, 235
"Communazi," 78–81; "Red-Brown"
    kinship, 47, 80
Communist International, 24, 69, 94
Communist Party, xxvii, 4, 25, 26,
    42, 62, 65, 66, 116, 169, 242, 269n4–
    270n5; Central Committee, 33, 76
Communist Party USA. See CPUSA
Communist Third
    International, 100
"Communist threat," 4
Coryphaeus, 23
"counterrevolutionaries," 54
"counterrevolutionary scum," 18
CPUSA, 115–116
Cripps, Sir Stafford, 78
Crozier, Brian, 254n5
Currie, Laughlin, 137
Curzon Line, 34, 147
Czechoslovakia, 37, 48, 63, 78, 81,
    87, 89, 97–98, 112, 146–147, 173,
    243, 257n1

Davies, Joseph E., 31
Deane, John R., 220
"democratic alliance," 102
Democratic Party, 270n5
"demythologization," 228
Deutscher, Isaac, 258n3
Dimitrov, Georgi, 66, 68, 96,
    151, 254n6
diplomacy, in Stalin's
    industrialization, 57–60
Djilas, Milovan, 124, 160,
    217, 269n2
Djugashvili, Josef Vissarionovich, 13,
    45, 78
Dreiser, Theodore, 257n3

"Dropshot," 271n8
Dubcek, Alexander, 226
Duclos, Jacques, 219, 270n5
Dulles, Allen, 219
Duranty, Walter, 31

Eastern Europe, 3, 30, 32, 72, 103–104, 162, 215, 218, 221, 257n1
Eastern Front, 13, 23, 40, 54–55, 74, 145, 163, 180, 217, 241, 243
Eastman, Max, 19
Economic Problems of Socialism, 95
Eden, Anthony, 121
Eighteenth Party Congress, 33, 77, 98;
    Stalin at, 111–112
Eisenhower, Dwight D., 271n8
Eisenstein, Sergei, 170, 268n5
England, 5–6, 12, 32, 45, 79, 88, 131, 134, 136–137, 146–147, 152–153, 168, 173, 180, 184
Erickson, John, 210
Estonia, 35, 62, 147
Ethiopia, 93
Eurasia, 12, 30, 133–134, 198
European Union (EU), 90
Extraordinary Commission to Combat Counterrevolution, 53

Falin, Valentin, 271n8
Far East, 30, 44, 49, 54, 57, 83, 136, 149, 270n4
Fascism, 67, 96, 98, 104, 238, 240
"Fascist aggression," xii, 23, 195
Fascist Germany, 195, 230–231, 233
"Fascist horde," xix, 51
Fascist Italy, 46, 80, 92, 111, 117, 139, 184
Fascist Man, 47, 80
FDR, 105–106, 107, 108, 109–111, 119, 121, 124, 131–132, 134, 135, 137, 138, 140, 141, 218, 270n5
Finkelstein, Lawrence, 261n3
Finland, 4, 8–9, 37, 39, 73, 109, 112, 121, 124, 136, 144, 150, 152, 159, 194, 210
"Finlandia," 124

"firm rebuff," 83
Fitin, Pavel, 203
Five-Year Plans, 45, 59, 101, 109
Foster, William Z., 220
"Fourth Squadron of the Red Air Force," 42
France, 5–6, 32, 37, 40, 45, 48, 52, 55, 65, 78–79, 81, 87–88, 96–97, 140–141, 146–147, 151–153
Franco-British Munich appeasement policy, 146, 153
French Revolution, 18

Gaddis, John, 269n4
Gallup Poll, 121
Gareyev, Makhmut, 75
Gazeta, Nezavisimaya, 166
Gelfand, Leon, 76
"Generalissimos," 23
General Staff of World Revolution, 64, 70, 100
Geneva Conference, 87
Genoa Conference, 40, 74
George, David Lloyd, 44
George, King VI, 168
Georgia, 52
Germany: pocket battleships, 43; and USSR relations, foundation of, 38–41; military and Red Army, collaboration of, 41–44
German Communist Party, 66
German Fascism, 232–233
Germanism, 45
German Nazis, 67
German October Revolution, 167, 253n4
German Pavilion, 108
German-Soviet Boundary and Friendship Treaty, 148
German-Soviet Commercial Agreement, 149
"German spy," 39
Germany, 31–35, 38–42, 46–50, 62–64, 68–69, 71–79, 81–82, 122–123, 146–153, 156–158, 180, 182–184, 186, 208–210, 229–231, 267n3–268n6
Gleiwitz raid, 198, 210

Goebbels, Josef, 17, 20, 32, 40, 74,
    183–184, 187, 257n5
Goering, Hermann, 184
Golikov, Filipp I., 171, 180
Gorbachev, Mikhail, 160, 226
Gorodetsky, Gabriel, 254n7
Grande Armée, 196, 208
Great Depression, 110, 117
Great Fatherland War, 60, 62,
    189, 249
"great game," xi, 13, 198
Great Patriotic War, xviii, xxi,
    xxxii, 9, 13, 15, 43, 197, 200,
    217, 236, 246, 253n4, 256n9,
    268n6, 271n8
Great Russian chauvinism, 45
Great War, 74, 93
Green, Michael, 224
Gubel, Minei, 266n3

Halder, Franz, 164
Harbor, Pearl, 57, 106, 118, 122, 187
Haushofer, Karl, 134, 183
Haze, Paul, 42
Henderson, Sir Neville, 186
Hess, Rudolf, 180
Hicks, Granville, 257n3
Hitler, Adolf, 11, 44, 97, 182
Hogan, Willard N., 91, 261n3
Hoover, J. Edgar, 124
Hopkins, Harry, 137, 139
House of Representatives
    Committee on Foreign
    Affairs, 220, 258n1
Hungary, 48, 62, 81
Hussein, Saddam, 26

Imperialist pacifism, 95
imperialist war, 39
inter-imperialist tension,
    encouraging, 56–57
"iron curtain" speech, 104, 216
"iron rule," 186
Italy, 3, 11, 38, 46, 65, 72, 80, 93, 98,
    104, 118, 122, 151
Ivan, Tsar III, 14, 129
Ivanov, Robert, 136

Japan, 3, 12, 38, 56–57, 72,
    82–83, 92–93, 96, 117–118,
    120, 122, 134, 136, 183–184,
    187, 194
Jewish Bolshevism, 183
Johnston, Eric, 62
Joint State Political Directorate.
    See OGPU

Kaganovich, Lazar
    Moiseyevich, 267n3
Kalinin, Mikhail, 196, 267n2
Kandelaki, David, 77
Kapelle, Rote, 201
Karelo-Finnish Republic, 237
Kellog-Briand Pact, 88
Kennan, George V., 54
Khan, Genghis, 32
Khrushchev, Nikita, 28, 105,
    168, 169–171, 174–176, 242,
    258n3, 266n1
Kipp, Joseph W., 211, 268n7
Kirov, Sergei, 28
Klimovskikh, Vladimir Ye.,
    22, 189
Korean War, 124, 270n4
Kosygin, Alexei, 177
Krivitsky, Walter, 68
Krupskaya, Nadezhda, 19
Kutuzov, Mikhail, 196
"Kutuzov medal," 268n5
Kutuzov strategy,
    approval of, 208–210
Kuznetsov, Nikolai G., 181

Lapteva, Yelena, 88
Laski, Harold, 257n3
Latvia, 35, 37, 48, 62, 81, 147,
    154, 194, 229
League of Nations, 5–6, 62,
    75–76, 87–88, 90–92, 95–96,
    125, 127, 145, 194, 210;
    Preparatory Commission, 88
Lebedev, Lev, 76
LeMay, Curtis, 271n8
Lend-Lease, 119–123
Lend-Lease Act, 119

Lenin, Vladimir, 3; United Front
   tactic, 66–70
"Lenin cult," 17
Leningrad, 28, 52, 149, 200,
   234, 237
Leningrad Party, 95, 263n9
Leninism, 47, 80
Leninist-Trotskyite strategy,
   82, 257n1
Lenin Old Guard, 253n4
Lithuania, 35, 37, 48, 62, 81, 147–148,
   154, 194, 229
Litvinov, Maxim, 63, 92, 100,
   105, 131, 153
London Disarmament
   Conference, 139
Louis, King XIV, 141
Lvov, Prince, 39
Lytton Commission, 210
Lyulechnik, Vladimir, 187

Machiavellian methods, 21–23
Maisky, Ivan, 135, 180
Maksimovich, Maksim, 100
Malenkov, Andrei, 174
Malenkov, Georgi, 59, 175
Malik, Yakov, 217
Mandela, Nelson, 226
Marshall Plan, 140, 222, 269n3
Martirosyan, Arsen, 174, 253n4,
   256n1, 257n1, 260n8, 263n5,
   265n5, 266n3, 271n8
Marxism-Leninism, xix, xxi, 24,
   29, 43, 50, 93, 94, 111, 124, 126,
   144, 160, 197, 203, 216, 217, 226
"master politician," 13–16
McNeal, Robert H., 261n4
Medvedev, Dmitri, xx, xxv, 89, 223;
   decree, fallout from, xxii–xxiii
Mein Kampf, 50, 67, 76, 98, 169, 185,
   197, 257n5
Mercader, Ramon, 256n4
methods and accomplishments,
   of Stalin, 17–24; legacy, of Stalin,
   23–24; Machiavellian
   methods, 21–23; Stalin cult, 17–21
Mikoyan, Anastas, 177

Molotov, Chuev, 179
Molotov, Vyacheslav, 33, 75
"Molotov Line," xxvi, 181, 199, 214
Molotov-Ribbentrop Pact, 157
Moscow, 4–6, 32–35, 63–64, 72–78,
   87–90, 92–94, 103–104, 132–133,
   149–152, 159–162, 168, 183–186,
   239–248, 253n1–255n9, 257n4–
   267n3, 270n5–271n11
Münzenberg, Willi, 65
Munich Conference, 6, 112
Mussolini, Benito, 6, 45–47,
   72, 79–80, 93, 184, 187, 257n5
"mutual nonaggression pact," 76–77

"national Bolshevism," 34
National Socialist Germany, 143
NATO, 222
Nazi Germany, 5–6, 9, 28,
   43, 46, 67, 92, 101, 117–118,
   121, 135, 138, 144, 147,
   151, 154
Nazism, xx, 183, 185
Nazi-Soviet Friendship Pact, 82
"Nazi-Soviet honeymoon," 62, 72
Nazi-Soviet Nonaggression
   Pact, 69, 80
Nazi-Soviet pacts, xxii, 143–160;
   gaining territory by, 159–160;
   global carve-up, 149–150; new
   tensions, 151–158; specifics
   and protocols of, 146–149;
   Stalin's defense policies,
   controversy over, 144–146
neo-liberalism, 47
Neutrality Law of 1935, 120
Nevsky, Alexander, 268n5
New Deal Congress, 118
New Economic Policy (NEP), 57
New Order for Europe, 49, 82
New World Order, 94
New York World, 103, 108
Nicholas, Tsar II, 39, 73
Nineteenth Party Congress, 95
NKGB, 119
NKVD, 4, 29, 31–32, 65, 76, 94,
   97, 121, 157, 162–163, 171,

209–210, 218–219, 223–224,
    255n1, 270n5
Nonaggression Pact, 35, 69,
    80, 147, 196
North Atlantic Treaty
    Organization. *See* NATO
North Korea, 18, 270n4

Obshchestva, Istoriya
    Sovetskovo, 174
Oberkommando der
    Wehrmacht. *See* OKW
Office of Strategic Services
    (OSS), 107
OGPU, 65
OKW, 134
Old Bolsheviks, 26–30, 44
Operation Barbarossa, pre, 161–190;
    additional observations and
    issues, 182–190; early German
    success, 163–164; Stalin,
    behavior on June 22nd, 164–168,
    new versions of, 172–182; Stalin,
    first reactions, 162–163,
    historiography, development
    of, 168–172
Operation Sea Lion, 162
Operation Typhoon, 164
Operation White, 262n5
Order of Red Banner, 224
Orthodox Patriarchate, 167
Ottoman Empire, 48, 81

Paris Peace Conference, 37
Pavlovich, Lavrenti, 176
Peaceful Policy, 224
People's Commissariat
    for State Security. *See* NKGB
People's Commissariat
    for Internal Affairs. *See* NKVD
peredyshki, 55–56
personal qualities, of Stalin, 9–11
Petrograd, 39, 46, 53, 73, 92
Pieck, Wilhelm, 157
Poland, 21, 35–36, 48, 52, 63,
    81–82, 99, 104, 144, 147, 151,
    153, 161, 174, 187, 196

Popular Front, 6, 21, 96, 123;
    tactic of Stalin, 66–70
Poskrebyshev, Aleksandr, 165
Preparatory Commission,
    League of Nations, 88
"preventive war," xii, 4, 146, 155, 182
pro-Communist National African
    Congress (ANC), 226
Prussia, 40, 71
purges: historiography on, 30–31;
    justification of, 27–28
Putin, Vladimir, 40, 51, 196

Quadpartite Axis, 150
Quadpartite Pact, 151

Radzinsky, Edvard, 31, 174
Rapallo Treaty, 41
Red Air Force, 42–43, 61, 200, 206
Red Army. *See* RKKA
Red Navy, 182, 232
Red Orchestra, 201
Red Square, 46, 167–168
Red Terror, 18
Reinsurance Treaty, 40
Republic of China, 46, 83, 227
Republic of Mongolia, 44
Republic of South Africa, 226
"revolution," 8
"revolutionary" mission, 91
"revolutionary state," 72
Revolution Day, 168
Ribbentrop, 33, 47, 77, 80, 143, 146,
    150, 184–185, 187, 199, 209, 230,
    255n7, 259n6
RKKA, xxvi, 8–9, 21–22, 29–30, 40–42,
    54, 97–99, 163–164, 179, 181–182,
    193, 196, 200, 204–208, 210–212,
    229–234, 239–241; and German
    military, collaboration of, 41–44
Roberts, Geoffrey, 270n4
Rolland, Romain, 257n3
Roman Empire, 93
Romania, 21, 35, 37, 48, 63, 81, 104,
    152, 154, 156, 174, 187, 207, 221
Rome, 46, 76, 80
Roosevelt, Eleanor, 137

Roosevelt, Franklin D. *See* FDR
Rosenberg, Alfred, 184
Russian Communist Party,
    xxiii, 24, 26, 155
Russian Empire, 48, 159
Russian Federation (RF), xviii, 40, 51,
    89, 145, 193, 219, 258n2, 265n5
"Russian state," xviii
Russophilia, 45, 78
Rybkina, Zoya, 202
Rzheshevsky, Oleg, 271n8

Savushkin, Robert, 211
Schlesinger, Arthur, Jr., 219
Second Congress of Soviets, 92
second dictator, twentieth
    century's, 3–16; advantages
    enjoyed by, 4–5; bluff, use of, 13;
    diplomacy as weapon, 7–9;
    personal qualities of, 9–11;
    unique dictator, 3–4; west
    and America, dealing with, 11–12;
    western leadership, contrasts
    with, 6–7
Selassie, Hailer, 93
Sherwood, Robert, 139
"Shturmovik," 61
Social-Democratic parties (SDs), 66
Solzhenitsyn, Aleksandr, 39, 73,
    254n1, 255n1
Sorge, Richard, 162, 178, 187
South Korea, 112
Soviet A-bomb, 218
Soviet Army, 103, 112, 158,
    215, 217, 269n1
Soviet Caucasus, 124, 202
Soviet Civil War, 37
Soviet Comintern, 65
Soviet Commissariat
    of Internal Affairs (NKVD), 76
Soviet Communism, 124, 154
Soviet Communist Party, 139;
    Central Committee, 68
Soviet diplomacy, early, 52–55
Soviet-Finnish War, 159
Soviet foreign policy, 43, 51–70, 124;
    broken treaties, trail of, 62–64;

Comintern factor, 64–65; early
    Soviet diplomacy, 52–55,
    peredyshki, 55–56; encouraging
    inter-imperialist tension, 56–57;
    popular front tactic of Stalin,
    66–70; Stalin, emphasis on
    defense, 60–62, industrialization,
    diplomacy in, 57–60; united
    front tactic, by Lenin, 66–70
Soviet-German Nonaggression
    Pact, 34
"Soviet government," 75, 76,
    87, 97, 197
Sovietism, 24
Soviet Man, 47, 80
Soviet Pavilion, 123
Soviet Political Dictionary, 224
Soviet Pro-German posture, 71–84;
    Brest-Litovsk Treaty as precedent
    (1918), 72–76; "Communazi" factor,
    78–81; early roots, 71–72; European
    waters, Stalin navigates, 81–82;
    Far East dangers, 82–84; Soviet
    initiatives, 76–78
Soviet Republic, 9, 35, 48, 52–53, 57,
    72, 75, 80, 91, 99, 115, 140
Soviet Union. *See* USSR
Speidel, Helm, 43
Stalin, Joseph: alleged
    greatness, assessing, 225–228;
    among Big Three, 134–142;
    broadcast to Soviet Union
    people, 229–234; current
    biography, 235–236; defensism of,
    112–113; at Eighteenth Party
    Congress, 111–112; emphasis on
    defense, 60–62; future, America in,
    105–142; greatness, poll on,
    xxiii–xxiv; hints, significance
    of, 114–115; industrialization,
    diplomacy in, 57–60; Kremlin,
    37–50, currents of Europe, 48–50,
    German-soviet relations,
    foundation of, 38–41, red
    army-German military,
    collaboration of, 41–44,
    soviet-fascist, totalitarian

kinship of, 44–47; new, 222;
  speech at Kremlin, 237–238;
  and state interests, 126–130;
  on West's plans, 113–114
Stalin, Mark, 256n1
Stalin cult, 17–21, 236
Stalinism, 169, 228, 271n11
"Stalin's Himmler," 206
Steinhardt, Lawrence, 135, 183
Stettinius, Edward R., 119
Sudoplatov, Pavel, 128, 137, 257n4,
  264n8
Suvorov, Viktor, 224, 254n5

Tanaka Plan, 50
Taubman, William, 28
Third Communist
  International, 43, 53, 64
Third World, 21, 24, 65, 82,
  102, 155, 270n4
Tolstoy, Alexei, 141
trade diplomacy, 57
Treaty of Berlin, 38, 71
Treaty of Brest-Litovsk, 38,
  39, 55, 71, 74
Treaty of Nonaggression, 147
Triandafillov, Vladimir, 44
Trotskyism, 26
Truman, Harry S., 135
Tukhachevsky, Mikhail, 8, 31,
  41, 44, 99–100, 189, 258n3,
  263n13, 265n5, 268n6
"Tukhachevsky-Trotsky"
  strategy, 265n5
Twentieth Communist
  Party Congress, 168, 169, 170

Ukraine, 33, 48, 54, 59, 169,
  176, 200, 207, 214, 237
Ultrix, Theodore J., 259n1
"Uncle Joe," 111
Union of Soviet
  Socialist Republics, 7
unique dictator, 3–4
United Front tactic, by Lenin, 66–70
United Nations (UN), 6, 87, 94, 108,
  136, 221, 269n1

United States, and USSR,
  alliance, 123–126. See also
  America
UN Security Council, 90, 216
U.S. Senate Judiciary
  Committee, 262n6
USSR: and fascist, totalitarian
  kinship of, 44–47; and German
  relations, foundation of, 38–41;
  and United States, alliance, 123–126

Versailles Treaty, 37, 48, 81
Victoria, Queen, 128
Vissarionovich, Iosif, 171, 235
Vissarionovich, Josef, 29, 128
Vlasik, Nikolai, 164
Volkogonov, Dmitri, 165, 171
Voroshilov, Klimenti, 99
Vozhd', preparation for war, 25–36;
  historiography, on purges, 30–31;
  Kirov case, 28–30; merging home
  front, 25–27; purges, justification
  of, 27–28; watershed year, 31–36
Vyshinsky, Andrei, 31

"wait-and-see attitude," 153
War Communism, 18, 58
Warsaw Pact Alliance, 222
watershed year, 31–36
Wehrmacht, 193–214;
  Barbarossa, 200–201;
  costly errors of Stalin, 205–206;
  Kutuzov strategy, approval of,
  208–210; military defense plan,
  of Stalin, 210–211; RKKA,
  preparedness of, 211–214;
  Russian Gleiwitz, prevention
  of, 210; Soviet weaknesses,
  206–208; Stalin bluffs, 198–200
Western Allies, 11, 13, 40, 49, 71, 84,
  109, 156, 158, 161, 177, 221
Western Catholicism, 58
Western Special Military
  District, 21, 214
Wheeler, Burton K., 119
White, Harry Dexter, 137
White House, 106, 119, 134, 137, 140

Wilhelm, Kaiser, 40, 71, 230
Willie, Wendell, 152
Wilson, Woodrow, 37
Winter War, 8–9, 189, 202
"world-historical" game, 128
"world revolution," xviii, 15,
    24, 26–27, 31, 63, 65, 69, 84,
    124, 125, 155
World War I, 20, 37, 40, 46, 48,
    72, 99, 117, 146
World War II, ix, xxxii, 8, 10, 63, 104,
    110, 169, 196, 217, 265n4
"worldwide agreement," 88

Yagoda, Genrikh, 29
Yakovlev, Aleksandr, 226, 259n3

Yalta Conference, 141
Yaroslavsky,
    Yemelyan, 266n3
Yeltsin, Boris, 51
Yezhov, Nikolai, 29
Yugoslavia, 132

Zakoretskiy, Keistut
    Aleksandrovich, 224
Zamyatin, Yevgeny, 18
Zhukov, Georgi, 13,
    84, 171
Zhukov, Yuri, 145, 271n8
Zhurnal, Istoricheskiy, 174
"Zinoviev letter," 114
Zionism, 265n5

About the Author

ALBERT L. WEEKS, graduate of the University of Chicago and Columbia University, is a veteran analyst of Soviet and Russian political and military affairs. Former Senior Soviet Analyst with the U.S. Department of State and Professor Emeritus of New York University, he is the author of a several books and many published articles in the civilian and military press here and abroad, including Russia. His latest work is *The Choice of War: The Iraq War and the Just War Tradition* (Praeger, 2009).